D1761447

Layout Design

Published in October 2010

British Library Cataloguing in Publication Data:
A catalogue record for this book is available
from the British Library

ISBN 978 1 84425 635 8

Library of Congress catalog card number 2010924935

Published by Haynes Publishing,
Sparkford, Yeovil, Somerset BA22 7JJ, UK
Tel: 01963 442030 Fax: 01963 440001
Int. tel: +44 1963 442030 Int. fax: +44 1963 440001
Email: sales@haynes.co.uk
Website: www.haynes.co.uk

Haynes North America Inc.
861 Lawrence Drive, Newbury Park, California 91320, USA

Printed in the USA

While every effort is taken to ensure the accuracy of the information given in this book, no liability can be accepted by the author or publishers for any loss, damage or injury caused by errors in, or omissions from, the information given.

Acknowledgements

As is invariably the case, this book could not have been written and illustrated without advice, assistance and input from all manner of folk. So I'd like to thank the following friends and colleagues – and if I've missed anybody off the list, my profuse apologies!

Special thanks are due to Adrian Colenut and the Uckfield Club for allowing me to raid their photographic archives, to Andrew Bluett-Duncan, Don Leeper and Simon de Souza for unrestricted access to their layouts, and to Dave Doe for constructive criticism and technical support.

I'm also indebted to Bob Barlow, Vincent de Bode, Chris Challis, John Chambers, Terry Cole, Matthew Doe, Ian Everett, Ted Farmer, Barry Fitzjerald, Gordon and Maggie Gravett, Rodney Hall, Paul Karau and Wild Swan Publications, Chris Lamacraft, David Lane, Gwilym McCoach, Barry Norman, Pendon Museum, Peter Ross, Nick Salzman, Winfried Schmitz-Esser, Dirk Schoemaker, Tim Shackleton, Mick and Yvonne Simpson, Jim Smith-Wright, Henry Tasker, Tim Venton, Len de Vries, Bob Wills and Martin Wynne.

Layout Design

Iain Rice

CONTENTS

INTRODUCTION

This is a book about compromise and deception – the two aids without which the eternal circle of realistic railway modelling can never be squared. My guiding principles in respect of layout design have always run along these twin lines, with the second – getting the thing to *look* right – being the arbiter that guides the choices made from the range of almost invariably far-from-ideal options that practicality presents. Very few aspiring modellers can ignore the constraints of space and cash (or rather, the lack of same…), while none of us can ignore the march of time. A successful layout design is, above all, one that is *achievable*. If I had to sum up this philosophy in a couple of pithy lines, they would read: 'The man (or woman) who never made a compromise never made a model railway', closely followed by 'What *looks* realistic *is* realistic'. These tenets are my first and ultimate laws of railway modelling.

There are many possible ways to design and build a model railway, to meet a wide range of priorities. The goal to which I have directed my own efforts over the past four decades has been towards the creation of models which appear as natural as possible, and which capture as far as I am able the *ambience* of the prototype. Well-observed subject matter, realistic viewpoints, the elimination of jarring elements, the integration of the trains and their setting into a cohesive whole, and a style of presentation that sets off the modelling while 'managing' the point where it has to stop – these are the factors that have underpinned my aspiration. I haven't got there yet – and almost certainly never will; so the present work is my attempt to set down what I've learned on the journey thus far.

Iain A. Rice
Bridestowe, West Devon
May 2009

ABOVE: *The wide open spaces of New Zealand's Caterbury Plains are captured to perfection on Peter Ross's ambitious multi-deck Sn31/2 layout in Christchurch, New Zealand. Here, a characterful NZGR 'WA' class 2-6-4T shunts the limeworks siding at Amberley, on the upper section of the layout. The modelling here is a bare two feet deep, but the subtle backdrop – with the foothills of the Southern Alps dimly visible through the haze – expands the scene to its natural limits. The 'sky' extends up out of the field of view, and the model is lit by carefully-concealed flourescent tubes with appropriate 'daylight' colour values. A truly realistic layout.* Author

BELOW: *One of the most realistic and best-observed pieces of modelling I've ever clapped eyes on: a New Zealand mountain shepherd's 'batch' on Barry Fitzgerald's stunning Sn31/2 layout in Timaru, New Zealand. Note the perfect colour match between foreground modelling and the backdrop; it's almost impossible to tell where the two meet.* Author

1 PRELIMINARIES: Philosophy, Scales and Standards, Terminology

'Define your terms, Rice!' my old physics master used to thunder from the blackboard, back in that distant age (somewhere between the disappearance of the dinosaurs and the emergence of Bob Dylan), when I was but a lecherous, pimply sixth-former. Well, 'Ben' Franklin may have failed to make a physicist of me, but his mantra as to the need for definition seems somehow to have stuck. So I'll start this essay by attempting an exposition of the concept that lies at its heart: realism.

Always a good first move is to see what the etymologists make of the word. Consulting the trusty *Shorter Oxford*, I find three basic meanings – of which the second seems appropriate and straightforward enough: *(in art or literature): The representation of things in a way that is accurate and true to life.* Wikipedia agrees, asserting that *Realism in the visual arts and literature is the depiction of subjects as they appear in everyday life, without embellishment or interpretation.* Taking a transatlantic slant, *Webster* has it that realism *is the theory or practice of fidelity in art and literature to nature or to real life and to accurate representation without idealization* (with a 'z'). All of which is pretty unequivocal: a realistic model must be one that tells it exactly like it is – or, more often – was. Boiled down, factual, no frills, and devoid of any personal preferences or interpretation.

Well, I don't know about you, but I find the concept of such a clinical approach to railway modelling somewhat sterile. I'd contend that creating a truly realistic model railway amounts to more than simple

ABOVE: *One of the first exhibition layouts to be constructed in an uncompromising quest for realism was Barry Norman's seminal 'Petherick', which created a considerable stir when first exhibited in the mid-1980s. Far from being the traditional afterthought, Petherick's superbly-executed scenic setting was the fundamental component of the design; the railway was almost an extra!* Barry Norman

BELOW: *The realistic benchmark for most people: 'Pendon'. Ultimate fidelity to prototype for each individual model, the highest standards consistently applied, and a breathtaking scope to the whole uncompromising project; a truly outstanding achievement. Although full of lessons and inspiration, 'Pendon' cannot really be held up as a viable role-model for the individual modeller. A mite more pragmatism is needed when you have to do it all yourself!* 'Pendon' Museum

unswerving factual and dimensional veracity to subject. The best layouts I know offer something greater than any sum of numerical or historical parts, in that they also capture the *intangibles* of the subject. A truly convincing model railway can trigger the same emotional responses that draw us to the lineside in the first place and evoke the feel, the atmosphere, the unique ambience and character of a particular setting or railway. Put simply, the most realistic model railways have *soul*.

The elusive quest

But how do you define and measure such an elusive quality? Mere mathematics won't do it; numerical accuracy in matters of scale dimension doesn't in itself produce realism. Indeed, you soon run up against the conundrum of the model full of scale shortcomings that is somehow more convincing than one that ticks the dimensional boxes to three places of decimals. Perfection of manufacture is no guarantee, either; many models end up being more perfect – crisper, squarer, shinier – than the real thing. Often, it's the little imperfections in a prototype that actually give it its essential character. No, it seems to me, that the most satisfyingly realistic model is one that not only offers a believable visual representation of its subject, but one that also evokes the elusive 'atmosphere' that is such a powerful conveyer of conviction. In that, it is often more akin to a grainy 'art' photograph than a pin-sharp multi-mega pixel digital snapshot; even, in some cases, more equivalent to a surprisingly impressionistic painting – although abstract art it certainly ain't! The somewhat indefinite qualities that give a model railway 'atmosphere' are, however, hard to pin down in print. To my mind they are almost all to do with two key attributes: accuracy of observation, and consistency of execution.

Learning to observe – to really *look* at something and perceive exactly its visual essence – is a key skill for any artist. As I would argue strongly that the best scenic model railways can be considered works of art fit to be compared with any other genre, then it's a key skill for modellers too! Observation – or informed perception – is critical at several points in the layout-creation process. It will help decide exactly what prototype elements need to be modelled to produce the desired result and determine the form, proportions and colouring of these chosen subjects. And – at the later planning and throughout the constructional phases of the model – the same analytical eye can evaluate the 'look' of what has been achieved and its conformity to the objective. The ultimate realism of a model railway, I reckon, depends to a very large extent on the quality of the perception that has informed the modelling decisions. While there are many possible ways of actually *constructing* a satisfying and homogenous miniature scene, if the subject is badly observed in the first place, then the result will never convince. A beautifully crafted error is still an error!

Homogeneity is all about harmony, not just of subject matter, but also of the appearance of the model: texturing, finishes, lighting, detail levels and – especially – colouring. It is about giving every modelled aspect of the layout – track, trains, topography, trees, structures, figures and 'accessories'

BELOW: *My own attempts at realistic railway modelling have largely centred around relatively small layouts and cameo-format dioramas. Achieving a convincing result in a truly tiny space takes a lot of effort and attention to detail, and calls for the use of every artifice in the book – especially in the matter of backdrops and scale compression. This is 'Trerice' – all 7 square feet of it!* Len de Vries

– equal emphasis and modelling effort, in a quest for a believable whole. The real world is, after all, utterly consistent in these matters. Homogeneity is also about taking care to blend everything seamlessly together, avoiding anomalies and 'sore thumbs'. In order to achieve this state of modelling nirvana, the qualities of each component are subjugated to the needs of the scene as a whole.

Hard-nosed realism

Before setting off to explore the essentially artistic realms of 'atmospheric' layout design, however, it is time to re-visit the dictionary in search of that alternative meaning of 'realism' – the one that is more about feet on the ground than elusive visions. *The practice of accepting a situation as it is and dealing with it accordingly*, says the *OED*. *Webster* is more helpful in our context, adding: *…rejection of the impractical and visionary.* What such hard-nosed realism amounts to in railway modelling is eschewing wishful thinking in favour of a proper understanding of the practicalities; pipe dreams remain no more than a cloud of noxious vapour unless there's some way of turning them into a tangible result. Whether we like it or not, there are certain immutable laws of nature that restrict what is possible on a model railway; inconveniences such as gravity, the properties of materials, the behaviour of electricity and light-waves, and – more prosaically – things like our skill level, age, financial and family circumstances and non-modelling commitments.

I know of quite a few beautifully observed and otherwise visually realistic model railways, for instance, that simply don't *work*. Trains constantly derail on poorly laid track or slip to a stand on uneven gradients. Poorly-planned electrics lead to operational impasses – not to mention frequent unplanned halts, miniature firework displays and expensive-smelling whisps of smoke. An unhappy choice of coupler and a lack of the necessary access lead to endless frustration in shunting. Too much complexity all too often results in a maintenance nightmare, while an unrealistically ambitious choice of standards makes for painfully slow progress or – more likely – to a subsequent slippage of the goalposts; what price consistency then?

Then there are the very great number of layouts that are destined never to be finished, usually due to lack of practical realism at the design stage. Over-ambition is a key stumbling block, both in terms of the scope of what is attempted and the standards aimed at. All too often, the design reaches well beyond the scope of the resources available. Other reasons for aspirant layouts becoming skip-fodder include: skimping the design of baseboards, the essential foundation of the whole edifice; not taking account of the need to make things transportable and adaptable in the face of the (often unforeseen) need to move house; lack of a clear set of objectives – the layout that 'loses its way'; and – possibly the commonest failing of all – unworkability in the basic concept due to a failure to understand the limitations of what is physically possible. Realistic layout planning is just as much about taking account of these plebian practicalities as it is about the pursuit of truth in the art of railway modelling.

Essential qualities of a realistic layout

Before considering these nuts and bolts of layout design, it seemed useful at this point to nail my flags to various masts and set out the basic qualities that I believe are essential in order that a model railway can be considered 'realistic' in the visual sense. Although these criteria may be dismissed as mere subjective opinions, I like to think that my assertions can be backed by analysis of the physical factors at work, by practical experiment and – most tellingly – by example.

So – what are Rice's 'essentials of a realistic layout'? I return at once to the two 'key attributes' already noted, observation and consistency. To convince, a model railway needs to depict something that is believable in the first place; realistic layouts need realistic ingredients. Even if the actual subject of a layout is totally fictitious, it needs to draw firmly on reality to inform that fiction. Many of our finest model railways depict scenes that are rooted in imagination – but every element making up that scene will be true to life, meticulously researched and observed. That these elements will then be individually well-modelled goes without saying, but what is equally important is that they are modelled in a *complementary* manner, so that

BELOW: *One of the leading exponents of the ultra-small 'cameo' format has been the irrepressible Ian Everret, who has produced some little gems. This is the canal lock and bridge on 'Clecklewyke' – unmistakably set in West Yorkshire. A sure eye for colour and detail and some beautifully executed modelling really bring this scene to life, even if an ex-NER G5 is a slightly unlikely engine in these parts. But that canal looks wonderfully wet and decidedly murky; it's a branch of the Huddersfield system, and hence 'narrow'.* Ian Everett

ABOVE: *The natural view. This stunningly convincing shot was taken on Gordon and Maggie Gravett's 1:50 'Pempoul', and demonstrates unequivocally the key components of truly realistic modelling: accurate observation (study the foreground vegetation!), utter consistency and homogeneity, an effective backdrop, and a natural viewpoint and lighting. A very long way from the trainset…* Gordon Gravett

their qualities are compatible in terms of texture, colour and general feel. In other words, consistent in quality; the real world is 'all of a piece', and a realistic model needs to appear likewise.

Realistic layouts also need to look *natural* – they need to present the spectator with the same viewing experience that would be had while observing the real thing. Which means they need to be seen from a natural viewpoint, equating to the relationship that one would have with an equivalent prospect in reality. This 'natural viewpoint' thus needs to take account of the *subject* of the model – particularly its topography. Not too many panoramic mountain-top views to be had in Lincolnshire, for instance… I would also suggest relatively few of us are aficionados of the hang-gliding or helicoptering that seems to provide the favoured viewpoint for so many layouts. What this quest for naturalistic viewpoints means in practice, of course, is that the model needs to be displayed at a height that puts it in an appropriate relationship with our eye level, such that the horizon-line (which in reality is always precisely *on* eye-level) will fall naturally within the height of the backscene.

Ah yes – the backscene. In my book, an absolute essential for any layout with pretences to realism, not only providing the over-arching sky that is such a fundamental component of any outdoor scene, but also cutting out distractions behind the model. A good backscene can do far more than that, of course, adding depth and distance to our modelled scenes and taking away the confines of our oft-cramped sites. Backscenes are a key element in any attempt to represent the world in a natural way, and understanding how they function is another critical aspect of realistic layout design – which is why I'll be devoting much time and emphasis to them.

And then there's the matter of natural illumination. We live in a star system that has but one sun, beneath an atmosphere which – at the northern latitudes in which the UK was located last time I looked – filters out a lot the 'hot-end' red-yellow solar radiation to give the cooler, blue-tinged light that is such a predominant characteristic of the British environment. Many models of British railways, by contrast, are

BELOW: *How much less convincing this picture of Vincent de Bode's 'Flintfields' would look if deprived of its backdrop. This restrained but highly effective piece of scene-painting was executed by Len de Vries, using an airbrush and acrylic paints on fine-weave roller blind fabric. This removable and rollable backcloth is some 18 seamless feet long.* Vincent de Bode

RIGHT: *A highly convincing depiction of the everyday; the canal bridge on David Lane's 'Saffron Street'. Top-class modelling and accurate observation play a big part in creating such realism – but so does the background of real sky. This is not only blessedly free from seams and shadows, but provides light that looks natural because it is natural! Trying to replicate this with artificial sources is a tall order…* David Lane

BELOW: *My attempt at a 'cool but sunny' autumn day on 'Bodesmeer' shows just how far off-beam you can be with artificial light even when – as here – a mix of sources is employed: 'warm white' fluorescent low-energy bulbs, blue-white LED lamps, and a few quartz-halogen fittings with wide-angle reflectors. The background is a plain wall in off-white.* Dirk Schoemaker

sited on some strange planet with many suns, flooding the surface with light whose colour temperature suggests close solar proximity (or no atmosphere) and a probable surface temperature that would happily melt lead. Layout lighting is another topic on which I have much to say…

The last ingredient in my 'basic realism' formula concerns not so much the model itself as the way it is presented to the viewer. I've already touched on the matters of display height, the role of the backdrop in excluding unwanted background, and the need for appropriate lighting. What I'm concerned with now is what happens around the edges of a model – how the design manages this artificial 'end of the world'. Coming up with some effective way of 'framing' a model – hiding things that need to be unseen (the edges of the backscene, the fiddleyard, light fittings) and separating the modelling from surrounding distractions – is a further requirement of the realistic layout. Far from being some mere add-on afterthought, I regard these 'peripherals' as a fundamental and integral part of realistic layout design.

The road to realism

I don't know about you, but before setting out on any of life's little adventures I like to have a clear idea of just where I'm trying to go and a pretty good idea of how I'm going to get there; it's a philosophy that I find holds good for everything

BELOW: *Vincent de Bode's 'Flintfields' has long set a standard for realistic display and very well thought-out presentation. With a relatively deep scene front-to-back of 43in (1,100mm), the relatively generous front viewing height of around 12in (305mm) calls for a tall backscene – 23in (600mm) in this case. All this makes for happy proportions, but calls for considerable infrastructure.* Adrian Colenutt

ABOVE: *The essential armchair-modelling appendage – a squared-paper notebook, preferably, as here, spiral-bound so it opens out flat. This dog-eared specimen is Lidl's finest, all 99p's-worth. The magnifier, by the by, is useful for discerning detail on maps and plans in books, often reproduced rather small.* Author

OPPOSITE: *Typical pages from notebooks, giving an idea of the sort of thing that I typically scribble during the 'armchair' phase of layout-designing: a perspective rough of a design proposal for a cameo layout ('Boduan' – see Chapter 10), and a baseboard schematic for a shelf layout. Other pages might contain lists of all sorts, outline specifications, prototype data, product information and ideas I've stolen from somebody else!*

from papering the parlour to – well, building a model railway. What has never ceased to surprise me, however, is just how many people set out on the latter endeavour with only the vaguest notion of what they're trying to achieve and no notion whatever as to how they expect to get there! In my experience, 'making it up as you go along' in the matter of railway modelling rarely results in anything other than an unconvincing, ill-functioning hodgepodge.

There are a great many things to consider before embarking on the creation of something as many-faceted and complex as a model railway. Quite apart from focusing that all-important 'mind's eye' vision of the finished model – hopefully crystal-clear but all-to-often, I fear, somewhat rose-tinted and distinctly fuzzy around the edges – there is the small matter of working out just how you're going to turn this glittering aspiration into an achievable reality. It's all very well dreaming up something of a scope to rival Clapham Junction, but fitting it into the spare bedroom and financing it from the small change of the household budget might *just* prove problematic. Before rushing off to the model shop for trains and track and to the D-I-Y store in a (near impossible!) quest for knot-free lumber and unwarped ply, a spot of 'armchair modelling' is no bad thing.

'Armchair modeller' has traditionally been a disparaging term – usually used of one who, on stern winter evenings when *real* railway modellers are confronting intractable constructional challenges in arctic attics or sub-zero sheds, is to be found comfortably ensconced in a favourite chair at the fireside contemplating in vivid mind's-eye detail the magnificent layout he will – one day – create. Well, I'll allow that idle dreaming never got much practical modelling done, but I'd certainly argue that time spent in careful contemplation of not only the aspiration, but the means of execution of a new model railway is rarely time wasted. Thinking through a proposed layout in detail can often save time, money and frustration at the construction phase. Fortunately, such contemplation is well-suited to those all-too-frequent occasions in modern life when one is condemned by circumstance to unwonted idleness; some of my best ideas owe their conception to traffic jams, interminable long-haul flights, or tedious journeys on that that new breed of train carefully engineered to prevent you from seeing out of the window.

In the context of these odd moments of not-so-idle contemplation, I'm a great advocate of the notebook – by which I mean humble sheets of paper between cardboard covers, for all you children of the electronic age. I never go anywhere without the latest in a succession of dog-eared spiral-bound volumes of squared paper, which I usually find in Herr Lidl's cut-price emporium in both A4 and A5 sizes for mere pence. Allied to a trusty Tesco pencil with a rubber on the chewing end, these unprepossessing volumes are my most indispensable layout-designing tool. From the resulting grubby pages of schemings, scribblings and sketchings are my complete designs derived.

The Holistic approach

You will have noted that word 'complete' – which, like the dual-context 'realism' of my introduction, has two distinct meanings: complete as in finished, and complete as in all-embracing. Tradition, it seems, holds that a track plan is the only blueprint needed to build a model railway – whereas I've always argued that a 'track plan' is just what it says, and that a complete model railway design needs to consider a great deal more than the mere disposition of the permanent way (PW). In my book, layout designing is about resolving *all* the issues involved: track disposition, certainly – but in relation to overall topography and the rules of visual harmony and proportion, taking into account the way the finished model will be viewed, the desired style of operation (including such factors as the couplings chosen) and the intended control philosophy. Careful consideration will need to be given to all those essentials of realistic modelling already identified – as well as too a host of pragmatic but important factors such as layout environment, the need for portability, constructional methods envisaged and the budget, time and skills available. Any meaningful layout plan will need to show a lot more than mere track arrangement, and will need to be accompanied by a great deal of additional material.

In fact, I've found that only certain aspects of a layout design can usefully be presented in the form of a plan –

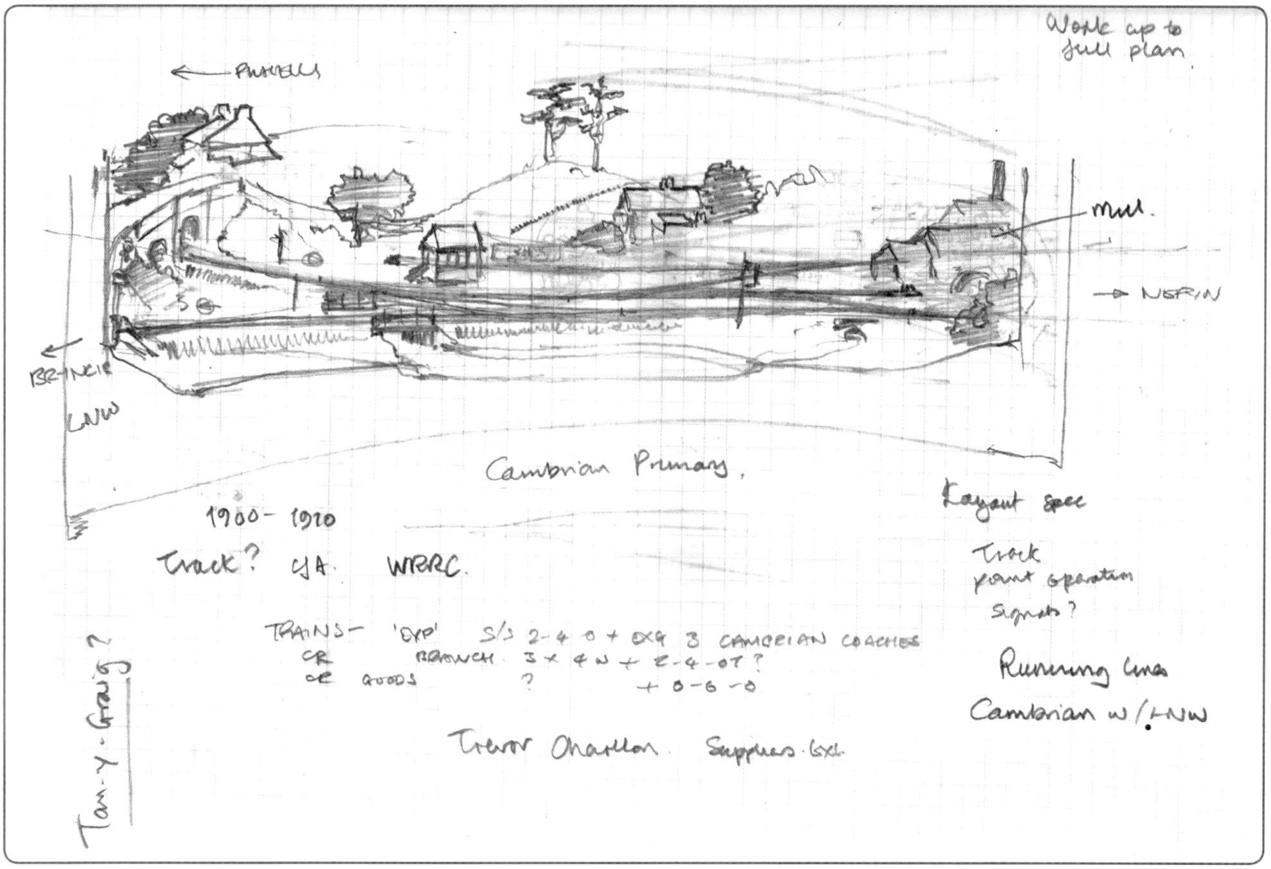

Work up to full plan

Cambrian Primary.

1900–1920

Track? WRRC.

Layout spec

Track
point operation
Signals?

Running lines
Cambrian w/LNW

Trevor Charlton. Supplies

Tan-y-Graig?

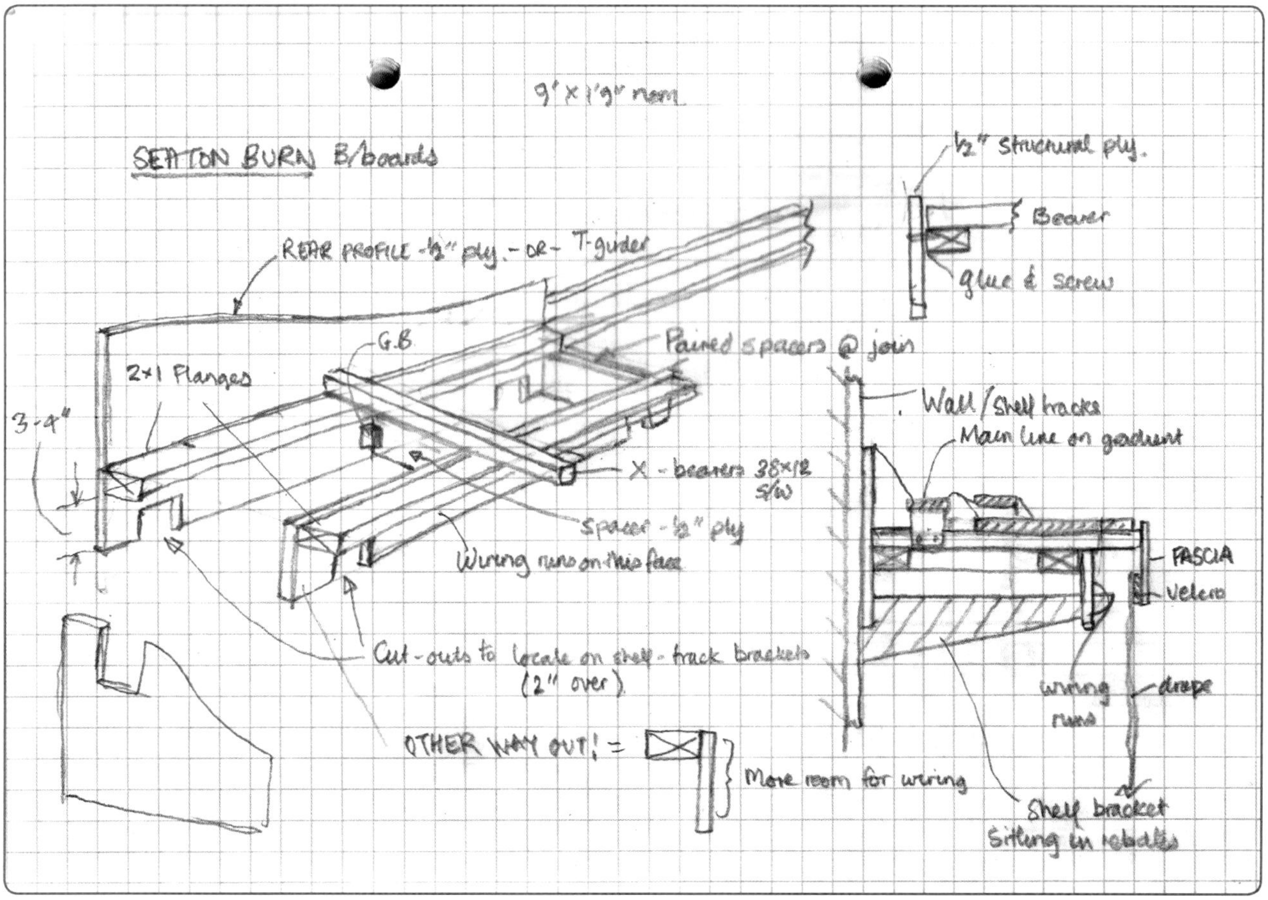

9' x 1'9" room

SEATON BURN B/boards

½" structural ply.

Bearer

glue & screw

REAR PROFILE ½" ply. – OR – T-girder

Paired spacers @ join

2x1 Flanges

Wall/shelf tracks

Main line on gradient

X-bearers

Spacer – ½" ply

Wiring runs on this face

FASCIA

Velcro

Cut-outs to locate on shelf-track brackets (2" over)

wiring runs

drape

OTHER WAY OUT! =

More room for wiring

Shelf bracket sitting in rebates

which is where a lot of CAD-style model railway design software falls down. Just as published layout designs are (or should be) accompanied by detailed notes, diagrams and prototype pictures, so our detailed layout planning drawings will need to be fleshed out with a copiously-illustrated prototype rationale and a comprehensive-written specification, documents over which it is well worth taking considerable trouble. A thoroughgoing layout specification is a vital tool both at the design stage, where it helps to clarify and direct thinking, as well as during the construction phase – when it keeps you true to your intent when submerged in the glue and sawdust.

Such a thorough and wide-ranging approach to designing a model railway demands considerable time and effort and represents a good work-out for the *'leetle grey cells'*. Far from consisting merely of armchair musing, 'holistic design' (if I might be permitted a modicum of ersatz jargon) is actually a pretty active pursuit. It embraces a wide range of disciplines, from prototype research through surveying, scale drawing, finding out how the other guy did it (why make your own mistakes when others have done it for you?), practical experiment, evaluation of what the trade has to offer, gaining a good understanding of the technicalities involved, project planning and even such mundane necessities as budgeting. Pipe dreams, alas, have price tags… However, all this hard-nosed nuts-and-bolts stuff is guided and informed by the underlying intent – the personal set of aspirations and priorities that hopefully crystallised during that spell of fireside musing.

Size matters: the influence of scale and standards

One of the key decisions in planning any model railway is choosing the scale you're going to work to. Often, this is predetermined by a pre-existing commitment to one particular scale and probably a set of associated wheel and track standards. But, there are occasions when a 'clean-slate' start is envisaged, in which case there are a number of factors to ponder. I'll have a bit to say about the practical pros and cons of the various scales elsewhere, but here I'm more concerned with the *ethos* of the various sizes, and the style and nature of the model railways to which they seem best suited. For if I've arrived at one conclusion in my many years of dabbling in modelling in a variety of sizes, it is that there's a lot more difference between the scales than any simple matter of mathematics. Rather, they engender different modelling *philosophies*. Although homogeneously realistic scenic model railways have been successfully built in all of the 'miniature' scales from 2mm/ft up to 0, the weighting is overwhelmingly tipped toward the smaller sizes. Above 7mm scale, the sheer size of individual models in relation to our typical field of view mitigates against the creation of panoramic and inclusive scenes of the sort proposed in these pages, while the requirement for a very high level of detail if such large models are to convince would render any such enterprise impracticable for normal mortals.

The balance of diminutive size and modelling potential offered by 2mm scale (1:150 proportion, in round figures) makes practicable projects of real scope, and some ambitious and superbly consistent panoramic models have emerged – notably the Model Railway Club's 'Copenhagen Fields' and the Manchester Club's 'Chee Tor'. These are both remarkable and ambitious fine-scale group projects, big in size and scope if small in scale. Keith Arme's 'Chipping Norton' espouses similar standards on a more modest footprint. The Croydon Club's 'Acton Main Line' uses mainstream N scale standards but still hits the highest levels of realism and atmosphere. To my eye, the chief virtue of 2mm scale is this ability to convincingly portray (to a surprising level of detail) a more generous slice of reality than is usually possible in the larger scales; it allows scale-length trains to traverse a worthwhile tract of landscape. The rather tautological flip-side of this 'broad brush' virtue is that 2mm is, I find, far less successful when used for truly tiny layouts. It's a truism that when there's not a lot to look *at*, you tend to look *closer* – and that's when the small size is at a disadvantage. Only the most accomplished 2mm fine-scale models can stand such scrutiny; in N, oversize wheel-flanges and chunky couplings – not overly apparent when the trains are viewed from a distance in a setting – become obtrusive and destroy realism.

Completely the opposite is the case with 0 scale, at a proportion of 1:43.5 the size *par excellence* for the detail-freak, but an intimidating prospect when it comes to realistic landscape modelling. We've become accustomed to encountering mind-blowing examples of the loco-builder's art in 7mm. scale, models replete with every last nut, bolt, rivet and split-pin. But have you ever come across a similarly-complete scale rendition of a full-grown English oak? The

LEFT: *A layout that really exploits the potential of British N scale is Graham Hedge's 'Stoney Lane Depot', which portrays an entirely convincing slice of workaday contemporary South London in a modest space. An apt choice of subjects, acute observation, and some wonderful structure modelling make for realism and atmosphere in spadefulls– something apparently not lost on younger viewers! Clever design, skilfully reworked stock and the use of less-obtrusive Kadee couplings largely mitigate the normal N drawbacks.* Adrian Colenutt

better part of two feet tall, with accurately textured bark, twenty-thousand odd twigs and half a million leaves? No? Neither have I. For the good and simple reason that to make such a model would take most of us half a lifetime. Yes, it *is* possible to produce truly realistic homogeneous scenic layouts at this size, but to do so takes a careful choice of subject, a lot of time and great skill. Which is why such models are exceedingly rare. Leaving aside the remarkable and legendary (if unfinished) Norris layout of the 1950s (created by the wealthy and inspired patron who was able to command the services of a modelling genius, Bernard Miller), I can call to mind only a few modern examples: Martin Welch's 'Hursley' (which created an absolute sensation when first seen) and, principally, the work of one supremely-gifted artist, Gordon Gravett. Gordon has given us the Tal-y-Llyn dioramas, the wonderful (but ultra-compact) 'Ditchling Green' and now the truly stunning 1:50 'Pempoul' – in the opinion of this scribe one of the finest – if not *the* finest – scenic model railways yet built in *any* scale.

It's the sheer amount of work involved in working to anything like the full potential of 7mm scale that mitigates against large scenic 0 gauge layouts that can be truly classed as 'realistic'. There have been quite a few aspirants – but to my eye only the merest handful of contenders, most notably 'Pempoul'. Almost always, the trains, track, signals and structures are superbly modelled – but are let down by the landscaping and presentation, which is rarely to anything like the same standard. Homogeneous they ain't! Many large 0 gauge layouts are really little more than glorified test-tracks on which to run collections of individual models. There is a healthy and wealthy collector's market in high-quality 0 gauge equipment, but the vast majority of such models are finished to 'exhibition' standards – the perfection of finish being a large component of their collectability and value. Toning-down the gloss to blend such a model with scenic layout colouring would impair this value; weathering it to a realistic working condition would probably render it almost worthless! Therefore, in my experience, the most successful 0 gauge layouts have been modest affairs, relatively small and simple, where the modelling workload is far more manageable and standards can be kept uniformly high. To me, layouts like 'Ditchling Green' and Martin Brent's witty and affectionate 'Arcadia' actually exploit the potential of 7mm scale far better than the more ambitious essays. My philosophy with regard to realistic modelling in 0 is definitely 'less is more'; I regard it as the ultimate scale for a small layout.

Which brings us to the 'median scales' of 3.5mm/ft 'H0' (1:87 proportion) and 4mm/ft (1:76.2). The former is by a huge margin the most popular modelling scale worldwide, being shared by the USA and most of Europe. In a UK context, a few dedicated souls cling to British-outline H0 for its combination of compact size with accurate track gauge, but the overwhelming majority of modellers working in H0 here are modelling US or European prototypes. The predominant 'British' scale is, of course, 4mm/ft – usually associated with the inaccurate but pragmatic 00 compromise of using the H0 track gauge of 16.5mm, but having a healthy and growing proportion of modellers working to finer scale track and wheel standards: 18.2mm gauge EM or exact 18.83mm gauge P4. But it's the *scale* not the standard I'm concerned with here – and the overwhelming virtue of both 4mm and H0 is that they are adaptable to a wide range of modelling intent. They offer something of the landscape and structural modelling facility

ABOVE: *Many scenic 0 gauge layouts are relatively small and based around urban/industrial themes, thus avoiding the need for much in the way of landscape modelling. This is Nigel Bowyer's 'Napier Street', seen at the Uckfield show in 2004. Typically, this layout uses the potential of the large scale to present a small but richly-detailed scene which permits intricate and realistic shunting.* Adrian Colenutt

BELOW: *The world's most popular railway modelling scale is H0, 3.5mm/1ft, 1:87 proportion – big enough to offer real scope for ultimate realism and fine detail no matter what the subject. This wonderfully-observed scene (look at those convincing coal piles – the 'angle of repose' is spot-on) is part of 'Ericus Quay', a stunning P87 diorama built by Winfried Schmitz-Esser. The model depicts part of the historic port of Hamburg between the wars.* Winfried Schmitz-Esser

LEFT: *A model in the 'Median' British scale – 4mm/ft, 1:76.2 proportion – but far-from average in subject. This is Corrieshalloch station on Simon de Souza's P4 layout based on the Highland Railway's projected (but never built) line to Ullapool. The scale is large enough to allow plenty of detail and to facilitate scratchbuilding, but small enough to offer the scenic scope needed to model the Western Highlands of Scotland convincingly, as here.* Author

associated with 2mm scale in conjunction with levels of detail and fidelity that can rival 0. In choosing these scales you can indeed enjoy the best of both worlds, working at a size amenable to layouts ranging from the megalomaniac to the minimal. Their long popularity has also ensured massive and comprehensive commercial support, rendering them both affordable and accessible.

The adaptability and strong commercial backing of N, H0 and 00 tends to make them the 'default choices' of modelling sizes and standards for the uncommitted; they're the only ones offering a wide choice of affordable RTR (ready-to-run) models and lots of kits. Certainly, if you're after a quick and easy result then opting for one of these mainstream, commercially supported scale/gauge combinations is the way to go. But if the journey – in the shape of rewarding modelling challenge – is as important as the result, then it is always worth looking to the fine-scale derivatives of the popular scales, or considering the two 'minority' scales: 3mm/ft 1:100 proportion TT and 3/16in/ft 1:64 proportion S. These sizes bracket the median scales and offer their own unique combinations of virtues – of which individuality is not the least with 3mm giving much of the scope of 2mm but offering mechanical and detailing potential more akin to 4mm. It allows you to use modest spaces for similar subjects to 4mm, but with significantly less cramping and greater landscaping potential. S sits between 4mm and 7mm scales, and is entirely a finescale discipline with accurate wheel and track standards. It permits detailing levels comparable to the best 0 scale, but is usefully more compact and considerably more amenable to most aspects of scenic modelling.

The standards crunch

Second only to the general choice of scale comes the selection of precise scale/gauge combinations and wheel and track standards within that scale: N or 2mm finescale? 00, EM or P4? 0f or Scaleseven? There are some notes on the practicalities of these various options in Chapter 4, but here I'm concerned with the effect a given choice of standards has

BELOW: *Opting to work in a true minority scale like 3/16 in/1ft, S – with a mere handful of kits and components available – usually poses a considerable modelling challenge. But allied to a subject – such as the Bishop's Castle Railway – for which almost nothing is available commercially in any scale, choosing S makes perfect sense and unlocks considerable modelling potential. This is 'Lydham Heath', by Barry Norman.* Adrian Colenutt

on the overall layout design – the basic premise being that there's precious little point in donning the hair shirt of finescale standards if you don't then apply the same degree of fidelity and modelling quality to all the other aspects of the layout. Indeed, it is my experience that a really well-observed and executed layout in a 'compromised' standard like N or 00 is usually far more convincing than an unevenly-modelled fine scale essay. Put another way, if time and resources are limited, then sticking with the ease and convenience of mainstream standards and putting the effort into getting the best out of them in the context of the overall layout will probably give a more realistic and satisfactory result than taking the hard road of finescale. The considerable additional work and cash demanded can all-too-often result in skimping elsewhere – and then bang goes that all-important consistency.

In a design context, then, the overriding quest for homogeneity will affect not just the track and wheel standards chosen for the execution of the project, but may well dictate the scope and form of the layout itself. How so? It all comes back to my holistic design thesis, to the consideration of all aspects of the proposed layout in concert; marrying such fundamental design decisions as the degree of scale fidelity with intractables like space, time, money and scope becomes far more critical. This is a key point, worth analysing in specifics. So let us take an extreme case and suppose you have decided (as an increasing number of modellers *are* doing), that you will work to exact-scale track and wheel standards and that all your locomotives will be built from the finest 'super kits', replete with every nut, bolt and rivet, fitted with full working inside valve gear and capable of the minutest inspection from a range of two inches through a jeweller's eye glass. These paragons will, of course, haul matching rakes of handbuilt carriages with full interiors, or long trains of wagons detailed inside and out and fitted with sprung suspension and superdetailed etched running gear. What then are the implications for all the other aspects of the layout?

Well, for a start, if you opt for finescale track then the chances are you'll be building all the pointwork yourself; even in the popular 4mm scale. While good 'fine 00', EM and P4 flexible track is to be had, mass-produced ready-to-use pointwork isn't. Constructing it will consume a great deal of time, effort and money and call for a considerable level of skill. If track-building's not your cup of tea, then you'll be paying someone else another big bundle of money to do the job for you. Whichever way you look at it, your fine scale PW will inevitably call for several times the investment of resources that would be entailed in sticking to 'mainstream' 00 standards and using the functional but comparatively inauthentic products of Messrs Peco. Faced with these unpalatable facts (for such they are, and no amount of wishful thinking will make them otherwise), many modellers opt to trim their fine scale trackplans to a believable minimum, trading quantity for quality in a classic 'less is more' approach. That's the tack I've often sailed on.

As with the track, so with the locos and stock – although here, the law of diminishing returns also rears its ugly head. Whereas in the matter of track, scale-railed, fully chaired, correctly gauged 4mm fine-scale PW is palpably

ABOVE: *Spot the 00 error… Opting for fine standards using scale rail sections and fully chaired track, and looking across the result at close to eye level, the lack of width between the railheads is unapparent. However, just like EM or P4, this approach calls for hand-built turnouts. The visible plain track on 'Maiden Newtown' may be C&L flexible, but the matching pointwork is all tailor-made using the 'ply and rivet' method with C&L plastic chairs applied cosmetically. Off-scene, however, Peco rules supreme!* Author

RIGHT: *No. 7715, the '57XX' GWR pannier tank I use on 'Trerice', has a modified and detailed Bachmann RTR body on an aftermarket, fine-scale chassis. It's not as refined or complete as a state-of-the-art kit (wot, no working inside valve gear!) but in the context of the layout these deficiencies are not unduly apparent. The model probably has about 90 per cent of the 'full house' look – for about 40 per cent of the effort and a quarter the cost.* Author

more realistic than off-the-peg 00 (or, rather, H0) Peco Streamline, the same isn't true of many contemporary RTR models – locos or rolling stock. Yes, a skilfully built and (especially) well-painted P4 Mitchell GW '45XX' 2-6-2T (to take a random but specific example) *will* be superior to an equivalent Bachmann 00 model – correct to gauge with finer wheels, more refined in it's detailing, a little more delicate about the sheet-work. But it won't be *that* much better, certainly when viewed from a couple of feet away in the context of a layout. The days when most RTR models incorporated substantial compromises in dimensions and proportions, had grossly coarse-scale wheels, incomplete valve gear, poor-quality mechanisms, crude paint finishes and lacked any but the most basic of details are long gone. Ditto for rolling stock. Going the high-end kit route is trading a lot of time and money for a relatively small gain in realism.

The pragmatic trade-off

Of course, there's more to the standards choice than mere pounds, pence and workbench-hours. A lot of modellers opt to work in fine scale and build their locomotives and rolling stock from kits or even from scratch because doing so is what they want from the hobby. Indeed, for many such people, the layout is often subordinate to the trains – being more by way of a showcase-cum-test-track than a prime objective. Realism and homogeneity may well be sacrificed on the altar of rivet-counting and the quality of individual models. This observation is, I hasten to add, not a criticism so much as a matter of observing differing agendas. Standing this 'quality-v-time' argument on its head, I have long advocated a rather less proscriptive approach in the matter of selecting ingredients for my own P4 layouts. So long as a model lives in happy homogeneity with the rest of the layout, I don't much care if it's modified RTR, kit-built, kit-bashed, bodged, scratchbuilt or trawled from some unknown source on eBay. Adopting this stance enables me to cut the odd corner without compromising the overall result – even if I maybe loose a few status points down at the clubroom when I confess that my new '45XX' is a tarted-up second-hand Bachmann with a drop-in wheel conversion rather than *echter-schloss* Mitchell with a custom paint job.

Taking all these factors into account, the 'benchmark standard' that you choose to apply when scheming out a layout will have a direct and fundamental impact on the size and scope of what you can realistically contemplate. In almost all cases there will be some trade-off between the ultimate possible standard and that which is attainable; either you settle for a less-exalted benchmark or accept a more modest layout in terms of scope. Speaking personally, I've long been wedded to fine-scale wheel and track standards and a relatively high (but far from 'ultimate') level of detail – so I've learnt to trim my aspirations as to layout size and complexity accordingly. It's a formula that has served me well, and even today – when I have a 10 x 20 foot layout space at my disposal – I still find myself opting for a modest scheme with a simple subject, a straightforward track plan and a limited structure count.

ABOVE: *The pragmatic choice: 00 fine scale. Andrew Duncan would have liked to have built his 4mm scale GWR 'Weymouth Lines' layout to EM or P4 standards – but that would have demanded curves of far wider radius than the available site (a long but narrow cellar) could have accommodated. Adopting fine scale 00 permitted tight curves on hidden sections while giving a realistic appearance to the visible areas of the layout – the more so as these were designed so that you are generally looking across the tracks at close to eye level, when the gauge error is less apparent.* Author

A design, moreover, calling for only a few extra items of motive power and rolling stock over what I have to hand. That way, I'm happy I can maintain my desired modelling standards and – given that I'm now in my early sixties, increasingly afflicted by Parkinson's, and far from rich – get the thing built over a reasonable timescale so that I can accomplish the work and still have something to enjoy in my dotage.

In advocating such a trade-off I'm not seeking to suggest that the achieving the very best standards is the sole province of the small layout; a visit to Pendon – as well as providing its usual shot of 22-carrat inspiration – will demonstrate that even the largest of model railways can be constructed without undue compromise. Not utterly *without* compromise, mind; when setting Pendon's wheel and track standards, Guy Williams chose to stick with less-accurate EM rather than adopting 'exact' S4 – a decision taken in the cause of manageable maintenance. But Pendon can anyway hardly be taken as a valid role-model for the *individual*; what you see today is the result of more than 50 years of effort involving many skilled and dedicated modellers working as a team – in itself a considerable achievement – and a total expenditure that must by now be numbered well into the millions. If Pendon has an overall lesson to teach, it is perhaps that it reveals the true cost of achieving ultimate quality.

Many hands?

Pendon, in common with a number of other outstanding layouts that have been seen in recent years, is a team effort – and involving more people is one obvious way of easing the size/standards/man-hours crunch and expanding the possible scope of a project. It is not, however, a sure-fire answer in the face of that overriding homogeneity requirement, as you've then got the problem of getting several modellers to work to the same exacting standard. Pendon uses an 'apprentice scheme' to school aspiring and appropriately-gifted contributors in their tightly-defined techniques and standards, with the ultimate arbitration of appointed team leaders looking after the quality control – an approach that works well in the context of an 'invitation only' group of like-minded modellers with compatible skill levels, clear aims and good leadership.

Achieving a consistent result is much more difficult in the context of a looser group such as typical model railway club. Here – in true democratic spirit – the layout must embrace the input of all, no matter what their skill level or aspiration. This is *not* an argument against club layouts per se, which fulfil an invaluable role in the hobby as a whole, but it is a recognition that the laissez-faire element inherent in their constitution is not likely to produce a particularly homogenous or realistic result. But then, that's a requirement that usually lies some way down the 'target list' when such a layout is being designed, if it figures at all. Club layouts have other fish to fry: inclusion, enjoyment, the chance to learn, a collective result with which a lot of people can identify, and the creation of a something which can entertain both operators and spectators when exhibited. It's a different hymn-sheet, but no less musical…

The other established way of easing the standards/man-hours crunch in creating a layout is to buy someone else's time and skill for all or part of the job – the 'cheque-book' approach to railway modelling. It's fashionable among the hair-shirt end of the hobby to look down disparagingly on those who resort to the fountain-pen in a quest for quality or, indeed, for a model railway at all. But the fact is that in the world of modern high-pressure commerce, there are significant numbers of people who have to work such long hours at such demanding jobs that finding the time and energy needed to build even the simplest of layouts to any sort of standard is out of the question. However, this same group is usually not short of the sort of disposable income which makes it possible to use the services of professional builders. Track, structures, locos and stock are the usual candidates for 'farming out' and it's not uncommon to encounter whole layouts equipped entirely with a mouth-watering collection of professionally-built models. Envy of such high-priced excellence may *just* account for some of the disdain directed at their owners…

In fact, unless counted among that tiny handful of die-hards who build every last thing themselves from scratch, we're all cheque-book modellers to some degree. Buying a kit is buying someone else's time and skill; and if that kit

ABOVE: *'Treneglos' is a beautifully executed and realistic fine scale 00 layout that demonstrates unequivocally that a like-minded group of people (in this case, the 'Withered Arm Group' of the Stafford Railway Circle) can work together to produce a truly consistent result.*

It also demonstrates the intelligent use of modern, state-of-the-art RTR as a springboard for a layout of high quality. Yes, this is a form of 'chequebook modelling' – but the result is no mere collection of nice-but-unrelated models. Adrian Colenutt

is an ultra-sophisticated 'super kit', you're actually buying rather a lot of both! At a rather less elevated level, the most typical of 'mainstream' home layouts, one using RTR locos and stock, ready-made track, plastic kit structures and off-the-peg accessories, is just as much a creation of the credit card as the most highfalutin custom-built job costing ten times as much. Even most 'finescale' layouts – mine being absolutely typical in this – depend for most of their ingredients on commercial sources of one sort or another. However, it's what you do with all this largesse that makes the difference; it's all too easy to cook an inedible meal from the finest ingredients…

No matter how large or how modest the amount of money spent, using 'bought-in' models of whatever provenance will inevitably bring you up against that over-riding problem in the quest for realism: getting everything to a common standard. A problem it is too, even if all you aspire to is matching the excellence of the best current RTR. Ascend to the heights of the top end of the custom-built, no-expense-spared stratosphere, and it's horribly easy to end up with a collection of models that, while faultless in themselves, just don't 'gel' in the context of a layout. This is particularly true in the matter of finish; many professional model painters are attuned to the requirements of the 'showcase' collector, who requires a faultless, usually bright-and-glossy 'exhibition finish'. Admirable though such models may be when displayed in isolation, they're invariably far too 'in your face' when placed on a layout. However, pointing an airbrush loaded with your favoured 'crud' mix at such a model in an effort to 'blend it in' is a tad more daunting than doing the same to a mass-produced RTR model with

ABOVE: *My 'Woolverstone' layout, built in 1988 to try out many of the ideas contained in this book, is an example of practical realism. Rather than aiming for the ultimate, 'Woolverstone' was conceived from the outset as a layout with only a moderate level of detail, facilitated by the extensive use of the Wills Scenic Series kits and building materials sheets. These ensured consistency of texture and detailing, a key ingredient of realism.* Author

a tenth the price tag! (Although it must be said that much modern RTR equipment is so well-finished and so admirably restrained in its colouration that the need for such toning down is greatly reduced.)

Setting a quality benchmark

There are a great many factors to consider here – some to do with that minds-eye vision of what you're seeking, but many of them hard practical limitations as to what is possible, in the light of restrictions and requirements resulting from circumstances or other design decisions. For it's an inherent characteristic of the design process that amendments of any one aspect have implications for all the others. As a key example of this interaction of factors in benchmarking, let's return to the thorny question of detail level – which, thus far, I have, I'll confess – treated in a somewhat simplistic manner; it's time to examine this in more detail.

So – although every single object in the real world is complete to the very *last* detail, we're only actually *aware* of this when we choose to concentrate our attention on some small part of reality. Much of what is out there we're simply oblivious to, either because we can't physically see it (hidden behind something else, too small, too far away, lacking illumination) or because our minds filter it out as irrelevant and distracting. The real world may be uniformly and completely detailed, but we don't *perceive* it as such – and taking account of our perception is a key element of realistic design; it's the flip-side of observation.

So here's something else to throw into the benchmarking pot – helpfully, in this instance. Cut it which way you will, there's one inescapable fact about detail on a model: if you can't actually *see* it, then it serves no useful purpose! But how much detail you *can* see on the various elements of a typical model railway scene will depend very much on the way the layout is presented to the viewer – in particular, the height at which it is displayed and the distance and direction from which it is actually viewed. This is where the modern approach of displaying layouts close to eye level pays dividends, in that it puts the viewer in a much closer and more natural relationship with the modelled scene. This is such a fundamental relationship that I'd place display height at the top of the list of key decisions in planning any layout, which is why it figures large in the next chapter.

The way a layout is going to be seen affects virtually every other aspect of the design, none more so than the business of determining the modelling input needed to realise it. Cutting down on the amount there is *to* do frees up resources to raise the standard of what *is* done – so anything that can be accomplished in this direction has a direct influence on the benchmark chosen. Tailoring this modelling input isn't rocket science. I've never seen the point in, say, fully finishing all four sides of a building when only two of them are visible. Similarly, there's precious little point in going to the trouble of fitting an interior to a building of which only the roof and chimney-pots are visible, or one sited so far from the viewing position that you can't actually see into it. And then, if we're modelling realistically, our observing eye will tell us we need to take account of 'distance recession', the falling off of perceived colour and texture (and detail basically *is* colour and texture) as things get further away. This occurs even within the depth of our modelled scene, to a degree determined by the available width. At 4mm scale, an object sited at the rear of a scene a mere two feet deep and viewed from a couple of feet in front of the layout is actually the equivalent of reality seen from a hundred yards away. At that range, you'll see the front door of a house – but not the button of the doorbell...

Perceived detail design

Looked at from another angle, taking account of this 'visibility factor' in respect of detail is a useful way of boosting the achievable benchmark. If you adopt an approach to detail that says 'I'm only going to put it on if it can be seen from the layout's normal viewpoint and viewing distance', then you can dramatically reduce the man-hour requirement without compromising the conviction of the end result. This in turn

ABOVE: *Here is the opposite end of the detailing and architectural modelling spectrum to the plastic pragmatism of 'Woolverstone': the mill stables at Orford Haven, on the East Suffolk Light – Bob Barlow at his inspired best. This is very much a 'Pendon' approach: everything built uncompromisingly from scratch using laborious techniques (those bricks are chads, applied one at a time!). Acute observation ensures that nothing is missing, nothing is out of place, and all is utterly consistent. This one small corner probably consumed more man-hours than all the buildings on 'Woolverstone' put together; but both approaches can produce a realistic result.* Alan Dench

may well enable you to raise your overall game somewhat, by diverting effort into those areas of the layout that are most apparent. Indeed, you can build on this approach by planning the model to draw the eye to these areas while 'backing off' and allowing a bit of respite elsewhere. There is such a thing as the layout with too *much* detail – resulting in a modelled scene that is excessively 'busy' and overwhelmed with visual clutter. In reality, when faced with such a prospect, our inbuilt 'mind filters' exclude irrelevant detail – so it pays to do the same on our model; that perception/observation factor again.

I call this approach – planning around the use of restricted and graduated detail levels within a scene – 'perceived detail design'; it's a benchmarking technique that I've made extensive use of throughout the planning and construction of my own layouts. It may well seem at odds with my emphasis on homogeneity, but that's where the observation comes in; if there's one motto that should be writ large in the annals of realistic railway modelling, it's the old adage that starts: 'If it *looks* right…' My aim is to create a model railway that 'looks right' when seen from the intended viewpoint – something of which the informed, observing eye is the best judge. As well as governing the presentation, opting to plan a layout around careful selection and modelling of perceived detail can govern other design decisions – like the choice and placement of subjects within the scene and the constructional techniques chosen to build them. A model railway conceived along these lines is really very much akin to a stage or film set – something which is contrived to be thoroughly convincing from the stalls or the camera position, even if an obvious sham from all other directions!

Trains in the landscape

Thus far, of course, I've been considering the fixed elements of the model railway – the setting, rather than the actual trains. The big difference between these two principal components is that the trains move, whereas the setting – by and large – doesn't. (True, alas, even of those things that *should* move – like running water, figures and animals, road vehicles, wind-blown grass and trees…) In particular, trains can travel between the different areas of our modelled scene – passing from foreground to mid-scene and into the background. So far as detail level goes, this mobility means that you often can't use positioning, orientation or scenic recession to assess what is appropriate for locomotives and rolling stock. In fact, a moment's consideration will suggest that they all need to be detailed to 'full foreground' standards as the likelihood is that at least some of the time, that's where they'll be! Which is jolly convenient, as most of us like our locos and stock to function as stand-alone, well-detailed models in their own right, rather than regarding them simply as items of hardware incidental to the layout. So opting to up the detailing ante on the trains is rarely a hardship – except in that the quality and finish of all the stock needs to be to a common high standard.

In the overall layout context, applying a higher-than-average level of detail to our trains isn't too much of a problem in the consistency stakes, as the extra detail simply won't be apparent when they're in less-prominent areas

BELOW: *Often regarded as the 'trains-in-the-landscape' scale par excellence: 2mm scale. Relatively few model locomotives in this small size, however, can stand 'stage front' close-up examination. Here's one that can – Mick Simpson's scratchbuilt 2mm fine scale ex-NER G5, seen on 'Wansbeck Road', Mick's affectionate but accurate portrayal of a workaday mining-town branchline in Co. Durham's coal country.* Mick Simpson

of the layout. What is essential, though, is to keep the *colouring* right in the context of the setting, particularly the intensity of the colours and the degree of gloss in the finish. This will obviously call for something of a compromise where equipment can occupy different parts of the scene at different times. However, given the modest scene depths we're usually working with I find that this is rarely a problem. The effects of visual recession are subtle and provided the tonal values fall within the range of the layout as a whole then the observing eye is not offended. If it is, then it's time to get the airbrush out for a tad of toning down.

There's a corollary to this conundrum, in that you might well want to capitalise on well-detailed trains by arranging the layout design to place them for the most part in areas of the scene where they can be fully appreciated. So, for instance, if you *are* going in for engines with full working inside valve gear, then you'll want to ensure that there is at least some trackage on the layout on which this refinement can be appreciated – that is, located and presented in such a way that the locomotives can be very much 'front of stage' and viewed slightly from above. This requirement will affect not just the track-plan but also the display height, nature and extent of the foreground and probably the layout lighting.

Terminology

Before moving on to consider the actual processes – theoretical, factual, visual and practical – of layout design, I must return briefly to the exhortations of Franklin the physics master and define a few more terms. Like all specialised disciplines, model railway layout design has developed a vocabulary all its own, much of which uses common terminology in a specific way. To avoid confusion, it seemed a good idea to round off these preliminaries by taking a brief look at the main bits of jargon in which I'm apt to indulge.

There being no official arbiter of correct 'model railway speak', I hasten to point out that the following are my own interpretations of the various terms; that said, these definitions are the sense in which I'll be using them in these pages, so there is some relevance where usually-accepted meanings are a bit vague. Whether we like it or not, railway modelling does demand a *modicum* of precision. Some words, thankfully, retain their wider meaning. The word 'scale', for instance, still defines the numeric modelling scale whether given as a scale name ('British N scale', H0, 0), a proportional ratio (1:148, 1:87, 1:43.5) or expressed in the familiar bastard (mixed unit of measurement) 'linear' fashion as 'so many millimetres to the foot'. But what is probably worth reiterating at this point is that some common descriptions of 'modelling scale' are not strictly *scales* as such, but rather refer to scale/gauge *combinations*.

This can be very confusing, especially in the case of N. Here, the letter used on its own simply denotes the use of a track gauge of nine millimetres – but add the word 'scale' and it has a decidedly different connotation. Or rather, a pair of connotations, for 'British N Scale' uses a scale ratio of 1:148 on the 9mm gauge, equating to a linear scale of 2.06mm/ft and giving an erroneous full-size track gauge equivalence of 4ft 4½in – whereas 'European/American N scale' uses a ratio of 1:160 on the same 9mm track gauge, a linear scale of 1.91mm/1ft, which gives an accurate full-size track gauge equivalence. On the other hand, 2mm *Finescale* (which pre-dates N by a clear 40 years) uses a linear scale of *exactly* 2mm/ft with a ratio of 1:152.4 and a (spot-on) track gauge of 9.42mm. How they coped with all those decimals decades before the invention of the electronic calculator I'll never know! Fortunately, in practice, there are rarely any problems in all this N mishmash; few prototypes short of the Channel Tunnel call for a mix of 1:148 and 1:160 scales, while the difference between 1:148 and 1:152.4 is small enough to be visibly insignificant.

Things aren't quite so bad at the British 'median' scale of 4mm/1ft. Yes, there are three 'standard gauge' alternatives: 00, EM and P4 – but they all use 4mm/1ft scale and the 1:76.2 ratio, albeit with differing track gauges and wheel standards. 'Standards' in this context refers to a defined set of dimensions covering precise wheel profiles and a full set of track parameters – but the word does also creep in rather more subjectively when it's used to describe the level of quality and detail aspired to. 'Superdetail standard' was an old chestnut, expressing aspirations as to high quality and completeness. In the context of this book, I use the concept of 'benchmark quality' to define the modelling yardstick at which the layout as a whole is aimed.

Specific layout design terminology

There are some general terms that I use in a very specific way when analysing the designing process. So 'site' in layout planning I take to mean a location where a model railway can take up residence on a permanent basis. This hallowed enclave I look at not just as a set of linear dimensions in plan, but very much as a three-dimensional space, in which vertical dimensions are as important as horizontal area. Other important site factors include the quality of the environment, nature of the building in which it is situated and the suitability for purpose. One of the fundamental aspects of a layout site is the type of 'footprint' it can accommodate – this being the precise shape that the layout can take: L-shaped, linear, circular, teardrop, C-shaped, hollow rectangle, hollow oval, solid rectangle, U-shaped and curvilinear, are all possible footprints. Many sites are amenable to more than one possible footprint, while the dimensions of the site will determine the all-important footprint proportions.

The 'subject' of a layout is its content, usually described in the form of a brief summary. Thus 'large branchline terminus', 'small classification yard', 'medium-sized MPD' and 'country junction' are all classic subject descriptions, which can be made more precise by adding a little basic detail: 'Two-platform branchline terminus with three-road goods yard, single-stall loco shed and dairy' gives a pretty fair idea of what we're talking about. Larger and more complex layouts might, of course, have several subjects, in which case the summary becomes rather more of a list: 'Four-platform terminus with freight and parcels depot, two-road loco shed with turntable, carriage sidings, classification yard and junction'. An apt

LEFT: *Truly realistic prototype modelling: looking along the yard on Chris Lamacraft's wonderfully-convincing EM rendition of Hemyock, terminus of the GWR Culm Valley branch. Atmosphere!* Author

choice of subject(s) and the successful reconciliation of the demands thus made with the space available is a critical and fundamental aspect of layout design.

Allied to subject is the concept of 'scope' – which essentially comes down to how much of your chosen subject you're going to try to represent. This is often dependent on the scale chosen; for instance, with a given site and subject, the 'scope' options may range from modelling only part of a station in 0 through the whole station and immediate environs in 4mm scale and the station complete with landscape surroundings in N. The scope of a layout may also be determined by choice and interests, which can also have a fundamental impact on the choice of subject. It was traditional in years gone by to restrict the scope of a model railway purely to the railway itself; trains and track took up 100% of the available space, with everything beyond the boundary fence being deemed of no significance or interest. By contrast, the modern school of scenic railway modelling – epitomised by layouts like Barry Norman's 'Petherick' – often calls for a relatively small and simple subject – in railway terms – to be sited on a generous footprint in order to give plenty of scope to model the landscape setting.

'Format' in layout planning simply refers to the basic nature of the model railway. 'Continuous run', 'terminus to fiddleyard', 'end-to-end', 'linked scenes' and 'out-and-back' are all basic layout formats – broad categories into one or other of which all model railways fall. Format descriptions can usefully be made more precise and informative by being a bit more proscriptive and adding footprint and subject information: 'L-shaped branchline terminus/ approach section/fiddleyard' or 'Continuous run oval with one-side staging feeding large though station'. These three parameters of layout design – footprint, format and subject – are inextricably linked and often in conflict; the challenge is to arrive at the best trade-off between them.

'Prototype' has a range of meanings in layout design terminology, all to do with the relationship of the subject with the real thing. Strictly speaking, then, a 'prototype' layout is one that sets out to replicate an actual place at a given date as accurately as possible. True prototype layouts are rare animals, as most real locations pose intractable problems of size, footprint, orientation and operation. Much more common is a 'prototype-based' layout, which takes an actual location as a starting point, but adapts it as needed to make a workable proposition for a layout. A 'prototypical' layout, on the other hand, may represent a subject that had no existence in reality, but does it in such a way that everything included in the model is accurately modelled from life. The last general meaning of 'prototype' as a layout describer refers to the railway company whose practice is being followed and often the period being modelled – in which context, it's usually appended to the subject description: A *1930s GW* branchline terminus, a *pre-WW1 LNWR* classification yard, a *BR-era ex-GE* country junction. Often, the company and period to be modelled is the first aspect of a layout design to be fixed, with the nature of the subject being subsidiary to this 'prototype choice'.

'Freelance' is a description long-used in railway modelling, being applied to a model railway which follows no actual prototype. In the days when RTR models were crude and few, kits non-existent and definitive prototype data much harder to obtain, there was a tradition of railway modelling in which the 'prototype' was entirely dreamed up by the modeller, who became his own loco designer, architect and structural engineer; the results were often entertaining, but rarely realistic! Later, the term came to mean an assemblage of models of subjects of random provenance, along the lines of the immortal Madder Valley.

BELOW: *Possibly the last word in off-the-wall esotericism goes to my near-neighbour Nick Saltzman, who models the broad gauge Bristol & Exeter Railway in 3mm fine scale. In common with the majority of model railways, 'Bagborough' represents a fictional location but follows prototype practice faithfully – although a lot of people find that a little hard to believe when confronted with this model of the B&E's 'steam carriage' No. 29 Fairfield, built in 1848!* Adrian Colenutt

2 SITE, HEIGHT AND LIGHT

In my introductory ramble around the whole business of layout design, I made much of the wisdom of considering *all* the aspects of a layout while planning it – including the various practical parameters. However, such practical planning can't be carried out in a vacuum; it's a process that needs to be informed by a good understanding of what works and what doesn't, of the alternative ways of arriving at a desired result, and of the traps that lie ever in wait for the unwary. Much of this necessary know-how comes from experience – a commodity hard-won in the business of layout-building, something that most sane people attempt only a few times in a lifetime.

By that measure, I am not a sane person. At a rough reckoning, over the past four decades I have built or had a goodly hand in some two dozen or so layouts, ranging from the miniscule ('Hepton Wharf', all of 3ft 9in long), to large American affairs covering several hundred square feet. Most, however, have been at the smaller end of the size spectrum, and the vast majority have been portable and exhibitable. Scales have been mostly 3, 3.5 and 4mm/1ft with the odd dash of N and a frosting of 0 gauge. And yes, a few of these essays were flops of one sort or another, abandoned before completion, as fatally flawed or short-lived due to shortcomings of design or ill-considered methods of construction (usually in the matter of baseboards). So what I offer here by way of practical planning advice is the result of this modelling life-time's worth of mistakes, misjudgements and occasional excesses of wishful thinking.

Site before subject?

The practicalities of designing a model railway start with the site – something which is almost always subject to the Fifth Law of Railway Modelling. That's the one that says 'Whatever space is available for a layout is neither quite big enough nor quite the right shape to contain whatever it is you'd ideally

ABOVE: *This is the 'Maiden Newtown' segment of Andrew Duncan's fine scale 00 'Weymouth Lines' layout, shoehorned into a series of somewhat-cramped cellars beneath a large Edwardian villa. The space shown is some 12ft long but only a shade under 6ft wide – a dimension that dictated the adoption of 00 rather than a more accurate gauge for the inside-viewed oval format. The misspelling of the name Maiden Newton is deliberate, to acknowledge the compromises that have had to be made.* Author

BELOW: *The other traditional layout site has always been the roof-space, but that also usually has drawbacks. The attic housing 'Pixton Magna', Bob Wills's own 4mm scale model railway, is long – nearly 30ft – but rather narrow and somewhat lacking in headroom, with very low eaves. The resulting linear layout is arranged for seated operation and has the backscene painted directly on the wall/ceiling.* Author

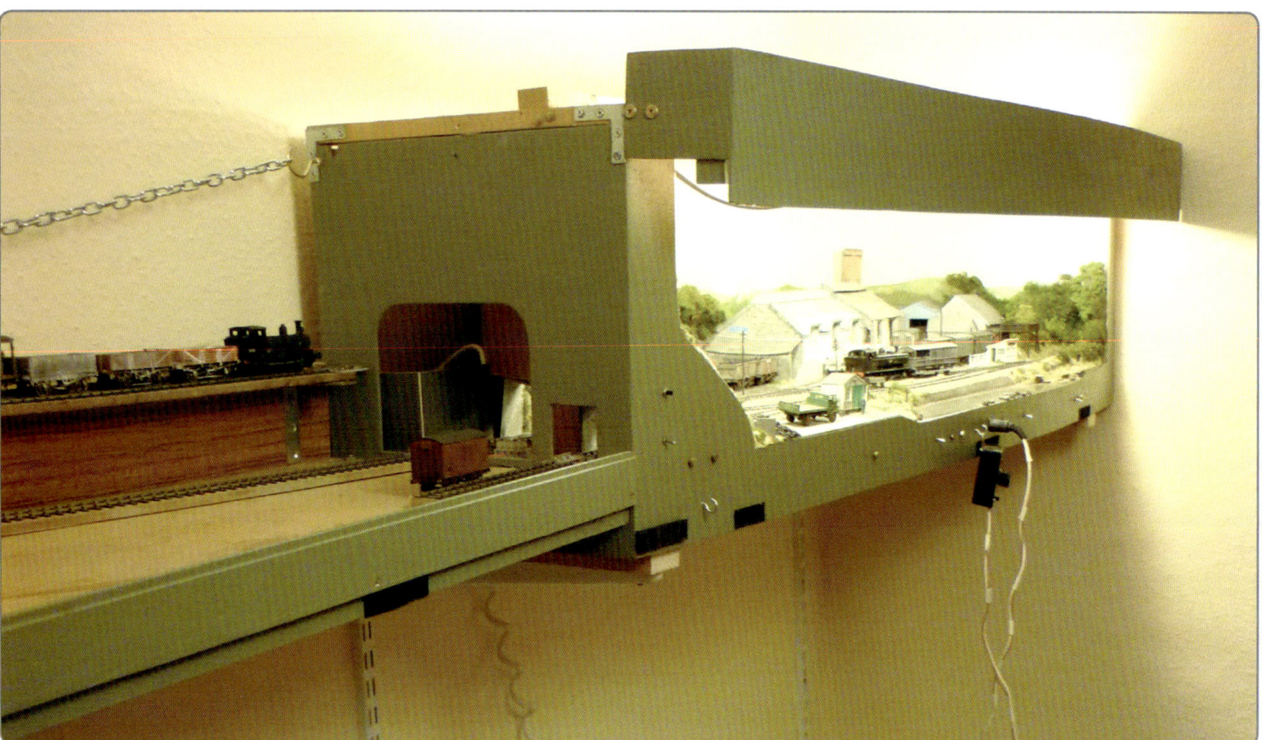

ABOVE: *Probably one of the most common layout configurations nowadays is a shelf-format model wall-mounted on shelf track. Here is 'Trerice', perched thus in the corner of the spare bedroom in my cottage; there are bookshelves beneath it now.* Author

like to put on it.' Most of us come at the site-seeking question from this angle; we've got a fair idea of the 'what' but not the 'where'. There's a lot of chicken-and-egg about model railway design, however, and one of the first such imponderables is whether it's better to seek your site first and, having found it, to then cast about for a subject and layout format compatible with the space you have available. That's often easier than fixing on a subject first then seeking an amenable site. Whichever way you go about it, though, what matters above all else is the nature of the layout footprint the site can accommodate – that is, the shape and proportions of the space. That is what really dictates the nature of the model railway it will be possible to contemplate.

Reconciling site, scale and subject where all three are pre-determined is one of the most challenging aspects of layout design. As a professional designer, it's the conundrum over which one is most frequently consulted. Obviously, every case is different, but as a general rule, something has to give; it's the point at which the First Law of Railway Modelling ('The man who never made a compromise never made a model railway…') starts to bite into ambition. Usually – with scale and site as 'givens' – it's the form and scope of the layout that has to bow to that compromise. Main line aspirations can conflict with minimum radii, or lack of longitude cramp the loop lengths and clearance points called for by lengthy trains. The vertical clearance available may compromise structures, scenery or display height, while no amount of wishful thinking can alter the separation required for one track to bridge another – or overcome lack of sufficient space for the gradients needed to accomplish this.

All of which is why, in pragmatic terms, it's easier to let the available site suggest the nature of the subject. That's not to say that clever design and 'thinking outside the box' can't overcome some of the conflicts between aspiration and available area, but by and large certain shapes and sizes of site suit certain formats of layout which, in turn, suit certain types of subject. To give an everyday example, a shelf of modest width along a typical spare-bedroom wall or two sits happily with a classic terminal-to-fiddleyard format – which need not *necessarily* be a branchline terminus – but is much harder to reconcile with, say, a junction or a large MPD. When determining site possibilities, I've often found it worthwhile to sacrifice ultimate area to good proportions if this then provides a footprint better suited to the sort of subject you really want to model.

Site selection practicalities

I set down some general thoughts about the suitability of various types of layout site in my earlier book *Railway Modelling The Realistic Way*, with special reference to places to *avoid*. So if some of the following seems familiar, apologies! Actually, much of the site-selection process comes down to common sense, but there are one or two less-obvious pitfalls to reckon with. Rather than concentrating too much on negatives, I'd rather set out an ideal to aim for, and use that as a site-assessment benchmark. So – what characteristics make for an ideal home for a small-scale scenic model railway?

Well, top of the list I'd place the *habitability* of the space you're considering. We're looking for somewhere that's temperate, clean, dry, free from draughts but well-ventilated and insulated and preferably having suitable illumination. These are all factors which affect the well-being of railway modellers – but they have an equal impact on the well-being of model railways. It is my firm conclusion that if the human element isn't comfortable, the model won't be either. So any space being considered as a layout site must be one in which you'll be happy to spend a considerable portion of your time.

Next on the tick-list comes the obvious question as to the size and suitability of the space available – which is not simply a matter of feet, inches or millimetres, but of proportion, vertical clearance, accessibility and the need to take account of things like doors and windows, domestic access to power or service points, cupboards or other storage, and vulnerability to conflicting uses of the space. Most critically, the usefulness of a given site depends on the 'footprint' that it offers and the relationship this has with the requirements of subject and scale. As a rule, long thin sites are the least scale-dependent, while squares and smaller rectangular sites are the trickiest to reconcile with things like curve radii, point formations, and train lengths. I can't really think of a shape or size of site that forms a generally applicable 'ideal', but if I had to plump for desirable qualities it would have to be generous unfettered wall length or a rectangular site with the long side at least twice the length of the short side, preferably more.

I suppose the most typically available sites that tick at least the most important of these boxes are: the whole or partial use of a room in the house; a reasonably-sized garden shed; an outbuilding or detached garage; an integral garage; an attic and, occasionally, a cellar or basement. The less-domestic of these sites will almost certainly call for a degree of adaptation to render them usable – chiefly in the matter of providing adequate insulation and appropriate heating/ventilation, plus a floor which is level, stable and comfortable to stand on. In a concrete-floored garage, shed or basement, carpet is a necessity rather than a luxury, believe me! One domestic space increasingly being looked to for modelling space nowadays is the conservatory or 'sun lounge'. I have considerable reservations as to the suitability of such rooms as layout environments, however. They are intended to make the most of the available sunlight – a commodity which is generally 'bad news' for model railways, often leading to fading of colours, degradation of some plastics

BELOW: *This is the solution that I used for some 20 years: a purpose-built shed in the garden. Actually, in this case, two conjoined sheds; the original off-the-peg 12 x 8ft garden shed at right, later joined by the custom-built slate-hung structure on the left, which measured 4 x 3 metres. The combined L-shaped edifice housed my office, library, workshop and up to four small layouts – two displayed, two on storage racks.* Author

ABOVE AND BELOW: *The ultimate in no-site layouts – one you could almost tuck under your arm and stroll off with! But even in a space as small as this, high levels of realism and satisfying visual design are perfectly achievable, as John Bruce so convincingly demonstrates with 'Lower Peak Wharf'. Note the nicely balanced composition, the lack of obvious parallels in spite of the rectangular footprint and, in particular, the subtle, but beautifully observed changes in ground level. As the close-up shows, this is also a layout which can withstand close scrutiny.* Adrian Colenutt

and excessive temperature variation. Unless it benefits from some measure of climate control and possesses decent blinds (or the layout can be provided with suitable drapes), I'd rule out a conservatory as a permanent layout site – but they're often a good place to erect and work on a portable layout that is normally kept elsewhere.

No-site layouts

Thus far, I've proceeded on the assumption that a *permanent* home for the layout is what we're seeking, somewhere it will live both for display and while being worked on. But such a dedicated site is not the only option; there's a long tradition in the hobby of layouts that enjoyed no such luxury, being designed to be readily dismantled and moved for stowing away when not in use and amenable to erection wherever or whenever there might be a suitable space. Such iconic lines as Peter Denny's 'Buckingham Branch' (which started life perched temporarily above

ABOVE: *Don Leeper positions the goods shed on 'Hepton Wharf', the minimum-space P4 cameo layout originally built in basic form over the two days of Scaleforum in 1993. Although now accoutred with elegant presentational aids, the actual self-contained layout module (up to the top of the backscene) measures just 45 x 21 x 15in, with the separate fiddleyard module adding another 21in. Truly portable, and you can store it on-end where space is really tight.* Author

the furniture in a London bedsit) and John Charman's 'Charford' (built in a domestic caravan) were conceived thus.

If a layout is designed along such ultra-portable 'now you see it, now you don't' lines, then there's no reason why it need demand *any* dedicated display space, so long as there's somewhere suitable to store it and a place (or places) to set it up when required. The combination of the occasional use of a spare room or study with a suitable cupboard or out-of-the-way shelf has saved many a modeller from layoutlessness. There are a number of advantages to adopting such an approach, which is (as you might have surmised) one I've long used myself. Apart from the advantage of being able to actually have a layout in the first place, such a model is almost entirely relocation-proof, while it lends itself readily to the 'hobby within a hobby' that is exhibiting. There are constraints and drawbacks, of course. The 'no site' approach hardly lends itself to large and complex subjects (although it is perfectly amenable to the use of larger scales), while you have to put quite a lot more effort into the design and construction of baseboards and electrical systems on such portable layouts, which also need to be fully self-contained in the matter of backscenes and presentation/lighting.

Permanence-v-portability

All indoor model railway layouts come into one of three categories: they are either permanent, transportable or portable. The truly permanent layout – one built 'all of a piece', integral with and dependent upon the building or room in which it is housed – is something of a rarity these days. Historically, however, this was a very traditional form of construction and a lot of layouts large and small were planned and built thus. Well-known permanent layouts have included such icons as the Norris 0 gauge layout, Beal's 'West Midland', Jim Russell's 'Little Western' and Ken Northwood's 'North Devonshire'. That all these are now but footnotes in the history of the hobby demonstrates the chief drawback with permanence: come the *need* to move it, then partial or total destruction of the layout is often the only option.

Nowadays, most layouts – no matter how large or how normally immobile – are usually built to be *transportable*. That is, they are designed to be dismantled into sections which are of a form that it is practicable to move – albeit with some difficulty – should the need arise. Such transportability can be arrived at in a number of ways. At the most basic, the layout can be arranged to break down into conventional self-contained but complete sections for re-erection 'as is' on an equivalent site. Much more flexible is to design the model as a series of 'key locations' – stations, yards, junctions and so on – built as robustly-framed and self-contained modules that are readily movable, linked by lightly-framed sections of non-movable plain track and

LEFT: *Designing a layout in demountable sections has many virtues, including avoiding the need to do everything in situ. Here, the trackwork for the north end of Yeovil Pen Mill takes shape on the Duncan family's kitchen table. In its final, high-level location back down in the basement, this part of the layout would be all-but impossible to work on. 'Yeovil' is made up of three trackbed sections and several removable 'jigsaw' scenery modules.* Author

LEFT: *This view looking down on the 2006 Uckfield Model Railway Show reveals the two most popular formats for home/exhibitable model railways in Britain: the shelf-type 'fiddleyard to modelled scene' and the hollow-centre, continuous-run oval with the subject on one side and a fiddleyard on the other.* Adrian Colenutt

landscape which are regarded as 'sacrificial'. This removes the requirement to find a site of similar size and footprint to the original on removal, as the various 'key modules' can be reconfigured and reassembled to suit any suitable space. The modules can even be dispersed and used as starting points for several completely new and different layouts. This approach has much to commend it and is now increasingly being used for some of the more progressive of the large 'basement buster' layouts in the USA, so many of which have finished up as scrap.

Truly portable layouts take the whole business of sectionalisation several steps further, as to be successful they need to be straightforward and quick to erect/dismantle and easy to move. This calls for accurate but rapid locating and retaining arrangements, folding or readily dismantled layout supports, integrated electrical and lighting systems, appropriate weight, robustness, shape and size of sections, and suitable transport or storage solutions. The lively British exhibition scene has seen the art of the truly portable and fully self-contained model railway brought to a high degree of sophistication, with great ingenuity and often a high degree of constructional refinement displayed in the way such layouts are arranged to come apart.

Readily demountable layouts have other virtues. For a start, they are easy to work on in comfort, as the appropriate board(s) can be set up in any suitable location (such as out in the garden on a nice day) and supported at a height and orientation best suited to the task in hand. This is especially relevant where a layout is designed for 'standing eye-level' presentation (typically 50+ inches from the floor) – a height that's great for viewing and operation, but often a Royal Pain when it comes to construction and maintenance. Portable layouts are also highly adaptable and versatile, being easy to re-configure or extend and amenable to different methods of mounting, viewing and operation. Ultra-portable or 'no site' layouts are also a tradable commodity, for the precise reason that they make no proscriptive spatial demands beyond a modicum of storage. This has given rise to a modest but steady market for good-quality 'pre owned' portable/exhibitable layouts, especially those of modest size. If you're going to put a lot of effort into a model, giving it an extended life in this way may well be a consideration.

Formats and footprints

These two fundamentals of layout design are irretrievably intertwined and always need to be considered in concert. In the context of the type of realistic model being considered here, the possibilities are usually somewhat limited, as many traditional layout formats – such as the multi-circuit round-and-round oval with umpteen stations and trains continually passing through the same scene on different tracks – are so inherently unrealistic as to disqualify themselves. And with them go the typical associated footprints – the solid rectangular tabletop or the room or attic so crammed with baseboarding that there is scarcely room for the operator. By and large, most realistic layouts use the basic format of a hidden staging or fiddleyard feeding a modelled scene or scenes. The two most common footprints for such layouts are the linear 'shelf form' with the hidden and visible trackage in line, or the continuous-run oval with the staging on one long side and the modelled scene on the other.

The 'shelf' in some form or other is probably the most common and most versatile layout footprint both for home use and for many exhibition layouts. I'm using the term here to describe a basic layout structure that is relatively long compared to its width, usually straight along the back edge (but not necessarily the front) and self-supporting. It can occupy a straight-line footprint, be arranged as an inside or outside 'L' or 'U' or set at informal angles to give a less-regular right-of-way. Such 'shelf-form' layouts are normally viewed from one side only (the front, hopefully!) and lend themselves readily to the addition of backdrops, overhead lighting rafts, presentation fascias and other adjuncts of the realistic layout. They are also easy to sectionalise, support and transport and are relatively simple to make.

When it comes to seeking layout sites in the home, shelves are often the most viable answer. They form an intrinsic part of the everyday domestic environment, so appropriating or adding one for the railway isn't usually too tall an order. Domestic shelves are also normally backed by domestic walls, which makes the provision of that all-essential backdrop relatively simple, as well as providing

BELOW: *The intractable backscene problem for the outside-viewed oval – or, in this case, circle. This is one of my favourite exhibition layouts, the Keighley Club's 0 scale NER 'Runswick Bay', an original concept and a stunning piece of modelling. But – as this rather poor snap shows all-too-clearly – a convex backdrop is not really effective at cutting out distracting background over much of the scene, as you can always 'see round the corner'.* Author

for an easy means of support; shelf-track could have been invented for railway modellers!

But it's the basic *shape* of shelf forms – long but relatively narrow – that makes them so suited to realistic models, as they're closely akin to the sort of footprint most often occupied by a real railway and its environs. Shelves can be built in a wide range of shapes and proportions and generally adapted so suit most model subjects and layout formats. Long associated with the classic terminus – fiddleyard layout format, they also work well for 'through' subjects (fiddleyard either side of a modelled scene) and in the context of a series of small, self-contained modelled scenes linked by 'blind trackage' – often in the form of removable 'link tracks'. Shelves invariably have nice square ends, so it is usually relatively easy to manage the 'edge of the scene' in a crisp and convincing manner; such things are much harder to contrive on oval layouts viewed from the outside, where convex curves in the 'sky' and being able to 'see around the corner' make life extremely difficult when it comes to getting the trains offstage gracefully and believably.

Indeed, so intractable is that particular problem that many of the most realistic outside-viewed continuous-run oval exhibition layouts actually consist effectively of a shelf-form scene as the 'display' side, discreetly linked to hidden return curves and a completely concealed staging yard. Two of my favourite such layouts – the Croydon Club's 'Acton Main Line' in N and Gordon and Maggie Gravett's magnificent 'Pempoul' in 1:50 scale – are arranged thus. To those who decry so grievous a 'waste' of viewing space, I'd suggest either adding subsidiary but self-contained 'end scenes', or the use of a front 'shelf' scene deep enough to contain at least a goodly portion of the end return curves within it. Indeed, there's no law that says operators of an oval exhibition layout *have* to stand in a hole in the middle. With handheld controls and staging/fiddleyards accessed from the outside at the rear of the model, the whole thing can be landscaped and operated from without – which allows the front scene to be as deep as you like. Tim Venton's ground-breaking 'Clutton' P4 layout shows the way, with an oval footprint fully modelled for virtually all of its depth, with only the rearmost portion (housing the staging) being 'off scene'. 'Clutton' is operated (very visibly, and greatly to the interest of spectators) from the layout front corners; the signalman has a proper lever-frame signalling panel, with the train-driver standing off to one side or other as required.

BELOW: *The ultimate way to do exhibition ovals, in my opinion: Tim Venton's ambitious 'Clutton'. It is an innovative and seminally important P4 layout combining Barry Norman's 'deep scene' doctrine with the authentic interpretation of an actual location, and a true-to-prototype operating system based on the real working timetable. Note the 'signalbox' console at bottom right. Personally, I'd have taken that backscene right to the ends of the scene and sacrificed a little bit of modelled real-estate, but I think the basic concept is spot-on.* Tim Venton

Ovals as a layout footprint work visually much better when viewed from the *inside*, when they can be arranged as a continuous surround-scene with no 'end' at all – a scene, furthermore, which extends beyond the natural edge of one's field of vision, just as reality does. This is probably the ideal for a home layout that has no 'second role' as an exhibition showpiece – for the inside-viewed oval is the one footprint that is totally incompatible with a British-style exhibition. There are a few very large 'inside the oval' permanent exhibition layouts in the USA that are situated on an upper floor and accessed by central staircases or ramps from below; but on this side of the Atlantic, the continuous-scene oval arrangement is probably confined to domestic loft layouts and one or two large-but-impressive private essays built by the seriously well-heeled. Much more prevalent here is the around-the-walls, shelf-based oval with a lifting flap or duck-under in one side or corner for access; that can readily be contrived in spare room, shed or garage sites.

Going around the walls of a rectangular site in this fashion generally makes quite good use of the available space and lends itself to the creation of realistic scenes. But it is just a bit limiting in terms of footprint and certainly isn't suited to every type of subject. Something a little less 'rigid' and freer in form can offer more scope for curved track alignments – which are not just an integral feature of many prototypes, but are often highly desirable from the visual point of view when composing a model scene. Creating such 'free form' or 'amoebic' layout footprints with curvilinear outlines and 'peninsula' or 'teardrop' shapes is not too difficult on a stay-at-home model but is a pretty tall order for a portable exhibition layout – especially one incorporating that all-important backdrop and scene-containment presentation.

It's this relationship between the modelled scene, the backdrop and the 'nothing to do with the model' surroundings that is so fundamental when it comes to preserving the illusion of reality on a model railway. And in this regard, there are a lot of layout footprints and formats that, while they're perfectly viable in a practical sense, are extremely difficult to present realistically along the lines I'm advocating. This is especially true of 'island' or 'peninsula' footprints that call for all-round viewing or are otherwise unsuited to being split into discreet self-contained scenes by integral backdrops. However, there is an alternative approach to integral backscenes that can work well in this sort of context – the 'remote' background sited at some distance behind and surrounding the model and against which it can be viewed from any angle: sort of 'surround-sky'. The project studio in the *Model Railroader* offices at Waukesha is arranged thus, the walls being painted to provide an all-round sky background against which any layout or section of layout can be photographed from any angle. On a much more modest scale, the Mk 2 version of my 'East Suffolk Light' (which was a whole 6½ft long and lived on top of a bookcase) was also arranged thus; the entire wall in front of which it sat was painted a neutral 'sky grey' – a shade against which the model looked pleasingly natural.

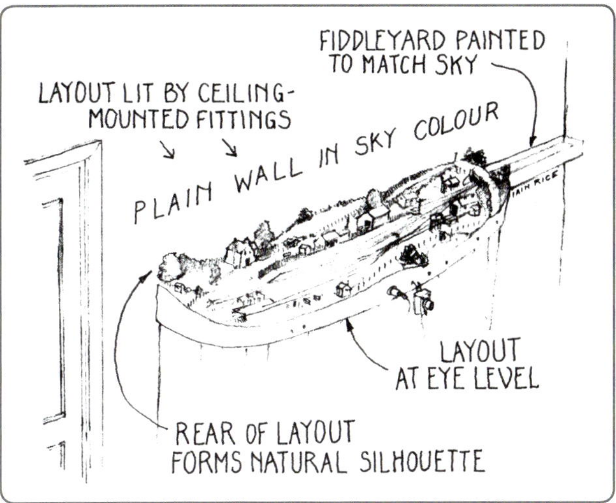

ABOVE: *A plain wall as a backdrop.*

Because of their ease of construction, ready portability, suitability for self-contained 'complete scenes', and compatibility with most layout formats, I tend to favour the shelf-form footprint for most of my models and designs. That is not to suggest that I'm thinking in terms of simple rectangular slabs – far from it! Hard, straight lines are rare in the British landscape, while even in purely abstract terms gently flowing curves are far more pleasing to the eye than harsh rectilinearity. So, while I generally stick with a straight back edge to the baseboard structure for simplicity of construction, the actual boundaries of the modelled scene – the backdrop at the rear and the form of the front edge and fascia – are almost always curved to some degree, albeit often quite subtly.

Layout mounting heights

In the context of realistic design, the height at which a layout is to be mounted in its normal location is a fundamental design decision, as it will determine the relationship with viewing eye level and hence the 'naturalness' of the view obtained. Theoretically, the viewer's eye-level should coincide *exactly* with the horizon-line incorporated in the layout – whether that's represented physically by being painted on the backdrop or merely inferred by the disposition of the landscape and structures. In practice, it soon becomes evident that there's some leeway in this correlation; actual eye level can be 2–3in above or below the 'true' position without the error being particularly apparent – which conveniently accommodates differing eye levels and gives a bit of flexibility in mounting height for a given subject. Too low is better than too high, however, as it's easier to bend the head slightly than stand on tippy-toes! There's a lot more on the whole business of eye levels, viewpoints, perspective and fields of vision in the 'visual design' section of Chapter 8. But whichever way you go about it – if you want a realistic view, you can't mess with nature; so it's best to aim at the right height.

Being linked to eye level, this 'right height' will vary, of course: by a little, depending on the stature of the viewer –

LEFT: *Eye levels and viewpoints related to layouts set at different heights. The traditional tabletop mounting at left puts the horizon-line well above any normal backdrop, with the layout distant from the viewer and only occupying part of the field of vision. Eye-level mounting, on the other hand, gives a natural horizon-line and presents a 'close to' view of the model, which occupies the whole field of view.*

or by rather more, depending upon the outcome of another fundamental design decision: whether the layout is intended for standing or seated viewing and operation. In the case of a portable exhibition layout it's quite possible, of course, to mount the model at different heights for different situations – that's what I do myself with those of my tiny trainsets that I inflict upon a hapless public. At shows, I present my handiwork at a height appropriate to the standing eye level of the average adult, while at home, the same layout will sit at an altitude suited to me perched on an ordinary roll-around office chair. Even where a layout is normally mounted at high level, it'll probably be necessary to bring it down off its elevated perch to work on it in any degree of comfort.

I am but a modest fellow in the vertical sense, teetering to a tad over 5ft 7in (67in/170cm) in my socks on a good day. That elevation gives me a standing, looking straight-ahead eye-level of about 62in (158cm), but a seated equivalent ranging from only 45in–50in (115cm–127cm), depending upon the height of the seat. However, you don't normally view layouts standing or sitting to attention and looking straight ahead; rather, one tends to bow one's head and lean forward slightly, which typically lowers eye level by an inch or two. I've found in my own case that good practical values for mean eye level are 60in (152cm) standing and 46in (122cm) seated. A taller person would add a few inches to these figures, while lesser statures would shave a bit off.

Taking advantage of that 'degree of leeway' with regard to true eye level, and allowing for the fact that tall folk can stoop a little if needs be, then I've found that by mounting my layouts for exhibition with the nominal eye level/ horizon line at a 'golden mean' height on the backscene (see Chapter 8 for chapter and verse on this) and the top-

BELOW: *Please excuse the ropey quality of this 20-year-old snap, but it is the only picture I have of 'Woolverstone' in its then-controversial high-level exhibition display format, circa 1989. The track level was 58in above the floor, with a continuous plain backdrop and deep upper lighting fascia. To give an idea of the heights, Chris Lamacraft (operating) is a svelte six feet, Rice at right, a stocky five-seven.* Monty Wells

BELOW: *Although true eye-level mounting as applied to 'Woolverstone' is still comparatively rare, many exhibition layouts are now being displayed at greater heights, typically in the range 48–54in above the floor, which certainly works much better than traditional tabletop height. Here's Karl Crowther's EM gauge 'Kentside' on show at Uckfield in 2004 – a good example of modern exhibition layout display practice.* Adrian Colenutt

of-baseboard datum/nominal track height set between 51in/130cm and 56in (142cm) above the floor, I get a display height that seems to work well for most people and with most subjects. With a viewing aperture depth of 10–12in and a backscene height around 15in, the bottom edge of the upper lighting fascia finishes up around head-height. Setting the baseboard at these sorts of elevations also accords well with the NMRA's recommended track height for 'walk-around' layouts of 54in for comfortable operation. To save carting a forest of tall, spindly legs around to exhibitions, I achieve this elevation using 'mini-trestles' designed to sit on top of ordinary, 30in (76cm) high tables of the sort found at almost any exhibition venue. As my baseboards are normally at least 4in (10cm) deep below rail level, these mini trestles only need to be around 18–20in (45–51cm) high.

Back in the attic at home, however, there isn't the headroom for such an elevated mounting and anyway I prefer to view and operate my trains from the comfort of that adjustable office chair. With the seat set at an elevation of around 15in (38cm) my mean eye level is 44in (112cm), so the baseboards sit on brackets to give a track height of 40in (102cm) above the floor. This not only gives me a natural view within the restricted headroom available – which limits backscene height and dictates the position of the lighting fascia – but keeps the layout at a height at which it's reasonably comfortable and convenient to work; 40in is not a great deal higher than a typical kitchen worktop.

Scene heights

We don't just have to consider the height at which we set our 'track datum' above the floor, of course. The other part of the viewing equation is the vertical depth of the actual scene itself, from ground level to the 'top of the sky'. Real skies don't have tops, of course – but when we look at the real world, what we see is constrained by the limits of our field of vision, which, in the vertical dimension, is (fortunately) quite restricted, especially above eye level and most particularly at close range. Typically, we're not aware of anything situated immediately above us and close to our plane of vision, while the upper edge of our 'sight envelope' only extends upwards with distance by a relatively small amount. All of which is jolly handy from a layout-designing point of view, as it means that we can site upper fascias and layout lighting beams at a modest height from the floor without them intruding, while the upper edge of our backscene need not ascend to the heavens.

The other 'given' in choosing a suitable scene height is the subject and scale of the model. Mountainous topography, a lot of tall trees or seriously big buildings are *physically* going to call for plenty of vertical elbow room, considerably more than would be needed for a low-lying, pastoral landscape. Headroom that appears spacious for N scale is likely to look a tad cramped in 0, where the bulk and height of the trains, structures and things like signals are about 400 per cent greater. The combination of subject and scale usually dictates a minimum scene height; the judgement then is how much beyond this minimum you opt to allow. There's no law that says the scene height has to be a constant – although

ABOVE: *'Treneglos' is in so many ways an excellent example of a realistic layout, but I don't think that this particular presentation sets it off at its best. The combination of a high-mounted lighting fascia with a relatively low upper edge to the backscene (for practical operational reasons) leaves a very distracting visual gap, as well as exposing some rather unsightly woodwork. I'd close the gap between layout and lighting fascias considerably by lowering the latter to the point where it concealed the 'top of the sky' – and take the opportunity to rearrange that bracing to set it above the new visual cut-off point.* Adrian Colenutt

I'm convinced that the 'top of the scene', be it upper front-mounted fascia or backdrop top edge, is best kept straight and level. But with a typical 'profiled' layout fascia following the rise and fall of the groundwork, the scene height can easily vary by several inches in line with the topography being modelled.

BELOW: *A well-proportioned, realistically modelled and effectively lit scene on the Dutch H0 layout 'Geervliet'. This relatively shallow shelf-format layout (it's about 16in/400mm front-to-back) enables a generous front viewing height to be used without calling for a towering backscene. The backdrop is lit with a wash of fluorescent light, warmed up by a few tungsten down-lighters.* Author

The ideal height for a modelled scene is to a large extent dictated by these practical considerations. The visual 'top edge' of the layout can most readily be defined by the use of a lighting fascia mounted immediately above the front edge of the layout – which, if aptly placed and related to the height of the backscene, can readily hide the 'top of the sky' by cutting off the line of sight just below that point. This is a simple set-up ideally suited to 'shelf form' layouts, which can often be surprisingly effective with surprisingly modest scene heights when mounted for eye-level viewing. The ideal front fascia height and/or total height needed for the backscene will, however, depend on the depth (front to back) of the modelled scene; deep scenes either need taller backdrops or lower front fascias. Barry Norman's 'Petherick' – which was five feet deep – used a front fascia mounted only a eight inches or so above the mean ground level of the scenery, while Vincent de Bode's 'Flintfields' – 1.2 metres deep – has a backdrop 60cm tall

The alternative to using this 'front cut off' is to either take the backdrop up far enough to extend well beyond the edge of the normal field of view, or to place a fascia or drape immediately above the top edge of a backdrop high enough to reach 'top sight line' level. Such a view-block will 'frame' the visual field and, importantly, hide any intrusive background clutter, as Don Leeper has done with the rear drape on 'Hepton Wharf' in the illustration. The 'high sky' approach is usually only an option on unmoving home layouts, but the latter solution can work well for portable/exhibition layouts; it combines especially well with the use of a backdrop 'wash light', as described in the 'lighting' section below.

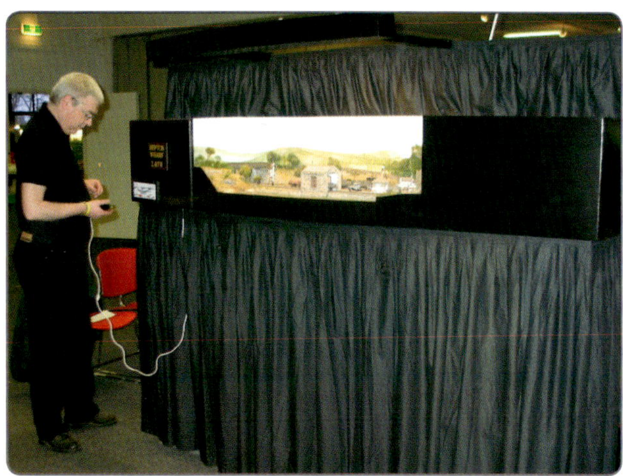

ABOVE: *'Hepton Wharf' in its fully developed 'through' format with a fiddleyard each end – set up for display at the 'Rail' exhibition at Houten, Utrecht in 2008. The upper of the two ruffled drapes (which, unlike flat curtaining, don't show creases) is actually set behind the top edge of the backscene, to cut out high-level distractions. The 'flying' lighting beam just visible at the top of the picture carries paired dichroic light fittings. Operator John 'JC' Chambers is busy figuring out the new, 'simplified' control system…* Author

Exhibition viewing heights: children and wheelchair users

One last general design point relating to high-mounted layouts, particularly at exhibitions – that is, the problem of their visual accessibility to those who lack sufficient stature to view them properly: young children and folk who are confined to a wheelchair. In the case of the kinderen, there arises at once the question of the 'target audience' at whom the layout is aimed. There would obviously be very little point in building the sort of model railway that would appeal to younger viewers (which is not *necessarily* 'Thomas') then mounting it in such a way that they can't even see it! But the same argument holds true the other way; there's equally little point in going to a great deal of effort to produce a sophisticated fine-scale super-realistic layout then displaying it a height that benefits only those least able to appreciate it. Horses for courses, in other words. Children can anyway be elevated – by means of a step-up stool or the loving arms of their parents – to a height from which they *can* see – an exercise that is not *too* onerous, given the attention-span of the average seven-year-old faced with a model on which very little appears to be happening!

However, appropriate mounting height is much more of a problem in the context of an adult viewer confined to a wheelchair trying to access a standing-eye-level mounted layout; the experience must be intensely frustrating. Obviously, the ideal would be a support system that allowed the model to be lowered in a controlled way to an appropriate height when the situation so demanded; but that's a tall order and I haven't come across any practicable

BELOW: *Viewing aids for high-mounted layouts.*

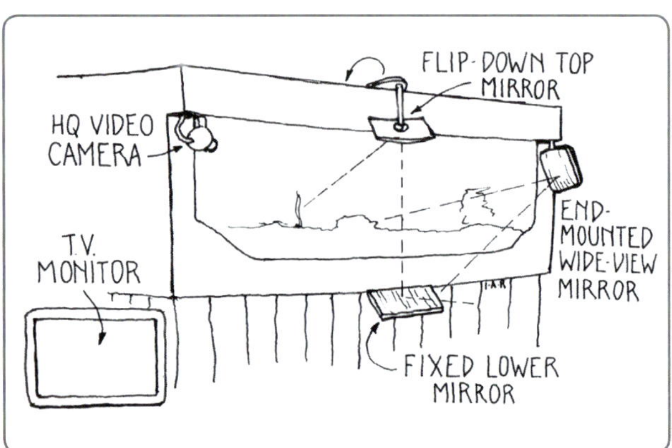

way to achieve this even for the sort of small self-contained layout I usually build. Ramps adequate to elevate a wheelchair to an appropriate viewing height seem to be equally impracticable. The only answer appears to be the provision of some form of visual aid, of which a strategically sited and angled mirror or two is the simplest. Slightly more sophisticated is a simple lightweight viewing periscope or – best of all, and more in keeping with the 21st century – the combination of a decent miniature video camera or cameras trained on the model coupled to a monitor mounted at a suitable height and location.

Layout lighting

The most thoughtful and apt of layout mountings is a bit of a waste of time if you can't actually *see* the modelling due to lack of suitable illumination. It has long been a source of amazement to me just how many layout-builders seem content to take a chance on whatever ambient light might happen to be available when displaying their models, both at home and at shows. The problem has been most acute at exhibitions, where many venues are very poorly lit and certainly don't furnish enough lumens to allow fine modelling to be appreciated – in which context, a solitary cheap B&Q spot-lamp up a pole at either end of the layout is scarcely much help either! In aiming for realism, the lighting has an important additional role – that of replicating the atmospheric conditions and resulting light quality under which the prototype would be seen. In my experience, contriving a really good lighting set-up is one of the most powerful tools in the realistic layout-designers armoury.

In fact, successful layout lighting has to meet a whole range of criteria. Not only does it have to provide an adequate level of illumination over the whole model (including objects at the extreme front and rear corners of the scene), it has to do so without producing excessive heat, without being obtrusive in itself and without throwing unwanted or contradictory shadows. It also needs to provide an appropriate *quality* of light, one that is as close as possible to the daylight values associated with the nature of the modelled scene. In which context, going for the 'yellow heavy' bright mid-summer look is not always the best choice; indeed, walking around exhibitions, I seem to come across a lot of English pastoral scenes illuminated by searing sunlight more appropriate to high noon in Arizona! Gentler lighting representing muted sunshine or even an overcast day is often more effective and kinder all round to the model.

Shadow management

Shadows are often the cruellest giveaway on our models; they are, after all, the means by which we perceive shape, detail and texture. Harsh lighting – of the sort often associated with high-powered quartz-halogen spotlights – produces stark cast shadows that can over-emphasise relief and rob the modelling of all subtlety. Also, point sources like spotlights throw strongly directional shadows that can often look most unnatural – never more so than when they contradict one another, suggesting that the layout represents some extra-Terrestrial landscape basking in the light of several stars… From this

ABOVE: *Shadow management on backdrops – always a knotty problem. The pole just to the left of the hoarding shows what we're trying to avoid – a shadow falling vertically on what should be a horizontal surface. This can be avoided by using a vertical scenic element – such as the hoarding shown – as a 'shadow catcher', or by careful positioning of shadow-casting objects so that they're either in contact/very close to the backdrop (hiding their own shadows), or far enough away so that the shadow falls naturally on the ground.*

point of view alone, I tend these days to shun such 'point' or focused-beam light fittings in favour of diffuse sources like fluorescent tubes of one sort or another (in which category I include the current generation of low-energy 'bulbs') as well as 'dispersed' or wide-angle incandescent fittings and those 'new kids on the block', high-power LEDs. All of these sources have the important benefit of not throwing intense or 'hard' shadows.

The importance of 'managing' shadows when lighting a model can't be over-stressed; it's far from easy to keep them consistent as to direction and intensity and prevent them straying onto the backdrop – and the 'shadow on the sky' is a classic giveaway! Avoiding such anomalies needs consideration at all stages of design and often a bit of trial-and-error during construction; just moving an object – especially something upright and tall like a telegraph pole, tree or streetlight – by an inch or two can often 'shift' a shadow so that it falls naturally on the ground rather than obtrusively on the backdrop. The other dodge is to interpose a 'shadow catcher' – some vertical modelled element on which a shadow might naturally fall – on or immediately in front of the backdrop at the appropriate location. Hedges, trees, grassy slopes, rockfaces, walls, fences, advertising hoardings or structure façades are all suitable candidates. In this context, it's worth pointing out that objects sited very close to the backscene will often hide their own shadows, while something that's actually in contact with the backscene won't throw a shadow in the first place. I had a 'sky shadow' problem with the chimney of the clay dry on 'Trerice Mk 2' when the structure was transferred from the original layout – as is all-too-evident in some pictures! But a combination of some juggling-about of position for this vital appendage plus the provision of an overhead 'wash light' for that corner of the backscene eventually cured the problem.

Backdrop illumination

In reality, of course, the sky is 'bright'; it is, after all, the source of the illumination by which we view the world. I have yet to come up with a way of producing a convincing illuminated *backlit* backdrop, which would appear to be the ideal solution. The problem is – what do you make it from? MDF and card are impervious to light, fabrics have a weave that's all-too-apparent when you shine a light through them and paper is almost impossible to keep flat and crease-free. Something like opaque acrylic sheet formed to shape would probably be suitable, provided you could make it seamless, but that still leaves the problem of applying colour to the sky and distant landscape. An it's an unfortunate fact that back-lighting almost always shows up brush-marks and other aspects of a painted backdrop that detract from its realism. More experiment needed!

What I *have* found to work well both in illuminating the 'sky' and killing unwanted shadows is to use fluorescent-sourced 'wash' lighting positioned immediately at the head of a conventional backscene which is painted in translucent colour coats over a ground of several dense coats of 'brilliant white' emulsion paint. These ultra-white paints contain a goodly dose of phosphors to give them their brilliance, which can react with the ultra-violet component of the wash light to give a degree of luminescence to the whole backdrop. The drawback is that the strong vertical lighting thus produced is merciless in showing up brush marks and other unwanted textures in the 'sky' part of the backscene – for which reason I never use a brush for this work, applying all the paint (including the white base coats) by spray, roller or pad, which at least gives an even and unobtrusive overall texture.

Lighting: practical considerations

There are a few bits of physics to digest when contemplating layout lighting solutions, starting with the make-up of those elusive waves. So – 'white' light is defined as being made up of the full range of frequencies, not all of which are visible. At the low end we have infra-red, which we sense as radiated heat, while the upper end gives us ultra-violet which we perceive as glare and which produces direct heating and even chemical degradation of any surface that absorbs it. Light is said to be emitted by a 'source' and falls on 'surfaces' which reflect or absorb it to varying degrees – the process which enables us to perceive colour and form. The light-sources we typically use for general domestic lighting are 'incoherent'; that is, they emit unphased light of varying frequencies going every which way, unless they are gathered up by a reflector or lens and sent out as a beam, as in a spotlight.

Beam-emitting spotlights of one sort or another are widely used to light model railways – but they have a number of drawbacks; they are strongly directional, while the pattern of illumination they typically produce is a circular 'pool' of light with a 'bright spot' at the centre and a fairly rapid fall-off towards the edges. The amount of light thrown by any source (except a laser, which is something else altogether!) onto any surface also diminishes by the *square* of the distance from the source. In other words, a given lamp situated two feet away from a model only produces a quarter the level of illumination that it would give if sited a foot away. Standing things on their head, this means that to get the same level of illumination with the twice-as-distant lamp, it would need to be *four* times as powerful as the near-mounted source. The trouble is, typical high-power light sources such as quartz-halogen incandescent bulbs bring additional problems to the layout lighting equation in terms of unwanted heat (they emit a very high infra-red component), glare and scatter (stray ultraviolet) and increased loads on the wiring. And while 'invisible' light obeys the same square law as the visible with regards to fall-off with distance, it's a different matter when it comes to reflection-v-absorption. It's an unhappy fact that the sort of matt-surfaced materials usual in model railways tend to absorb non-visible infra-red light and the associated heat rather than disperse it – which is not good news for the layout as a whole. It was, after all, a quartz-halogen lamp directed at close range onto just such a matt surface that caused the disastrous fire at Windsor Castle!

Although powerful incandescent sources mounted at a suitable distance from the layout (a yard or more is prudent) are reasonably effective in lighting some types of model, they are not very efficient and at the heights associated with eye-level display, often difficult to support and somewhat obtrusive – see the picture! You *can* buy 'cool' high-powered incandescent sources suited to close mounting, in the form of 'Dichroic' lights, which use special (and costly) filters, coatings or reflectors to eliminate infra-red component from the light-beam and produce high-intensity illumination of accurate colour temperature. Don Leeper used a couple of miniature 3,800K 50-watt Dichroic fittings – fitted with 'barn door' baffles to prevent light spill – on 'Hepton Wharf', mounted about 26in from the model on a 'flying' light-beam situated above the viewer's heads. That's an elegant 'de luxe' lighting solution for a very small layout like 'Hepton', but not really suited to anything much larger.

The alternative to a 'spot' or 'point' source like an incandescent filament is a 'diffuse' lamp – one which emits light uniformly and omni-directionally over an area of surface. Such sources have a correspondingly uniform pattern of illumination, free from 'bright spots' or areas of steep fall-of; they also cast softer and less-defined shadows and are largely non-directional. The most common 'diffuse' light sources are, of course, fluorescent tubes and the new generation of 'low-energy' lamps designed to replace the old GLS tungsten-filament bulb. Low-energy lamps are simply a form of 'folded' or 'coiled' fluorescent tube, with the associated electronics miniaturised and incorporated in the lamp base rather than being housed in the sort of bulky and heavy fitting associated with conventional 'strip

lights'. Fluorescent sources emit virtually no infra-red but are comparatively high in ultra-violet, dependent on the exact mix of light-emitting phosphors coating the tube. Such heat as is associated with fluorescent lighting derives almost entirely from the electronics powering the lamps and is rarely a problem as it's not a component of the light. As well as *running* cool, fluorescent lamps are generally associated with 'cooler' light qualities, as they work at higher colour temperatures than incandescents; the new 'low-energy' lamps, however, are usually quite a bit warmer than strip lights, as they're mostly designed to exhibit colour values closer to an 'old-fashioned' pearl light bulb. Fluorescent sources are far more efficient than filament lamps, producing a lot more illumination for a lot less power.

Lighting colour values

You'll have noticed several references to 'colour temperature' in the above descriptions, given in the form of a number quoted as so many 'K'. This is the 'Kelvin number', a precise method of describing the colour value of a light source. The figure represents the temperature (measured in degrees Kelvin) above absolute zero to which an inert 'black body' would have to be heated to give off light of a given colour – a value quoted, simply, in 'Kelvins'. The confusing bit is that the 'hotter' the source gets, the 'cooler' the emitted light. Think of heating a bit of metal with a flame; it goes from 'straw' through dull red, red, orange and yellow to white and finally blue-white and violet. So, the higher the colour temperature, the more the light colour tends to the blue end of the spectrum. To put this information into a form relevant to layout lighting, then most normal domestic 'general service' incandescent bulbs operate in the range 2,800–3,200K. 'Daylight' photofloods are rated at 3,400K – but actual daylight is cooler still, about 5,000K at noon on a clear, bright sunny day. Fluorescent light sources range from about 3,500K 'warm white' through 4,500K 'white' to 6,000K 'daylight' tubes. The relationship between colour temperature and light colour isn't linear, by the way; doubling the Kelvins doesn't result in a light that's twice as 'blue'.

ABOVE, LEFT AND RIGHT: *Trouble with lights! Here are a couple of examples of set-ups I'd regard as less than ideal. Although 'Deurne' has a full backdrop, very well executed and nicely integrated fascias and drapes and a pleasantly unified (if rather bright) colour-scheme, the use of 'spots up poles' for illumination is somewhat incongruous. Unfortunately, the heat output and beam pattern of these 150W spots means they needed to be mounted a good distance from the model – which makes them all too visible, a source of glare and distraction. It is difficult to see why lower-powered hidden sources couldn't have been used in this instance…*

'Forks Creek' is another very nicely executed layout that uses very high-mounted lights – a good 8ft off the deck, where they struggle to light up the model! In this case, they're hidden by a fascia, but this is way too high up to perform any scene-framing/top-of-sky hiding function. Combined with a lowish backdrop, the result is a very distracting gap and a lot of unnecessarily exposed woodwork. It would be so simple to alter this arrangement into an effective set-up! Author

These nice round numbers are, of course, typical values measured under laboratory conditions. By contrast, the colour temperatures appropriate to layout lighting need to take account of the 'perceived' light values under which we view the real world – that is, light which has been reflected by the various elements making up the landscape and filtered through our far-from-transparent atmosphere. Reflected light is light from which a wide range of frequencies have been removed by absorption on striking the reflecting surface, which leaves only the residual frequencies to bounce back into our shining orbs and give an object its particular perceived colour. Perceived reflected colour is determined both by the colouration and finish of the objects being illuminated and by the colour temperature of the illumination – which is why it's such a good idea to paint your models under the same lighting as that under which they'll be viewed. Practically, on a scenic model railway, the exact colour values of the actual models are arrived by appropriate painting rather than by fiddling with the lighting.

ABOVE: *This stunning outdoor picture of David Lane's 'Saffron Street' is not only a great 'Wow!' picture of some superb modelling, but an eloquent demonstration of the difference truly natural lighting makes to the whole look and atmosphere of a modelled scene. Trying to replicate this 'look' – those distant trees against a seamless, uniformly lit and boundless sky – is the toughest challenge facing the railway modeller in search of true realism.* David Lane

Which leaves us to address the 'filtering' property of the atmosphere, which is what determines the light quality under which we view reality and which we need to try and replicate on our models. In Britain, our temperate-but-northerly situation and unique maritime climate means there's usually a fair amount of moisture – both as water vapour and fine droplets – suspended in the atmosphere. This is held to account for the characteristic 'softness' of our daylight for much of the year, contributing both to our often-overcast skies and summer heat-haze. The atmosphere also contains a mass of fine particles – soil-derived dust, micro-organisms, animal detritus and all manner of pollutants – which, mixed together with the water, act as a filtering medium that scatters, refracts and absorbs light and alters perceived colour values enormously. Whereas the water reflects and scatters the light, raising the 'white' component of the light and giving the 'cool' values associated with typically British overcast conditions, dust particles tend to absorb the blue-white component of the light and so 'warm' the perceived colour values.

Under clear skies, 'bright daylight' has a colour value of around 5,000K, but by the time this light has been filtered through the atmosphere and reached our retinas the 'perceived' colour temperature can be anywhere from a warm 3,000K – well into the yellow end of things – to a decidedly chilly 8,000K or more, decidedly 'blue'. The former tends to be associated with summer, the latter with the other 50-odd weeks of the year. This is because on a warm, sunny summer's day the atmosphere is full of convection currents lifting and circulating lots of dust particles, whereas at cooler, more sunless times the dust lies, but there are more water droplets floating about.

In fact, such generalisations are false as the amount of direct sunlight has an overwhelming influence on these perceptions; a stray cloud on a hot day can easily send the Kelvins soaring into the 'cool' 6,000+ range as it obscures the sun, whereas on a sunny snow-free winter's day the perceived light colour can get very close to 'warm' summer values, for all that, actual air temperatures might be below freezing. There won't be as much dust in the air, but the very low angle of the winter sun means it's shining through a lot more atmosphere. I've attempted to illustrate these different lighting conditions in the pair of snaps below, showing bits of the same landscape under very different conditions.

BELOW, LEFT AND RIGHT: *What a difference a spot of direct solar radiation makes! As soon as the sun shines, the yellow component of the daylight soars and everything takes on a much 'warmer' aspect. This is largely irrespective of the air temperature; it was actually colder (–1°C) when the sunny snap was taken in early December 2008 – the snowy day the following February registered a 'tropical' +2°C! The daylight colour values here are in the order of 3,500K (low winter sun) and 7,500+K (heavy overcast/snow). The two pictures were taken from the same viewpoint and show the Lew Valley in West Devon.* Author

Practical lighting solutions

So much for the theory; but what does it all amount to in practical terms? Well, bearing these theoretical factors in mind is a good guide when selecting light sources to give layout lighting appropriate for the subject you're depicting; all that then remains is to devise a suitable mounting for them! There are quite a few factors to consider here: size and weight of fittings, power rating and wiring requirements, heat dissipation, the avoidance of unwanted shadows, reflections and glare, and the location of the lighting in relation to the layout. Basing the lighting on cool-running 'emitter' sources such as fluorescent tubes, low-energy bulbs or LEDs enables you to choose the option of close-mounted fittings of relatively low power, but rather limits how 'warm' you can make the colour values. I've found it is usually necessary to mix light from sources of quite different colour temperatures to give the right effect; such mixing results in an 'average' colour value over the scene as a whole – and that, I find, is what you need to get right.

While I choose my light sources depending on the effect I'm after, I go for cool-running lamps and close mounting if I can. So, for a typical 'bright British summer's day' look, I aim at around 3,500°K as an average colour temperature, which I find I can get from main lighting using mid-range fluorescent lamps 'warmed up' with secondary incandescent sources – normal 2,700K GS light bulbs or 3,000K quartz-halogen for a bit of extra sparkle. So, for instance, 'Trerice' – which aims for a 'hazy sunshine' look – uses a very simple and basic set-up combing two 18W 'cool' coiled-tube 4,000K fluorescent low-energy bulbs and a single 21W 'U-tube' 3,200K lamp equivalent to a pearl tungsten GLS lamp. These lamps are mounted about a foot above the front of the layout in a radial pattern.

'Trerice's' lights are just normal domestic bayonet-cap lamps held in ordinary batten-holders. Apart from economy and ease of sourcing, using 'universal' fittings like this means it's easy to change the colour values by simply swapping lamp types. The fittings that offer the most scope in this direction are those designed to take GU10 miniature 250V lamps, which you can now obtain in a huge range of types and colour temperatures. These range from straightforward tungsten-halogen reflectors or energy-saving fluorescents at around 3,000K through quartz-halogen reflectors at 3,500K, quartz Dichroic and 'golden white' LED lamps at 3,800K to 'white' 4,500K and 'blue white' 7,000K' LEDs. This range and interchangeability opens up the possibility of a GU10-based 'universal' layout lighting system, where the same basic hardware could be configured at will by choosing lamps to suit any application, as well as allowing such refinements as fine-tuning to suit lighting conditions at a particular exhibition venue.

Combining such a versatile and compact lighting set-up with an upper front fascia and overhead dust/falling-object damage protection is particularly easy to arrange on the typical shelf-form layout – whatever its footprint – by use of a 'top deck' shelf sited above the layout and arranged along the lines shown in the diagram. In a domestic setting with a wall-mounted shelf-form layout supported off shelf track, adding such upperworks is simplicity itself; slot in a few extra shelf brackets and away you go. Self-contained portable/exhibition layouts are a little more problematic, in that the upper deck and lighting will need to be supported off the main baseboard structure in some way – a classic case of the importance of designing 'in the round'. It is a great deal easier to incorporate such structural provision from the outset rather than trying to tack it on later. And you *know* how I know this...

ABOVE: *Modern lightweight GU10 light fittings on the replacement light beam for 'Bodesmeer', seen under construction in a bit of a hurry before the Proto-87 convention at Utrecht in 2009. These fittings are very cheap – what you see here are two four-lamp spot strips at £7 a pop from B&Q including a quartet of 50W quartz-halogen reflector lamps. I used a mix of quartz-halogen, blue-white LED and low-energy lamp mini-fluorescent sources to light the layout.* Author

BELOW: *Lighting set-up for a typical shelf layout with a 'top deck' carrying a mix of T4/T5 super-slim fluorescent tubes (including a backdrop 'wash' light) and a few wide-angle low-voltage 25W Halogen down-lights for a bit of sparkle. All these fittings are sold by DIY centres for use below wall-mounted kitchen units. Note the ventilation slots in the deck.*

3 BASEBOARDS AND OTHER BORING BITS

Building a model railway is a bit like attending an old-fashioned tea-party; you have to chew your way through the bread and butter before you can cut loose with the cream cakes. I do actually know a couple of modellers who like woodworking enough to be quite happy designing and building baseboards, but for most of us it's nothing more than a chore, a necessary prelude to the fun parts of the layout-building process – laying track, sculpting scenery and siting structures. The only other cloud on this hedonistic horizon is the irksome necessity of adding the wiring and switchgear needed to make everything work. However, it's an unavoidable fact that the baseboarding is what underpins the whole edifice of a model railway – and its structural integrity and fitness for purpose are thus a key factor in the success of the whole enterprise. Likewise, the wiring and control systems lie at the functional heart of the model, both in terms of reliability and operational realism, so they also demand careful consideration in design and execution.

It'll come as no surprise, then, when I suggest that in adopting a holistic approach to designing a model railway, the baseboard demands thought very early on in the proceedings and you won't go all that far before needing to take account of the intended mode of operation and associated control system. As I have discovered to my cost, neglecting these aspects of the job leads nowhere but the vale of tears. Baseboards, in particular, have long been the subject of unquestioning non-design; not so long since, it seemed that almost every layout featured in the *Railway Modeller* had 'four- by two-foot rectangular baseboards with a half-inch fibreboard surface braced with two-by-one softwood butt-jointed on twelve-inch centres'. Given the size and number of the knots and the amount of 'shake' found in much of the 'joinery pine' then on offer, the fibreboard actually did quite a good job of holding this feeble 'bracing' together! The flat and floppy affair that resulted made a woefully inadequate support for the track and offered precious little scope for effective landscaping.

In the context of an of all-embracing layout design as advocated here, deciding upon an apt set of underpinnings for that superb, smooth-flowing track and mind-blowingly realistic scenery is without doubt one of the most important practical design decisions. The underlying rule here is that it's the needs of the model that dictate the design of the base structure, not t'other way about. In the school of realistic design, where we may well be using irregular or curvilinear footprints with a complex topography in the model, as well as seeking the best presentational options – including the all-essential backdrop – then evolving a suitable base structure isn't easy. This is why I'm now going to take a quick skit around some of the possible options.

ABOVE: *Even a very small layout like 'Clecklewyke' requires a surprisingly large amount of infrastructure – especially when it is a portable exhibition model which needs to be easy to move, quick and easy to erect and dismantle, and truly reliable in operation. Much thought (and not a little experiment) goes into devising and constructing all these unexciting underpinnings – which are as fundamental to the layout as track and scenery.* Ian Everett

Traditional baseboard systems

With the traditional British softwood-and-board 'tabletop' approach to baseboarding just described, it was very much a case of building the baseboard, then coming up with something to stick on top of it; the two operations bore very little relation one to another. In layout design terms, you were stuck with a world made up of flat four-by-two rectangles a

ABOVE: *Modern American open-grid benchwork; this is the commercial 'Mianne' system, based on lightweight I-beams with a thin MDF web and hardwood top and bottom flanges, bolted together at leg-tops or with joiners. The trackbeds and scenery are on bearers and risers supported off the grid.* Author

bit like shrunken ping-pong tables, on which you were trying to model a subject – the British landscape – that was anything *but* flat, not to mention notably short on rectangles! The only scenario to which such a baseboard might be remotely suited would seem to be a layout set in the fen-country; but even then, you'd have a problem: how to model the ditches, drains and counter-drains with which such scenery is seamed? As I found when trying to model the Dutch landscape on 'Bodesmeer', there's a surprising amount of verticality even in topography that, at a casual glance, seems 'flat'.

In the USA they have always gone in for plenty of verticality in their model railroads, many of which are set in terrain that's positively precipitous. In which cause, they have long since devised alternatives to the flat tabletop to serve them as a layout supporting structure – or 'benchwork', to use the appropriate vernacular. The most traditional format was the 'open grid', which uses a rectangular-plan timber structure not unlike the bare 2 x 1 framing of the traditional British table-top, but a good deal beefier (4 x 1 is usual) and far freer from knots, lumber across the water being of notably better quality than what we're usually palmed off with here! This framing is set at a 'datum' level which equates to the lowest point in the scene it is supporting. Often, such open-grid benchwork is assembled from a commercial manufactured modular system using patent fasteners and bolts to hold it together – a method of assembly that is quick and easy.

The open grid framing is used as a base to support all the separate elements making up the rest of the layout. Where there is a yard, depot or other substantial area of level trackwork, then it will be surfaced, tabletop-style, with sheet material to form a suitable trackbase, packed as necessary to give it the right elevation above the 'grid datum'. Elsewhere, the framing is used merely as an anchor-point for risers supporting separate trackbeds tailor-cut for the various running lines and set at elevations appropriate to the intended topography. In the USA, such trackbases are normally cut from half-inch structural ply, often laminated to a further half-inch layer of 'Homasote', a compressed-paper based softboard that takes pins and spikes well. The resulting inch-thick sandwich offers considerable topographical possibilities in its own right! Away from the track locations, the actual landscaping is supported by ply 'scenery profiles', also fixed to the 'grid' framing; the traditional landform surface using chicken-wire tacked to the ply profiles to support a 'hard shell' of paper towels dipped in runny 'Hydrocal' plaster.

While not as limiting as the British mini ping-pong table, such modular frames are often restricted to rigid geometric outlines and are dimensionally determined by the fixed spacing of the cross-members, which are usually based on a 12in grid. These cross-members form the part of the base structure to which the various layout elements are usually secured, so their spacing is important. Such modular grids also tend to need a lot of support, often standing on a veritable forest of legs. In the mid-1970s, these limitations inspired the late Linn Westcott – then editing the *Model Railroader* – to look around for something that would be less restricting as to footprint and offer a far more adaptable system of support. He was also looking for a benchwork system that was cheap, used readily available materials and hardware, was easy to build for non-carpenters, and which could be self-supporting over a reasonable span rather than needing more legs than a millipede.

The L-girder system

What Linn came up with was an irregular ladder-style framing based on the L-girder – a simple but immensely strong structural member made of two inch-thick planks of wood screwed and glued together at right angles, so that each element braced the 'weak' dimension of the other. The 'L' was used inverted and made so that the horizontal flange sat on top of the vertical web. By making the vertical component of the girder quite deep – typically, six to eight inches – it was possible to produce a relatively lightweight beam that would support the very substantial loads associated with typical plaster-based 'Rocky Mountain whoopee' scenery, and to do so over a considerable span without deflection. The much-narrower 'top flange' both braced the upright and provided a convenient means of attaching the other structural element of the system, the cross-bearer. These were simply lengths of suitable stripwood – usually 2 x 1 or 3 x 1 – cut to whatever length was needed and screwed to the top flange from beneath.

L-girder is a truly flexible system of benchwork. The girders can be made to any length, depth or span and require relatively few supports. They can be grouped in pairs or more as required, be set at any distance apart without any need to be parallel one with another. The cross bearers, too, can be set at any convenient angle and spacing and

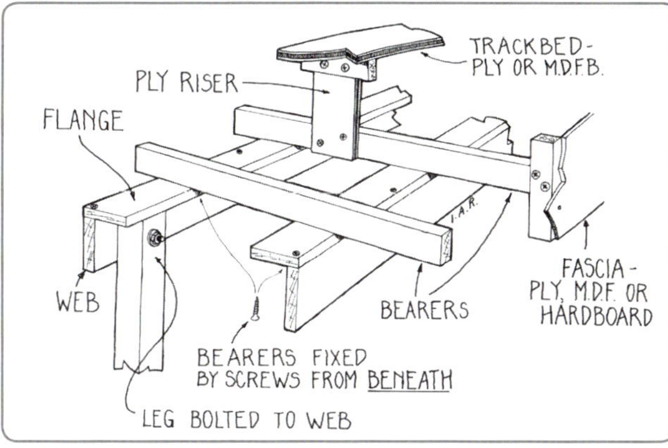

ABOVE: *A basic L-girder baseboard system.*

be made to any length required by the layout design; they can overhang the supporting L-girders by a considerable amount. Even when a layout is substantially complete, cross-bearers can be added, subtracted, moved or replaced by those of a different length. The system favours a wide range of footprints – including the irregular, curvilinear outlines pioneered by layout designers like John Armstrong. L-girder benchwork is very quick and easy to build and is highly adaptable. Even if a layout is subsequently scrapped and dismantled, the basic structural elements can be readily salvaged for reuse.

L-girders have proved to be a very good supporting system for layouts that stay put. If push comes to shove, it *is* possible to move a layout built onto L-girder framework – provided that it has been designed from the outset with this possibility in mind, so that it at least comes apart in manageable chunks. But the nature of the L-girder ladder frame – extremely stiff in the vertical plane, but far from rigid in the horizontal – means that it does not offer good lateral support when being handled; usually, it's the trackbeds and scenery that hold the frame in alignment, not the other way about. With care, you can get away with this lack of lateral location on a very occasional basis; but for layouts that need to move regularly, traditional ladder-frame L-girder is pretty much a no-no. For truly portable baseboarding, we need something far stiffer in the horizontal plane.

Portable sectional baseboards

Americans, by and large, don't build portable layouts, whereas in Britain they predominate – probably the reason why the L-girder baseboard system has never really caught on here. Older British sectional/portable layouts tended to use baseboard technologies derived from traditional 'grid frame' permanent-layout practice: substantial glued-and-screwed timber frameworks, usually surfaced with a high-density chipboard like 'Weyroc' – widely adopted on account of its smooth, flat surface, relative stability and moderate cost. Grid-frame baseboards could certainly be made strong, stable and rigid – but they were normally limited to geometric linear outlines and some variation of 'tabletop' format and tended to be heavy and unwieldy. The strength and integrity of such a frame depends to a great extent on the quality of the timber used, the properties of the adhesives holding it together and the skill with which the various joints have been made. The real Achilles' heel of the grid frame is the almost exclusive reliance on butt joints which, as any carpenter will tell you, are inherently weak. Even leaving aside the limitations of the traditional boiled-bone carpentry glues used in pre-PVA days, unless the joining faces were dead square and true, the actual glued area in contact would be minimal. Even if the joints were reinforced with nails or screws, these only go into the end grain of the butt piece, offering relatively poor location and weak retention. One suspects, however, that few modellers would be up to the sort of nifty mortice-and-tenon work really called for.

The growth of the British model railway exhibition circuit and the resulting demand for readily portable layouts soon triggered a quest for stronger, lighter and more versatile baseboard systems – a quest aided and abetted by the increasing range of materials and adhesives becoming available. Plywood in a range of thicknesses and qualities was joined by other manufactured wood or wood-fibre-based sheet boards like high-density particle boards, blockboard, insulation boards, oriented strand bond sheet and the now-ubiquitous medium-density fibreboard (MDF). To go with these materials we now have high-strength resin-bonded PVA woodworking adhesives like Evo-Stik's 'Resin W' and manly construction adhesives like 'No More Nails'. Of these materials, it was the better grades of thin (4–8mm) ply and the smooth-faced, stable and acoustically 'dead' MDF – available in thicknesses from 2mm up to 40mm or so – that offered the most promise.

BELOW: *The demands of the British exhibition circuit have spawned some very sophisticated and ingenious baseboards and layout-supporting systems. Few are more hi-tech and refined than the lightweight ply structures designed by Steve Ridgeway and Trevor Edwards for their evolving 'Rose Grove' layout, seen here 'straight out of the van' at Scaleforum 2009.* Author

ABOVE: *A ply-framed 'eggbox' lightweight baseboard.*

Lightweight glued-ply baseboard structures using thin sheet were soon being produced to a variety of formats; properly designed with adequate bracing, such ply baseboards can be amazingly rigid and very strong. Initial efforts usually focused on composite ply beams to replace the timber sections in a traditional grid-pattern framework, but the more innovative modellers soon started to take advantage of the properties of ply sheet and resin-reinforced adhesives to produce far more adventurous and versatile all-glued baseboard structures. Usually, such lightweight ply baseboards are deep-section fabrications in 4–5mm thick material used in 'eggbox' fashion to produce a well-braced and rigid structure. Such 'eggbox' boards can be made to any outline you like, curves being no problem as the thin ply is easy to form. The basic 'eggbox' approach has seen considerable development in recent years, to the point where we're now seeing lightweight baseboards that incorporate trackbeds at different levels, landscape formers and backscenes within their basic structure. These are what I term 'integrated' baseboards, on which more anon.

BELOW: *Ply baseboards can be made in many ways. This elegant framework built by Don Leeper for a cameo baseboard uses a box-beam spine girder and ply cross-bearers. The fascia is a stressed member, as is the foot of the backdrop. The result is a very strong structure of modest weight.* Don Leeper

Sheet foam baseboards

Sheet-foam baseboards fall into two categories: those based on thin (10mm or less) foam-cored sheet or board, like the paper-surfaced urethane-cored 'featherboard' used extensively in display and advertising (free source: the skip at the rear of your local supermarket!); and those using 'Styrofoam' rigid *extruded* foam polystyrene insulation sheet. Note that this extruded sheet is a very different animal to traditional beaded 'expanded polystyrene', which is horrible soft, floppy stuff quite useless for baseboard building. The styro-foams are very different, having an even, dense closed-cell foam texture and a smooth, continuous 'skin'; they are also flame-retardant and come in a variety of grades and densities and thicknesses of 50mm, 75mm, 100mm and 200mm. Medium-density blue general-purpose Styrofoam sheet 50mm or 75mm thick is the most readily available option – but even that's none too easy to find, being stocked only by dedicated insulation outlets. Builder's merchants can usually get it to order, but you won't find it at your local DIY emporium. Sheet sizes are usually nominal 8ft x 4ft 2,440mm x 1,220mm or 10ft x 2ft (3,000mm x 610mm). It's not a cheap option – expect to pay £30–£50 per sheet – which generally puts foam baseboards in the same price bracket as good-quality ply jobs.

The thin sheet foam-cored boards are generally cut with a Stanley knife and straightedge and fabricated – in similar 'eggbox' fashion to glued-ply baseboards – with the help of a hot-glue gun. Such a baseboard shares many of the virtues of a ply structure – although I find foam-core board less accommodating of curves than thin ply. Fabricating such boards out of foam-core does save quite a bit more weight, but personally I'm not convinced that this is *necessarily* a good thing; layouts that are *too* light lack resistance to the inevitable knocks and nudges when being displayed at exhibitions, as well as being somewhat prone to resonant vibration. A *bit* of weight in a portable layout helps keep everything in place and damps out unwanted noise, I find. The rigid Styrofoam insulation sheet, being both denser and far thicker, is obviously heavier than foam-core board. If completely unframed, 50mm is the minimum dimension at which most such sheet is rigid enough to be self-supporting over the area of a typical portable baseboard, but laminating two or more layers together produces a very much stronger structure, as does adding a little ply bracing. The usual practice is anyway to add a thin ply 'perimeter frame' to foam-constructed baseboards, as much to give a fascia finish and to protect the foam from transit knocks as for any structural benefit. The result is surprisingly strong and robust, light enough for ease of handling but heavy enough for stability, and acoustically pretty inert.

Apart from light weight and ease of construction, the other advantage of Styrofoam insulation sheet is that it can readily be laminated to any desired thickness and carved

ABOVE: *Sheet extruded-styrene foam baseboards for 'Pempoul'. Strictly speaking, these are a composite foam/ply structure, with the ply perimeter facing and bracing providing a proportion of the structural strength. All-foam baseboards do without such bracing, but tend to use thicker foam, and more of it. As good-quality extruded foam is quite hard to source by the sheet (and tends to be pretty expensive when you do find it!), then the composite approach can look very attractive.* Gordon Gravett

and sanded to shape to produce landforms as an integrated part of the base structure. Both Gordon Gravett and Barry Norman use foam in this way, covering the basic landform with a skin of plaster-bandage or paper-towel 'glueshell' to protect it and form a basis for the landscape textures. You can also lay track straight onto the foam without any need for an additional trackbase layer – provided you use a suitable adhesive. Although not *quite* as vulnerable to petroleum-based contact adhesives as traditional expanded polystyrene – which will vanish like snow in the desert sun given even a whiff of something like traditional Evo-Stik – you still need to use a water-based construction adhesive like 'No More Nails', Evo-Stik 'Impact' solvent-free or 'Unibond Extra' to stick Styrofoam sheet. And be prepared to wait, as these adhesives can take a long time to cure when laminating foam. To cut and shape the foam, it is nicest and cleanest to use a purpose-designed hot-wire cutter – but failing this a fine-toothed wood saw or serrated knife (I use an old bread-knife) will suffice. To smooth the rough-cut contours you can use a 'Surform' type wood-rasp and coarse abrasive papers – although this can be somewhat messy! A good industrial-style or bagless vacuum cleaner is a good idea too.

Integrated baseboards

The sort of laminated-foam 'landform' structure just described is a good example of an 'integrated' baseboard – one where the supporting structure forms an integral part of the

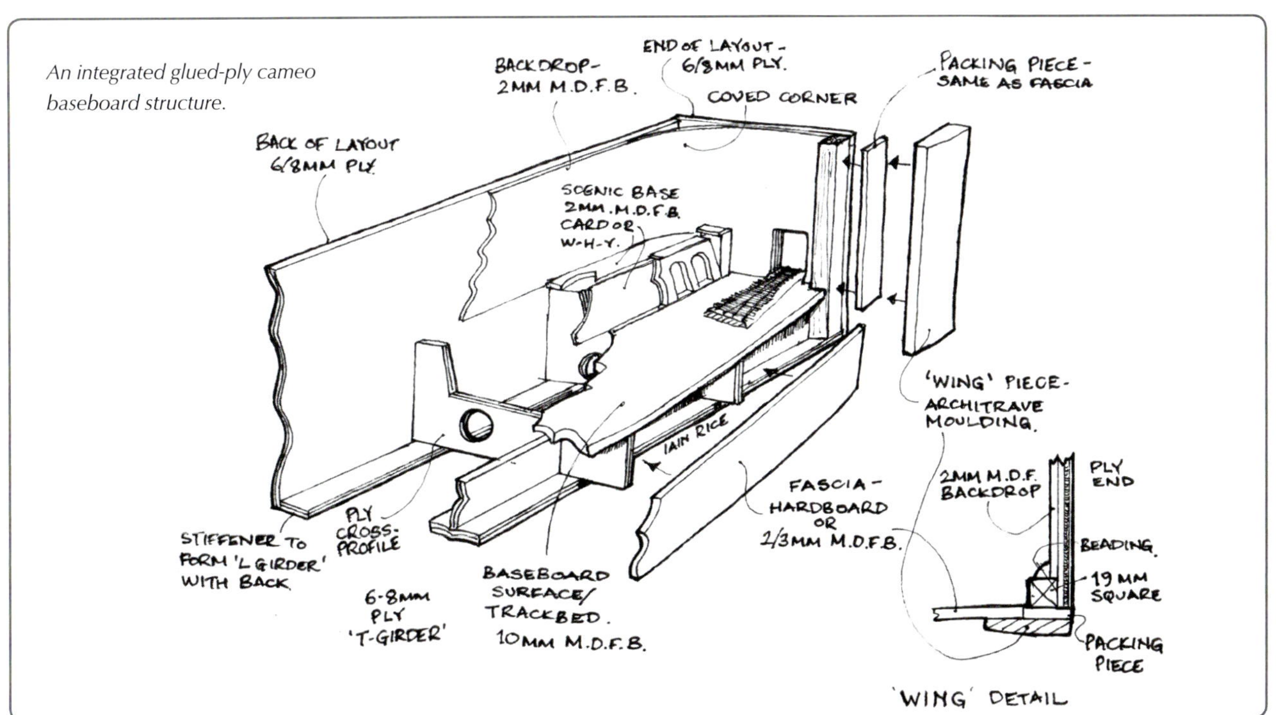

An integrated glued-ply cameo baseboard structure.

ABOVE: *'Hepton Wharf' is a pioneering example of a fully integrated cameo layout; everything you see here is part of a single homogeneous glued-ply structure that incorporates the lighting and layout power supplies, as well as the modelling, backdrop and presentation. Moving and storing such a layout is simple, but practicable overall size is limited.* Author

BELOW: *For true and easy portability, the self-contained cameo takes a bit of beating. Here is 'Trerice', tastefully gift-wrapped in plastic sheet and gaffer tape, perched on the roof of my long-serving Volvo, after the 700+ mile hike from Devon to Den Bosch in the Netherlands. The inside of the car was taken up by Ian Everett's 'Humber Dock', the occasion being the 2006 'Rail' exhibition. As well as displaying the model, the cameo structure also protects it well in transit.* Author

modelled scene. Truly integrated base structures are conceived to provide not only a mechanically rigid subframe and a series of suitable surfaces on which to lay track, but also to take account of such visual aspects of the model railway as the basic landscape form and the provision of a backscene. Taking things a stage further, a 'fully-integrated' baseboard structure might also incorporate further display-related elements like backdrops, fascias, side-wings and lighting beams and provide such practical adjuncts as integral electrical compartments for power supplies and control gear. It can even include such refinements as inbuilt stock-storage, stowage for extra fiddleyard cassettes and the like, and even a toolbox. I know of one exhibition layout so thoroughly integrated that it even boasts its own on-board Espresso machine!

An example of such a fully integrated baseboard structure is the self-contained 'cameo' style of 'micro layout' – of which 'Hepton Wharf' is a pioneering example, built in 1993. Here, one sophisticated glued-ply structure incorporates not just the layout – complete with full-height backscene – but also a complete display system with fascia and 'side wings', fiddleyard, integral stock-box and power supply. 'Trerice' is similar but has an integral lighting beam/top fascia as well. Such a baseboard does a very good job of protecting the model as well as supporting it, and makes for an immensely strong and robust structure that is very easy to transport and store. 'Trerice' can be stored on end if need be, and a couple of years ago – suitably wrapped in waterproof sheeting – it went all the way from Devon to s'Hertogenbosch in the Netherlands and back on the roof of a car without any ill effects.

Fully integrated portable baseboards like this aren't suited to every type of model railway, being influenced by scale, subject and size. They are limited to fairly modest footprints and scene heights, as they can easily become unwieldy if made too big; ideally, they want to be no larger than about coffin-sized – six foot long by a couple wide and a foot-and-a-half high. A structure this big will go through a normal doorway in the upright position and up and down most stairways. Of course, you *can* make fully integrated glued-ply baseboards in sectional form for bigger scenes, but their real forte is the single-section self-contained small layout. My own experience is that they are best suited to 'single span of view' scenes (See Chapter 8 for an explanation of this concept), in the 'miniature' range 4ft 6in–6ft. The huge advantage of this sort of integrated layout in an exhibition or 'no site' context is the speed and ease with which it can be brought into use – more or less 'plug and play', in contemporary argot. Also, it is harder to lose or leave behind vital adjuncts (like power supplies) if they're built-in.

'Disintegrated' layout structures: the jigsaw approach

Diametrically opposed to the 'integrated' all-in-one approach to model railway supporting structures described above, is the concept of a model railway that comes completely to pieces, rather like a giant 3-D Chinese puzzle. This is what I call 'Jigsaw Construction', an idea I first described in my 1990 book *An Approach to Model Railway Layout Design* (Wild Swan Publications). The original starting point for the jigsaw concept was a quest to get away from the visually intrusive 'dead-straight geological fault' of the baseboard join – something that bedevils all sectional-portable model railways and rose to particular prominence on the new generation of 'broad brush' scenic layouts exemplified by Barry Norman's 'Petherick' and the Barlow-Rice 'East Suffolk Light'. It was in an effort to disguise such a join on my 1984 'Butley Mills' layout that I came up with the notion of bridging the offending crevasse with removable scenic modules that plugged unobtrusively into the landscape by following 'natural' boundaries within it – hedge-lines, walls, riverbanks, road-edges, structure margins and the like.

From this starting point, it was but a step to the concept of the layout in which the scenery was entirely made up of such removable modules, leaving the actual baseboard as a very simple supporting frame on which the only fixed

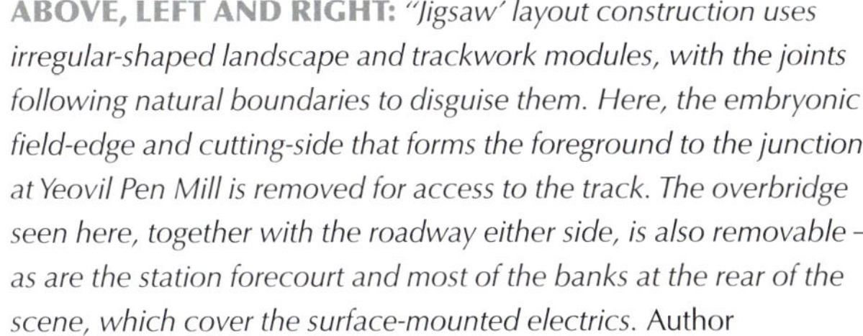

ABOVE, LEFT AND RIGHT: *'Jigsaw' layout construction uses irregular-shaped landscape and trackwork modules, with the joints following natural boundaries to disguise them. Here, the embryonic field-edge and cutting-side that forms the foreground to the junction at Yeovil Pen Mill is removed for access to the track. The overbridge seen here, together with the roadway either side, is also removable – as are the station forecourt and most of the banks at the rear of the scene, which cover the surface-mounted electrics.* Author

elements were the trackbeds with the track, wiring and point control systems attached thereto. My first true 'jigsaw' model was the P4 Bringewood Chase layout 'Leintwardine', built in 1990–91; here, the baseboard was little more than a simple ply 'tray' of suitable outline with the PW, mechanical point-control system and wiring mounted thereon. The point rodding and wiring were all surface run, being hidden by the removable scenery modules. The only scenic modelling on the actual baseboard was that lying below track level – a small area of the foreground. Virtually all the layouts I've built since 'Leintwardine' have used the jigsaw principle to a greater or lesser extent. A good example is my Dutch-prototype P87 exhibition layout – born in 1994 – where the entire town of Bodesmeer is made up of a series of 'jigsaw pieces' that come off when the layout is moved, which not only allows the delicate structures to be properly protected for transit, but allows highly accessible surface-mounted wiring and point actuation and a very simple baseboard that folds up for transport.

Also in the Netherlands, my friend Vincent de Bode (for whom Bodesmeer was named) took the jigsaw principle a stage further on his ground-breaking 'Flintfields' P4 exhibition layout, where the actual baseboard consists solely of a 'spine' – in the form of narrow (6–15in wide) frame supported off a pair of modest glued-ply 'box beams' located beneath the actual trackbed. The jigsaw modules that make up the scenery in its entirety are lightweight, self-supporting cantilevered structures that simply plug into this spine, located by 'tongues' fitting into the gap left between the top of the frame and the ply trackbed, spaced off by a few centimetres on bearers at suitable intervals. That the whole of 'Flintfield' – 14ft x 4ft, complete with a 2ft deep backdrop and overhead lighting raft – could be moved with a Fiat Panda (original model!) speaks volumes for the potential of the jigsaw system! The snag (of *course* there's a snag!) is that such a layout takes a lot more time erecting

RIGHT: *Spot the join... One of the two main section joints in 'Bodesmeer's' folding baseboard runs smack through the middle of this picture – it lies directly beneath the bridge and roadway, bisects the level crossing then cuts across the square to run straight through the vestibule of the white-fronted Golden Lion Hotel at the rear of the scene. However, only in the fragment of road fronting the bridge and in the brick paving of the level crossing can you see any evidence of a join; otherwise, the unwanted chasm lies completely hidden beneath the removable 'jigsaw' modules making up the Station Square and the bridge with its apron. The whole town of Bodesmeer is a series of such modules.* Author

ABOVE: *How do you transport a 14ft x 4ft exhibition layout with a tall backdrop, lighting system and supporting structure, plus a four-man operating crew and all their luggage, in a modest family hatchback? Well you make it come apart jigsaw-fashion and shift it in a pair of compact weathertight boxes on the roof-rack! Vincent de Bode checks the vital restraining straps.* Author

and dismantling, being the complete antithesis of the plug-and-play integrated layout.

On a more down-to-earth note, jigsaw construction has a range of practical advantages. Apart from the ease of transport already noted, the various individual pieces making up the jigsaw can be constructed at any convenient size and shape, allowing them to be worked on at the bench rather than in situ on the layout – a particular advantage where this last normally sits at high level for viewing. Each piece can be constructed using the methods and materials best suited to the needs of the subject, as it effectively forms a self-contained modelling project (although subject, of course, to our over-riding consistency requirement). Jigsaw landscape pieces can be readily removed to allow free access to the track and other infrastructure elements of the layout; they particularly facilitate 'above decks' of mechanical point and signal actuating systems and wiring – far easier to install and maintain than traditional 'underground' systems. Even on the most permanent of layouts, these are worthwhile virtues.

Generic layout systems

There is still quite a lot of unexplored territory in the whole jigsaw concept. It's a form of model railway construction that opens up some exciting design possibilities as well as having a range of visual and practical advantages. The facility to be able to separate the jigsaw modules making up the landscape setting from the railway infrastructure proper – track, electrics, point control system and so on – means that you can change, improve or alternate all or any part of the setting without the need to 'go back to square one' and rebuild the entire layout. This ability to adjust the scenery at will enables you to, for instance, present the same subject at different periods – providing alternative buildings, landscape features, street furniture, vehicles, figures and so on as appropriate to different timeframes simply by building alternative interchangeable jigsaw modules for key elements of the scene.

Taking this facility for interchangeability a stage further, you could accommodate widely differing prototype interests on a single layout by having two complete sets of scenic modules to fit a given track formation, which could then be 'dressed up' to represent, say, the LMS in the gritty industrial North West one day and the SR in rural Hampshire the next – giving scope for two complete sets of rolling stock. Adopting this sort of generic approach is certainly one way of extending the scope and potential of a small layout or restricted site, and gets the maximum use out of a single set of model railway infrastructure – the part of any model railway most demanding of time, effort and money. Yes, such an approach does embody a degree of compromise that probably won't appeal to finescale purists worried by the finer points of PW practice, but it's certainly not incompatible with a realistic result (or set of results!) and is a good solution for those who tend to build or accumulate collections of locos and stock rather larger or more diverse than can be comfortably accommodated on a typical single-subject small layout.

Generic spine design

One stage further down the interchangeability trail from even this is the somewhat radical concept that I've christened the 'Generic spine' system, a notion that I conceived while working on the design of 'nTrack' modules in the USA. The 'nTrack' and other similar communal modular formats are based on a system of highly portable individually built layout modules, constructed on defined footprints and having common standards, track centres, electrical circuitry and joining systems. These modules can then be combined in an almost infinite variety of ways to create a range of entirely different layouts. The idea is that individual modellers (who might lack the space or inclination to construct a conventional layout) concoct a module or modules which they then bring to a 'meet' at a suitable venue, where the various modules can be combined into a common layout – often a very large affair indeed! Such layouts are rarely realistic as a whole, the content and subject of each module being down to the preferences of the builder; the *quality* of the modelling, though, is often very high.

My idea was for a system where the modules are restricted to the actual model railway infrastructure, consisting solely of trackbed sections – complete with PW, electrics and point control – supported on matching sections of plug-together box-beam 'spine'. Track centres/alignments and electrical systems (easy with DCC) would be sufficiently standardised for these modules to be combined in different ways to allow alternative track configurations, almost like sophisticated train-set sections. Jigsaw scenery modules would then plug, Flintfield-style, into this spine; again, alternative scenic sections would facilitate the representation of a range of different subjects in a totally realistic way. Given the money and effort needed to produce high-quality infrastructure – particularly where hand-laid fine scale track is involved – then such a way of extending the 'return on investment' seems to me to be worthwhile; a way of spending more time eating cake and less chewing your way through the bread-and-butter. Arriving at a situation where a number of track modules and a suitable selection of scenic jigsaw pieces were available would allow a group (or even an industrious individual) to, for instance, offer exhibition managers a choice of layout configurations and subjects, or simply to ring the changes to maintain interest.

Transportable baseboards: Mini L-girders

Layouts not designed to be carted about pose a rather different set of requirements as to baseboarding. A lot of the sophisticated solutions called on in the cause of ready portability are simply not necessary for stay-put models; something far more straightforward – such as L-girder – will usually suffice. In the traditional American form, L-girder benchwork is usually pretty hefty – being conceived for the type of heavyweight permanent layout prevailing on that side of the Atlantic. For the much more compact and modest affairs usually found on these shores, something far less substantial is usually adequate – in which role I've successfully employed a variety of miniaturised L and T-girder structures. The simplest of these are based on the type of fine-sawn kiln-dried 50mm x 25mm 'battening' widely available in bundles from chain DIY outlets like B&Q. By and large, this stuff is a great deal straighter and freer from knots than a lot of so-called joinery pine (especially if you spend a bit of time winkling out the best bits!) and, if glued-and-screwed in the proscribed 'L' fashion, makes a compact, 75mm x 50mm girder that is quite strong enough for most UK applications; the same material – used upright or flat on its side – also serves as cross-bearers. This 'mini' L-girder frame is very cheap and simple to make and is my usual choice for non-portable baseboarding.

I've also made extensive use of ply-webbed or all-ply mini L and T-girders where weight and vertical stiffness are a consideration; a 4in-deep ply web glued and pinned to a 'top flange' of either ply or stripwood makes for a structural member that is very light and compact but extremely stiff in the vertical plane. I often use this type of beam as a basic structural member for glued-ply baseboard assemblies, particularly for shelf format boards designed to be carried on shelf track. Used with the flange at the bottom and combined with ply cross-formers designed to slot over the

ABOVE: *Mini L-girder baseboard framing on the extension to my 'Cade's Green' layout.* Author

BELOW: *Ply mini girders.*

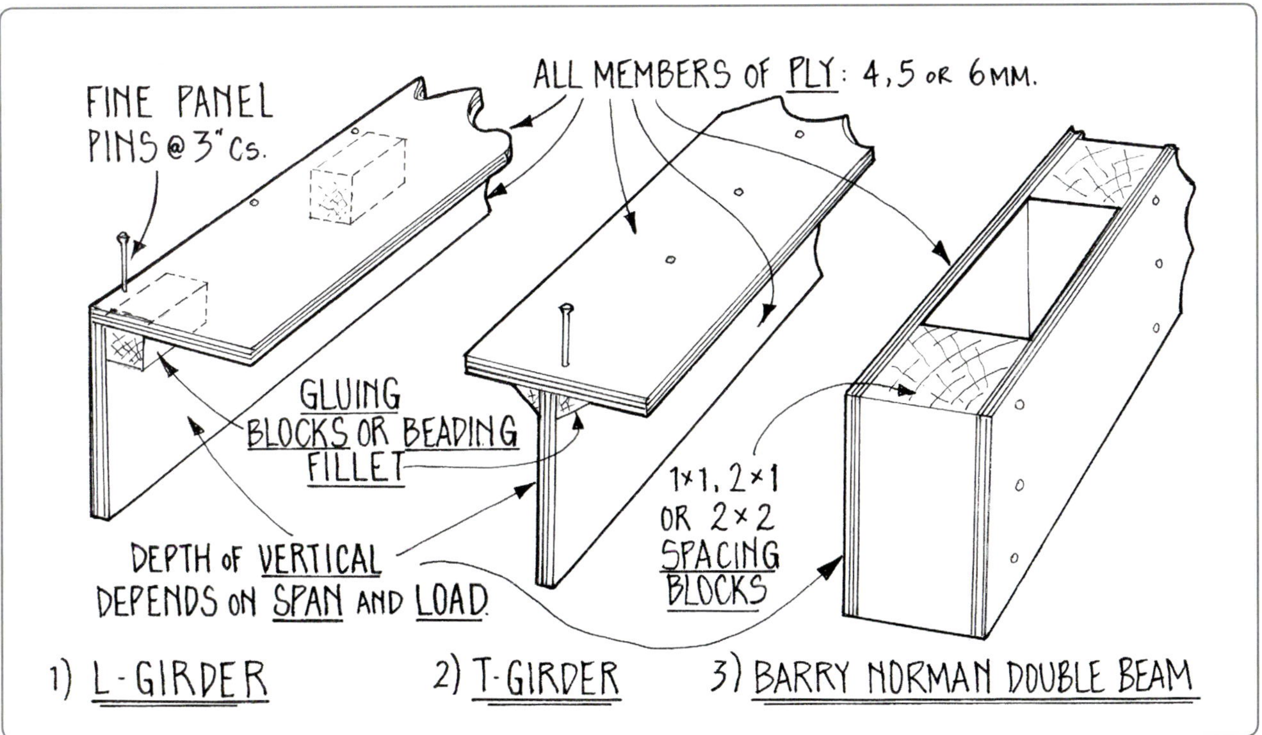

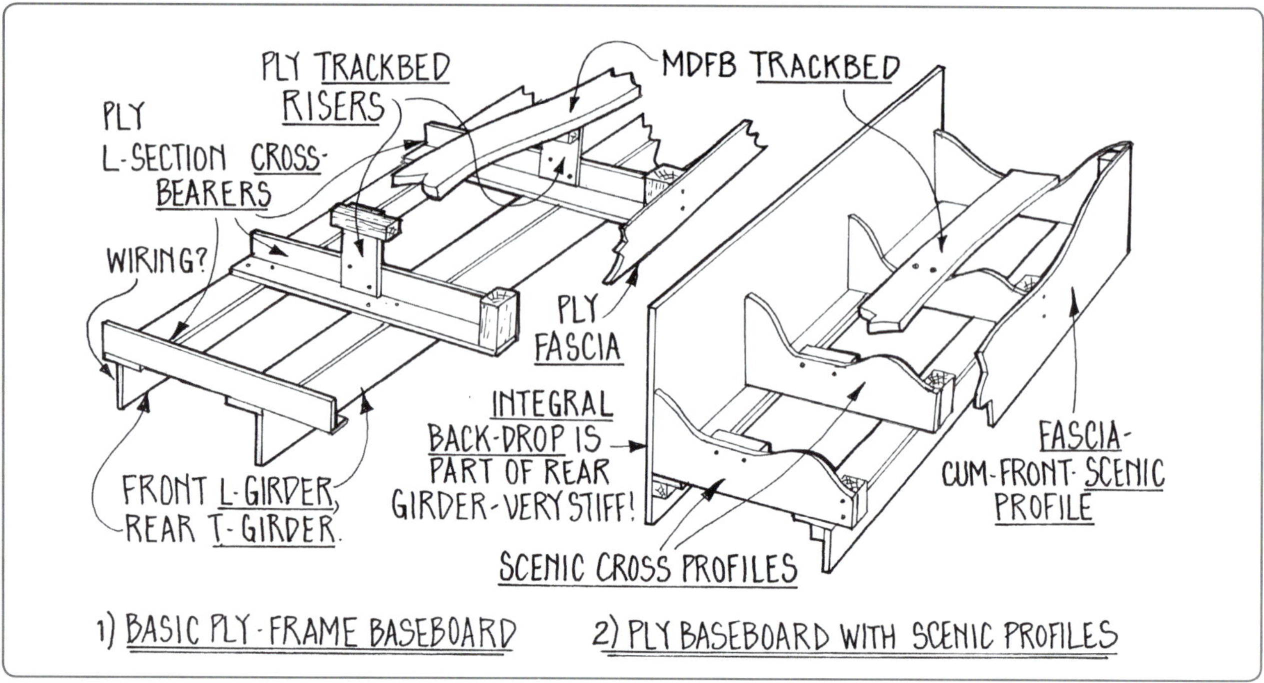

ABOVE: *Ply-beam baseboard structures.*

vertical web of the girder, with all the joints reinforced with gluing blocks, it makes for a quick, easy and versatile but very solid ply baseboard structure that can be adapted for anything from a simple flat shelf to a fully integrated mountain-scenery design.

Baseboarding summary

All the preceding verbiage is but a cursory skit around the possible ways of devising a supporting structure suited to a realistic model railway. As I hope will have become evident, I believe there's a great deal more to this baseboarding business than any mere simplistic bashing-together of a few two-by-four rectangles. The appropriate solution for any given model depends on a number of factors – of which scale, subject, size, situation and degree of permanence are but the most obvious. It's almost impossible to generalise as to 'best' choices, but these days I find myself designing around mini L-girder, glued-ply and laminated foam structures in combination with jigsaw scenery principles more and more often, even for non-portable layouts. Whatever the baseboard, I always aim for as few joints as possible, while arranging a seamless backdrop is a fundamental part of the layout-structural equation. But the really important thing, so far as layout design goes, is to think very carefully about what you're trying to achieve and to explore all the relevant possibilities thoroughly; 'non-design' is not an option!

Baseboard supporting systems

Whatever the nature of the baseboard structure, it needs to be supported at the height called for by the presentation and viewpoint decided upon. There are two basic options: support the layout directly off of the floor or hang it on a

LEFT AND RIGHT: *Support trestles for high-level layouts. These can either be sturdy, full-height affairs as favoured by Ian Everett, or the pragmatic and more readily portable mini trestles I use for my own layouts, which are designed to sit on a normal table of the type available at most exhibition venues.* Author

wall, shelf-fashion. Or, in the case of a dual-purpose home/exhibition model, both: wall-hung at home, free-standing at shows. In the context of a typical long/narrow home layout using shelf-form baseboards positioned against a wall, a domestic shelf-track system makes wall-mounting such a simple option that these days I scarcely consider anything else. All my own layouts sit-on wall-mounted brackets when in residence *chez moi* – either heavy-duty twin-slot 'Spur' track or – more economically – the lightweight single-slot track of unknown brand but good quality sold by some DIY outlets.

For obvious reasons, portable exhibition layouts have to be floor-mounted in some way, either using bolt-on or socketed legs attached directly to the base structure, or by sitting the latter on some form of self-contained, free-standing support. Over the years, I've tried both approaches, my conclusion being that a system independent of the layout is infinitely preferable – in which role I have found the simple, robust free-standing A-frame trestle to be a satisfactory answer. For a start, such trestles can be made more-or-less universal, rather than being tied to a given layout; provided they are wide enough, they can be used with just about any type of baseboard structure or layout style. As such trestles are very easy to make height-adjustable they can be readily tweaked to fine-tune display heights, while the addition of a single screw-type levelling foot on the bottom crosspiece allows them to be made extremely stable. A-frame trestles are very easy to make, fold flat for storage and transit, and – given appropriate timber sections and stout hinges – are quite strong enough for any load we're likely to put on them.

To display my own models at shows I have a selection of such trestles, some of them dating back more than two decades and having seen duty beneath a succession of layouts. More recently, I've taken to using 'mini-trestles' about 20in tall, designed to sit on a normal six-by-two foot table of the sort found at most exhibition venues; as such tables are normally 30in high, sitting a 20in trestle plus a baseboard around 4in deep puts the track height on the favoured 54in level suited to standing eye-level viewing. These mini-trestles are a lot less unwieldy to cart about than full-height 5ft versions. I also take advantage of the vertical stiffness and strength of glued-ply integral or L-beam baseboards to keep the number of trestles to a minimum. You don't always need support over the full length of a layout anyway, as fiddleyards and the like can often be cantilevered from the end of the layout proper. On 'Trerice' for instance, a cameo having a full-height integrated baseboard/display frame, the fiddleyard is simply suspended from the top of the framing using steel picture-hanging wire, like half a suspension bridge. I like to think it adds a Brunelian touch.

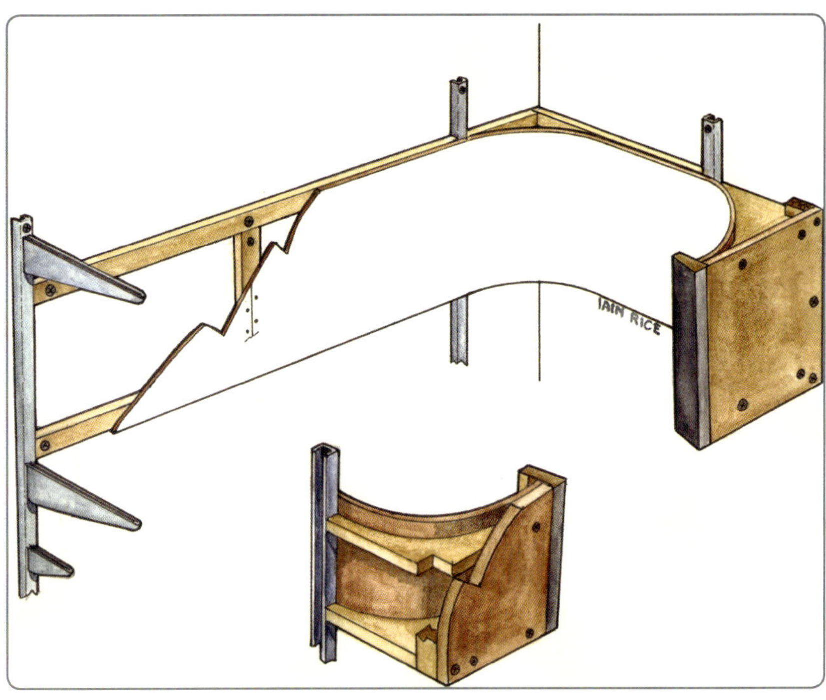

ABOVE: *A wall-mounted backscene.*

Backdrops: the essential adjunct

As I argue consistently throughout this book, a backdrop of some sort is something no realistic layout can do without, and its provision is therefore a prime structural requirement. Unfortunately, it's no sinecure. For reasons already touched upon in the lighting notes in the previous chapter and expounded upon at length in Chapter 8, for an effective and natural-looking backscene we need a surface that is truly vertical, tall enough to reach the upper limit of our field of view, completely smooth, joint-free, without angular changes of direction, and generally concave in form. Corners need to be 'coved' – curved on as wide a radius as possible – and the whole thing needs to be lit evenly and in such a way that it has no evident shape. In the case of portable exhibition layouts, the backdrop also needs to allow access for operation as well as being easy to erect/dismantle and transport. All-in-all, a pretty tall order!

Only in the case of the permanent home layout or the completely integrated cameo style of exhibition layout is the provision of such a backdrop relatively straightforward. In the former case, the backdrop can use the walls of the room in which the layout is situated, either directly as a surface to paint on or, more frequently, as a means of support for a structure incorporating the desiderata listed. This is my preferred approach, using small-section timber and ply for framing as in the diagram, with smooth-faced, ultra flexible 2mm-thick MDF sheet as a surface. This last is available for modest cost from the better timber merchants in 8ft x 4ft sheets; it cuts readily with a Stanley knife and you can curve it smoothly down to radii of six inches or less. I attach it with copper-finish (non-rusting) lost-head panel pins, with Resin-W glued splice plates at any joins. Joint-lines and

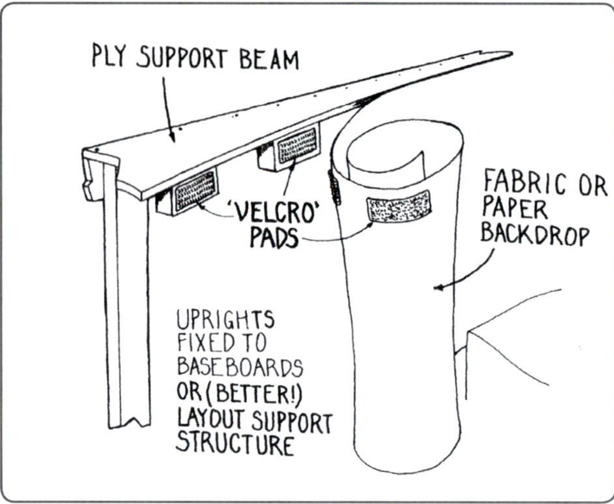

ABOVE: *Rollable backdrops.*

pin-holes are carefully filled with fine-surface filler (with a drop of Uni-Bond added for improved adhesion) and sanded smooth. The whole surface is primed with brilliant white emulsion applied with a roller to avoid brush marks. In the case of the cameo, the materials and techniques used are much the same, with the addition of a stiff and well-braced ply backing sheet that forms an integral part of the baseboard structure.

BELOW: *Highly effective rollable (paper, in this instance) backdrop on Rodney Hall's 'Llanastr'. Admittedly, this is something that is relatively easy to achieve in the context of a very small layout, but the same principle (on roller blind fabric) is used for 'Pempoul', 26-odd feet long.* Author

This leaves the sectional/portable layout as the 'problem child'. How much of a problem backscene provision for such a layout is can be seen at any exhibition, where even today the majority of layouts will lack this vital appendage. There are two basic alternatives: use a sectional backdrop – either free-standing/add-on or integrated with the baseboards – and accept (or try to disguise) the resulting 'cracks in the sky' every few feet; or use a free-standing or detachable backscene based on either reinforced paper or fabric, that can be removed and rolled up for transport. Roller-blind fabric – a fine cotton-weave material treated with a stiffener/filler – has proved ideal for this, as demonstrated by Vincent de Bode on 'Flintfields' and now adopted by Gordon Gravett and other leading scenic modellers. The only real difficulty is in sourcing such material 'off the roll' in sufficient lengths and cut to an appropriate width. It can be obtained in either off-white 'raw' form or dyed in basic sky-blue or neutral grey shades, and can be readily painted with acrylic or emulsion paints, applied sparingly. The infrastructure required to support such a fabric backdrop (which can, of course, be easily curved for concave forms and coved corners) amounts to little more than a suitably aligned top 'hanging rail' – either free-standing or supported off the baseboards – to which the fabric is simply clipped, pinned or Velcro'd. The diagram gives a typical arrangement.

Operating position

While normal home layouts are obviously designed to be operated and viewed from much the same frontal position, this is often not the case with exhibition layouts. Tradition has it that such things should be run from the rear, with the layout sited twixt operator and audience with the control panels and so on positioned accordingly. This is certainly one factor that has led to the perpetuation of the 'train set' style of table-top presentation with an ineffective six-inch strip of backscene –

ABOVE: *The traditional operating set-up for exhibition layouts, with the model mounted very low and operated from behind – practical, but not a great aid to realistic presentation.* Adrian Colenutt

ABOVE: *The modern alternative: realistic presentation with a higher-mounted model, a full backdrop and front operation; Simon Challis's P4 'Cheddar, S&D'.* Adrian Colenutt

usually with the operator's midriff towering above the top of the sky; not, I'd suggest, much of an aid to realism!

The combination of eye-level display and full-height backdrops advocated in these pages obviously tends to rule out this traditional approach – so what are the alternatives? Well, some advocates of realistic display have chosen to keep rear operation, but to elevate the operators by siting them on some sort of platform so that they can look down on the layout, God-like, from above the top of the backscene – where, of course, they are hidden from the gaze of the audience by the top fascia cutting off the sight-lines. This 'men on a box' approach can work well enough – 'Flintfields' is operated thus – but has several drawbacks. For a start, it's very much 'hands off' as it does not permit ready access to the model from the operating position in time of need – which calls for a very high degree of reliability from the trains and, especially, from the auto-couplings essential to such a modus operandi. Also the necessary infrastructure can be bulky and hard to transport – although, with typical de Bode ingenuity, 'Flintfield's' ply operating 'box' is used to transport the layout's jigsaw scenery modules, so is dual-purpose.

But if you rule out the *rear* of the layout as the operating position, then that leaves the front and sides of the modelled scene as possible alternatives. Far from being a 'second best' option, I'd argue that up-front operation has many advantages over skulking behind the scenes. Quite apart from anything else, if I'm going to be operating my model railway for hours on end, why shouldn't I also enjoy a decent view of the action? As the whole point of a well-presented exhibition layout is to give the audience the best possible view of the modelling when standing in front of it, it would seem to follow that that is also the best place from which to oversee its animation. My experience is that, far from being an impediment to viewing for the audience, having the operator on their side of the layout has a number of benefits. For a start, a lot of people are interested in how the railway is actually *being* controlled, especially if this is being done in an authentic manner using realistic hardware; with the operator and his equipment visible, they can *see* what's going on. It is also relatively easy (although demanding of concentration) to answer questions and talk to the audience without needing to bellow across the backscene, while being 'up front' enables you to exercise a greater degree of supervision over those among the throng with an urge to 'finger-poke'. So for 20 years now I've been exhibiting layouts operated from in front, standing to one side of the modelled scene except when needing access elsewhere.

Although quite readily accepted these days, such a break with tradition was seen as somewhat radical when initially advanced back in the 1980s. Certainly, when I first exhibited my 'Woolverstone' layout in 1989 with the track some 60in from the floor, a full-height backdrop and front operation using hand-held controllers and 'dispersed' control, it came in for a lot of flak. Subsequently, a change in attitudes and a number of technical developments in control hardware have helped gain acceptance for front operation, and some innovative layout-builders, like Tim Venton with 'Clutton' and Gordon Gravett with 'Pempoul', have integrated the layout's controls and operating position very much as part of the overall display. However the detail is arranged, deciding upon front or rear operation is obviously a fundamental aspect of display – and hence baseboard – design. It will also have a fundamental impact on the disposition of the control system and associated wiring.

The vital spark

Wiring is another necessary evil that, while never a bundle of fun, can often become a bundle of trouble if not taken properly into account at both the design and constructional phases. The one thing it should *never* be is an afterthought – which is precisely what it usually is! Layout wiring is another aspect of 'traditional' railway modelling practice which, like the two-by-one-and-softboard baseboard, has seemed to go unaltered and unquestioned for decades. You built your solid-topped baseboard, then strung the necessary wiring as

LEFT: *Traditional below-baseboard wiring is all well and good if, as here, you can turn the layout on its back to work on it. No problem with a small affair like 'Hepton Wharf', here being rewired in 2007 after 14 years service, but often not possible with larger or more permanent layouts; also not really practicable for emergency repairs in mid-show!* Author

a mass of Technicolor spaghetti beneath it – right where you couldn't see it, thereby engendering loads of angst as you tried to figure out what was connected to what whilst working on track, signalling and so on from above that same baseboard. And, of course, the relevant wiring was just where you couldn't get at it without either turning the layout over or crouching on your back 'below stairs', trying to manipulate a hot iron and molten solder directly above your own head. Whatever happened to self-preservation?

BELOW: *Surface-run wiring being installed at Yeovil Pen Mill on Andrew Duncan's 'Weymouth Lines' layout; everything to the left of the track lies beneath the removable jigsaw scenery modules carrying the cuttingside and bridge abutments of the A30 overbridge, while the wiring at bottom centre lies beneath the island platform, which is also readily removable.* Author

I built several layouts with just such inaccessible wiring before I got around to asking myself "Why am I doing this? Where lyeth the tablet of stone?" I suppose it follows on from the domestic tradition that buries domestic wires and water pipes beneath the plaster and wallpaper of the best parlour, but I never understood the sense of that either! I soon found that positioning my wires where I could both see where they went as well as get at them with ease paid huge dividends in both layout construction and maintenance. Nowadays, I run virtually all my layout circuitry in accessible 'wireways', surface-mounted runs of grouped circuits – usually sited along the rear of the layout, either along the top rear edge of the baseboard or on an outside vertical face of the rear baseboard framing. Where this 'rear mount' isn't practicable – as on a shelf layout hung from a wall – I run the wireway along a front framing member or on purpose-provided 'wiring batten' mounted beneath and behind the line of the fascia. From these main wireways, individual wires or wiring bundles lead off to feed the track sections or devices like point motors, uncoupler magnets and signals either via surface-run wires hidden by removable scenery modules jigsaw style, or through conduits buried in permanent scenery. The conduits are simply plastic tubing through which the wires can easily be fed. I use either flexible neoprene tube (automotive fuel line, obtainable for a few pence a metre from motor factors) or, more prosaically still, plastic drinking straws.

Of course, the positioning of wiring conduits or surface-run circuitry needs to be allowed for in the layout design – a part of the planning process in which a generous hand is never misplaced. Nowadays, in a search for reliability, I aim for a high degree of redundancy (duplication of electrical pathways) in my circuitry, and in routeing my wiring I'm always careful to allow space for a few extra cables if need be; sticking a few extra drinking-straw conduits in while building the scenery takes negligible effort at the time but can pay rich dividends when you want to add an extra uncoupler magnet or track section. It might be argued that

burying wires beneath scenery is asking for trouble – but it's my experience that very little ever goes wrong with a simple piece of wire, especially one well-protected in a conduit or surface wireway; the trouble almost always occurs where that wire is connected to something else. In my scheme of things, these joints are always get-atable, either in the drainage cess of the track or in the main wireway behind the backscene. If you do need to replace a length of wire for whatever reason, feeding a new bit of flex through a conduit or stringing it along the baseboard surface is simplicity itself.

Behind-the-scenes electrics are especially valuable on exhibition layouts, where most problems can then be discreetly dealt with while standing concealed behind the backdrop, whistling nonchalantly. In fact, I often take this 'backstage' approach a stage further by also installing point motors and other electro-mechanical devices behind the backdrop along with the wires, whence they are connected to the turnout or whatever via simple mechanical linkages. Mounted thus, reluctant point motors can be prodded or lubricated back into life when necessary or – should they have perished in the line of duty – be manually operated or even replaced.

Infrastructure planning

Having just expended quite a slab of text and not a few illustrations dissecting in some detail topics that might be regarded as somewhat peripheral to the business of layout design, I'm hoping that I've demonstrated that the opposite is in fact the case. In my philosophy, proper consideration of the underlying infrastructure is a vital and central part of the layout design process. There are new materials and resources coming along all the time, and every new layout project offers the opportunity to re-examine the possibilities and devise better methods of doing what we've always done – as well as perhaps suggesting a few things that maybe nobody's tried before. The foundations of any edifice always merit a little pencil-chewing time.

ABOVE, LEFT AND RIGHT: *Concealed control... The two Seep solenoid motors controlling the double junction at the south end of Pen Mill, together with a pair of stacked micro switches taking care of crossing polarity for the junction diamond, and the busbars and isolating switch for the Yeovil South End DCC power district, all live beneath the cattle dock and adjoining bank – again made to be easily removable.* Author

BELOW: *Here's my current thinking on exhibition layout power supplies – a separate, discrete 'power box' supplying all the necessary voltages via a multi-way cable and plugs – SCART type in this instance. This universal box, built to service 'Hepton Wharf' and its successor layouts, provides several independent 16V ac circuits for traction, 24V ac for solenoid-powered accessories, 12V dc for motor-drive point actuators and lighting, and a 20V ac DCC Power Bus, plus mains sockets for soldering irons and lighting – all protected by independent fuses.*

4 THINGS YOU CAN'T IGNORE

Many of the aspects of layout design discussed in these pages are concerned with matters of *choice*. This chapter looks at the other side of that coin, the areas where there *is* no choice: the things you *have* to take into account to build a workable layout – whether you like it or not! For, like their full-sized counterparts, model railways embrace a complex and finely balanced set of requirements and associated engineering solutions that are fundamental to their functioning: curve radii, clearances, gradients, loadings and tolerances have an impact on any railway, whatever the size. To this 'universal' list we can add a few extra requirements specific to small-scale electrically powered models: workable track and wheel standards, accurate alignments, electrical propriety, and scale conformity. Ignore any of these strictures, and the thing simply won't work properly.

ABOVE: *The scale trade-off. At one end of the 'miniature' spectrum, 7mm/1ft 0 offers heft, robustness, excellent running, ease of handling and the potential for very high levels of detail. What it doesn't offer is much scope in a small space, although compact urban/industrial/ dockside shunting layouts – like Rob Cottrell's 'Ellis Road' – have become a popular option.* Adrian Colenutt

Scale choice: practical implications

There is an obvious trade-off between the size and proportions of the layout footprint available and the scale you choose to work in. However, it is not necessarily a case of straight linearity – bigger footprint = larger scale – as the small matter of subject comes into the issue. A modest footprint that is cramped in area or wrongly proportioned for a conventional station-based layout in 4mm scale might well work wonderfully for, say, a dockside/industrial prototype in 0 – but only if there's sufficient height available to accommodate the greater bulk of models in the larger scale. If headroom is really tight, then a smaller scale is almost always a prerequisite for a realistic model whatever the site, unless you box really clever and pick a subject that would, in reality, be vertically confined. I know of one minimum-space, minimum-height (8in!) 0 scale layout that represents the *interior* of a 'roundhouse' locomotive shed – entirely convincingly, as the 'top of the scene' (the underside of the shed roof) can be contained at scale height within the limited space available. A good solution for, in this case, a dedicated loco builder/ collector with little interest in scenic modelling or even running trains – by no means an uncommon breed in 7mm scale!

Some parameters, of course, remain the same whatever the scale – chief among which are gradients (a universal constant) and turnout crossing angles, which have similar implications for track curvatures, divergences and clearing points at any size. Electrical, baseboard structural and mechanical integrity requirements are also universal. Some common differences in practice between the various modelling sizes are more a matter of tradition than hard practical diktat; manual point-operating systems, for instance, are rarely used in N – for no particular mechanical reason that I can discern, other than the almost-universal

BELOW: *At the opposite extreme of the size range – 2mm/N – a similarly modest site offers very considerable scope and facilitates the modelling of surprisingly expansive subjects, like the broad slice of South London so tellingly captured by Graeme Hedges' 'Stoney Lane Depot'.* Adrian Colenutt

employment of Peco turnouts and hence the presumption that clip-on Peco point motors are the way to go. In all scales, there's a large practical implication in the choice made over the sourcing of track, in that opting to use mass-produced pointwork limits your options to the types and geometries available. This in turn may throw up some quite intractable layout-planning problems – the layout with an awkward kink in the track due to the use of a turnout with not-quite-right geometry is a hoary old modelling chestnut. It is 0 scale which has the most limited selection of ready-to-use track, while adoption of fine standards in any scale presumes hand-laid pointwork – definitely something to be factored into the scale choice decision.

Curves

These are the real layout-designing crunch point in almost any scale larger than 2mm and on virtually any footprint; only on straight-line layouts or those with a fortunate combination of site, scale and subject will they fail to figure as a cause for concern. On almost any oval/continuous run design calling for return curves or right-angled bends on L or U-shaped linear footprints, curve radii are a headache-inducing limiting factor. As the modelling scale gets larger and the fidelity to scale gets closer, the problem of accommodating workable curves becomes ever more intractable – and that's before worrying about what they're going to *look* like! Most modellers are aware that running line curves on virtually all model railways are somewhat tighter than they are on the prototype – but it's only when you sit down and start doing the sums you realise just *how* far off the scale mark we are!

The root of the problem is, of course, 'the prototype' – principally in the shape of locomotives (rolling stock generally being much less of a problem). I reproduce below the official weight diagram of the BR Standard Class 3 2-6-0 – by no means a large locomotive, and one of very modest coupled wheelbase (a couple of inches shorter than a GW '57XX' pannier tank and over a foot less than a 'Jinty'). But, you will note the proviso as to the minimum permitted curve radii appended at the foot of the drawing: 6 chains, or 4½ chains 'dead slow' (figures common to all the BR standard types). Yes, the figures given are 'without gauge widening', the provision of which might shave off another quarter-chain or so. Flexible wheelbases notwithstanding, diesels do only slightly better – as you'll see from the other diagram reproduced, that for the Class 55 'Deltic'; the minimum 'dead slow' radius is given as 4 chains, or 3.8 with maximum gauge widening. So for practical purposes, 4 chains minimum for a main-line loco is about it – which dimension tellingly scales out at a shade over 20in radius in 2mm scale, 31in at 3mm, 41in in 4mm and no less than 73in in 0. Dedicated dock shunters and industrial engines with ultra-short wheelbases, extra sideplay and special flange profiles might in reality squeak around curves as tight as 1½ chains – giving absolute minimal 'quayside curve' values for the scales as 8in, 12in, 16in and 27in respectively.

Comparing these figures with the sort of curve radii prevalent on most model railways is depressingly revealing. Taking the 4-chain 'limit' figures for the main-line engine as a benchmark, I think it is true to say that ruling curves on running lines of 20in in N, 3ft 6in in 4mm and 6ft in 0 would be regarded by many modellers as being pretty reasonable if not actually generous! But in the real world, the minimum curve on a main running line rarely got anywhere near this limit, rarely straying below 10 chains or so (and that with a severe speed restriction). Only on minor branch or mineral lines or within station limits and on yard tracks – all situations where speeds are normally low – would tighter curves be tolerated. Even then they were problematic; it's worth noting that the infamous 'severe curve' that triggered the 1906 Salisbury smash was of 8 chains radius, limited (many said insufficiently) to a relatively brisk 30mph – although the boat train involved in the

BELOW: *BR Standard Class 3 2-6-0: Weight diagram.*

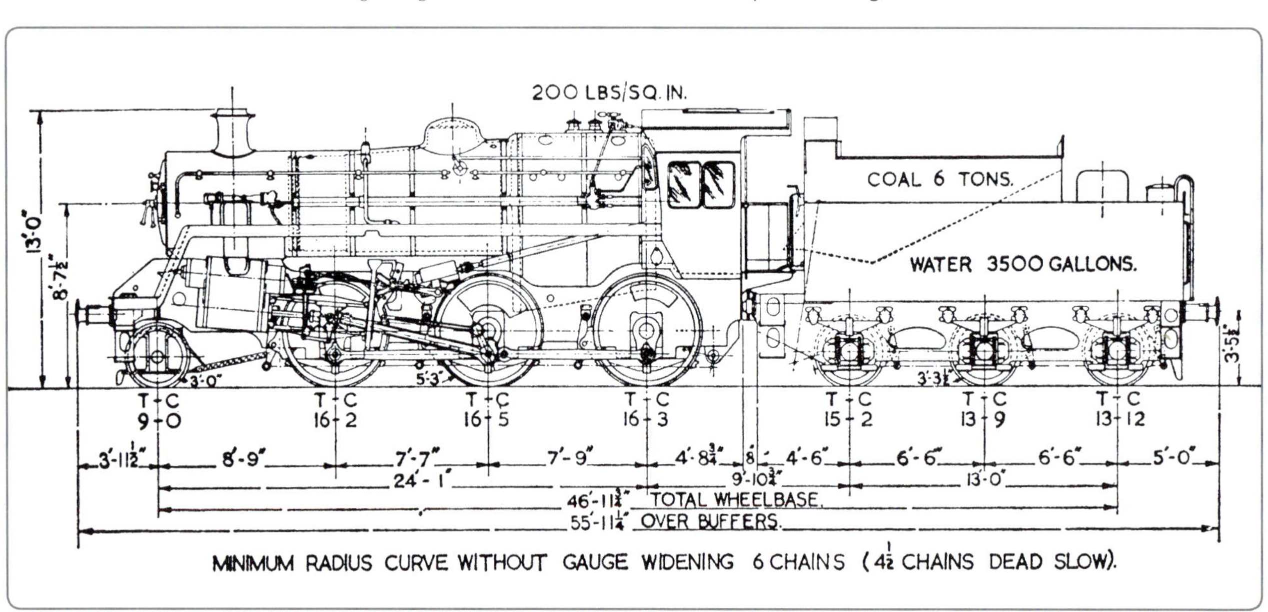

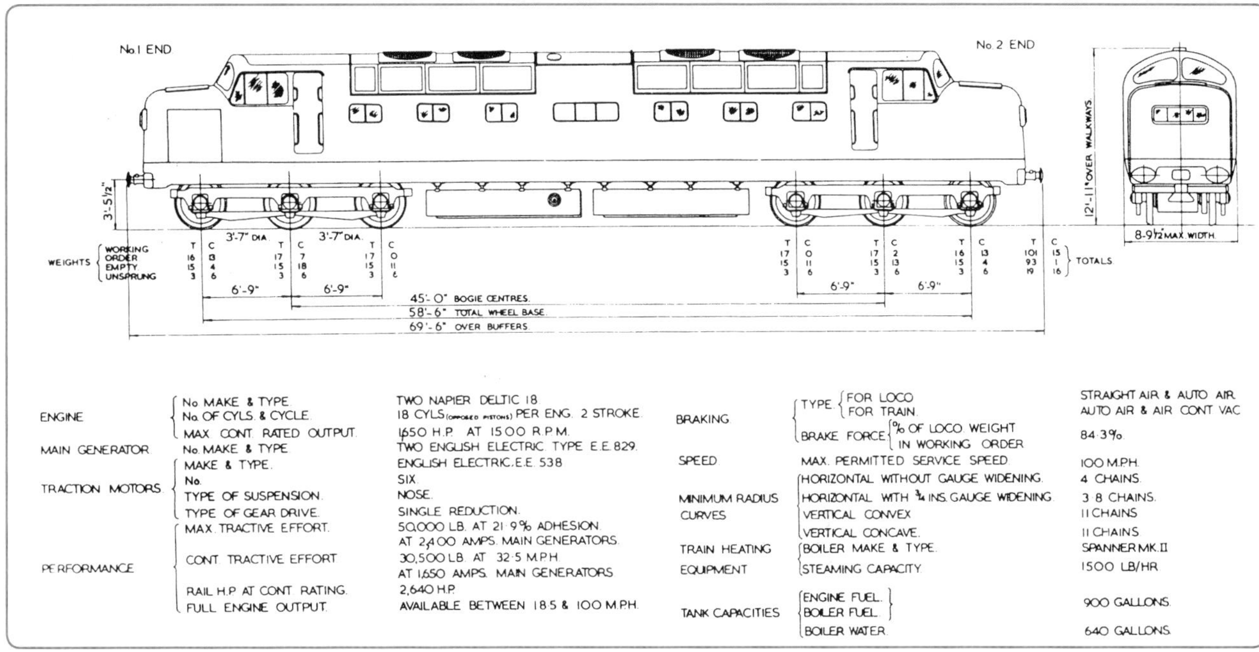

ABOVE: *BR Class. 55 'Deltic': Weight diagram.*

disaster was evidently travelling a great deal faster than that! And yes, 8 chains *does* scale out at 3ft 4in radius in N, 7ft at 4mm/1ft and a whopping 4 yards in 0!

And that's the 'limiting' situation; in *Railway Construction*, by W. Hemingway-Mills – a prototype railway civil engineering textbook published in 1898 – a desirable value for the mean radius of 'speed unrestricted' curves on main lines in open country is given as 80 chains, or 1 mile, although use of suitable super elevation could reduce this figure somewhat! Some degree of speed restriction was deemed advisable on curves of less than 40 chains radius, and anything under 20

BELOW: *The running-line limit in reality: Bulleid SR 'Battle of Britain' light Pacific No. 21C162 17 Squadron squeals its way around the 8-chain curve from Borough Market towards London Bridge; the 7-chains of the innermost curve of Borough Market Junction (from the Waterloo direction towards Cannon Street) was on the absolute minimum; yet even this scales out at 6ft radius in 4mm scale!* Author's collection

BELOW: *A typical 'main line' 0-6-0 would sneak around curves down to about 4 chains radius; anything tighter called for special locomotive types with ultra-short wheelbases, generous sideplay and special flange profiles. Here is one such, an ex-G&SWR Drummond 'Dock tank' of the 322 class, seen in colliery service after sale by the LMS in 1934. Note the long top link on the three-link coupling, to ease coupling-up on ultra-tight curves.* Author's collection

ABOVE: *A tight situation in reality – the serpentine reverse curve on the old South Eastern approach to Dover, here being negotiated by the 'Pullman Club' boat train behind a Wainwright D class 4-4-0. These curves are about 15 chains radius, with check rails and doubtless speed-restricted; a trifling 13ft or so at 4mm scale.* Author's collection

chains was regarded as 'tight', warranting speed restriction and sometimes check rails. One suspects these were 'ideal' values for new construction, proposed with the benefit of hindsight; certainly, many railways built before 1890 used far tighter curves, being laid out in an era when anything over 40mph was 'going some'. By the turn of the 19th century, many of these sharply curved alignments were proving a severe impediment to the general speeding-up of express trains then taking place. An 'easy' road like Brunel's GW London–Bristol main line, which used continuous flowing curves of very wide radius, was far more amenable to sustained high speed than the Stephenson/Locke model of long straights connected by severe kinks, as on the LSWR main line. That Brunel's route needed virtually no modification for 125mph line speeds on the advent of the HSTs says it all, really!

LEFT: *The model limit: in N scale, ultra-tight curves – such as the 9¾/11in radius 'end return curves' on the Launceston MRC's 16ft x 2ft 'Lydtor' layout – are quite practicable and even visually not entirely unbelievable (although longer stock looks much less happy). In reality, such a curve at 2mm scale equates to a flange-squealing dockside 2-chain radius at full size.* Author

Model curves

Mechanically speaking, we modellers don't have to worry about many of the problems that the prototype has to contend with in running around curves; with their lack of mass, low centres of gravity and negligible inertia; our model trains can take sharp curves at speeds that would spell disaster for the full-sized equivalent. When we get into the pragmatic realms of the 'compromise' wheel and track standards used for N or 00, with their whopping running clearances and generous sideplay allowances, we can get away with absolute murder on the curvature front! On the prototype, running clearance (the gap between the outside faces of the wheel flanges and the inside faces of the running rails) is around an inch and typical sideplay allowance not much more – values that reduce to a few tenths of a millimetre when scaled down, even at 7mm/1ft. By contrast, 00 running clearance is typically 1mm (the precise figure depends on the flange profile, which is not standardised), while sideplay on individual axles can be anything up to 2mm, unhampered by cylinders, slidebars and valve gear usually set at correct scale centres outside wheels, that are gauged 12½ per cent too close together. Small wonder, then, that the 4mm RTR makers can persuade even their largest 00 locomotives to squeak around 18in radius curves – well into dock-tank territory in reality.

It's an inescapable fact that the 'finer' the wheel and track standards to which a model is built, the smaller these clearances and allowances become and the wider the minimum radius that will be needed to make things work (never mind look right!). This has a significant impact in the choice of standards; in 4mm scale, while a 00 model – even one using relatively fine-scale wheels – can usually be persuaded around sub-24in radius curves, the same prototype built strictly to P4 standards (with a running clearance of 0.28mm, only very slightly greater than the true scale value) would probably struggle at twice that radius – although there are a few clever 'tweaks' that can be used to ease the problems slightly. EM, which has a running clearance of around 0.7mm – even if limited scope for sideplay – generally 'splits the difference' and manages curves around 1.5 x the 00 minima. Both EM and P4 standards call for gauge widening of up to 0.2mm on

LEFT: *The fine scale crunch. The main line on Simon de Souza's P4 'Corrieshalloch' curves through the station at around 70in radius, representing just about the acceptable fine-scale minimum for many larger types of engine – although locos and stock of modest pre-Grouping size will scrape around 42in or so, a dimension which most 00 modellers would regard as pretty generous.* Author

sharper curves to ease flange binding problems; 00 does quite happily without.

It is this ability to negotiate drastically underscale curves without problem that made 00 a practicable standard for trainset use when Hornby-Dublo and Trix set out to produce small-scale model trains before the Second World War – an ability subsequently engineered into commercial N scale models, which have even more generous (in proportion to size) running clearances. Acute curve negotiation is the key capability that has helped keep 00 and N as the mainstream commercial standards, as they permit the creation of continuous-run layouts on restricted footprints. It is worth pointing out that the 'wide' second and third standard radius curves offered by Hornby in 00 today are still only 17¼in and 20in.

'Railway' curves

Thus far, I've been discussing track curvature in terms of plain circular curves of fixed radius. That's the sort you get with train-set sectional track and over the years has become the traditional way of thinking about all curved model railway track. Reality, however, is somewhat less straightforward, in that prototype track rarely describes such simple fixed-radius arcs. Rather, it changes direction over a complex alignment in which the curve is entered on a very wide radius which progressively tightens down to the limiting value (a 'parabolic' or spiral curve), over a distance that will vary with topography and line speed. The actual limiting radius – which is still the nominal figure quoted for the curve – may only hold over a relatively short distance before the process is reversed and the bend eases back out to the straight (if there is any!) once more. A curve of this type is known as a 'railway curve' and is normally precisely described mathematically.

These 'spiral easements' or 'transitions' are designed to avoid abrupt changes of direction and to smooth the passage of a train into and through a curve. They are almost universal on passenger-carrying lines, and freight-

BELOW: *This beautiful shot of a train on the ex-NBR West Highland line of the LNER shows a train rounding a transitioned curve – one with a tight ruling radius, if the check-rails are anything to go by! The diminishing radius of the curve from the rear of the train to the locomotives is clearly evident.* Author's collection

only or mineral branches or locations where speeds are very low can do without them. Visually, they are also the feature that gives so much British track it's characteristically sinuous quality, with curves flowing gracefully from the straight or blending smoothly one into another. All of which means that transitioned curves are obviously a feature we need to reproduce on our models in the quest for realistic appearance – quite apart from the fact that they benefit the smooth running of our model trains every bit as much as they do the prototype. If you're so inclined, you can find the mathematical formula by which such curves are calculated and laid out by prototype PW engineers – the various fine scale societies generally include this information in their 'manuals'. If, however, like me, you don't find differential calculus too entertaining, you can arrive at a perfectly workable and visually convincing result using nothing more than the Mk 1 eyeball, aided by the fact that if you anchor one end of a length of flexible track and bend it from the other, it naturally takes up a nicely parabolic curve.

Incorporating easements does, however, have implications for the amount of space needed to accommodate a curve of a given limiting radius on a model. Whereas a circular curve of, say, three feet radius (scale/gauge immaterial) can allow a 180° 'return curve' for an oval or U-shaped layout in a footprint 6ft 6in or so wide, add easements and that figure will spread to 7ft 6in or more. Where the three feet represent a limiting radius determined by the locos and stock you're intending to run, then it simply may not be possible to add easements. However, if the stock does permit the use of a lesser curves, then it may be better – both visually and practically – to accept a *tighter* limiting radius, but one approached by transitions. Personally, I would always opt for transitions; indeed, in designing my own 4mm scale loft layout I made just this choice, preferring a 3ft 9in ruling radius with transitions over the 4ft 6in circular curves that would otherwise have been possible in the same space.

Practical values for realistic curves

So where does all this leave us in our quest for curves on our models that are not only functional but visibly acceptable? The first thing to say is that, thankfully, we don't need to try to stick to anything like the ruling values quoted by Mr Hemingway-Mills; indeed, if we did, the result wouldn't looked 'curved' at all, as a 70ft-radius '80 chain' curve in 4mm scale would be, visually speaking, indistinguishable from a dead straight line. Even if we move into the realms of his 'tight' 20-chain curve – 17ft 6in at 4mm scale – we still wouldn't get much impression of curvature, and the result certainly wouldn't look 'tight'. As is so often the case, merely doing the sums and reducing everything by a precise scale ratio does not result in a model that equates to our perception when viewing the real thing.

This is largely due to the difference in the physical distances from which we gaze on a model as opposed to our normal standpoint when viewing a full-sized scene. In looking at a typical small-scale model from a yard away, what we are trying to replicate is the look of the real thing seen at a considerable distance. The precise implications of

ABOVE: *The curve from Exeter St. David's up to Exeter Central looks pretty much like a hairpin bend when photographed from the end of Platform 5 – about 80 yards away. OK, this is a fairly tight curve by prototype standards – about 12 chains. But that's 10ft 4in at 4mm scale – and a 10ft 4in radius model railway curve viewed from a yard away wouldn't look like this!* Author

this visual relationship and the mechanisms at work in what we perceive are examined in some depth in Chapter 8, but in the context of selecting suitable curve radii what matters is the effect of this distance and the related foreshortening in making real curves *appear* far tighter than they actually are. This effect is even more pronounced when using multi-lens viewing aids such as binoculars or telescopes, or looking through the viewfinder of a camera with zoom or telephoto optics. A 'long' telephoto lens can compress curves to an almost comical degree, giving trains running over them a distinct 'Disney cartoon' look.

Well, we may not want to emulate Disney but we *do* want our curves to look suitably curved. So the value we actually need to work around is a curve of a radius that, viewed from our yard or so away, *appears* to match that of the prototype seen at many times that distance – the exact equivalence depending on the scale of the model. A little experiment will soon suggest that to obtain the right degree of visual 'tightening' on our model actually calls for curves of mean radii very considerably *below* strict scale values, which is very good news indeed! As with so many aspects of realism in modelling, the critical eye is the best guide to determining what is appropriate. I've found that even on the largest of layouts, the most convincing effect is often created by curves that may well be some way below the maximum that is physically possible on the site or footprint, although the incorporation of transitions is invariably vital to getting the correct 'look'. But, to be specific, I've rarely found any need to go beyond a scale 'ten chain' benchmark for a believably generous-looking curve on main running lines on model railways. That's 15ft 2in in 0 scale, 8ft 8in in 4mm and around 4ft 4in in 2mm – figures which are a great deal more attainable than the 'prototype' values.

So much for the 'top' end; but what of the bottom?

Well, while it's actually quite hard to gauge the 'sharpness' of curved trackage viewed unadorned, as soon as a locomotive or a rake of carriages enters the equation it becomes painfully apparent when the radius strays too far on the tight side. End throw, bogie displacement, coupling gaps and centre overhangs all give the game away, especially with larger locomotives and longer coaching stock. Persuading model trains to physically squeak around sub-minimal curves is one thing, but making them *look* believable while doing so is quite another! There is a definite 'lower limit' to visually realistic track curvature, a minimum radius below which the trains start to look faintly ridiculous even if still functioning adequately. Easements can help in avoiding the giveaway 'sudden jink' by which a model train tends to run onto a tight curve, but there is still a point beyond which the whole process just looks plain silly.

However, the ability to negotiate such unseemly bends is still valuable as often, use of small-radius curves on hidden portions of the layout will permit wider, more realistic radii in the visible areas. My friend Andrew Duncan's 'Maiden Newtown' layout is a good example of this approach. Sited in a narrow basement a scant 6ft wide, advantage was taken of the ability of trains built using 00 'fine' standards to run reliably around curves of only 2ft 6in radius to squeeze in the 180° return curves needed for a continuous run. These eye-watering semi-circular bends are, however, strictly 'off scene'; the sweeping visible curves through Maiden Newton station itself are a far more relaxed: a 7ft 6in ruling radius with long transitions means that they really 'look the business' with a GW 4-6-0 and a rake of 'Toplights' snaking smoothly through them.

The minimum 'visibly acceptable curve radius' for a given scale is not a figure that can be set in stone, as it depends to a considerable extent on the subject being modelled and the nature of the trains being run. On the sort of freight-only mineral branch represented by my P4 'Trerice' model, inspired by the Wenford Bridge line, I found that prototype curves in the order of 5 chains radius (52in at 4mm scale) could come down to a scale 3 chains (about 30in) on the model and still look credible; that's the ruling radius on the 'loop' road, around which my P4 '57XX' pannier tank or '45XX' 'Small Prairie' will grind, 'dead slow', while looking perfectly at home. More into the mainstream, many rural branch lines had curves well below 10 chains radius, especially in hilly country and where only small locomotives were used. There are a couple of choice examples here in my West Devon neck of the woods, where the GWR Launceston branch leaving Lydford Junction turned through more than 90 degrees on a 7-chain radius curve dating from broad gauge days, while the Princetown branch abounded in curves down to a mere 6 chains. To get the right flange-grinding look in 4mm scale would probably call for radii of around 30–33in – perfectly workable even in P4 with the appropriate locomotives – in both these instances, the versatile (and flexible!) GWR 'Small Prairie'.

Rather than go through every possible prototype permutation of train type and track curvature in prose, it seemed more useful to put together a table encompassing a range of typical situations: lines of differing stature, the locomotive types typically used thereon, some associated prototype curve values and ballpark 'visibly acceptable'

BELOW: *Pragmatic curve parameters.*

		TYPICAL MAX. M.P.H.	PROTOTYPE CURVES (Ch.)		MODEL EQUIVALENTS (IF CORRECT TO SCALE)				PRAGMATIC MODEL CURVES						
LINE TYPE	LOCOS		TYPICAL/	MIN.	2MM	3MM	4MM	7MM	2MM/N	2MM/FS	3MM†	4MM/00	4MM/FS	7MM/FS	
MAIN LINE	4-6-2/4-6-0/	<80	40		17'6"	26'0"	35'0"	61'0"	3'3"	4'6"	5'4"	6'6"	7'6"	14'0"	T
(UNRESTRICTED)	2-8-0/2-10-0			25	11'0"	16'2"	22'0"	38'0"	2'6"	3'3"	4'3"	4'9"	5'6"	10'6"	M
* MAIN LINE	AS	<35	20		8'9"	13'0"	17'6"	30'6"	2'6"	3'3"	4'3"	4'9"	5'6"	10'6"	T
(RESTRICTED)	ABOVE			8	3'6"	5'2"	7'0"	12'2"	1'9"	2'0"	2'3"	2'9"	3'6"	6'6"	M
SECONDARY/	4-6-0/2-6-0	<60	30		13'0"	19'4"	26'0"	45'8"	3'0"	3'9"	4'6"	5'9"	6'6"	12'0"	T
CROSS-COUNTRY	4-4-0/0-6-0			15	6'6"	9'8"	13'0"	22'10"	2'3"	3'0"	3'9"	4'0"	4'9"	8'6"	M
SUBURBAN	2-6-2T/2-6-4T														
BRANCHLINE	0-6-0/0-6-0T	<45	15		6'6"	9'8"	13'0"	22'10"	2'3"	3'0"	3'9"	4'0"	4'9"	8'6"	T
(PASSENGER)	0-4-2T/2-6-2T			7	3'1"	4'6"	6'2"	10'8"	1'4"	1'9"	2'0"	2'6"	3'0"	6'6"	M
BRANCHLINE	0-6-0, 2-8-0,	<25	10		4'5"	6'6"	8'10"	15'3"	2'3"	3'0"	3'9"	4'0"	4'9"	8'6"	T
(FREIGHT ONLY)	0-4-0T			5	2'3"	3'3"	4'5"	7'7"	1'3"	1'6"	2'0"	2'6"	3'0"	6'0"	M
MINERAL/DOCK/	0-6-0T/	<20	8		3'6"	5'2"	7'0"	12'2"	1'6"	2'0"	2'3"	2'9"	3'6"	6'6"	T
INDUSTRIAL	0-4-0T			1½	8"	1'0"	1'4"	2'4"	6"	8"	1'0"	1'4"	1'4"	2'4"	M

* JUNCS, URBAN AREAS, STATIONS, MOUNTAIN SECTIONS, ETC

† FINESCALE 13·5 & 14·2MM

CHAINS	1	1½	5	7	8	10	15	20	25	30	40
2MM/FT	5¼"	8"	2'2¼"	3'1"	3'6"	4'4½"	6'6"	8'9"	11'0"	13'0"	17'6"
3MM/FT	7¾"	1'0"	3'3"	4'6"	5'2"	6'6"	9'8"	13'0"	16'2"	19'4"	26'0"
4MM/FT	10½"	1'3¾"	4'4"	6'1½"	7'0"	8'9"	13'0"	17'6"	22'0"	26'0"	35'0"
7MM/FT	18¼"	2'4"	7'7"	10'8"	12'2"	15'3"	22'9"	30'6"	38'4"	45'8"	61'0"

ROUNDED TO NEAREST ¼"

and 'minimum functional' curve radii for the popular scales and track/wheel standards. I hasten to add these are only pragmatic guidelines derived from a modicum of research, my own experience, and a lifetime of trial-and-error. As always, I'd advocate the full-size mock-up and due experiment as the only way to determine the best compromise (for that is what it is: Rice's First Law applies) for a particular situation. But, hopefully, the table will form a useful starting point.

Clearances

Immutably linked to track curvatures are track clearances, of which there are a number of significance. While the 'running clearance' – the slack between the outside faces of the wheel-flanges and the inside face of the rail-heads – may not have an obvious impact in layout planning, its effects do, in that they help determine the minimum practicable curve radii discussed *ad nauseam* above. Much more obviously relevant are the 'loading gauge clearances' – the amount of space that must be left above, beneath and to the sides of the strict cross-sectional envelope occupied by the trains. This envelope – the 'static loading gauge' – is strictly defined on the prototype and from 1923 to about 1970 was common to virtually the whole of our railway network, with the exception of a few 'restricted' routes. This uniformity wasn't always the case, however, and in the pre-Grouping period railways used varying loading gauges. Although the allowable width did not stray more than an inch or two beyond the nominal nine feet, the Scottish maximum height of 13ft 6in exceeded the Sassenach norm by a full eight inches, while the odd English line – such as the LBSCR and GNR – adopted even more expansive standards. After the 1923 Grouping, a composite loading gauge based on the Scottish model was adopted, and all non-conforming stock either altered to fit or restricted as to route availability. Since the later 1970s, modern practice has moved away from the old 'static' standards to complex dynamic envelopes which take account of the movement of the vehicle when running and factors like 25kV overhead electrification, compatibility with Europe and 'tilting' trains.

The loading gauge clearances that matter most to us in planning a model railway are the inter-track and structure clearance gauges, which determine the distances between trains on adjacent tracks as well as the minimum clearances between the train and fixed elements of the railway infrastructure such as signals, buildings, bridges and station platforms. These can be seen in the 'clearance diagram' hereabouts, which is based on Railway Clearing House drawings. It must be stressed that these are all *minimum* figures; normal practice was to ease these where possible or appropriate, although the 'six foot way' was maintained over the vast majority of ordinary double track, in the interests of a standard formation width. The vital inter-track clearances – the 'six-foot way' and 'ten-foot way' – need especially careful consideration, as they are affected by the accuracy (to prototype) of the track gauge as well as by the curvature of the track; the latter consideration can also affect the lineside structure clearance.

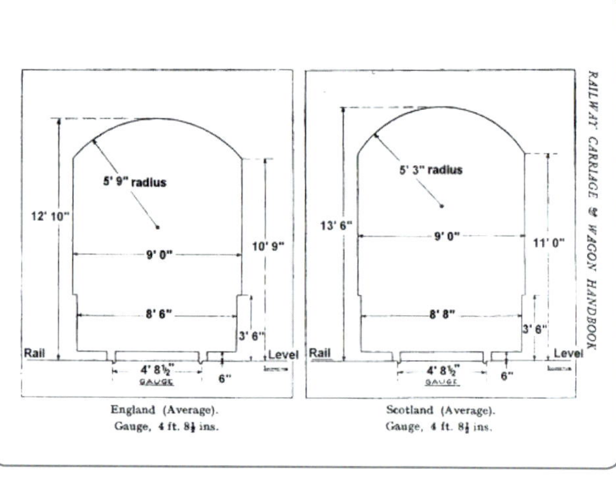

ABOVE: *Historic (pre-Grouping) loading gauges.*

On the British prototype, at least until recently, these minimum load gauge clearances have been far from generous; normally, a scant 24in between the coach sides of trains passing one another on straight double track, and a bare yard to trackside structures. Even today, with 100 mph.+ line speeds and associated greater degrees of super elevation, these values still hold for much of the UK rail network – which, among other compromises, accounts for the rather 'top tapered' profile of much modern rolling stock. The traditional spacing of double track – the six-foot way – is so called because at full size this was the actual and precise minimum distance between the *outside faces* of the running rails. The ten-foot dimension is that between the rail faces where a running line adjoins a loop or siding – the extra 4ft being there to allow clearance for personnel on the ground between the tracks.

BELOW: *RCH composite loading gauge.*

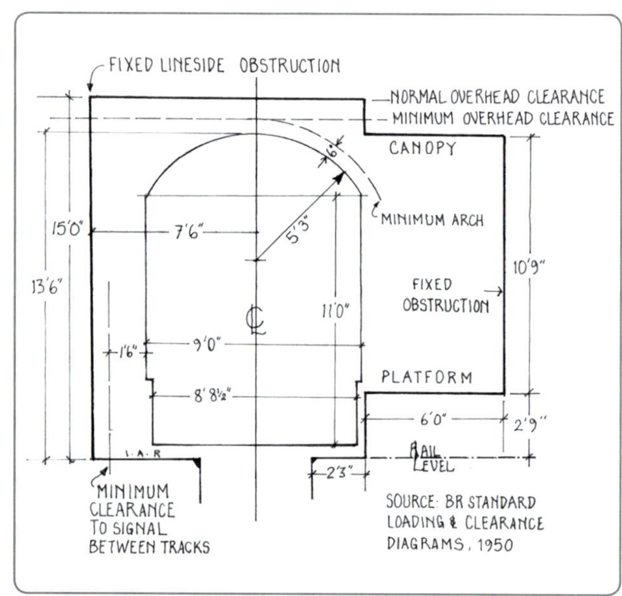

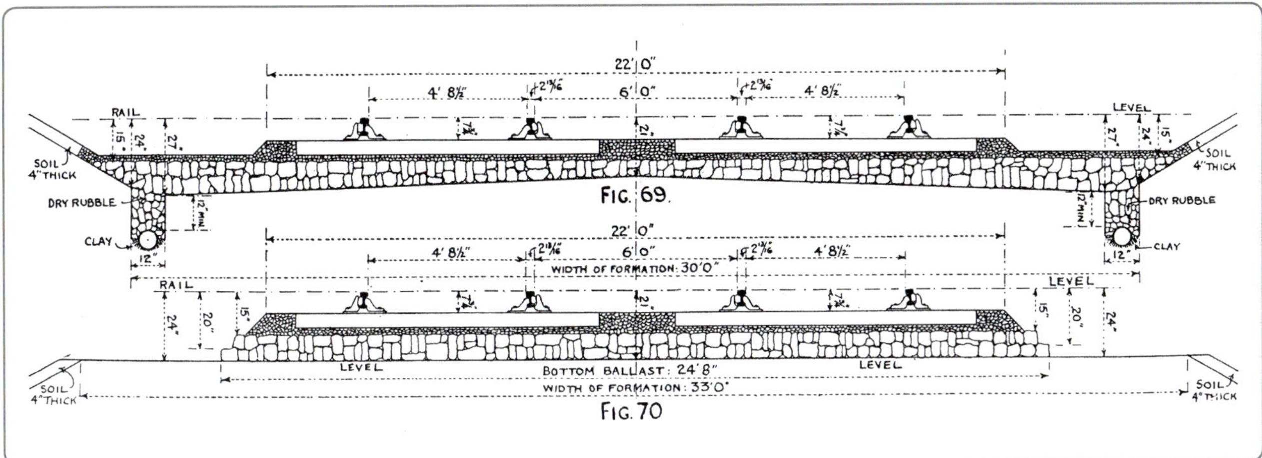

ABOVE: *Typical double-track formation.*

In miniature, it is the six-foot way and the lineside structure clearance that can cause most problems, especially on tighter-than-scale curves. For a start, the six foot way is only six *scale* feet when the track gauge is true to prototype; in 00 you need to make a small but significant adjustment. In this context, I find it is much safer to consider the centre-to-centre spacing of adjacent tracks – which, allowing for a rail head width of 2¾in, is actually 11ft 2in at full size. I err a tad on the plus side of this dimension and use 'scale' centre-to-centre values of 24mm for 2mm scale, 45mm in 4mm and 80mm in 0. But these 'scale' values only hold good for prototypical curves – which, as already suggested, did not usually stray below a radius of around 7 chains on running lines, especially double-track ones.

The equally important structure clearance gauge is measured from the track centreline on the prototype, the long-held minimum figure being 7ft 6ins. That applies to anything fixed – bridge piers, buildings, signals or other lineside furniture. What *isn't* defined on the RCH diagram is platform clearances; while the 'normal' platform *height* is given – 3ft above rail level – no value for coping clearance is quoted. In practice, this was always related to the track curvature, if any, and the characteristics of the rolling stock in use on a given line. Usually, the dimension from track centreline to the edge of the coping was in the range 4ft 9in–5ft 3in. This lack of a standardised platform clearance proved problematic on the prototype, especially when amalgamations, groupings and nationalisation brought locomotives and stock designed for one railway on to the lines of another. There are several well-documented instances of cylinder-casings and bufferbeam ends meeting platform copings, with expensive results!

All these clearances have implications for model railways and need taking into account when designing a layout, especially if things – as so often happens – are a tad on the tight side. Usually, the 'true scale' values are not much use to us as they only take account of the end-throw and mid-point overhang of locomotives and rolling stock when running on prototypical curves. Using the sort of grossly underscale radii we're usually faced with will call for suitably increased allowances if our trains are not to knock seven bells out of platforms, bridge piers and signal posts – not to mention sideswiping stock on adjacent running lines! We normally need to increase these clearances somewhat even when working to fine scale standards; no matter that the trains manage to miss one another or the scenery by the proverbial fag paper – if they're too close they'll still *look* wrong. Such inadequate clearances are usually far more apparent than a millimetre or two of extra breathing space.

Adding that extra millimetre or two to strict scale clearance values isn't anyway unprototypical, as the quoted figures are minima and are often 'eased' in reality. It's hard to pin down convenient 'allowance' numbers that can be usefully and universally applied, as there are a lot of factors involved. The best approach, I find, is a little trial-and error with a suitable mock-up of the proposed curves and the longest/most intractable items of rolling stock, as that provides a definitive answer for a given set of circumstances. And don't forget we're not only seeking to establish workable clearances, but clearances that *look* right. In this context, it's worth pointing out that where ready-made pointwork is being contemplated, assembling two turnouts 'back to back' as a running line crossover will give a pre-determined six-foot way that's hard to vary. The result, in all probability, will be rather more than anybody's six feet, and can often look a bit odd if universally applied. In N, Peco turnouts used thus give a track centre-to-centre distance of 1¼in (32mm) – equivalent to a whopping 16ft; in 00, the corresponding figures are a far more reasonable 2in (50.8mm), scaling out at 12ft 8in. The latter is in the 'reasonable' range of believable values for the 'six-foot' in 4mm, but the N scale figure looks way too wide; on our 'realistic' radii, you can take a scale yard and more out of it.

Fouling points

A 'fouling point' is the precise spot on two diverging tracks at which the minimum clearance between adjacent trains is obtained. It's usually quoted as a 'fouling distance' – a measurement from the toe or crossing nose of a turnout to

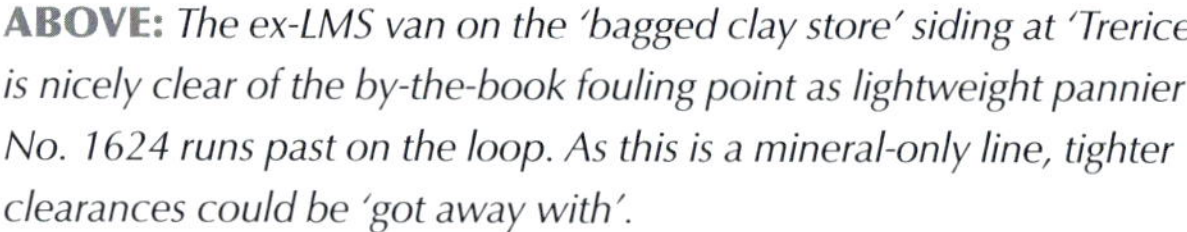

ABOVE: *The ex-LMS van on the 'bagged clay store' siding at 'Trerice' is nicely clear of the by-the-book fouling point as lightweight pannier No. 1624 runs past on the loop. As this is a mineral-only line, tighter clearances could be 'got away with'.*

In the second picture, J15 No. 65454 is on the loop at 'Cade's Green' – a general passenger-carrying running line. The cattle van on the dock siding at lower left is clear of the fouling point, which in this situation is protected by a single-bladed trap point. Author

the point at which an item of rolling stock can be 'parked' and be legally clear of the through or running line. The pictures should hopefully make this clear… It's the position of this fouling point that is of the most immediate relevance in a layout-planning context, in that there is a direct relationship between turnout angles and associated curve radii and fouling points – and that relationship is what decides the useful capacity of loops and sidings. This is a stricture that needs careful checking at both the planning and constructional phases, especially where the usual lack of space calls for such things to be set at a minimum value on a model. A siding which won't *quite* hold the required number of wagons 'in the clear', or a loop laid a tad too short to allow a loco to run round a favoured train formation, is a frustration that's all too easy to arrive at! Once again, mocking things up at actual size is often the best way to determine an appropriate choice of turnout angle and curve radius. While you can *physically* 'get away with' under-scale clearances, trains that come too close together will never *look* convincing. The only exception to this generality is diverging sidings within goods yards well clear of the running line, or turnouts on industrial or mineral lines. In those situations, the relevant fouling clearance was usually the minimal miss that was as good as the proverbial mile!

Gradients

Those of you intending to model the GNR in the Lincolnshire fens can skip this bit. But for almost any other prototype, track that's entirely dead flat is highly unlikely; in our undulating island, a large percentage of the British railway network was inclined to a greater or lesser extent. Many of these changes in level are very subtle – but as with so many subtleties of the prototype, including these minor ripples of the PW and their relationship to the topography and earthworks adds a surprising degree of realism to a model. On larger layouts, especially those depicting the hillier parts of the country, longer and steeper gradients may well be necessary for veracity to prototype; they are also often a practical necessity where one track has to bridge another. Even on the smallest

BELOW: *'Cade's Green' plan, showing the short 1-in-42 gradient.*

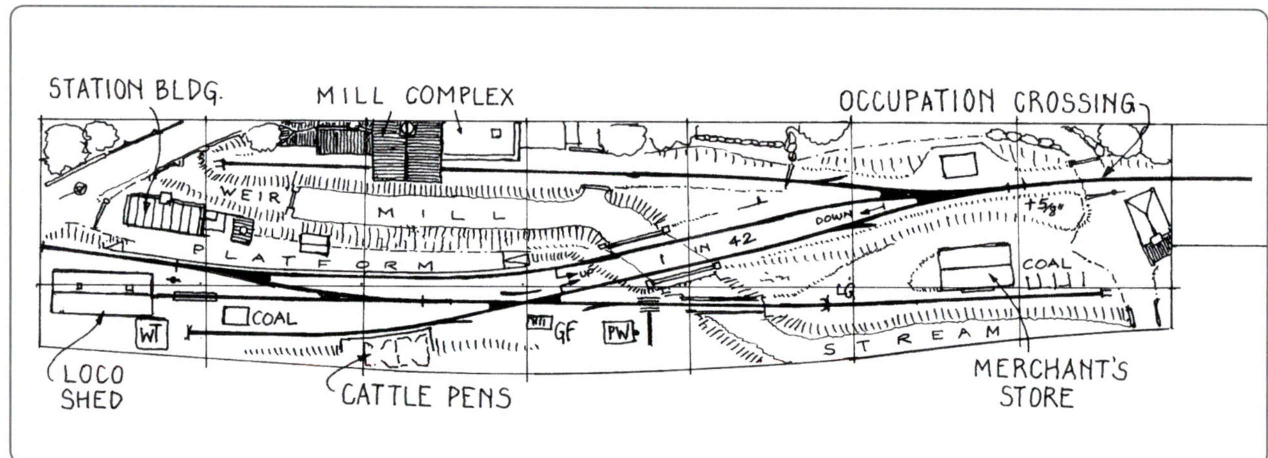

and least hilly of layouts however, departing from the flat adds both visual and operational interest, even when the resulting differences in level are only a few fractions of an inch.

An example of this vertical minimalism is my little East Anglian branch-line terminus, 'Cade's Green' – the current Rice project, illustrated by the sketch plan. From this you will note that the running lines rise at an inclination of 1 in 42 from the platform end as they head out of the station towards an (off-scene, at least for now) river crossing. The resulting gradient may be less than a yard long (the whole layout as it stands is only 7ft!), but the resulting 5/8in difference in elevations at the top of the incline places the stop blocks of the goods siding at a visibly lower level than the main line as it crosses the lane and heads into the fiddleyard. This minimal difference imparts a gentle slope to the road up to the crossing and adds a slight undulation to the rough grassy bank separating the goods yard and running tracks. The 'mill siding' at the rear of the scene, which leaves the main line at the top of the grade, is likewise at a slightly higher level than the platform road. All very far from mountainous – but a lot more convincing and visually interesting than having all the trackwork on an identical level.

Even a tiny gradient like this one can have an operational impact, however. Trains leaving 'Cade's Green' are on the 1 in 42 before they're really rolling, and the branch passenger engine – an F5 class 2-4-2T – often slips a little (in nicely prototypical fashion, fortunately!) if you're heavy-handed with the 'regulator', or a milk tank too many has been hung onto the rear of the coaches. In P4, with pinpoint axles, you can't leave standing wagons on that 1 in 42 slope while shunting; at least, not without working brakes! But then, you couldn't in real life. The trifling gradient on 'Cade's Green' thus add both realism and challenge to the operation of the layout.

ABOVE: *A famous prototype gradient: Talerddig, on the ex-Cambrian Railways main line between Moat Lane Junction and Machynlleth. This is the western approach to the summit, inclined at 1 in 54; a stiff climb in anybody's book, calling for the double heading of most trains in steam days.* Author

Prototype gradients

Realistic layout design starts with the prototype, so it's worth taking a look at the implications of inclined track at full size. A gradient on any railway is only practicable if the trains running thereon can get up it – so determining an acceptable inclination is as much a matter of establishing the train's ability to climb hills as it is any mere matter of topography and earthworks. Train resistance – the key parameter in the traffic-working equation – is hugely affected by gradient, and has a dramatic effect on the practicable load that can be hauled. The invaluable Mr Hemingway-Mills gives a table of specific figures for the fall-off in train weight with adverse gradient which are very revealing. An 0-6-0 goods engine developing 12,900lb of maximum sustained tractive effort is quoted as being able to shift a theoretical maximum of 900-odd tons on the level – but only 390 tons up 1 in 100, 240 tons on 1 in 75 and a mere 163 tons up 1 in 50. (For those of you raised on percentage values for slopes, British railway gradients are traditionally quoted as 'fractional inclines' – the number of linear units along the railhead needed for one unit of rise.)

As these figures show, anything steeper than 1 in 100 is enough to cause major operating difficulties on the prototype. Such notable main-line banks as Shap and Beattock were both 1 in 75 at their steepest, while the 'Long Drag' of the Settle and Carlisle has a ruling grade

BELOW: *A train cresting Hemerdon bank – the nearly 3 miles of 1 in 43 by which the South Devon main line ascends the lower slopes of Dartmoor. Such a gradient inevitably calls for double heading or banking (in extreme cases, both!). Here, a 'Hall' is piloting a 'King', and the top of the gradient shows clearly in the train.* Author's collection

ABOVE: *Britain's steepest gradient worked by adhesion alone – Hopton, on the Cromford & High Peak mineral line in Derbyshire, which reached 1 in 14. The steepest gradient I've found on a passenger-carrying route is the 1 in 27 of the Holywell Town branch in North Wales.* Author's collection

of 1 in 100 (although quite a lot of it!). Predictably more extreme were the gradients on secondary main lines in mountainous country, such as the LSWR's 1-in-70 ascent of northern Dartmoor, the Highland's 1-in-60 slog up to Slochd Mhuich, the 1 in 54 of Girvan bank on the Stranraer line, the Cambrian's 1 in 52 approach to Tallerdig Summit and the Somerset & Dorset's famed route over the Mendips, which had miles and miles at the ruling grade of 1 in 50. Some of the steepest prototype inclinations are found in the oddest places; for instance, the ruling gradient of the East Suffolk line north from Ipswich is an abrupt 1 in 43 – albeit only over short, sharp 'humps'. But the 'hilliest main line' prize undoubtedly goes to Brunel's South Devon Railway between Newton Abbot and Plymouth, engineered under the Atmospheric delusion and an operating bane ever since! Coming east, trains face the formidable 2¾-mile 1-in-43 Hemerdon Bank, the following descent from Rattery being at 1 in 44. But even these pale into insignificance when you consider the westbound climb up Dainton, which at one point gets down to 1 in 36 – a whisker steeper than the notorious 1-in-37 Lickey Incline by which the Midland's Bristol–Birmingham route scales the Severn scarp. These two formidable climbs (both still in use) stand as the steepest main-line banks in Britain.

On branch lines, gradients steeper than 1 in 70 are by no means uncommon. Only a mile or two from where I'm writing this, the trackbed of the GWR's Launceston branch climbs the Lyd Valley from Coryton to Lydford Junction over nearly 4 miles of 1 in 55, while trains to Princetown toiled up a ruling grade of 1 in 40. Steeper still were bits of the Brecon and Merthyr in South Wales, which strayed down towards 1 in 35 over curves quoted as being of 'less than 6 chains radius'. Non-passenger lines could be even more alpine; in the High Peak of Derbyshire, the superannuated ex-North London Railway 0-6-0Ts of the Cromford & High Peak charged their way up 1-in-14 grade at Hopton – albeit with trains that rarely exceeded four wagons. Not to be outdone, the Taff Vale's Pwllrhebog mineral branch in South Wales surmounted a fearsome 1-in-13 incline with cable assistance, using special locomotives with raised firebox casings to keep the crown plate covered with water when working at such a steep angle.

BELOW: *Mendip mountaineer: I built this model of Somerset & Dorset small-wheeled (5ft 9in) 4-4-0 No.18 for Henry Tasker's EM 'Bath to Midford' layout. Even with carefully set up compensation, a Portescap motor, the boiler full of ballast and a 'loaded' tender, it struggles to pull six brass coaches up the 1 in 45 gradients.* Author

Equivalent gradients

As I remarked in my preamble to this chapter, a gradient is a gradient and it doesn't much matter if it's on a real railway or a small-scale model, the practical implications are much the same. In choosing appropriate gradients for a realistic model railway, therefore, we have to bear in mind two factors: how steep the hill that we can actually surmount with our model trains, and how steep the gradient that an equivalent train could climb in reality. The former is not always the lesser problem; model trains that 'lose their feet' and slip to a stand on even a modest adverse slope are by no means uncommon. I know, I spent *years* trying to come up with a mechanical recipe for a 4mm scale 4-4-0 that would pull prototypical-length (six–eight coach) trains of etched-brass stock up the winding 1-in-45 grade from Bath Junction to Combe Down Tunnel on Henry Tasker's EM Somerset & Dorset layout.

Things would be bad enough if all other factors were

ABOVE: *The quest for tractive effort on gradients: the original chassis for Ken Northwood's* Eaton Mascot Hall*, with a Pitman DC71 in the tender and shaft drive, to allow the loco body to be filled entirely with ballast.* A. G. Ingram

equal; but they're not. Alas, the same perspective and visual compression factors that affect the 'look' of curved track on our small-scale models also come into play in our perception of inclines. For a gradient to look convincingly steep on a model, I've found that it usually needs to be made markedly *steeper* than the true prototype value. That 1 in 42 on 'Cade's Green' – a pretty severe 'hiccup' at full size – is, in practice, barely perceptible; a lot of people fail to spot it at a casual glance – although they'll soon discover it's presence if they try their hand at the throttle! Even those perceptive enough to discern the subtle difference in levels rarely come anywhere near the true value of the gradient when invited to estimate its severity; 1 in 60 or better is the usual guess. When trying to impart the feeling of a stiff climb on a model, therefore, I find it is usually necessary to exaggerate the track inclination by at least 20 per cent, probably a tad more. A model 'Shap' would thus pose a 1-in-60 challenge, while Henry's 'Pines Express' should really be faced with a daunting climb at 1 in 40; in practice, even the 1 in 45 settled upon has proved problematic.

Practical gradients for models

The rolling resistance of real trains is, pro rata, a great deal less than the average model. So, in spite of our plenitude of power, when all other factors are equal we're actually doing rather well to equal prototype hill-climbing performance, let alone better it. Only model locomotives that 'cheat' and use traction tyres will produce tractive efforts and levels of grip markedly better than their full-sized equivalents. Certainly, in 'scale' applications, getting our 'stiff' trains up prototypical gradients over sharper-than scale curves is quite a tall order – and that's before we consider the challenges posed by steeper-than-prototype grades, whether 'tweaked' for aesthetic effect or, more prosaically, needed to achieve necessary changes in level in too little space.

Fortunately, there are a goodly number of model railway engineering solutions that can be applied to ease these problems; after all, 'toy' trains have always been expected to climb silly slopes: 1 in 12 for Triang engines fitted with 'magnadhesion'! Adding extra weight has been the traditional approach, loading locomotives with lead in a search for sure-footed traction. On the late Ken Northwood's historic 00 gauge 'North Devonshire Railway', 1-in-100 ruling gradients, passenger trains of up to 16 coaches and freights loading to 65 wagons were the order of the day. To move these loads and get them up the hills with the technology then current, called for extraordinary measures. The 'King' that hauled the 16 Exley coaches of the 'Torreyman' had a hefty Pitman DC71 motor in the tender and a shaft drive to the loco, which was loaded with no less than 2½ lb of ballast! The big '72XX' 2-8-2T used on the 65-wagon coal train had a similar motor in the cab and firebox and 'Cerrobend' just about everywhere else; that one tipped the scales at something close to 3lb! The lights used to go dim when you cranked this behemoth up… To further aid traction, the NDR's track was laid 'floating' on soft foam-rubber underlay, which allowed it to flex under the weight of the trains and thus improve wheel-to-rail contact.

Certainly, wheel-to-rail grip is a key factor in hill-climbing on a model, where we're rarely lacking for adequate power. There's no doubt in my mind that the prototypical combination of steel for both wheel tyres and rails gives markedly more purchase on the railhead than the equivalent in nickel-silver – if not as much as that imparted by the neoprene-rubber traction tyres fitted to many RTR models in N and 00! Some form of suspension that keeps all the wheels firmly in contact with the railhead at all times is also a major boon both for traction and reliable pick-up and has a dramatic effect on hill-climbing ability. For the actual drivetrain, we need a motor that develops plenty of torque and an appropriate transmission with an apt ratio and low friction. Fortunately, this is very much the sort of thing you'll find in most modern RTR locos, and easy to arrange in kit-built models using Mashima can motors and multi-stage gearboxes like the High Level range. Even with all this sophistication, you will still need adequate ballast, although keeping this to the minimum that will do the job reaps benefits in terms of bearing and gear wear, electrical loading and motor heating. The loco should *never* be ballasted to the point where it can't slip and stalls the motor under load; that way lies a nasty niff and a bill for a new motor…

In tackling hill-climbing problems, don't forget about the impact of the train. On the NDR, great trouble was taken to reduce train resistance: those gleaming Exleys ran on special ball-bearing bogies, while every wagon on the railway had pinpoint bearings a decade before they came into general use. Reducing the train resistance by use of improved bearings à la Northwood certainly brings big benefits in the hill-climbing stakes. In most scales and circumstances, accurately set-up pinpoints offer the best performance; make sure they are neither too tight nor too sloppy, and that the bearings are clean and well-lubricated – for which graphite (a 5B pencil rubbed into the bearing cups) is far more effective than oil. Also, make a careful check to ensure no wheelsets are binding. It is surprising how often a flange-edge can come into contact with a bogie frame, or a slightly misaligned wagon brake-shoe rub against a tyre. Keeping the wheel-treads clean also makes a big difference to rolling resistance, while losing excess and unnecessary weight is an obvious step. Therefore, regular checking of rolling stock for free-running is always worthwhile. My personal test-rig for this purpose uses four feet of track inclined at 1 in 48 followed by a couple of yards on the flat. Stock released at the top of the incline is expected roll at least a couple of feet on the level, while anything over a yard is considered good going.

Point geometry

Flip back through the pages of the model railway press of a decade or two ago and you'll soon discover a long tradition of very ropey-looking pointwork on model railways; turnouts that resemble nothing you'd ever see on the prototype and which, one suspects, didn't work any too well on the model. Almost invariably, these abominations were associated with coarse-scale standards: 'Standard 0', 'Universal' 00 and embryonic N. If the advent of fine-scale standards has done nothing else, it has raised the general awareness of the precise nature of pointwork and the importance of the trackwork parameters it encompasses. Those adopting finer standards in the quest for realism soon come to understand that 'getting it right' with regard to point geometry is as fundamental to the functioning of a layout as it is to its appearance. As with the other aspects of the train/track interface, the closer you get to scale, the less you can 'get away with'.

Like so many aspects of the real railway, the design and geometry of pointwork is a very precise and subtle business. Things are the way they are for good and fundamental reasons, and if we try and monkey with these essential relationships – particularly in matters of 'lead' (distance from the tips of the point blades to the nose of the crossing 'V') and the associated curvatures and divergence angles – then we're asking for trouble. Pointwork flawed in fundamental geometry will never look other than unconvincing, even

BELOW: *The geometry of traditional British pointwork is characterised by its flowing nature and infinite variety, with turnouts custom-built to fit their locations – even if, as here, that's only a connection to a mineral line. No kinks or doglegs anywhere, with smooth curvature throughout the formation.* Author's collection

if stock lurches and bumps its way though somehow. In the cause of realism, therefore, sticking to prototypical pointwork geometries as closely as possible is a *sine qua non*. In layout design terms, this essentially comes down to making sure that you allow enough space to accommodate it without any need to distort the geometry in any way; most especially, ensuring that there's sufficient length available to preserve the correct 'lead'. In planning trackwork formations, accurate scale drawing is the least that's called for; better still is mocking-up the proposed arrangement in actual size using photocopied track templates or actual PW sections.

If you're intending to build your own track, you do at least have the widest range of options when it comes to fitting in the pointwork needed to meet operational requirements; you just do what the prototype does and tailor-make the track to suit the situation – obeying, of course, all the relevant rules of PW design. If you're stuck with using off-the-peg turnouts, however, your options are far more limited. Fortunately, the Peco range (pretty much the only choice in Britain) is reasonably comprehensive in all the main scales, with 0 gauge enjoying by far the best and most prototypical track, but suffering the most limited range. While the geometry of Peco's 00 and N offerings is not strictly prototypical – the use of a common crossing angle for all formations regardless of length scuppers any hope of that – it is quite clever and subtle and generally functions well in the 'mainstream' 00/N context for which it is intended. Alas, it is less successful in the matter of authentic appearance.

I suppose that what all this boils down to in the context of designing realistic layouts is that you're probably going to have to give the notion of using handbuilt pointwork some serious consideration, at least in 4mm scale. Track is such a fundamental feature of any railway that it calls for authentic reproduction, and as things stand with ready-to-use PW that's only possible in 0. At the other end of the size spectrum it's easier to get away with unauthentic PW in N scale; Peco's Code 55 'Universal Fine' does at least look reasonably credible. Departures from prototype are anyway not so apparent in the small scale, as you generally appreciate the trackwork as part of a broader scene rather than examining it in close-up. It's at the median 4mm scale that the lack of any authentic-to-prototype off-the-peg pointwork is most acutely felt – surely one of the fundamental anomalies of the hobby. Unfortunately, the proliferation of gauges and standards and the complex nature of British-prototype PW both mitigate against mass production of accurate ready-to-go 4mm scale pointwork, something that's been at the top of the hobby's 'wish list' for a very long time! Excellent, highly-realistic flexible track is available and scale track components are freely available for the construction of both traditional chaired BH steam-era and modern FB concrete-sleepered PW. Building 4mm scale pointwork isn't *that* difficult, but if it's really not your cup of tea then it may be a case of budgeting for custom-built track. Or moving house and stepping up to 0 scale. The custom track is probably the cheaper option.

ABOVE: *Prototypically subtle turnout geometry on Tim Venton's beautifully observed P4 layout 'Clutton'; this is model track you can believe in! The advent of fine scale standards has generally raised awareness of the importance of correct track geometry and anatomy.* Tim Venton

BELOW: *The safe way: mocking-up a proposed point formation with photocopied track templates will soon show whether or not things will fit. This is the embryonic station throat of Hepton Hey's high-level LNWR branch terminus.* Author

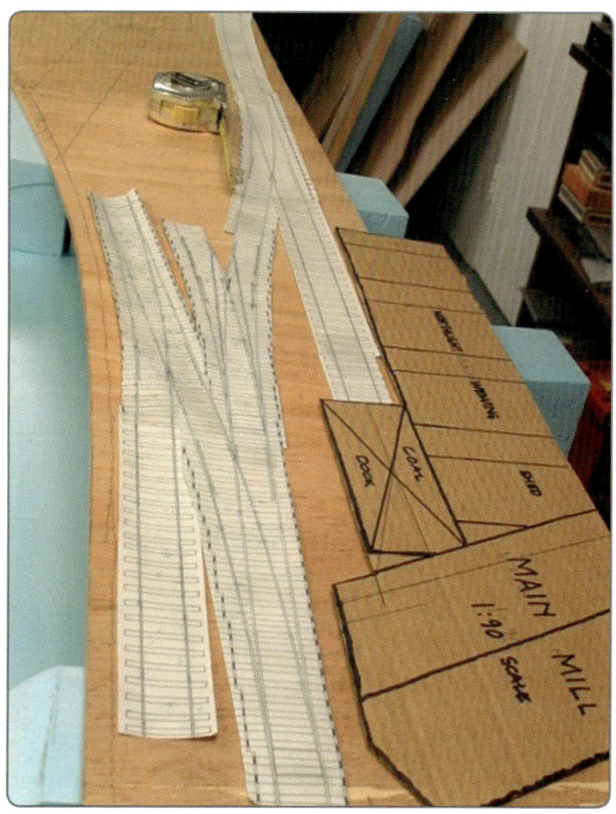

5 PROTOTYPE MATTERS: Inspiration and Sources

ABOVE: *Why bother to try to dream things up when reality offers you peachy and highly modellable tit-bits like this? No, I don't (alas) know where it is – but I do know if I were designing an NER layout and needed to include a road underbridge, I'd fall on it with glee as a prototype!* Author's collection

At last, we've reached the end of the bread-and-butter preliminaries and arrived at the peachy bit of the layout design process: picking and preparing the prototype ingredients that will be skilfully combined into our delectable dish of model railway realism. Easy-peasy, surely? Well, yes and no. Even given limitless resources, turning prototype inspiration into a workable model can pose a fair few problems; add on the usual constraints of less-than-ideal site, insufficient funds and not enough time, and we need to start boxing a bit clever as to exactly which prototype elements we choose to try to represent. In which context, it's as well to bear in mind that seeking suitable subjects to model goes a lot further than the trains and their immediate supporting infrastructure. To convince, a realistic model needs to have a close relationship with the prototype in *every* regard, not just in matters of railway minutiæ. As I suggested in my introductory chapter, accurate observation of reality and its careful reproduction in miniature is the key – and that goes as much for the landscape setting, civil engineering, vernacular structures and such environmental details as figures, animals, road vehicles and street furniture as it does for nuts-and-bolts railway hardware.

Although the vast majority of the layouts that I have confected over the past 40-odd years have been fictional in subject, they have always been made up of elements drawn directly from real life. I fancy you'd need to be very well-versed indeed in the finer points of full-sized civil and mechanical engineering, architecture, geology and topography before you could concoct convincing 'prototypes' completely from scratch. Far safer, I find, to model something that actually existed, even if you change its context by combining it with prototypes drawn from other locations. Better still is to select existing *groupings* of subjects – 'sub-scenes' or 'layout elements' – which are then carefully blended together to form an overall, cohesive whole. This approach – creating a layout by combining disparate bits of the prototype into a homogeneous and convincing whole – is what I term 'composite layout design'.

But before getting immersed in this rational reordering of reality, I feel it is a good idea to go back a step and examine the 'roots' of what we're trying to achieve; in other words, attempt to understand what it is that inspires us to try to model railways in the first place. Nailing down these underlying motivations is a useful way of arriving at a concise 'mission statement' – something that I've found a very useful design tool when it comes to evaluating alternatives. Such an exercise is, of course, extremely personal, and my attempts at analysis here are based on my own 'modelling history' and those of a few close friends; so I'll crave your indulgence if this seems a bit like a trip down Rice's 'memory lane'. Although, that said, as 'serious' railway modelling guinea-pigs go, I think I make a reasonable sample – and most of the sources from which I have derived prototype inspiration and knowledge are still valid today. Bus-pass aside, about the only good thing to be said for being the age I am is that I was able to experience – for a few brief years – the traditional steam-era railway, if not in 'full flower', at least in 'late bloom'. Try hard though they might, preserved lines never *quite* convey the true flavour of their working forbears.

Prototype inspiration

Question modellers of my generation (post-war baby-boomers) as to what it is that inspires them to try to build a model railway in the first place and you can probably distil the majority of the answers into a single emotive word: nostalgia. Most of us, it would seem, are modelling the railways we knew at first hand in our youth – which, in my case, means those of East Anglia and, more fleetingly, West Devon/North Cornwall, during the later 1950s and early 1960s. Well, certainly, that was when I *started* modelling, and my earliest attempts must have been inspired by railways that I experienced directly as – doings on the Island of Sodor apart – they were the only ones I *knew* about! Of course, as my knowledge widened I darted this way and that as each new possibility seduced me; from about 1963-on I set off on a twenty-year dalliance with the railways of an earlier era and subsequently, I've indulged in a series of pre-Grouping and light-railway diversions – not to mention the odd foreign flirtation. However, now that I'm homing in on senior citizenship I find I have come full circle; once again it is the late-1950s timeframe and those first-familiar railways and landscapes that most inspire me.

One suspects that the psychologists would tell us that in modelling our childhoods in this way we are attempting to recapture a time when life was less onerous and the world was fresh, new and exciting; it's the same imperative that keeps Rock 'n' Roll alive and sees otherwise sane people (me included) driving around in cherished old bangers with vague steering, a rough ride and no heater. That this propensity to try to recreate our own pasts through model railways is a well-established trend is supported by a quick perusal of the model railway press. Magazines of the 1950s are full of layouts set firmly in the pre-World War 2 'Grouping' period, while today's crop of 'contemporary' publications – those expressly eschewing steam in favour of compression-ignition – seem equally full of layouts featuring the BR 'Corporate Blue' era of the 1970s and 1980s; presumably today's 40-something modellers modelling the trains of *their* childhoods! Nowadays, even the 'Sectorised' era of BR counts as a historic/nostalgic choice.

ABOVE: *Preserved lines – or 'Heritage Railways', to use the current jargon – may inspire, but nowadays are apt to misinform, as they are very rarely 'true' to their origins now that 'celebrity' locos go on tour and Thomas brings in the families. Things were a lot truer to BR(W)/GWR type on the (original) Dart Valley Railway when I took this rather washed-out snap at Buckfastleigh in 1971 or so. No Thomas!* Author

BELOW: *The trains we knew: modellers of the generation following my own look back on the BR 'Blue Diesel' era with the same nostalgia that we post-war baby-boomers reserve for the swansong of steam.* Author's collection

My first short-lived attempt at a 'proper' prototype-inspired model railway (as opposed to a random train-set round-and-roundy) was an early 'seduction' – the result of a memorable ride over the ex-Cambrian Mid-Wales line when on a 'Freedom of Wales' trip with my father. (A reward for scraping through the eleven-plus school exam, as I recall, which would make it the summer of 1958.) It thus fitted neatly into an important sub-category of direct prototype inspiration: railways discovered whilst on holiday. The result (see snap!) – was entitled 'Rhayader'; cobbled together from second-hand Wrenn track with home-made cornflake-packet buildings, it unsurprisingly bore but the scantiest resemblance to either that unpretentious Radnorshire market town or the delectable Mid-Wales line. Railways encountered fleetingly in this way might light a spark – but often the fire of long-term allegiance fails to catch hold as the memory fades. I suspect that my early experience is fairly typical in this regard; I know that Rhayader soon came to seem as remote as Mars when viewed from my Essex home! The same was true of other 'occasional' childhood railway

encounters: the Waverly Route, seen on rare visits to elderly relatives who lived near Galashiels, the S&D in the Mendips glimpsed during farmhouse holidays in 1956–57.

No; far more immediate were the railways I saw every day. The 'Jazz' lines of East London (over which I went daily to school), the East Coast Main Line (to which I bussed or bicycled, 'ABC' in pocket, at weekends) and – most particularly – the ex-GE lines in North Essex, East Suffolk and South Norfolk (where I spent most of my school holidays, West Country fortnight aside). Although the 'Streaks' and express workings on the East Coast Main Line were the highlights of my train-watching youth, they didn't provide much scope for modelling; much though I might have lusted after a layout big enough to take an 'A4 and twelve' and the wherewithal to acquire same, my parents had other views on pocket money and the use of domestic space! The ex-GE minor lines I came to know so well seemed much more attainable in the context of the one available bedroom wall, for all that they were being closed at a distressing rate. When my 'home' line – Long Melford to Bury St Edmunds – closed in late 1961, closely followed by the abrupt disappearance of steam from East Anglia a scant year later, I responded by putting the clock back; I spent most of the next twenty years modelling the pre-World War 1 Edwardian era.

ABOVE: *The up-and-coming generation of 'serious' modellers are now turning their attentions to the 'Sectorised' BR network of the later 1980s and pre-privatisation 1990s. Both in modelling and stock-finishing terms this is no sinecure, as Jim Smith-Wright demonstrates with his ambitious P4 Birmingham New Street project.* Jim Smith-Wright

BELOW: *This gruesome affair is Rice's first prototype-inspired model railway, built in 1958 when I was 11, the result of a trip over the Mid-Wales. Airfix kits mixed with cornflake-packet home-builds and a Kitmaster GWR large Prairie. But even back then I was into backscenes, it would seem!* Author

BELOW: *And here is the real Mid-Wales line c1961 – still an inspiring prototype and one for which you could now buy an apt selection of locos and stock 'off the shelf', even in N scale.* Author's collection

ABOVE: *In common with most schoolboys of my generation, this was to me, the ultimate railway experience and modelling inspiration; watching express trains at speed on a principal main line. In my case, Gresley Pacifics on the ECML. This superb official postcard view from the LNER period has been in my collection since I was about 13.* Author's collection

BELOW: *This was the familiar railway scene of my formative years – and a life-long modelling preoccupation ever since: the ex-GE lines in East Anglia in their sunset years of the later 1950s and early 1960s. This is Wickham Market on the East Suffolk line – for which I made a bicycled beeline from my occasional summer domicile at nearby Brabling Green.* Lens of Sutton

RIGHT: *Literary and historical inspiration; three seminal sources for my own interest in pre-Grouping railway modelling. The colour postcards are the F. Moore's series produced by the Loco Publishing Co., of which I amassed a considerable collection; the books are essential classics.* Author

Literary influences

Books and magazines have always formed an important source of *information* for railway modellers; but the best of them have also been rich founts of *inspiration* – none more so, in my case, than Cuthbert Hamilton Ellis's *The Trains we Loved*, an accomplished whistle-stop survey of the pre-grouping railways of Britain. Here was a whole world portrayed in polished prose and affectionate art, a world of colour and romance and of dashing exploits just crying out to be reproduced in miniature. The railways Hamilton Ellis described so vividly were about as far removed from dreary, defeated, Beeching-butchered BR as it was possible to get; overnight, I became a historical modeller. This new direction was fuelled by a second classic of railway literature, F. C. Hambleton's *Locomotives Worth Modelling* – page after page of effusive enthusiasm accompanied by exquisitely detailed scale drawings. By no more than about page 10, I was set on becoming a loco-modeller.

The other important literary influence on the hobby has always been the model railway press – principally, in my case, *Model Railway News* under the incomparable Roy Dock. The *MRN* in the '60s was a wonderful magazine, forever pushing the boundaries of scale modelling and exploring the less-obvious aspects of the prototype. Like so many of my contemporaries, I was bowled over by W. S. Norris's fine-scale 0 gauge line, the early work of Guy Williams, Malcolm Cross's prototypical EM trackwork, and the stunningly convincing scenic modelling of George Illiffe Stokes. Jim Whittaker's GW coaching stock made your jaw drop, while the effervescent Maurice Deane was modelling the Wantage Tramway, the Jersey Railway and the Welshpool & Llanfair – all from scratch, and all apparently at the same time! And then there was the prototype gen: every month brought a Tom Lindsay 'Steam Roster' loco drawing and a meticulous Kenneth Werret wagon; rarely were either of 'obvious' subjects. The whole thing was an eye-opener; the achievements and ideas of other modellers have always been an important spur, and even today I still find those old *MRN*s inspiring.

The 1960s were also the period at which railway publishing generally started to take off, spearheaded by Ian Allan and David & Charles. Soon, pretty well every railway of consequence had a 'standard history', which provided background information and – in the form of accounts of lines proposed but never built – a rich fund of possible starting-points for fictional-but-credible models. To go with this bald historical material, there also started to appear books of old photographs, railway atlases and – even more useful to modellers – books combining station portraits with prototype layout diagrams. The model railway press also started highlighting 'suitable subjects for modelling', with

ABOVE: *The model railway press has always been an important source of information and inspiration, as well as practical know-how. The* Model Railway News *of the 1960s was a vibrant and charismatic publication that had a major influence on my modelling aspirations.* Author

BELOW: *Nowhere else in the world will you find such a cornucopia of railway books and periodicals as we have in Britain. Informed, inspired and copiously illustrated, many of these works have become classics of railway literature and form a prime source for modellers. Here are some significant volumes from my own modelling past.* Author

ABOVE: *How many railway images are there circulating out there in postcard form? Several million, without doubt. Although many of them are stock 'glamour' shots or static locomotive portraits, others cover lesser trains, stations and aspects of the railway infrastructure. Here is a random selection from my own collection.* Author

track plans, photographs and structure drawings. Of course, there were also the 'layout suggestion' articles, many of which had a prototypical origin. Leafing through the many pages on offer was as good way as any of discovering, not just a starting point, but the flesh to pad out the bare bones.

The photographic fount

When the first 'artistic' albums of railway photographs started to appear, we had another major source of prototype inspiration. I am quite positive it was Pat Whitehouse's two *Branch Line Albums* of 1962 and 1965, combined with the availability of the K's loco kits and fanned by the writings of Cyril Freezer in the *Railway Modeller*, that led to the rise of the 4mm scale GW branch-line terminus 'somewhere in the West Country' as the nation's favourite model railway theme! In my own case, it was the appearance of Dr Ian C. Allen's *East Anglian Album* in 1976 that rekindled my interest in, and affection for, the trains of my childhood; I could have been *in* a lot of those pictures! In fact, considering that East Anglia in the 1950s was a bit of a backwater in every way, it has been remarkably well served by railway photography of the highest order; the work of Dr Allen and Frank Church provides us with a wonderful record not just of the trains and landscape, but also of the tranquil fabric of life. These photographs, which so bring to life my own memories, have long been a major source of both inspiration and ingredients for my own modelling endeavours. Given the proliferation of railway photographic albums, which now cover just about every subject and era, I suspect most modellers of my generation will now find themselves in this fortunate position.

Photographs have always been the most important secondary source for railway modellers and historians, and we're fortunate that railways are among the best-documented of photographic subjects. There are literally millions of rail-related images out there, the oldest going back to the dawn of photography itself – for trains, then the marvel of the age, were amongst the first things to be photographed. Photography doesn't stop at the railway fence, of course, and covers just about every aspect of life. Postcards, in particular, are a major source, being particularly rich when it comes to landscape and vernacular architecture – information vital to the modeller bent on realism. Since my teens I have been an avid collector of old and not-so-old photos and postcards – rooted out from old shoe-boxes in the dingy back-rooms of bookshops, haggled out of antique shops, espied among the bric-a-brac in junk shops, jumble sales and clearance auctions, donated by friends or family and, latterly, bought from specialist dealers – who are to be observed rubbing their hands together when I hove in sight! After 45 years of this squirreling I now seem to possess several thousand such images, split roughly two-thirds railway to one-third general vernacular. When in search of inspiration for new projects, my bulging and battered albums are the first port of call.

Much railway photography has been devoted to the 'glamour' end of the business – dramatic shots of express trains speeding by or storming gradients, formal portraits of bulled-up engines and so on – but in model-railway inspirational terms I find these images less useful than the much more 'documentary' style of picture – pictures in which the railway is an incidental part of a more general view, or pictures of stations, structures, bridges and the like. Some of the most inspiring pictures in my albums have ne'er a train in sight. Fortunately, many railway photographers did occasionally take such snaps, while there are a wealth of railway company 'official views' – photographs taken purely to record some aspect of the railway infrastructure for engineering, valuation or publicity purposes. These non-train photos, while often a little dry, can provide a wellspring of inspiration for 'layout elements' as well as sometimes providing the starting-point for an entire layout project.

The quest for place

Thus far, I've been mostly been considering the *railway* side of the inspirational equation – which, traditionally, was all that mattered. However, in my quest to capture the atmosphere of place and period I'm just as interested in the landscape and vernacular setting, which for me is intrinsically linked to my appreciation of the trains. This is, I think, a common scenario; for a lot of people, it's the conjunction of the railway with a particular *setting* that inspires. So, rather

LEFT: *Documentary views of stations, yards, structures, locations and bits of infrastructure are the true bits of grit around which to grow layout design pearls. This superb view of Haxby, on the NER's York–Scarborough line in North Yorkshire, is as informative as it is inspiring, and forms a classic 'layout design element' in its own right.* Author's collection

than 'BR Eastern Region', my focus is very specifically the ex-GE minor lines in rural east and mid-Suffolk. However interesting I might find the legacies of the GWR and LSWR, it's the railways of West Devon and next-door North Cornwall that I'm actually trying to model, rather than the hardware of a particular railway company.

The common factor with both these scenarios is that the settings are familiar to me. Well, I'd better modify that a bit, as the East Anglia that I knew and loved (and am consequently trying to model) is the East Anglia of half a century since; these days, I find I'm completely out of touch with the place! And when I do go there I find dramatic and sweeping changes in the landscapes familiar from short-trouser days; where have all the trees and hedges gone? Only the general form of the land, the placid waterways, the peg-tiled and pargeted villages and those towering Suffolk skies are as I truly remember them. As for the railways – well, even before Beeching, the branchline closure axe bit deep hereabouts and a few subsequent decades of ruthless factory farming have often completely obliterated any traces of the old trackbeds. It's all but impossible to get any feel for a former railway's context when it has been totally expunged from a landscape that is itself greatly altered.

The situation in the West Country is, I'm glad to say, a good deal less depressing for the railway enthusiast. Although at the period I'm interested in modelling I had only a relatively scanty youthful acquaintance with the place, the impression these bleak moors, wooded valleys and towering sea-cliffs made upon me then tallies quite closely with what I see today. Having lived in West Devon for nearly forty years now, this is an environment that I probably know as well as one man can. While the Beeching cull closed many of the lesser West Country railways, there are still a good few survivors in either preserved or minimised form: Totnes –Buckfastleigh, Bodmin, Kingswear, the West Somerset to Minehead, the 'Tarka Line' to Barnstaple and the line over the Tamar to Gunnislake, plus the Looe, Newquay, Falmouth and St Ives branches in Cornwall. Even where the tracks are gone, much of the infrastructure remains intact; I walk my dog regularly along the alignments of the LSWR North Cornwall and Plymouth lines, the GWR's Launceston branch or the truly bucolic North Devon and Cornwall Junction. Not just the earthworks but most of the bridges are still in place, while rails in the tarmac mark out many a former road crossing. Buildings, too, are mostly still standing, with many a station inhabited and beautifully preserved. Small surprise, then, that these are railways I'm strongly drawn to as modelling subjects.

Personally, I find it very difficult to come up with a

BELOW: *Is there anything more evocative of a departed railway than this? The rails are still embedded in the roadway where once Beattie well-tanks nosed across the lane at Helland on their way to Wenford Bridge. As modellers, we can unpick history and recreate such scenes in miniature.* Author

ABOVE: *Place as subject; I model the former GWR because it ran through West Devon, not because I'm a devotee of all things Swindon. (Although a '45XX' and a fully panelled 'Toplight' are not to be sneezed at!) This treasured (if rather lacklustre) postcard shows Liddaton Halt, on the Tavistock–Launceston section, about 4 miles from my front door. The village in the background is Coryton, served by a station a good two miles further west down the valley!* Author's collection

convincing rendition of somewhere that I've never visited and for whose landscape I have no 'feel'; I'd go so far as to say it's all-but-impossible to *convincingly* model a setting of which you have no direct experience. Many of us choose to set our model railways in familiar or well-loved landscapes for just this reason; indeed, the setting may often dictate the railway subject. I model the former GWR because it ran through West Devon and the ex-LSWR on account of its North Cornish incursions, not because I'm a dyed-in-the-wool GWR or LSWR enthusiast. When faced with trying to design a layout set somewhere I don't know, almost my first move is to plan a field trip. However familiar one might be with somewhere from photographs or other secondary sources, when you actually get on the ground it's as if everything comes into focus or takes on a further dimension; often, your preconceptions prove to be well wide of the mark.

Picking a prototype

For a lot of people, this will be what our transatlantic cousins colourfully call a 'no brainer'; one or other (or several) of the inspirational sources touched on above will have wormed its way so deep into your modelling soul that there will be only 'one true way'. Some people are unswerving in their dedication to a particular railway company, period and geographical location, to the extent that they are utterly unmoved by all or any alternatives. Many of us, however (yours truly included), can see merit in any number of possibilities and consequently have more of a problem settling on a single theme and subject. When faced with this dilemma, there are two basic options: keep chewing away at the choices, gradually eliminating alternatives until one clear winner emerges; or decide to have a dabble at a couple of possibilities rather than putting all your modelling eggs into one prototype basket. Planning two (or more) modest projects in tandem or succession rather than a settling on a single ambitious long-term one is a perfectly valid and workable way of going railway modelling; I know – it's what I've been doing for the past four decades!

Traditionally, the most common starting point in choosing a model railway theme has been an often-fierce allegiance to the practice of a particular railway company; the avid GW enthusiast with the company monogram emblazoned on his neckwear (and quite possibly his underwear!), driving a Brunswick Green car and inhabiting a suburban bungalow decked out in 'Stone No. 1' and 'Stone No. 3', is something of a standing joke! But setting out to represent a particular pre-Group or Grouping company or the equivalent region of BR is as good a starting point as any; the refining process then becomes one of deciding which *aspect* of that company's operations you're actually going to model, and the geographical and other prototype implications of this choice. The problem is that the more mainstream starting points – the 'Big Four' grouping companies or BR – were truly vast undertakings, embracing every possible type of railway from remote mineral or rural branch lines to four-track raceways and labyrinthine stations, sprawling yards and convoluted junctions. Even contemporary Network Rail – with its eclectic mix of historic and 'of the moment' infrastructure and bewildering and ever-changing plethora of train operators – takes a bit of boiling down into an achievable, realistic modelling proposition. Without a matching 'second priority' – such as a particular type of subject or a defined geographic setting – narrowing the focus can still be quite an involved process. Indeed, in the face of so wide a range of possibilities, it is sometimes only one step removed from having no prototype allegiance in the first place!

Hard though the dyed-in-the-wool company man may find it to comprehend, there are many aspiring layout-builders who come to the task free from any such prototypical preconceptions. This I find particularly true of a new generation of modellers, young and old, whose interest in railways has been awakened by a visit to a heritage railway or by stumbling across the current generation of sophisticated and highly realistic RTR models and who seek to create a realistic and authentic layout without the benefit of background railway knowledge. Even amongst my own generation, I come in to contact with people who, while they may remember trains affectionately from their youth, took no particular interest in them then and thus have no personal fund of past enthusiasm on which to draw. In one way, being in such a position may be regarded as fortunate – in that there is now such a wide range of possibilities to choose from, but with no star to steer by, where do you start?

Well, modestly, would be my advice; think small and simple and keep the double task of research and modelling achievable. This still leaves the problem of selecting a starting-point – the one essential without which no journey, even a mystery-tour, can commence. Over many a year of helping people to make a start in just such rudderless circumstances, I've found that the two most helpful markers are a well-loved landscape or a favourite locomotive type. Either way, the one will help determine the possibilities for the other; both will involve a modicum of background digging to determine the trains appropriate to the setting or to put the favoured engine into a correct context. The former used to be the tougher option, but seeking 'the right trains' is greatly facilitated by the wonderful choice of kits and ready-built models available nowadays. How much more possible would my juvenile attempt to model the 1950s-era Mid-Wales line be today, when all the necessary railway ingredients – a 'Dean' or Collett '22xx' goods, an ex-LMS 'Mickey Mouse' Mogul, a GW 'B set' and a selection of authentic 'Grouping' and BR goods stock – can be so easily found ready-to-run in both N and 00? Even if I were bent on 0 scale or in essaying something hair-shirt in fine scale 4mm, all the kits and components needed are to be had. Selecting a railway prototype more-or-less at random to match a favoured location no longer has anything like the consequences that pertained not so long ago.

Refining the prototype choice

With the basic railway theme and setting decided upon, the next stage is to move the design of a layout from the germ of general inspiration to the specifics of a modellable subject – essentially, a process of refinement. There are some useful nut-and-bolt techniques to help accomplish this process described in the next chapter, but the point I want to labour here is the importance of getting this fundamental aspect of layout planning *right*. This means sorting out in your own mind *exactly* what your key prototype interests and

BELOW: *Picking a favourite loco type around which to base a layout is as good a starting-point as any. If your pin-up is as abstruse as mine, then you too will be modelling North Cornwall!* Author's collection

inspirations really are – the point at which the 'armchair' phase of just sitting and really thinking through all the possibilities pays such rich dividends. Above all, you need to be sure that whatever you choose to model is going to sustain your interest throughout several years of effort. I know of all too many model railway projects (several of my own included!) that have faltered and ultimately come to naught precisely because the underlying interest faded well before the work was finished. If you're not sure whether a particular theme is really for you, there's much to be said for a spot of toe-dipping with a small, simple and quick 'mini project' before you commit to a major undertaking.

Refining a general desire to model a given railway company, period and setting into the bones of a workable project is either very easy – in that you find a peachy prototype location just calling out to be modelled and have the space to do it in – or rather difficult, in that nothing seems to fit the bill (or the available footprint) and you're left with a series of disconnected threads that, while inspiring enough in their own right, don't somehow knit together into a cohesive whole. The hardest row to hoe in the sunny garden of realistic model railway design is trying to come up with something completely fictional that is convincing at all levels: landscape and vernacular setting, railway practice, trains, period detail. To accomplish such a feat requires rather more in the way of background knowledge – railway and vernacular – than merely modelling an actual location, when the disposition of everything is decided for you by your subject and what you really *need* to know about is restricted to that one place. Picking an actual location is thus the easiest way of refining a general prototype choice as it dramatically narrows the focus of the necessary research.

Going the other way, on the other hand, widens the scope of this task exponentially – which is either a chore you'd rather do without, or an aspect of the project you find as rewarding as the modelling itself. Your personal view on this facet of realistic modelling may well determine which of these two routes you choose to go down; but there's no gainsaying the fact that prototype research can be both time-consuming and – at times – frustrating. (Although, in my experience, it's when seeking material on a definite location that you most often hit a complete impasse, when there's one structure or feature that you *have* to model – but for which you just *can't* find the necessary information!) Researching for what I term a 'factional' model – something that, while it never existed, is nevertheless so closely based on what did that nothing jars or looks out of place – requires a thorough familiarisation both with the nuts and bolts of full-sized railway design practice as well as with the detailed nature and character of the supposed setting. A tall order indeed!

Prototype research

In my exploration of sources of *inspiration*, I've already touched on some of the main sources of layout-designing *information*: direct knowledge, books and magazines and photographs. To which I would now add a few others: maps and plans of all sorts, official railway publications, public records (whether rail-specific or general/historical), old movies,

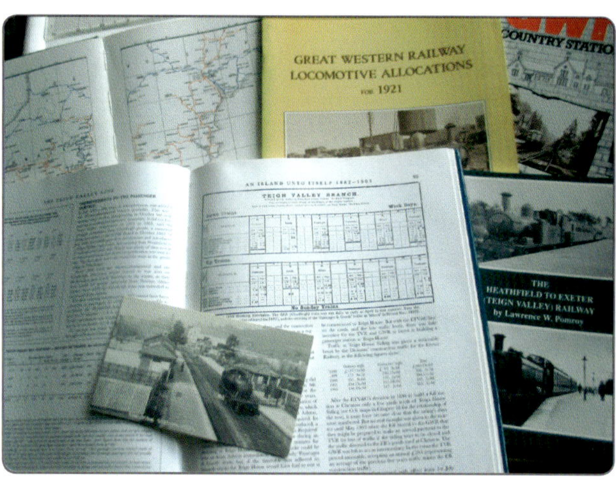

ABOVE: *These days, such is the depth and quality of the best 'line histories' produced by the specialist railway press that you can often find almost all your 'research' answers between one pair of covers. The example seen here (together with a few additional sources) is Peter Kay's superbly detailed account of the GWR's Teign Valley branch in Devon, published by Wild Swan: 285 pages covering less than 16 miles of single-track railway. You could easily design an authentic layout from this lot!* Author

direct observation and recording, talking to people who know more than you do and – not least in this ethereal age – the Internet. Just typing the right keywords into a search engine can unlock a veritable welter of resources. However, in researching for a model railway, as in all other quests, the first essential is decide what information it is you're actually looking for – which, in the case of general background research, is actually quite a difficult undertaking in itself! Nevertheless, time spent compiling a detailed list of questions will be time well spent, as the precise nature of a question will often suggest the best place to look for an answer.

Compiling such a research questionnaire is another one of those layout design tasks that can be comfortably and profitably accomplished at the 'armchair' note-doodling stage. As I'll explain in detail in the next chapter, lists and questionnaires are a key design tool in the actual process of layout design chez Rice – but for now I'll restrict myself to the peculiar nature of the 'need to know' background inventory. This is always an untidy beast, forever in a state of constant flux, new questions appearing at the foot as fast as those further up can be ticked-off as answered. So as not to get ahead of myself, I'll refer you forwards for my thoughts on the structuring of such a list; here, I'm concerned with content and purpose. Broadly speaking, what do we need to know and where should we best look for our answers?

Researching the railway

Given that we're looking for information to help us design the *layout*, the one thing we don't need to know all that much about at this stage is the trains. All we're really concerned with is their general nature and the broad outlines of the service. Basically, that comes down to defining the types of trains we're talking about, their overall length and the facilities we need to provide to handle them – loops, platforms, sidings, docks, sheds or locomotive depots (with or without turntable). More specifically, we need the critical dimensions and required curve radii and clearances for the largest locomotives and longest items of rolling to be accommodated, as these will form the 'limiting case' and will determine things like minimum turnout angles and their associated fouling clearances, the length of shunting necks and run-round loops and the nature of the infrastructure needed to accommodate the traffic. Getting accurate answers to these questions will not only avoid annoying practical errors like the not-quite-long-enough platform headshunt or slightly-too-tight turnout, but also the visual anomaly of, say, running a particular locomotive type over a bridge that quite patently would not, in reality, support its weight.

Answers to this first set of questions can be gleaned from a variety of sources. Train formations and permitted locomotive types found on a specific line or group of lines can be found definitively in working timetables (often in the form of route availability codes) or noted in guard's journals. Failing such documentary sources, this information can be gleaned from photographs or movie film of the actual trains – possibly the most authoritative source of all, showing as they do what *actually* went on! Motive power shed allocations can suggest also likely locomotive types, while official plans and surveys can furnish details of the permissible weight for a given bridge or structure. Sometimes, you need to deduce things like the relationship between a bridge and specific loco types from weight diagrams or route availability codes and the permitted loadings given for the route on which the bridge was situated. This is particularly relevant if you're going to use said bridge out of context in 'composing' a fictional subject.

Civil engineering

The next set of railway questions we need answering concern the civil engineering characteristics of our chosen prototype. In this context, what we're looking for is the practice of the (almost-certainly pre-Grouping) railway company that originally built the lines we're interested in representing. Even if we're modelling the here-and-now of Network Rail, much of the infrastructure we need to reproduce will have originated very much in the there-and-then. I was reminded of this mix of new and old only a few days ago, when stepping from the cramped confines of a gaudily attired Northern Trains 'Pacer' (admittedly, some way removed from the 21st century 'state of the art') into the sober and almost-unaltered mid-Victorian splendour of Huddersfield's grandly neo-Classical station – built in 1846/47 and surely one of the finest (and best-preserved) historic railway buildings in Europe. On my way thence from Sheffield (whose former Midland station is also magnificent) I had travelled over trackbeds originating with the Midland, Manchester, Sheffield & Lincolnshire and Lancashire & Yorkshire railways, crossing a series of splendid and lofty viaducts and threading bridges and tunnels built in the distinct and distinctive styles of those great companies.

Capturing this distinctiveness of engineering style is the key to modelling the railways built by these old companies at any point throughout their long histories and into the present. In the quest for realism and authenticity – even in the context of a 'factional' subject – it's something you have to get absolutely right. In my experience, the only sure way you can achieve this is to base all the infrastructure elements on real designs: bridges, tunnel-mouths, retaining walls and other masonry, goods facilities and details like incidental ironwork, fencing and woodwork. When you really start to look, it's amazing just how much of even our current railway infrastructure is well over a century old! While some companies – like the LNWR and GWR – developed very distinctive 'standard designs' for many aspects of their infrastructure, other railways used a wide mix of styles on different lines; indeed, many such structures originate, not with the pre-group company 'owning' the line, but by the preceding independent company which actually built it. Railways like the NER possessed several distinct families of structures, reflecting the practice of the constituent Stockton

BELOW: *Much of the civil engineering of our early railways was built to last the proverbial millennium and a lot of it is still very much extant. I took this recent picture of Southerly (Lake) Viaduct, on the LSWR's 'Mountain Division' between Okehampton and Lydford, to show detail of the masonry. Note the 'join' where the original 1874 single-line structure was widened in 1889/90. The corbel stones and sofits in the piers supported the wooden 'centreing' on which the arches were built.* Author

& Darlington, Stanhope & Tyne, and Newcastle & Carlisle railways; selecting an N&C structure for a Yorkshire-set NER layout would be as inappropriate as sticking in something based on a Brighton or Highland prototype.

Fortunately, a great deal of this historic railway civil engineering is still to be seen today, so can often be studied at first hand – a rewarding exercise in its own right. Once again, the field trip can bring rich rewards in uncovering subjects just crying out to be photographed, sketched and – ultimately – modelled. Railway civil engineering was a major professional discipline throughout the Victorian and Edwardian eras, and the publications of bodies like the Institute of Civil Engineers are full of detailed descriptions of railway infrastructure of all sorts. There are also a good number of textbooks on the subject, such as the Hemingway-Mills volume already quoted; these turn up quite frequently in bookshops and figure in many libraries.

As a topic, civil engineering has always been very thoroughly documented, with original drawings, plans and official photographs from the railways' own archives being well-represented both in the private collections of the professional institutions and the principal public archives: the National Records Office in Kew, the National Railway Museum at York, the Mitchell Library in Glasgow, the Railway Studies Library at Newton Abbot and, more locally, the various County Records Offices. If you're intent on researching a particular location, local museums and history societies will often also have relevant railway material in their collections (as well as being a valuable source of more vernacular material). A final source that can often yield surprising results are local newspapers – whose archives are usually available in microfilmed form at main libraries or County Record Offices.

BELOW: *'Without a train in sight' – yet, to the informed eye, unmistakably Great Western. If the characteristic corrugated-iron lock-up store and fire-bucket rack didn't give the game away, the 'too-wide' bridge (built for the broad gauge) would! This is Coryton, the epitome of a GW Devon rural wayside station.* Author's collection

Railway engineering

As well as the nature of the basic engineering of their lines – which could range from the 'monumental' scale of the various viaduct-and-tunnel trans-Pennine routes to the almost-negligible scrapings of the 'farmers lines' undulating gently across East Anglia – the old railway companies were equally distinctive in their detailed engineering. To the knowledgeable eye, the precise identity or pre-Group origin of many a railway can often be divined at a glance and without a train in sight, merely from the style of the lineside fencing, the precise nature of the PW or a finial atop a signal post! It follows without saying that these are facets of the prototype we need to get right if we're to have any hope of producing a convincing result on our model. This detail engineering is an even more complex area of study, as it covers so many aspects of the railway – some of them long-lived and 'fixed' (signals, buildings and structures such as footbridges or water cranes), others more transient, such as the track, signage and ancillary equipment.

Track, particularly, is a key 'signature' of both railway origin and period. While on a busy line the PW might be renewed every ten years or so, on lesser-used routes it can easily last well over half a century! This means that although traditional chaired bullhead track in all its many variations was usurped as the 'standard' by flat-bottom in the mid-1950s, there's still an amazing amount of it left even today. It is quite possible to find the very latest in hi-tech rolling

stock running over what is effectively pure steam-era PW. What is *not* possible, however, is to see steam trains (other than preserved ones) rolling over heavyweight Pandrol-clipped, concrete-sleepered FB track! At earlier periods – from the Grouping era back – it would be equally unlikely to find the trains of one group or company running over PW of a design associated with another. The further back you go, the more distinctive the PW becomes, so that while the LNER and SR of the 1930s might have shared a common '3-bolt' chair design, their predecessors had very different ideas! And anything running on 'baulk road' just *has* to be GW.

Just to add to the confusion, there is often a mix of 'internal' engineering design with 'bought in' components. The situation often arises where several different pre-Grouping railways (and hence their successors) might use the same design of signal, originating with an independent signalling contractor like Saxby & Farmer or Stevens – although often embellished with distinctive finials or painting schemes. Another such 'common denominator' is the graceful arched lattice-iron footbridge manufactured by the Butterley Iron Company, to be found on a number of lines from Scotland to the South Coast. Sorting out what is 'typical' of a given stretch of railway can be a tall order, as it's an area of study more or less specific to modelling and thus not always of concern to railway historians.

Architecture is the other major area of individuality, not just between the various railway companies, but also between the various lines that went to make up that company in its formative years, as already touched upon above in relation to the NER. Fortunately, as with the

ABOVE: *Beware the bought-in bits! This elegant lattice-iron footbridge is of a design manufactured by several leading ironworks and offered 'off the peg'. It could thus be found on the lines of different pre-Grouping companies – the Caley in this case, I fancy; but all the Scottish railways, the Midland and the GE, also used them, among others. This makes such a bridge a good choice for a 'factional' layout – especially as you can get a nice etched-brass kit!* Author's collection

basic civil engineering, much of the railway's architectural heritage is still in place and capable of being observed and surveyed at first hand (subject to the constraints of the laws of trespass!), while like the civil engineering, it is extremely well-documented in both official/professional records and through general railway or postcard photography.

Many railways did develop very well-defined 'schools' of architecture, such that the parentage of a structure is instantly apparent. These standard designs or architectural styles are a boon to the modeller of the 'fictional might-have-been', as they allow the selection of suitable structural prototypes for modelling in the knowledge that they are very much what would have been built had the railway existed in reality. Once you understand this architectural provenance, it is a relatively straightforward matter to find an extant or well-documented example of the type of structure you need to model. So, although the standard South Devon Railway 'cottage' station building at Coryton – on which prototype location my own 'Lydstowe' is based – no longer exists, I was able to obtain appropriate dimensions, interior layouts and architectural detail from the extant SDR stations at Marytavy, Lustleigh and Bovey Tracey, built to essentially the same design.

Railway history societies

As modellers, we need prototype information covering a wide spectrum of full-size railway practice, both constructional and operational. Trying to locate all this material from original sources is a considerable undertaking – but fortunately, also a process we can often short-circuit by benefiting from the researches of others. It's an endearing aspect of this hobby that many people make the fruits of their labours widely and readily available, often through the channels of the various specialist societies and interest groups. These form an important resource for the modeller bent on realism and authenticity.

Most specifically orientated to our needs is the Historical Model Railway Society, founded as long ago as 1950 to preserve, record and collate a wide range of material pertaining to the accurate modelling of our railway heritage. Now an educational charity, the HMRS holds a major collection of railway photographs and drawings and has an important library (all accessible to members directly or by post), housed in its permanent, dedicated headquarters building at Swanwick Junction (Butterley) in Derbyshire – also home to the Midland Railway Trust. At local level, the HMRS operates through active area groups, staging regular meetings, lectures and field trips. It also has a system of 'Company Stewards' – specialists who can almost always point you in the right direction when seeking information on a particular topic. As well as publishing its own regular journal, the HMRS produces substantial and authoritative books on a wide range of railway history. Alongside the modelling-orientated HMRS sits the other major 'broad-brush' research body, the Railway and Canal Historical Society – which, as it's title suggests, has a somewhat wider remit (nowadays, it also covers historic road transport as well). Although more academic in approach than the HMRS, the RCHS too has large collections of photographs, plans, maps and drawings alongside its documentary archives. The RCHS collections are particularly strong on early railways, tramways, mineral and industrial railways, light railways and other minor lines, and joint railway/canal undertakings.

Much more specific in terms of subject matter (although not always aimed at the needs of modellers) are the various 'line societies', dedicated to the preservation and researching of all aspects of individual pre-group or grouping railways, or sometimes geographical groups of railways, as with the Welsh Railways Research Circle or Cumbrian Railways Association. Many of these line societies work closely with the full-sized preservation groups and the NRM, while others with a modelling bent co-operate with the HMRS, often jointly sponsoring research projects or publishing ventures. Virtually all line societies produce regular journals, some of the very highest quality, as well as single-topic occasional publications. Many also make available drawings and copy photographs from their own collections. As well as these 'line' groups, other specialist organisations have sprung up to cover specific aspects of railway practice or particular groups of railway types. The Signalling Record Society has, for many years, done what it says on the tin, while the Tramway and Light Railway Society, the Industrial Railway Society (even older than the HMRS!) and the Irish Railway Record Society are equally explicit about their objectives. If you find yourself drawn to a particular railway or speciality, then membership of one of these dedicated bodies is a good investment; if you're not so committed, however, then the HMRS is probably the society to join, as it basically covers The Lot.

BELOW: *All in the family… I wanted to model the South Devon Railway 'cottage' station at Coryton – but it's no longer there. The all-but-identical building at Bovey Tracey is extant, however – it's now the town's heritage centre – and thus formed a valuable alternative source. This lovely Chapman postcard has 'GWR' writ all over it – note the baulk road at broad gauge track centres, spear and paling fences, and the elegant GW design of oil lamp.* Author's collection

Commercial prototype sources

As if all this voluntary collaborative effort is not enough, to the activities of the various 'study groups' must be added the commercial output of the very healthy British railway publishing industry, surely the most active such speciality in the world. Among an absolute plethora of railway periodicals appearing regularly (although not all monthly) are a good selection covering just about every aspect of our railway heritage: *Backtrack*, *British Railway Journal, Railway Archive, British Railways Illustrated, Steam Days, Steam World, Traction* and *Railway Bylines* are all general titles covering the broader

ABOVE: *The publications of the specialist societies are packed with the sort of accurate, detailed information that's invaluable for layout planning and actual modelling. Here is a random selection from my library – not all entirely rail-orientated; I like my trains in context...* Author

ABOVE: *Just a selection of commercial railway history sources. Most of these are general in scope but – as can be seen – there are also railway company-specific titles as well. Archive – an excellent industrial archaeology quarterly which always had good railway coverage – has now spawned a rail-only offshoot, Railway Archive.* Author

subject, while the *Great Western Railway Journal, LMS Journal, Midland Record* and *London Railway Record* (among others even more arcane) cover specific topics. The problem is that you can easily spend a small fortune and aeons of time on acquiring and ploughing through magazines that, while enjoyable and sometimes inspirational, don't actually tell you what you need to know! When researching, plucking relevant articles and photo-features from this mass of material isn't easy – but it's a process greatly aided by indexing. Many of the line societies publish regular 'digests' highlighting articles in the general press relevant to their areas of interest, while the magazines themselves and several independent sources produce detailed indexes of material by topic and origin. Spending a little time rootling through such listings can quickly narrow things down to a shortlist of 'must have' issues for each publication. Then it's down to a trawl around the back-number specialists or an approach to one of the library collections (HMRS, line society or local public library) for loan copies or photocopies of the relevant pages.

The 'historical' publications sit beside a plethora of 'news/current affairs' railway titles covering the more recent and contemporary scene: *The Railway Magazine, Rail, Rail Express, Modern Railways, Railways Illustrated and Today's Railways*. These are important sources for the modellers of the contemporary. To this 'of the minute' list must be added a further raft of periodicals devoted to the heritage railway (ie preservation) scene – less relevant as a direct source of modelling information, although often useful in letting you know what artefacts and bits of infrastructure are being rescued/restored and where they might be seen. But I have to say that, as an accurate depiction of 'how things were', a lot of preserved railways are somewhat suspect; much of what is lovingly illustrated in glorious digital colour in the pages of *Steam Railway and Heritage Railway* should be enjoyed for what it is rather than treated as a credible source of data! Indeed, so heterogeneous and fictionally liveried are the collections of some preserved railways that they rather come to resemble a 'because I like it' model railway in their juxtaposition of items and painting schemes that, historically, never came within a couple of hundred miles or a decade or two of one another!

Vernacular sources

So much for researching what goes on the *railway* side of the fence – but in the cause of realism, our need for authentic material extends just as much to the environment. Here, fieldwork is usually the best way of gathering the bones of what we need for convincing landscape modelling – but unless you're representing the strictly contemporary, you'll need to flesh those bones out with some historical material. Fortunately, this is usually pretty easy to come by from a variety of sources – many of them already familiar from the railway side of things. Photographs are both the most prevalent well-spring, and the most useful – particularly if they're dated. The proliferation of albums of the *'Just-About-Anywhere in Old Photos'* variety are a major provider of such images, although I have to say the standard of many of these books – both in terms of quality of reproduction and the accuracy and informativeness of the captions – leaves a bit to be desired. But the best of them are treasuries of both hard information and that elusive but so-important 'atmosphere'. A lot of the images reproduced in these books started out on postcards, and these are another valuable fount of local background information, widely available and rarely expensive. Never neglect what's on the *back* of a postcard; apart from all else, Post Office stamp-cancellings often give a useful starting-point for dating the image.

Another absolute treasury of both images and information are the various County or Regional magazines and general 'rural Britain' periodicals like *The Countryman*. Many years

ABOVE AND BELOW: *Vernacular sources. If you're intent on a layout which is in any way 'historic', then these are some of the places to look for information on the environment in which your railway will be set. The 'nostalgia industry' has deluged us with sepia-toned tomes – many of which are a bit suspect; I've found local history society or county library publications to be generally more reliable and informative. Regional magazines (especially old-established ones) are a great source, while for sheer inspiration and all manner of anecdotes and snippets, books like Archie White's classic on the East Anglian coast are hard to beat.* Author

ago now I lit upon a boxful of *The East Anglian* magazine in a bookshop in Lavenham; I bought the lot, some 85 copies stretching from 1950 to the early 1960s – a move I've never regretted, as these beautifully written and illustrated chronicles of local life and history have proved to be a near-bottomless well of information, inspiration and true local colour. An awful lot of what has gone into my various Suffolk layouts was gleaned from those pages. There have also been some evocative but authoritative travel books written about the various areas of Britain, usually on a county basis. The well-known and well-respected Shell Guide series was the work of some of our finest writers and illustrators, and can be found in library collections as well as in second-hand bookshops. Those same bookshops often throw up unsuspected treasures:; Donald Maxwell's *Unknown Suffolk* and Archie White's exquisitely illustrated *Tideways and Byways of Essex and Suffolk* were two such finds, books that have provided valuable grist to my modelling mill.

Thinking of mills reminds me that I have also gleaned much valuable prototype material from photo-albums aimed specifically at those with an interest in industrial archaeology. Watermills are a Rice passion and several have featured on layouts I've built, like the model of Heybridge Mill that dominated 'Butley Mills' – trawled from the pages of a wonderful volume somewhat ponderously entitled *Victorian and Edwardian Windmills and Watermills from Old Photographs*. A lot of what we're modelling as the settings of our railways comes under the general heading of Industrial Archaeology – which is yet another field rich in published material of all sorts, from the learned journals of bodies like the Newcomen or Trevithick societies through the various regional 'Industrial Archaeology of XXXX' series from publishers like David & Charles and related industry-specific books to general industrial archaeological periodicals like *Archive*. Within this wide field are books not just on process and extractive industries – principal justifications and traffic sources for many a model railway – but also on industrially linked transport and infrastructure, of which canals, tramways and worker's 'model' housing are but the more obvious examples.

On that vernacular note, the study and recording of old buildings is another discipline which has thrown up a huge body of written and illustrative material that can be a major source for us modellers. The monumental *Buildings of England* series of handbooks, edited by Nicklaus Pevsner and Bridget Cherry and produced on a county-by-county basis, lists just about every building of merit or historical importance. Alongside which, many towns or local history societies have produced their own booklets on interesting local structures and the vernacular peculiarities of their district. Once again, local libraries can often help in locating

LEFT: *Another specialist field with strong links to railways is industrial archaeology, again supported by a wide range of books, periodicals and specialist societies. The picture of Heybridge Mill featured in this spread was a key element of the design of my 'Butley Mills' layout of 1986.* Author

ABOVE: *And here is the resulting model of Heybridge Mill, which formed such a vital component of 'Butley Mills'; it hid the fiddleyard!* Author

these somewhat-obscure publications. Far more accessible (sold just about everywhere!) but no less useful, are the wide-ranging Shire Publications series of handbooks and albums, modest but informative tomes. They have lists covering such useful topic areas as Architecture and Street Furniture, Social History, Canals and Waterways, Industrial History, Road Transport, Local History, and Rural Life. Where else could you readily find pithy information on beach huts, pargeting, privies, thatching, cob buildings, signposts and milestones, pillar-boxes, farm buildings, water pumps, farm wagons, horsedrawn vehicles and machinery, heavy horses and harness, dry-stone walls, ploughing, sailing barges, steam shovels, limekilns, and the London Taxi? The list is almost endless, and all for only £5 a pop.

Virtual research

There is, of course, one further immensely powerful and far-reaching research corridor open to everyone with the necessary hardware – the Internet. While the Net may not have produced any new prime-source material, it has made what's already out there vastly more accessible – as well as enabling archives to be compiled, cross-checked and cross-referenced worldwide. The range of topics to be found lurking in the Ether is almost limitless, and both the railway and vernacular setting fields are amazingly well-covered. While local history sites and the like are generally free and open, don't expect too much direct access to railway archives, certainly not in a British context where so much material is in the hands of private individuals, traders and the various specialist societies – none of whom have any remit to make such material freely available in downloadable form. In the USA, where there's a powerful 'freedom of information' culture, much more original material *is* directly accessible via the Web, but UK prototype information sites tend – by and

BELOW: *There are some excellent and authoritative railway and vernacular history websites which can be invaluable. Here's one of the best I've come across, the Northumbrian Railways site (**www.northumbrian-railways.co.uk**). As one of my current projects is a Co. Durham colliery branch, this has been an absolute goldmine.* Author

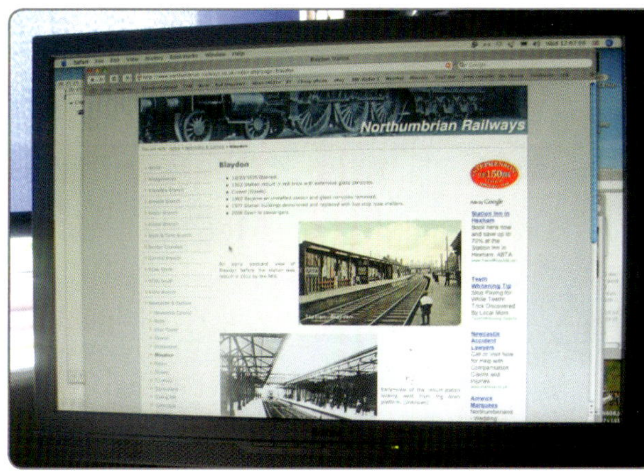

large – have an indexing or linking role, pointing you at the location of the source.

Nice though it would be to be able to directly access and download, say, the entire 'Lens of Sutton' photographic collection, the existence of on-line listings of the material available and the source from which it may be obtained makes a pretty good starting point. At present, though, the vast majority of this material is still retailed in conventional hard-print form; commercial considerations aside, the sheer amount of work and computer memory involved in scanning, indexing and archiving the umpteen-million railway images and source documents that are scattered in collections throughout the UK is pretty daunting. I expect it'll happen in time, but for now we still have to go the long way round. However, all that is not to under-play the invaluable role of the Internet as a stunningly fast and effective way of discovering what's out there. Typing a well-phrased query into a search engine will, in a few tenths of a second, throw up thousands of possible sources of information, while many specialist indexing web-sites list the locations of pretty much all the material available on a given topic. Looked at in this way, the Net is the world's fastest short-cut. I've listed some of the most useful 'portal' and indexing sites in the Sources appendix.

Fieldwork

No matter how much research material you amass from secondary sources, nothing beats a field trip for gaining a real first-hand understanding of a place. Even where – as in the case of East Anglia – actual railway remains are hard to find, such a field trip is still the best way to garner general background information to flesh out the photographs, maps and plans. Just walking around an environment with your eyes wide open, camera at the ready and notebook to hand, you'll reap a wealth of useful material. As well as establishing fundamentals such as typical landforms (How steep are slopes? What is the nature of the watercourses? What are the characteristics of underlying rocks and soils?), you can determine the nature and disposition of trees, hedges and general vegetation. Much vernacular architecture, by its very nature, is there to inspire and be recorded, even if you have to make allowance for modern 'improvements' such as ill-proportioned plastic windows, concrete tiles in place of slate or clay and ill-judged pebbledash or artificial wall claddings. First hand is also the best way to gain a true appreciation of colourings: of soils, stonework and other building materials, and of mosses, lichens, watermarks and other weathering agents; photographs, notes and a few suitable soil samples can be a big help when it comes to the actual modelling. Rummaging around can also uncover all manner of modellogenic minor details: odd bits of street furniture, old fences and field-gates, less obvious facets of the vernacular infrastructure such as characteristic street paving, drainage ditches or culverts.

Basic equipment needed for such general 'background' field trips is not extensive: the relevant two-and-a-half-inch OS sheet, a camera (preferably digital, as that gives you an instant results check, a macro-zoom facility and low-light performance a conventional film camera just can't match), a notebook and pencils, suitable transport, stout shoes and a packet of sandwiches should about do it. Oh yes, this being Britain don't forget the umbrella! The other truly useful tool is a laptop computer, the relevance of which is revealed in the section on archiving. In the field, while the camera is the primary tool, sketching is also useful; surprisingly often,

LEFT: *Field trip equipment, Rice style: 1:25000 OS map, 10-metre tape measure, notebook and pencils, somewhat-vintage digital camera (rangefinder type – better in bright sun, as you don't have to compose on-screen), laptop computer, lunch-box (with cheese-and-pickle sandwiches) and good big Thermos of tea. All fits in a rucksack for bicycle-born transport where possible.* Author

you just can't get where you need to be to take a particular photo, while a drawing can be usefully amplified with written notes. While you're physically in your area of study, don't forget to take a quick look in the local book, antique or junk shop in search of that battered shoebox full of old postcards and any useful locally-produced publications. Local libraries or museums are also well worth an hour or two; museums, particularly, are often staffed by people who are both enthusiastic and knowledgeable and who'll take delight in pointing you in the right direction over all manner of local matters. One very useful source that they may well hold are old local trade directories, which will tell you what sort of businesses and industries existed in your target area and period, as well as providing authentic names for the traders. Good material when compiling a rationale for a 'might-have-been' prototype.

Assembling a prototype source archive

You won't be far down the background research road before you find yourself drowning in a sea of disparate material: books, photographs, maps, plans, notes, sketches, photocopies, lists, old magazines, railway documents and pamphlets. Getting all this lot into some sort of order, such that it forms a usable archive to inform the layout-designing process, is a pretty tall order. At this stage, we're mostly interested in broad outlines rather than fine detail, which means that photocopies of material originating in books or magazines are adequate for our purposes – and a lot easier to file and refer to during the actual pencil-pushing business. A ring-binder and individual plastic page sleeves I've found to be the best way of managing such paper-based material, the file clearly divided up into sections classified by the aspect of the layout to which they relate: geography, landscape, vernacular setting, civil engineering and railway engineering – track, signalling and structures – all grouped by functional relevance: plain line, station approach, passenger station, goods yard, locomotive facilities. That way, all the reference relating to a particular aspect of the prototype *should* all be in the same place. Don't forget that, when actually designing the layout, all this prototype reference has to be consulted in conjunction with the material relating to practical aspects of the project – so make sure that ring binder's a good big one!

Nowadays, fortunately, we have an alternative to this sea of paper. I refer, of course, to that indispensable adjunct to modern life, the personal computer. Or, better still, the personal *laptop* computer – a device which could have been invented with the layout-designer in mind. A laptop enables us to assemble our mass of material into one simple, compact, instantly accessible cross-referenced but easily-portable source. That portability is a key asset; the laptop can be taken on field trips – to compare what you're looking at with other reference and to enter images and other material directly into the archive – while back at home, it can perch on the edge of the drawing board while you're designing and be kept at hand at every stage throughout construction. My battered and well-travelled Powerbook is now the second most essential item in my layout-designing

ABOVE: *A laptop computer is a great tool for assembling, storing and accessing a prototype archive, which can be brought together with site plans, design sketches, notes, lists and all manner of other design aids – all accessible at the click of whatever-it-is-you-click on a laptop!* Author

toolkit, giving place only to the humble HB pencil and pad without which I can do nothing! I'm not well-versed in matters computational, apart from finding Mr Apple's devices generally less intimidating to the non-technical than the 'other sort', so the only thing I would say about the actual machine is that for archiving work a bigger screen (mine is 15in) is to be preferred as it enables you to have several photos or other sources displayed at once – and at a decent size.

In conjunction with a desktop scanner and a digital camera, and using straightforward picture-manipulation, word-processing, spreadsheet and database software, the computer enables you to combine all the information from your various sources into one universal and easily-accessible format. It can happily handle photographs direct from the camera or scanned from prints or books, together with scanned notes and lists, documents, plans and drawings, weblinks and 'hard' information. The only fly in the ointment is that photos scanned in from printed sources like books or magazines will usually not reproduce cleanly, as the dot screen of the printed image interacts with the screen of the scanner to give a moiré effect. The way around this little difficulty is simply to take a snap of the printed photo with the digital camera, which seems to avoid the problem.

At the end of this lengthy inspiration-seeking, researching and archive-compiling process, you should have the answer to the first fundamental question on which the layout design will be based: the 'What?' All that now remains is to sort out the second part of the equation, the 'How?' That is the business of the actual formal design process, which is where we go next.

6 RATIONALES, LISTS AND LOGISTICS

Having sorted out our potential subject matter – at least in outline – and amassed plenty of prototype material to draw on, we can start on the formal business of turning this mix of raw material and general intention into a workable, detailed layout design. This amounts, I'd suggest, to rather more than scribbling a few lines on a beer mat or the back of an old envelope. In fact, as I see it, a fully fledged layout design comprises three or four discrete elements – the exact number depending upon whether the layout sets out to model an actual piece of railway, or something that is to a greater or lesser degree fictitious. The core trio, common to all subjects, are: the Prototype Archive, the Layout Specification and the Plan. To which those of us indulging in a little fiction need to add that fourth element, inserted immediately after the archive: the Layout Rationale – effectively, a document supplying a proper history and background for our fictional subject, something that the prototype modeller can draw directly from his archive.

Of that core trio, the plan is the centre point – for it's in the drawing of the plan that the 'What?' half of the design process meets the 'How?' Plan drawing and track planning – as distinct from the broader aspects of layout designing – is a fascinating discipline in its own right, and forms the subject of a separate chapter. Coming up with a good plan is no easy task, as every single potential piece of the jigsaw has to be considered from at least three standpoints: 'Is it prototypical?' 'Is it practicable?' and 'Will it look good?' The plan-drawing process is made considerably harder in the case of the fictional subject, as there's also the matter of deciding exactly what to include – something the prototype modeller doesn't have to worry about; his nemesis is usually squeezing everything in! A lot of people assume that designing without a prototype straightjacket is the easier option, an assertion I'd challenge; in such unfettered circumstances, it's all-too-easy to end up with an unlikely hodgepodge or to simply over-egg the pudding and try and stir too much into the mix. Refining the 'wish list' of possibilities is an important preliminary of the plan-drawing process.

The last element of the design, the Layout Specification, evolves alongside the Plan and provides definitive answers to the 'How?' part of the design equation. Carefully considering the execution of a layout project during its planning is the best way of ending up with something that's a pleasure to build rather than a series of 'How the

ABOVE: *Layout designing is the process of reconciling the prototypical aspirations with the practical limitations to create what is, effectively, the best possible compromise. Here we see key elements of the job: prototype data, a site survey, a detailed layout specification, plans and sketches.* Author

BELOW: *The plan, Moriarty, the plan… The centrepiece of any layout design, but by no means the only essential. Note that this proposal – which has pretty steep topography – also includes a set of levels, in the form of a vertical section.*

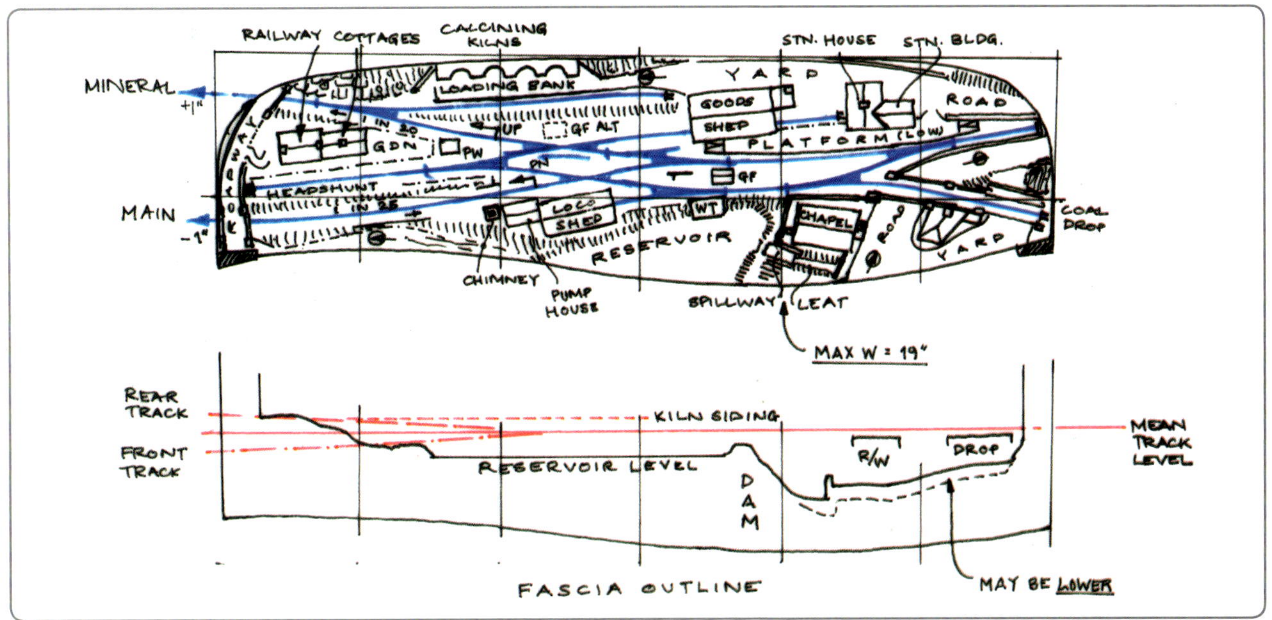

hell do I do/afford this?' headaches. The starting point for the evolutionary stage of the design process takes the form of the compilation of a pair of 'key lists' – effectively, the 'wish list' and the corresponding list of constraints. Refining the wish list while taking account of these constraints is a vital stage of the whole design business, as it determines the exact criteria to which you're actually designing. From this will spring, not just the content of the model, but the *precise* details – materials, methods, components, costs, required skills, timescales – of its construction. These details, rounded out with relevant technical and catalogue information and sources for the hardware or services needed, are the meat of the layout specification. Creation of a really useful layout specification is another task for which the computer is the ideal tool, for all the same reasons that make it such a good archiving aid.

The layout rationale

This is an aspect of layout planning that follows on closely from the compilation of a prototype archive; indeed, some might question whether it's a topic that belongs in this chapter at all – maybe it should have been included in the last? But I prefer to regard the creation of a layout rationale for a fictional subject as part of the design process, an important component of the written material that lies alongside the plan. For those many of us setting out to represent a line that in reality never got further than a speculative squiggle on a map – let alone something even more fictional or fantastical, involving the creation of landscapes and places that have no existence outside our imaginations – then setting down a carefully contrived and convincing justification of our make-believe is an essential (and enjoyable) part of the planning process. Basically, a layout rationale is a 'fictional history' – a document that sets out in some detail the economic, social and geographic background to what it is you're intending to model. I think it's very important to get this justification right – for if the underlying rationale is unrealistic and unconvincing, then what chance will the model have of ringing true?

As a layout-designing tool, the rationale is also important in determining the 'why?' that results in the definitive 'what?' Reference to the 'history' will influence a wide range of decisions about the content of the model, from the exact facilities needed through the engineering and architectural styles to be employed, the signalling and other proprietary hardware used, the nature of the railway's surroundings and the traffic that will be carried over it. The more fictional your subject, the more detailed and well-informed this rationale will need to be; conversely, the closer you keep to reality, the less you need to invent. For instance, a few years ago I designed a GW branchline terminus set in my former home-town of Chagford, Devon. This was strictly speaking a 'fictional' subject, in that no Chagford branch was ever completed, but in this instance, the fiction was only marginal, as such a line was proposed, surveyed and approved by Parliament (the Exeter, Teign Valley & Chagford Railway, 1883 *et seq.*). Parts of the Chagford branch even got as far as some earthworks before the money ran out! As the surveys and plans of this abortive scheme (and at least three others!) are still extant in the public record, the model design was simply based on the full-sized proposals and the accompanying rationale drawn directly from the prospectus of the real railway company.

Even if you choose to place a completely fictional railway in a real and defined geographic setting – as with Peter Denny's 'Buckingham, GC' or, come to it, the various iterations of the East Suffolk Light – then much of the necessary rationale will also already exist in reality, needing but a modicum of research and some modest embellishment to provide the 'prototype bones' of your layout design. That said, insinuating a fictional railway convincingly into

BELOW: *Fictional layouts need convincing rationales for realism. Although the whole 'East Suffolk Light' is but the merest fairy tale, a carefully researched and geographically accurate setting, together with the use of real subjects for vernacular structures, trains and details, gave the resulting models an air of verisimilitude. This is the quay at Orford Haven, precisely located on an inlet of the River Ore at Oxley Marsh.* Alan Dench, courtesy Bob Barlow

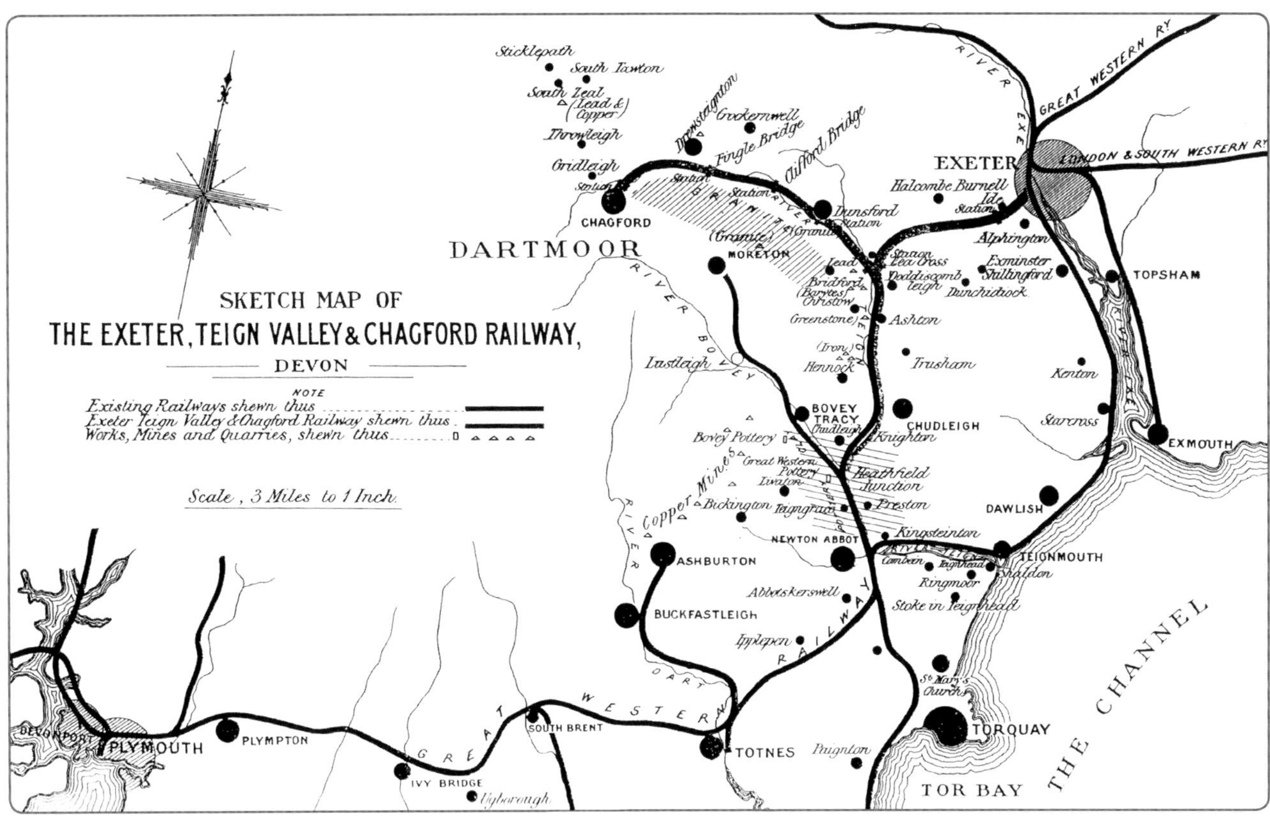

a factual setting is a challenge in it's own right, calling for some careful 'surveying' on the ground and plenty of painstaking map-work – in which context I've found the satellite-image-based Google Earth on-line mapping system an absolutely invaluable adjunct to the mandatory OS maps. Another popular halfway option is to modify an actual location to suit your own devices – which again should only involve a little tinkering at the margins of reality. I have a little convention in this regard, in that I marginally change the spelling of the place-name to reflect this departure from true-to-prototype modelling.

It's when you come to the totally imaginary subject that you have to work hardest in creating a believable rationale. In fact, unless you're intent on modelling the railways of Middle Earth or the Hogwarts Express, I'd suggest that wild flights of the imagination are both inadvisable and unnecessary; the composite approach – taking slabs of historical reality (railway and vernacular) and combining them in a fictional manner – works as well in concocting a realistic rationale as

ABOVE: *Choosing to model a railway that was proposed and authorised but never built can get you an instant rationale. Here is the 'sketch map' that accompanied the prospectus of the Exeter, Teign Valley & Chagford Railway, from the files of the Public Record Office at Kew.* Courtesy of PRO

RIGHT: *Ultimate layout rationale? Producing a complete fictional 'history' of your proposed railway is a lot of fun, even if it's a tad OTT to go to the lengths of a complete typeset book… The 'ESL' 'history', got up to look like an Oakwood Press booklet of the 1970s, uses pictures of the resulting models to 'illustrate' the fiction on which they were founded.*

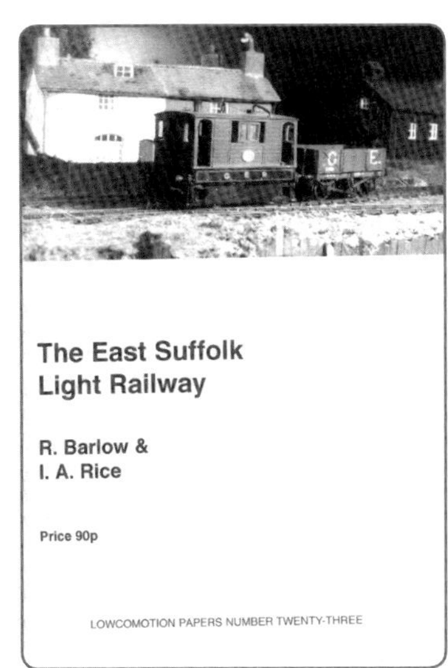

CHAPTER TWO

THE ROUTE DESCRIBED

The northern extremity and starting-point of the East Suffolk Light route lies in the end-on junction with the Mid-Suffolk Light's branch from Kenton Junction to Debenham. The actual point of junction lies 3 chains 16 yards north of the level crossing over the Cade's Green to Debenham road, which point also forms the limit of the ESL's Debenham station. Adjacent to the junction now lies the extensive Deben Vale creamery of the Ipswich branch of the Co-operative Wholesale Society; the current buildings were erected in 1935.

The Debenham goods depot lies immediately to the south of the road crossing, and consists of a commodious timber goods shed built by the Debenham & Ipswich Railway for the opening of the line, a loading bank and cattle dock. A crane of 30 cwt. capacity is provided, and there is stabling for a dray horse and extensive sack storage. Entering the station proper, the line passes behind the brick-built locomotive shed erected in 1924 to replace the earlier D& I structure destroyed by fire in 1920. The water-tank holds 3000 gallons and is replenished by a petrol-powered pump fed by the brook supplying Deben Mills;a small coaling stage is also provided.

The modest timber station building also dates back to the opening of the original D & I line in 1874, and stands at the northern end of the station on the remaining section of the original low platform; the rest of the platform was rebuilt, extended and raised during the late war. At the southern end of the platform the line crosses the mill brook on a short plate girder bridge, installed in 1934 to replace the original timber structure. The line climbs briefly at 1 in 42 past the coal yard operated by Messrs. D. Radleigh & Co, served by a siding off the loop line. A further siding serves the former flour mill, which now produces animal feeds.

Also situated at the south end of the station is the signal small cabin built in 1942 when the line was upgraded for military

Debenham and Ipswich Railway No.5, a 4-4-0T acquired from the North London Railway in 1889. It was designed by William Adams and built at Bow Works in 1865. The engine worked on the East Suffolk until 1905. *(C. Langley Aldrich)*

A view of the ESL's motive power depôt at Orford Haven, taken in 1900. The building in the right foreground is the original station, replaced when the line was extended to Butley and Orford. Latterly, it was used as an office and store. *(L & CRP)*

it does in producing a model that convinces visually. Writing a detailed history of the supposed line – perhaps using a real railway history as a model – can be both entertaining and educational. It's well worth taking the trouble to make it comprehensive, covering not just the actual location that you're intent on modelling, but the rest of the imaginary line of which it forms a part. Referring to the paper account of the non-modelled parts of your 'prototype' can inform the design of the bits that *are* being reproduced.

Indeed, a comprehensive rationale like this can serve more than one layout; several of my Suffolk essays (all three 'Debenham' layouts, 'Orford Haven' and 'Butley Mills') have been based on the common fiction of the East Suffolk Light Railway, the rationale of which eventually progressed to the point of a complete dummy vintage mid-1970s Oakwood Press-style 'Locomotion Paper' line history (available, of course, from all good fantastical bookshops, price 90 Gallions!). This effort was properly typeset, included maps, timetables and bogus documents, and was spuriously illustrated by suitable prototype photographs set alongside pictures of the various models. Bob Barlow and I found that fabricating such detailed background story fixed firmly in our own minds the various features of our subject, as well as throwing up a plethora of pertinent questions for the research list. It thus formed an essential part of the armchair phase of the layout design, playing an important role in compiling the all-important wish list. It was also a whole lot of fun in its own right, and with its aid we even managed to fool a few people into believing that the East Suffolk Light had actually existed!

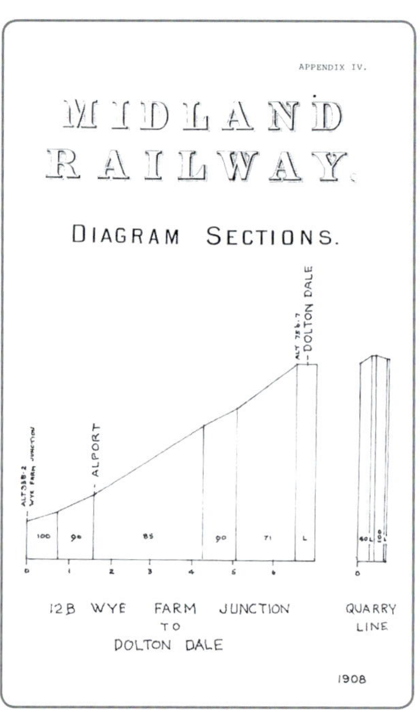

RIGHT AND BELOW: *A couple of pages from a very well thought-out and beautifully executed layout rationale, that for Gwilym McCoach's fictional but utterly believable 'Dolton Dale' – a branch line the Midland Railway never knew it had, set in the eastern Peak District. Here are the gradient profile and route-map – complete with authentic Midland Railway typesetting.*

MIDLAND RAILWAY DISTANCE DIAGRAM. SCALE 1 INCH TO 1 MILE.
(MATLOCK DISTRICT).
SHEET 14.
(Sixth Edition.)
APPENDIX III.

The art of the list

Ah yes, those lists. Much of my basic thinking in evolving and refining a layout concept revolves around the use of the list

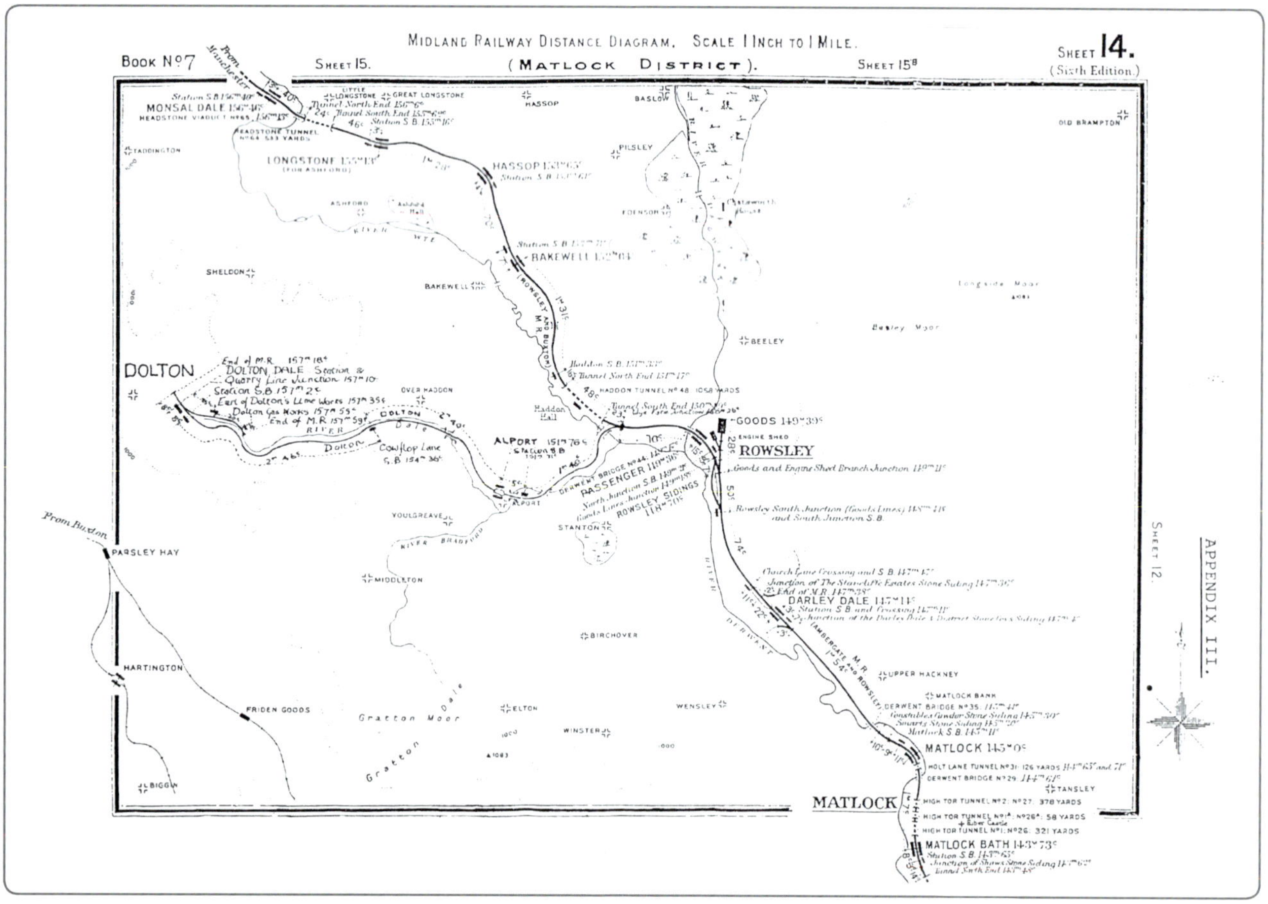

Hepton High Moor. - Exhibition Cameo, replace H-W

Same theme/Locale as Hepton Wharf - see ammended rationale. BUT based on ROSEDALE EAST. Period c 1920. To use H-W locos & stock + Rapid Shunter. Steam R/MOTOR?

Want List.
1) Coal Drop as Rosedale E
2) Calcining kilns " "
3) Rly. Cottages - Blakeney Junc
4) LARGE Chapel Holmfirth?
5) Loco shed (Middleton, C+HP.)
6) Station? Pass. trains?? What prototype?? – LEADHILLS & WANLOCKHEAD
7) Very plain stone goods shed of Rosedale E – NIDD VALLEY
8) Reservoir/engine pond with dam.
9) Large vertical component for scenery.
10) ONE-PIECE CAMEO
11) Plug-in fiddleyards with cassettes – L&Y only or L&Y/LNW. (See rationale)
12) Jigsaw scenics
13) Spine construction ??
14) Signalling (if poss.)
15) Plastic structures - Wills s/series
16) Remote point operation
17) To take Barton-Wright 0-6-0 (Ironclad)

Given List
1) Max length = 6'0" (to fit Volvo estate)
2) To use H-W support system + lights + drapes.
3) Median standard/spec as H-W PCB track?
4) Max gradient 1 in 25/4%. (and that's probably pushing it!)
5) Still DC, not DCC.
6) Auto couplings as H-W.
7) One-person operation
8) No Portescap motors - AMR H/H controller only.
9) Use new H-W power box

RIGHT: *Yet another page from the indispensable notebook – in this case, the initial 'druthers' and 'givens' for Hepton High Moor. ('Druthers' was a term invented by John Armstrong for a 'wants list'; it is, allegedly, a contraction of 'I'd rather', as in 'I'd rather have this than that…') Note that the lists throw up questions as well as answers!*

and its interrogative counterpart, the questionnaire. A well-constructed list not only sets out objectives of the design, but can also point the way to achieving them. My layout-planning lists take many forms: the key lists of wishes and constraints; the sources list (information to hand) and its counterpart, the research questionnaire, detailing those questions to which I need to find answers. Then there are lists of available resources: the locomotives and rolling stock available or around which the new layout will be structured, any stocks of unused material and components to hand and those items – PW, electrical components, signals or structures – reclaimed from previous layouts now departed. Hopefully, there might even be a disposals list of things not needed, choice titbits which can be slapped on eBay or the club bring-and-buy table and sold handsomely to offset the damage done by the inevitable shopping list. More practically, the nuts-and-bolts aspects of the design will throw up yet more lists: the materials list, task/technique lists (the jobs you will need to do and how best to do them), the tool list and, most importantly, the help list – 'people whose arms I can twist to do the jobs I can't tackle.'

The list of lists is long in itself, as lists beget more lists; but despair not, because they are the great refining and organising tool that enables you to boil things down to a practicable, achievable project. At the end of the list-making day, you'll end up with a few bits of paper (or, hopefully, a few megabytes-worth of computer files) that will form the basis of both the design and its execution. This forms the all-important layout specification which, besides setting out the technical basis of the design, will also incorporate a summary of the overall aims and objectives and a 'how I'm going to do it' project plan. Such a plan chez Rice usually comprises an optimistic budget, a rough timetable, a lengthy shopping list and a daunting task list, the latter tied to that essential arm-twisting help list. Organising these various lists – particularly the fundamental wish list – to be as concise and meaningful as possible is a good layout-designing discipline; it's all too easy to keep adding items, particularly to what might be termed the 'cake' end of things! Here, I find that the pertinent self-question is usually 'Can I do without a …?' rather than 'Wouldn't it be nice to have a …?' The key objective of the listing process is to refine and define the many criteria that go into a holistic layout design, to end up with the best – and best balanced – overall solution. This is a process that starts with the setting out of those two key lists – the first task in that all-important armchair phase of the design process.

Key lists

That doyen of American layout designers, John Armstrong, set great store by this duet, which he christened 'Druthers' and 'Givens' – effectively, a wish list and a woe list. Put baldly, the first of them sets out all the things you *want* to include in the layout – and the second enumerates all the reasons why you can't have them. The task is to reconcile the two. Compiling a prototype-ingredient wish list *can* be very simple, as at one extreme – setting out to model an actual location to the scale and standards to which you are already committed – it can be reduced to a single item as in: 'To build an X scale/Y standards model of the station/goods yard/junction/MPD or whatever at Z as it was in 19XX'. Effectively, the list becomes the layout summary in one step. Done and dusted, move straight on to

LEFT: *A peachy layout design element from a rather unusual old postcard; you don't often find expensive tinted cards like this depicting such a commonplace (but attractive and highly modellogenic) scene. This arrangement of wooded hillside, level crossing, MR signalbox, crossing cottage, lamp and fences would work superbly as one end of a shelf-layout scene.* Author's collection

LEFT: *Here's a design element to define a whole layout – a tramway (industrial, in this case) winding between the houses on a narrow right-of-way. This is the Leiston Tramway in Suffolk; it's figured high on the 'wish list' for several of my schemes.* Author's collection

LEFT: *Sometimes you find something so absolutely drop-dead gorgeous that you find yourself designing a complete layout around it. This is Marley Hill cabin on the Tanfield Railway, sited where the line to the incline head crossed the 'main line'. Coming up with a layout configuration centred on this track arrangement has proved challenging!* Author

the detailed practical planning… However, the further you get from such tight-focus prototypical simplicity, the longer and more complex the wish list of things to be modelled will inevitably become; with a typical fictional/might-have-been layout, you can soon end up with a bewildering range of candidates for inclusion. The job of the listing process is to effectively 'interview' each candidate and assess its pros and cons, gradually eliminating the more far-fetched and less practicable subjects until you are left with balanced and complementary grouping that can be brought together into a satisfactory design.

A prototype-ingredient wish-list is basically made up of all those things you've come across that are just crying out to be modelled and included in the design: the station buildings from X, the goods yard entry pointwork from Y, that gorgeous cast-iron overbridge from Z… If you're anything like me, this list of peachy must-haves would happily fill a site measuring several times the space available and account for a couple of decade's-worth of modelling time, and, of course, there will be many elements of the potential layout for which your list includes two or more equally appealing candidates. Deciding which of these many temptations you're going to give way to and choosing between alternatives for individual features is either a case of going with gut-feeling or, where this somewhat-nebulous indicator is absent, evaluating and 'scoring' the choices in such a way that a clear pecking order eventually appears. In most cases – where the list is modest and the options limited – this isn't too difficult to achieve with a spot of pencil-chewing and diligent reference to the layout rationale.

BELOW: *Not all the possible design elements that figure on the wish-list are major features; peachy incidentals such as this minor occupation crossing with its characteristic SR concrete-post fencing, 'double-X' gate with wicket and sloping approach path (it's in Bodmin, I fancy) has appeared in several Rice designs.* Author's collection

Where things are less clear-cut – typically where the starting-point is vague and the possibilities many, or where it's necessary to choose between several equally attractive and appropriate alternatives for specific elements of the layout – then it's useful to extend this ranking concept somewhat and evaluate each item a little more scientifically. This I do by scoring potential layout features according to specific criteria using a structured list, as described below.

Alongside the 'prototype ingredients' wish-list sits a second table of wants, covering the various technical, practical and artistic desiderata. This includes criteria such as the standards to be used, the quality benchmark being aimed at and the degree of portability required, as well as such fundamentals as the type of control (analogue DC or digital DCC, with or without sound), the sophistication of the lighting set-up and the presentational style and finish. Also on this list might appear the possible operating styles and control philosophies, some thoughts on couplings and on the fiddleyard solutions that might work. Some of these criteria are fundamental to the nature of the layout, and at many points in the design you're back to comparing options – in which case the ranking system suggested below can be useful.

List structuring

At its most basic, a layout wish list is just, well, a series of items set out in sequence – usually in the form of a column – on a piece of paper. That's useful, but by adding extra columns to this basic listing we can create something a great deal more powerful. So, for instance, such a list can be broadly prioritised by simply adding a column for a 'must-haveness' score – a measure of how important a particular item or feature is in context. To further sort the wheat from the chaff, we can extend this scoring principle: a 'leg-up' column can give an indication of the availability of suitable RTR models, kits, components, or other useful items, while a third extra column can indicate whether adequate prototype information is to hand. Yet another column can be used to assess the degree of effort or difficulty involved in including that particular feature, and so on.

For prioritising purposes, simply allocating a score out of ten under each of these headings enables an overall ranking score to be arrived at. These 'marks out of ten' are awarded in direct proportion to an item's desirability, availability or accessibility, and in inverse proportion to its difficulty or cost. So a 'must have' might score 9 for desirability but only 3 if there are no appropriate kits or bits, with a median 5 if there's a reasonable amount of data but perhaps only 1 if the thing looks like being a pig to build. Just adding the scores under all these headings together across the page gives an overall ranking number – yup, another column! And

New Hey - Wish List

	A	B	C	D	E	F	G	H	I	J
1	Item or feature	Des.	Acc	Info	Ease	Score	Kit/part	Information	Cost	Go For
2										
3	LNWR timber station	10	8	9	4	31	Parkside	Nelson P126-7	£30.00	√
4	LNWR timber platform	10	3	9	3	25	Scratch/stripwood	Nelson P121		√
5	LNWR Type 4 sig box	10	6	9	6	31	LRM kit	Nelson P54	£25.00	√
6	LNWR small goods shed	7	2	4	2	15	Scratch/styrene sheet	Nelson P142		
7	LNWR water tank (cf Alex Yd)	8	4	7	4	23	Scratch/styrene sheet	LNW Jnl?		√
8	LNWR tank w coal stage	6	4	9	3	22	Scratch/styrene sheet	Nelson P79		
9	LNWR Column w/tank	6	3	9	2	20	Scratch	Nelson P86		
10	LNWR 1-road loco shed	7	3	2	3	15	Scratch/styrene sheet	Nelson P72		
11	LNW Timber coal stage	8	5	9	6	28	Scratch/sheet ply or styrene	Nelson P78		√
12	Level crossing (LNW gates)	10	5	4	7	26	Anybody do an LNW gate?	?		√
13	LNW skew span bridge w jack beams	9	5	5	5	24	Scratch/Plastruct/Wills	LVW book		√
14										
15										
16	L & Y Ground frame (Rochdale yard)	9	6	6	4	23	Scratch/styrene sheet	Rys Rnd Rochdale		√
17	L & Y Railmotor halt	9	6	4	5	24	Scratch	L & Y Misc 2		√
18	L & Y Road overbridge (girder)	7	4	4	5	20	Scratch/Wills sheet abutments	?		√
19	L & Y lge goods warehouse	10	5	5	5	25	Scratch/Wills sheet/Langley wind	Ramsbottom		√
20	L & Y shunter's bothy	6	5	3	4	18	Scratch			??
21	L & Y loco service point (Rose Bank)	8	5	5	5	23	Scratch + MM casting	L & Y 150		√
22										
23	Low-relief mill (New Hall Hey)	9	6	8	5	27	Scratch/Wills sheet/Langley wind	Foxline bk 33		√
24	Terrace of houses (Bolton)	9	5	7	5	24	Scratch/Wills sheet/Langley wind	L & Y Misc 2		√

ABOVE: *Structured list with scores.*

if by now you're thinking: 'By golly, that sounds like a job for a computer spreadsheet' then you're spot-on; prioritised list-making is another task in which the trusty laptop is invaluable.

That being so, it's no problem to add a set of further columns for notes under the key heading of 'sources': somewhere to identify kit and component suppliers, the location of (or need to locate) prototype information, and who might be called on to provide assistance for aspects that need to be 'bought in'. These columns form the basis of lists in their own right: the 'shopping list', 'research questionnaire' and 'help list'. They can also incorporate cross-referencing to the prototype archive, to trade catalogues or websites and to the details of specialists whose services you might need. One last column that it is as well to add to the spreadsheet mêlée is that of cost – or at least estimated cost. Unless you're a great deal better-heeled than yours truly, the expenditure called for by the various options is a factor that has to be taken into account when making those final decisions.

The 'Givens' list

Compiling the 'givens' or 'woe' list is a lot easier than arriving at a properly pared-down wish list, if usually more depressing! Essentially, it starts by setting out the limitations of the resources available – space, time, skills, money, materials and equipment – as accurately as possible. It will also incorporate such do-not-ignore criteria as the ruling radius for running line curves, the length of the largest projected loco and maximum train length to be accommodated, as well as such determinants as the proposed mode of operation (see next chapter) and the associated coupling choice. If you're stuck with using mass-produced track, then the available turnout types, angles and radii will also feature, as will the possible point-operating systems. For portable/exhibition layouts, the nature and size of space available for storage, the limitations imposed by any 'pinch points' on the route from resting-place to outside world and the dimensional restrictions of the intended mode of transport are also all relevant. A givens list has no place for wishful thinking, and I've always found it prudent to err on the pessimistic side when quantifying consumables like time and money.

To be a useful design tool, a givens listing has to be clear and easy to refer to at a glance. In fact, although it may start out as a simple list, it will almost certainly be necessary to put the information it contains into a variety of different forms: tables, templates, overlays and graphs. The templates and overlays come in more at the drawing stage, but the tables and graphs are useful for displaying information like train lengths or the linear space needed for specific items of rolling stock, clearing points relative to different turnout angles, and possible train formations and loadings compared graphically with curves and gradients. I illustrate such a useful design aid alongside: the 'equipment length' table for my BR/GE efforts.

The layout summary and specification

At the end of a successful working-over of a wish-list, interjected by the odd shower of cold water from the 'givens', it should be possible to summarise the basic intent, theme and content of the proposed layout in a few pithy sentences. These will form a 'Mission Statement' (to use now-speak) for the whole project. Effectively, this is the answer to the question: 'This new layout you're thinking of building – what's it going be, then?' If your reply strays beyond about three or four sentences and includes any 'errs' and 'maybes', then you probably have a little more list-refining to plough through! Subject, style, size, scale and standards are the stuff of a summary. That for 'Hepton Hey' – derived from the wish-list illustrated above – reads thus: West Yorkshire near Huddersfield *circa* 1910 with high-level LNWR branch terminus/mill complex, low-level L&Y goods depot, canal basin and railmotor halt. Cameo 6ft 3ins x 2ft 4ins with foam-and-ply baseboards, integral DC controls, fiddleyards and lighting. 4mm scale, P4, high level of detail: 'small but exquisite'. A snappy, 50-odd words summing up weeks of agonising – coupled with a considerable amount of additional research – that eliminated all manner of potential ingredients: an engine shed for the LNW (not prototypical), a rail-served canal warehouse (over-egging the pudding) an engine servicing siding on the low level (no room), some fancy bridgework (not typical) and several peachy vernacular

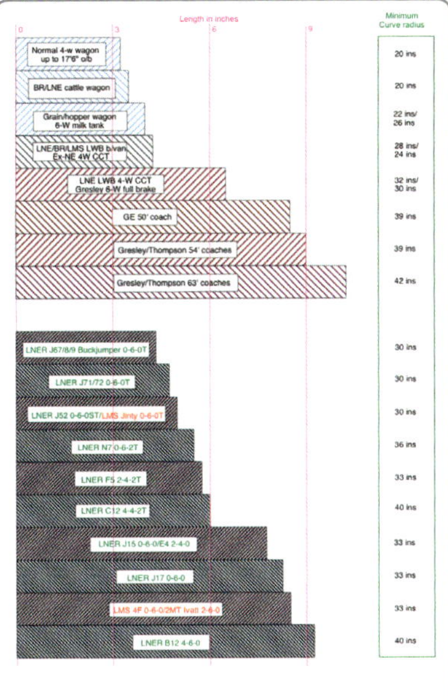

LEFT: *The chart of lengths and minimum curve radii for the locos and stock I use on my BR GE-section layouts. All the figures are derived from actual measurements and include allowance for couplings.*

buildings (not appropriate). It also pinned down such essentials as the exact location of Hepton Hey, the type of canal and its features, the status of the LNW branch and hence a typical track layout and suite of structures, and the origins and destinations of the trains and traffic. Much of this derived from the parallel establishment of the layout's rationale, as already described.

The layout specification covers much the same ground as the summary, but in exhaustive detail rather than concise outline. It also takes account of a further raft of considerations – practical and aesthetic – that go into the evolution of a fully-rounded design. A good layout spec includes precise particulars of *all* the various aspects of the proposed layout, set out under a series of headings. The ones I use are: baseboard structure, supporting system, presentation, lighting, trackbeds and PW, signalling, point and signal operating systems, layout control systems and wiring, power supply, landscaping (including surface textures, trees and other vegetation) and structures. Bundled together, I reckon this lot qualifies for the 'holistic' label to which I've attached such great importance! Each heading gets a page or several in the notebook during the armchair stage of the design, on which are recorded materials, fixings and adhesives, components, kits, tools and constructional methods to be used, any technical references in books, magazines or on the Web, catalogue references, sources and prices and so on. You can simply scan these pages into the computer to form your spec, but I find it's worth taking the trouble to create decent, workmanlike documents on the keyboard.

Layout logistics

If your layout is a strict stay-at-home, you can largely ignore these brief notes, which concern themselves mainly with those aspects of practical design related to the whole mad business of exhibiting. Strictly speaking, logistics is about the movement of information and supplies to a given point and end – but in model railway sense, the term is used to describe the whole business of making a layout disassemble and move readily and function well under exhibition conditions. Taking the trouble to really think about and plan in detail the means by which a layout goes together and comes apart always pays rich dividends, while making sure that what is intended to be readily portable is just that – light, wieldy, robust, and well-protected – is surely common sense. The exhibition layout with a baseboard module that is just a bit too long to reliably fit in any average estate car (5ft 6in for a Passat/Mondeo/Vectra/Octavia or similar, 6in longer for a Volvo V70/Saab 95/Citroën C5/Omega and Espace/Galaxy type people carriers) is a classic blunder, as are lumps of layout that are uncomfortably heavy or awkwardly-shaped. Come packing-up and going-home time, you'll bless the careful design that gives slick break-down, swift, neat and painless loading and a rattle-free ride home.

Detail design of exhibition layout infrastructure is a wide topic in its own right with the best examples exhibiting a high degree of sophistication, both in the matter of the layout structure and the way it is designed to pack away and move. The use of special crates and racks into which the various layout sections fit, carefully dimensioned to negotiate standard doorways, stairs and passageways and to readily fit specific vehicle types, equipped with heavy-duty castors and incorporating carrying handles, locking catches and anchorage points, are becoming increasingly common. Ingenious design often sees these transit arrangements doubling-up as the layout's supporting infrastructure at shows. The whole business has developed to the point of specific hardware becoming available, either adapted from other fields or custom-designed for the job: alignment and location devices, catches and securing systems, screw-adjusting 'levelling feet', ball-bearing slides for traverser or 'vertical stacker' fiddleyards and pivot systems for sector plates.

BELOW: *Sample of layout spec.*

Shaftesbury Layout Spec. **P.7**

Section 4: TRACK

4:01 Trackbeds:

Profile-cut from 12mm M.D.F.B. screwd to risers o/s line of PW..

4:02 Underlay:

a) Plain track: Woodland Scenics 4mm expanded vinyl strip. 1 pack required.
b) Turnouts: Carrs bonded cork 4mm; sheet or strip as required. 1 pack strip/1 sheet required

4:03 Underlay bonding:

Stuck to trackbed with Bostik 1 clear contact cement.

4:04 Plain running line:

C & L EM 3-bolt S1 moulded trackbase set out for 60' panels with SR-pattern closed-up joints. EMGS steel rail with railhead nicked for joints. Cosmetic joints to carry Riceworks etched 4-bolt fishplates. Sleeper base glued to underlay with Bostik Clear Hi-Strength. Peco pin on c/l at suitable intervals. Allow for 7m plain track (including station loop).

7 OPERATIONAL DESIGN

ABOVE: *Operation – the neglected art? A realistic model railway should not only look like the real thing, but work like it too. Ian Harrison brings a local working from Barnstaple into Tiverton Town station on Ted Farmer's EM gauge GWR layout. This is a truly versatile affair, bits of which can be exhibited in a number of forms as well as forming segments of a good-sized home layout that can be run 'by the book' and keep seven or eight operators on their toes.* Author

Determining how a layout is going to be operated is a decision that needs to be taken right from the outset, as it will affect virtually every other aspect of the design process. What I'm talking about here is not the *means* of operation – wiring, hardware or control position – but rather the underlying operating *philosophy*. 'Operating philosophy' or 'Operating stance' are terms better known on the sunset side of the Atlantic than here, being usually defined by reference to the lineside boundary fence. Thus, an 'outside the fence' operating stance is basically concerned with replicating the workings of the railway *as they appear to a casual lineside train-watcher*. That is, a succession of trains will pass the viewer (as on many exhibition layouts, in the form of a more-or-less-continuous parade), and maintaining an interesting, varied and entertaining procession is the primary goal of operation. At the opposite extreme, the full-monty 'inside stance' style of operation is a far sterner proposition, as it seeks to reproduce the proper working of the railway *from the point of view of the professional railwayman*. Here, the objective is to replicate as closely as possible the minutiae of full-size railway operation – strictly to timetable, observing all relevant rules and operating practices, employing only prototypical forms of communication, and often using all the appropriate documentation. Under this sort of exacting regime, relatively few trains will run, but those that do will do so properly, with prototypical intent and purpose.

There are degrees of fidelity within this broad spectrum, of course. While certain types of layout lend themselves only to a single, specific form of operation, many popular layout formats can be positioned somewhere towards the middle of a scale that ranges from 'random lineside parade' at one end to 'strictly by the book' at the other. While the typical British oval-format 'scene fed by staging' exhibition layout is essentially only capable of sustaining an 'outside' operating stance, this can still take considerable cognisance of the prototype niceties. Thus, the 'parade of trains' presented to the viewer can conform to a proper working timetable in many respects: train formations and headcodes, appropriate running speeds, observation of station stops or other operational requirements, and – of course – appearance of trains in the correct sequence. Further aiding the authenticity of the viewer's 'lineside experience', the line can be correctly signalled and the trains worked strictly in accordance with the signal indications, which can themselves be controlled by a properly worked lever-frame-equipped 'signalbox panel' complete with block instruments and bells, as on Tim Venton's superb 'Clutton'. This type of high fidelity 'outside' operation I would regard as being very close to the lineside fence, if not actually sitting right on it!

The pure by-the-book fully inside-stance operational main line layout is actually pretty rare on these shores, being rather more closely associated with large linear-plan American basement layouts. There are good reasons for this. The nature of working of many American railroads – usually single-track, relatively sparsely trafficked, unsignalled,

LEFT: *Here is the signalman's 'desk' on Tim Venton's 'Clutton' – probably the ultimate in authentic layout control. The lever frame is a complete (ie all levers present) replication of the real Clutton frame; it is fully interlocked both mechanically within itself and electrically with the single-line key token instruments. All the signalling (including ground signals) is present, working and controlled by the frame. Signalling communication is by bell-code, and working block instruments are installed. The 'model' signalman has to do pretty much everything his full-sized counterpart would have done.* Tim Venton

but centrally controlled by a dispatcher issuing written/telegraph orders or, for more-contemporary prototypes, by radio and CTC – lends itself far more readily to replication in miniature than does the typical traditional 'dense' British block-signalled, heavily trafficked railway, often double-track and effectively worked by dispersed control through a multitude of individual signalboxes. Few British 'scale' model railways anyway approach the site size and scope of the big US layouts, and here the torch of true 'inside stance' main line operation has largely been carried by a handful of clockwork-powered coarse-scale 0 gauge layouts – indoor or garden – of which the best-known have been John Ray's 'Crewchester', the Conway Model Railway in Harrow, North London, and the late Norman Eagles' 'Sherwood Section'. On such a layout, realism and authenticity in the modelling takes a decided second place to compression, complexity and uncompromising functionality; the late Cyril Freezer once memorably described the true 'operations man' as being '...quite happy to operate a string of tennis balls – provided they ran to timetable and obeyed all the signals'.

Authentic on the inside

However, that doesn't mean that the visually realistic style of British fine-scale layout is inherently incapable of supporting proper 'inside' operation. Far from it! Indeed, that most typical of British 'scale' model railways, the traditional steam-era country branch line terminus, is an example of a style of layout that can support absolutely by-the-book 'inside' operation, as it was in reality worked largely in isolation – timetable aside – from the rest of the railway network; pretty much everything that went on there can be reasonably authentically represented. Branch terminals enjoyed a high degree of autonomy; apart from the over-arching requirements of the Rule Book (often observed in the spirit rather than to the letter so far from the watchful eye of 'authority'!), they were usually subject only to the relatively gentle rigours of a none-too-demanding working timetable. That timetable was implemented by a small staff, under the direction of that awful autocrat, the Stationmaster. Of the various prototype roles under his command, the only ones we need to replicate on our model are those of the signalman, the goods clerk (to generate meaningful freight traffic), the crew of the branch passenger set (rarely more than one!), the

BELOW: *The key document on which real railway working is based is the Working Time Table. This is the prototype WTT for the Somerset & Dorset, and being able to replicate the workings detailed therein formed the chief design requirement for Henry Tasker's 'Bath Green Park to Midford' layout, determining many aspects of layout design.* Author

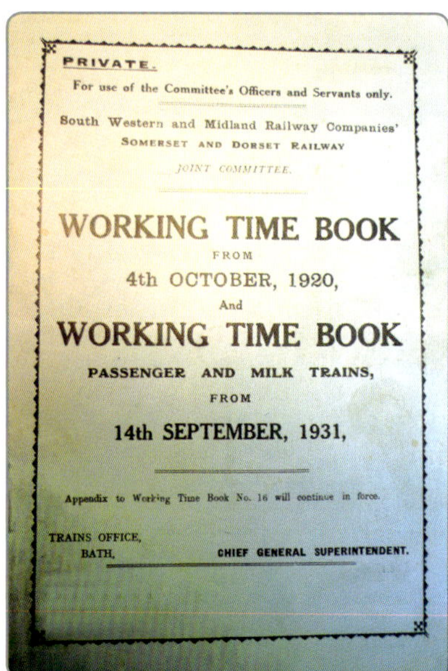

PRIVATE.

For use of the Committee's Officers and Servants only.

South Western and Midland Railway Companies'

SOMERSET AND DORSET RAILWAY

JOINT COMMITTEE.

WORKING TIME BOOK

FROM

4th OCTOBER, 1920,

And

WORKING TIME BOOK

PASSENGER AND MILK TRAINS,

FROM

14th SEPTEMBER, 1931,

Appendix to Working Time Book No. 16 will continue in force.

TRAINS OFFICE, BATH, CHIEF GENERAL SUPERINTENDENT.

RIGHT: *If you're modelling an imaginary prototype for authentic operation, then you'll need to come up with your own WTT (with due deference to the prototype at any point of junction with reality!). Here is an extract from the detailed WTT evolved by Gwilym McCoach for his fictional P4 'Dolton Dale' branch.* Gwilym McCoach

LONDON MIDLAND & SCOTTISH RAILWAY COMPANY.
(MIDLAND DIVISION).
Extracts from
THE WORKING TIME TABLE FOR FREIGHT TRAINS.
Effective 27th.September 1937 until further notice.

WEEKDAYS ONLY.

UP.

		Miles	Empties a.m.	Freight a.m.	W Cattle p.m.	Freight p.m.	Mineral p.m.
Dolton Dale	dep.	-	6.26	9.50	2.46	5.49	9.34
Alport	arr.	5 1/4				6.14	
	dep.	-	6.51	10.15	3.11	6.25	9.59
Wye Farm Junc.		6 3/4	7.0	10.24	3.20	6.34	10.8
Rowsley Sids.	arr.	7 3/4	7.7	10.31	3.27	6.41	10.15

DOWN

		Miles	Mineral a.m.	Freight a.m.	W Cattle a.m.	Freight p.m.	Empties p.m.
Rowsley Sids	dep.	-	4.41	7.45	8.30	3.50	7.34
Wye Farm Junc.		1	4.48	7.52	8.37	3.57	7.41
Alport	arr.	2 1/2		7B59		4B6	
	dep.		4.57	8.30	8.46	4.30	7.50
Dolton Dale	arr.	7 3/4	5A23	8B56	9.12	4B56	8C16

A:- Shunts Dolton Lime and Gas Works.
B:- Shunts as required.
C:- Shunts Dolton Lime Works.
W:- Wednesdays only.

.....2.

APPENDIX V.

crews of the once or twice-daily freight (including a shunter) and the crew of any through or special workings. All the other prototype tasks (apart, possibly, from the odd spot of PW or signal maintenance) are not relevant or reproducible in model terms.

So, in designing such a layout for 'inside' operation, what do we need to plan for? Well, for a start, we need an authentic and workable track layout, preferably drawn directly from a prototype, but certainly designed in accordance with strict prototype criteria. More on all that in the 'track planning' section of Chapter 9. The next requirement is closely related to track-planning – the provision and appropriate siting of all the necessary operational facilities, as determined by the demands of the working timetable (WTT), the traffic of the district, and the dictates of the operating department. For instance, if the WTT requires a coaching set to lie over while the yard is being shunted by the goods, it will be necessary to provide somewhere for said set to lie. And it will be the WTT as much as the dictates of the motive power department that determines the need for an out-posted engine and men – and hence the provision of the shed needed to accommodate them. As a 'common carrier', our railway also has to be in a position to handle *all* the traffic offering; in a country district, that will probably call for cattle pens (and a water supply), end-loading facilities, probably some basic lifting gear (a small crane, not always 'fixed'), a 'mileage siding' where carts can be backed direct up to wagons for loading, mineral-handling facilities – chutes, bins and so on – if appropriate, and perhaps a loading bank if a lot of parcels or 'smalls' traffic is worked. All that in addition to the basic provision of a goods lock-up or shed, weighing facilities and somewhere to handle coal – the one universal traffic.

The operating department will have a further raft of 'running' requirements: adequate loop or run-round lengths, shunting necks and shunt limits; sufficient stabling for the likely number of wagons required at busy times; carriage

BELOW: *'Model' branch-line station layouts, terminal and intermediate, as suggested by W. Hemingway-Mills in his 1898 handbook* Railway Construction. *Turntable aside, these are pretty typical examples of the genre. (W. H.-M. was a railway engineer in Ireland, where tender locos were usually used for branch workings).*

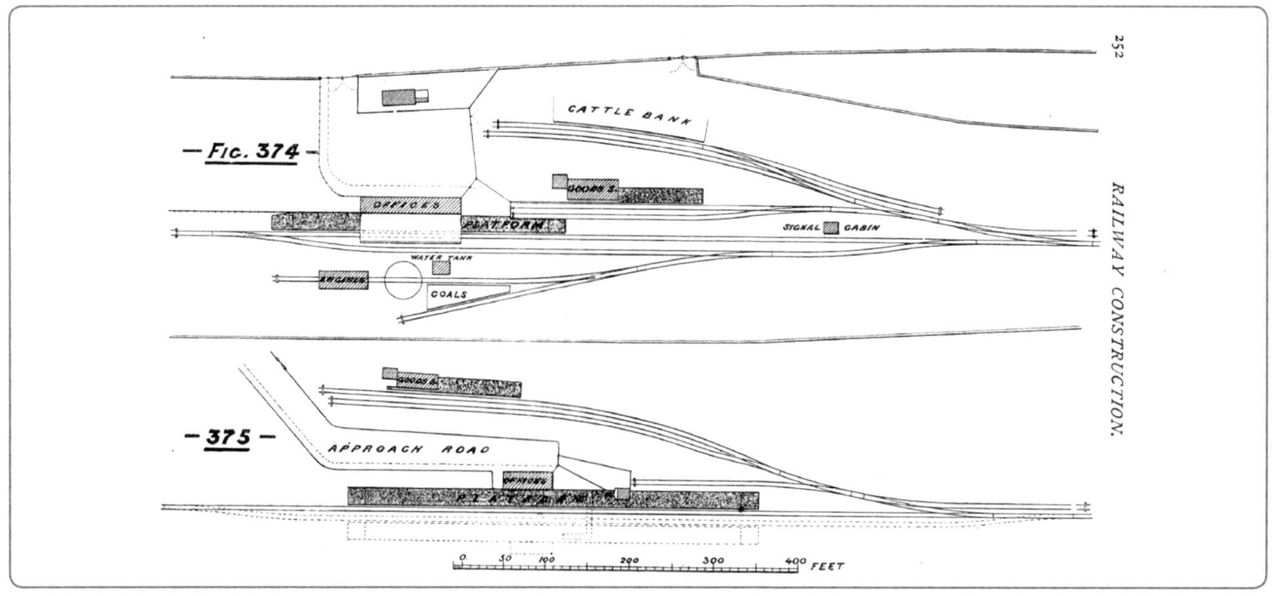

Private and not for publication. BR 29960

BRITISH RAILWAYS

REGULATIONS
for
TRAIN SIGNALLING
and
SIGNALMEN'S GENERAL INSTRUCTIONS

222 Marylebone Road, London, N.W.1 1st October, 1972

By Order of the Chief Executive

LEFT: *Signalling is a key component of any prototypically operated layout – and before you can get too far, some study of the rules will be required… After grappling with this complex and pithy little volume, my respect for the occupation of railway signalman went up several notches!*

cleaning facilities and somewhere to park a gas tank wagon if the branch passenger set is gas-lit; stabling for shunting or dray horses, or a garage for the 'road motor'. And, of course, those prerequisites of the steam-operated railway – an adequate water supply, fire-cleaning and ash-disposal facilities, some way of coaling stabled locomotives and a place to carry out routine light repairs. Then, of course, there is the signalling – an absolutely key element in any layout intended to operate realistically. Leaving aside mineral/industrial lines and the odd freight-only branch worked as an 'extended siding', virtually every move on every part of the British railway network was carried out under the direct control of a signalman and his signals. Many British railway facilities – minor country branch line terminals included – were amazingly fully signalled, not just with primary block signals but also with a whole range of subsidiary indications: intermediate and advanced signals, conditional arms, calling-on arms, and shunt signals, many of them in the distinctive form of the ground signal. For any layout with pretensions to operational fidelity, all this lot will have to be present and work in an authentic manner.

BELOW: *If realistic operation is intended, then correctly placed and working signals become a fundamental requirement. Here is the 4mm scale 'splitting inner home' for the Brideport branch at Maiden Newtown: exit to the main line on the left, entry to the bay platform on the right. The signal was scratchbuilt by the author using ScaleLink arms, Gibson laddering and MSE finials and balance arms; it is worked by a pair of modified miniature relays. The baseplate awaits blending-in…* Author

Of course, that's all for a traditional-era branch terminus in full flower; the later you come in modelling period, the more pared-down the facilities become. Those few branch lines that survived the post-war period of retrenchment have today been stripped down to the barest of twigs – effectively, extended sidings, devoid of pointwork or signalling and with facilities rarely amounting to more than a bare and weedy platform and a prefabricated shelter. With a few rare exceptions, freight traffic is a dim and distant memory, and passenger working amounts to no more than a solitary railcar or multiple-unit shuttling to and fro. I'm often accused of being 'anti modern' and resolutely stuck in the steam era, but the bare facts are that for modelling and operating interest on a modest site the contemporary 'subsidiary' railway has almost nothing to offer. I think even the hardest-nosed of 'here-and-now' diehards would have a job arguing the modelling and operational scope of a length of plain track, a buffer-stop and a solitary perambulating 'Pacer'…

Exhibition operation

The other operational design consideration for exhibitable, as opposed to 'home only' layouts, is the demands that actually running the layout at an exhibition will place on the operator(s) and equipment. A pattern of operation that is entertaining and involving when undertaken casually at home 'when the fancy strikes' can all too easily become over-demanding and highly tiring if you've got to keep it up over several hours in front of a critical audience. So, if you're designing a layout either principally as an exhibition model or as a home layout with exhibition aspirations, then the possible modes of operation need very careful consideration. There are a number of questions to ask yourself: How much do I *like* operation? How many other *competent* operators can I call on to help me at shows? (Bearing in mind that the number of people who *think* they can operate a model railway greatly exceeds the number who actually can!) How difficult will it actually be to run this layout at an exhibition? Is there some form of low-level basic train movement that can be carried out simply by an operator unfamiliar with the layout? How demanding is the operating pattern going to be in terms of wear and tear on locomotives, stock, couplings, point and signal mechanisms? How am I going to manage to keep things going in the event of equipment failure?

After nearly four decades of exhibiting layouts that have all been relatively small and, operationally, essentially exercises in intensive shunting, I have reached some fairly firm conclusions on the matter of exhibition operation – the principal lesson being that I've chosen to hoe by far the

ABOVE: *Merthyr (High St.) – a post-rationalisation branchline terminus, reduced to the most basic of track layouts and devoid of buildings, goods and loco facilities or signalling – and hence any vestige of operational interest...* Author's collection

hardest row! Ask any seasoned exhibitor and he'll tell you that much the easiest style of exhibition layout to operate and keep running reliably is a large continuous-run oval, preferably built in an undemanding standard like N or 00, devoid of fancy moves of any sort, and run simply as a parade of passing trains (preferably express passenger trains that can belt past the viewer at an impressive clip!).

In other words, the complete antithesis of the sort of small, freight-orientated 'shunting plank' or minor terminus to which I (along with many other finescale modellers) seem to gravitate. This is not to decry the continuous-run 'parade' layout; such models, with their capability for constant movement, continual variety and degree of 'spectacle', are the mainstay of most exhibitions, especially those aimed at a more general audience. You don't need to know anything about railways to appreciate such a layout.

Small, finescale exhibition layouts, on the other hand, rarely offer much in the way of spectacle. Their appeal lies in the combination of realism and high quality in the modelling and refinement and authenticity in the operation, and as such they attract a more knowledgeable (but far more critical!) audience. Such a layout, with its need for smooth, reliable slow running under fine control, continual stop-reverse-start operation, frequent coupling and uncoupling and the constant resetting of points to facilitate complex shunting moves, is infinitely more demanding both to build and keep running than anybody's main line oval. Not only must the equipment perform faultlessly, but the operator(s) will have to maintain a high degree of concentration to avoid 'pilot errors'. The lack of length of run endemic in all small layouts provides very little respite from the need to actually *operate*, while the complexity and demanding nature of this type of layout working means that it is not something you pick up in five minutes. If you are contemplating an exhibitable layout of this type, then the availability of skilled operators and the chance to practice and refine operation other than in the public eye is, I'd suggest, a prime consideration in determining what is practicable. This is yet another of the many less-obvious factors that can have a considerable impact on basic layout design.

BELOW: *An oval-format 'trains passing' exhibition layout, designed for straightforward operation to favour plenty of movement for wide audience appeal. As this example (the Crawley MRC's fine scale 00 'Well Street') ably demonstrates, such a layout can be realistic and authentic, while if enough skilled operators are available then there is scope for shunting that goods yard as well as maintaining the main line parade.* Adrian Colenutt

Control systems for authentic operation

If you're going to go to the trouble of designing a model railway to replicate as far as possible the various operational roles and tasks found on the prototype, then you obviously need to come up with a system of control that is equally authentic. Which, in the case of a traditional-era railway is, I'd suggest, not the once-obligatory 'mighty Wurlitzer' style of integrated layout control panel – bedecked with serried ranks of section, point and signal switches, housing umpteen controllers and boasting more coloured lights than Blackpool promenade. Nor is it the Wurlitzer's 21st century equivalent, the multi-function DCC keypad or, worse still, a normal alpha-numeric computer keyboard. Such things *may* be appropriate if you're representing to-the-minute contemporary CTC practice, but for all else they are utterly alien. A keyboard can do many things, but replicating the feel of traditional 'mechanical' railway working is not one of them!

Whatever the means of operating points and signals and managing section-switching or DCC-address allocation, there is one absolute fundamental that underpins any system of authentic model railway control: the total separation of the train-driving function from that of route-setting and signalling. This division is the basic principle on which the whole edifice of prototypical British railway operation has always been based, with the train drivers at all times under the jurisdiction of the signalman. The only exceptions to this rule are shunting moves made within a yard and the working of unsignalled trackage on minor lines, where train crews *may* be called on to throw the odd hand point lever or to open an occasional crossing gate. On a prototypically operated model, these two basic functions are distinguished in a control sense by only presenting the person taking each role with the means of fulfilling that particular function. Train drivers get a controller that enables them to vary power, speed and direction and maybe blow the whistle or horn, functions relating only to the actual engine they are supposedly driving. The signalman gets his lever frame and block instruments or a geographical or CTC panel. Both will be provided with a rule book and a copy of the WTT to guide them. Even if both roles are being taken by the same person, the two functions are considered separately; you set the road and clear the signals, then change hats and implements to drive the train.

ABOVE: *Prototypical control on Ted Farmer's 'Tiverton Town': mechanical lever frames to operate the points and signals, with home-made three-position block instruments (two instruments combined in a common casing and using coloured lights rather than a needle). On this non-DCC layout, a minimal electrical panel handles unavoidable section switching and uncoupler magnet actuation (the red pushbuttons). The trains are driven using handheld controllers in a 'walkabout' mode – but not by the signalman!* Author

BELOW: *Control: This is how the prototype did it – three-position block instruments in a signalbox, one pair of instruments and a bell for each direction. This is the old Sheringham East box, preserved on the North Norfolk Railway.* Author

In reality, these two basic functions – signalling and driving – have always been the sole means by which railways are physically controlled. On our electrically powered models, however, we have to handle additional operational tasks that the prototype does without: the switching-in and -out of track power sections on a traditional analogue DC layout, or the allocation of address codes among controllers on a DCC system. Here, DCC has a clear advantage; track power switching for operational purposes is eliminated, and controller allocation to specific locomotives is only an occasional task. On a traditional DC layout, however, section switching is a veritable pain in the fundament, and in my experience the source of the vast majority of 'pilot errors' during operation. Given that it is a non-prototypical control function, section switching can be handled in one of three ways: you can keep it entirely separate and regard it as a sort of 'offstage' task, like re-staging trains in a fiddleyard, or you can integrate it into either the signalling or driving roles. Most people opt for the former, either by adding the section switches to the lever frame or panel controlling the points and signals, or by using additional contacts in either the route-setting or signal indicating mechanisms to feed the track power to the appropriate sections. The current generation of microswitch-carrying mechanical lever frames greatly facilitate this strategy.

An alternative is to take the opposite approach, by allocating the task of managing the track power to the train driver(s), when it can be regarded as equivalent to 'putting on the handbrake' when the locomotive is stationary – very much a prototypical train-crew task. This is an approach I've used with some success on layouts – like my own 'Cade's Green' – that favour 'walkaround' operation with a hand-held controllers and 'dispersed' control (see below) with section switches or point operating mechanisms set into the layout fascia adjacent to the functions they control. Such a layout can easily be wired so that at all the places where a locomotive might need to stand while operations carry on elsewhere, there are suitable 'holding sections'. These are fed, not directly from the controller output or traction BUS, but from the adjacent 'running sections', of which they form a subsidiary part. All the rest of the track – although sectionalised as 'running sections' and switchable for controller-allocation or fault-finding purposes – is normally left 'live'. Under this system, when a locomotive draws up to a stand at a holding point, the relevant holding-section switch is operated to 'put the handbrake on'; and before that locomotive can move again, the brake must be 'taken off'. It's not so much a change in the way the control hardware is arranged as in the way it is regarded for operational purposes.

BELOW: *A state-of-the-art electro-mechanical lever frame at Maiden Newtown. This elegant affair, complete with turned-steel handles and prototypical catch-levers, was built by Andrew Duncan from parts supplied by the Scalefour Society. Red levers indicate home signals (no distants in this frame, alas); black levers are turnouts and whites are spares.* Author

Point and signal control

The precise means by which you intend to actuate points and signals is something else that needs careful consideration at the design stage. In the cause of realism, I think it is generally accepted that the objective is to try to re-create the prototypical arrangements as far as possible, at least in so far as they affect the hands-on operation of the layout. Thus, while a traditional steam-era layout may not go so far as using working mechanical point-rodding (although that's perfectly possible even in 4mm scale, as was long ago demonstrated by Ray Hammond on his 'Buntingford' P4 layout), the signalman should be presented with a proper lever frame, or at least a bank of switches arranged in the *format* of a lever frame. Real signalling die-hards can insist on fully functioning mechanical interlocking (also quite possible and, indeed, commercially available), although most of us will be more than happy to settle for proper levers with working catch-handles!

But even the steam era was not all 'long-lever, duster and heave' control; the arrival of power actuation of points and signals (or the replacement of semaphores with colour lights) in the late 1920s heralded the miniature lever or pneumatic slider frame, closely followed (at key locations and in all new installations) by the power-operated geographic signalbox panel, with its illuminated track diagrams and rotary point and signal switches – relatively easy to replicate in miniature. Not quite so easy to mimic are the slightly later route-setting panels, where a single switch on the panel controlled several turnouts 'on the ground' through a series of electrically locked relays. From these local signalbox panels developed the diesel-era route-setting CTC panel controlling a whole geographic district of railway. These panels were soon being computerised, leading by development to the contemporary systems of on-screen train control. CTC-style control can be applied authentically to a model railway – although few of us will be modelling an entire 'district'! However, while such panels *look* deceptively simple, the electrics involved are anything but!

Model lever frames can be arranged to support mechanical or electrical means of actuation, or a combination of the two. The current crop of etched-kit-based 'proper' frames, such as those produced by Ambis Engineering, Brassmasters, Model Signal Engineering or the Scalefour Society, can accept integrated microswitches either in place of, or in addition to, the mechanical functions. So there is no reason why you have to plump for one overall method of point or signal control for the whole layout; the prototype frequently didn't! Nowadays, we have a wide range of options for actually moving point blades and signal arms, ranging from traditional mechanical means like wire-in-tube, rodding with cranks or cable-and-spring through the traditional style of AC-powered

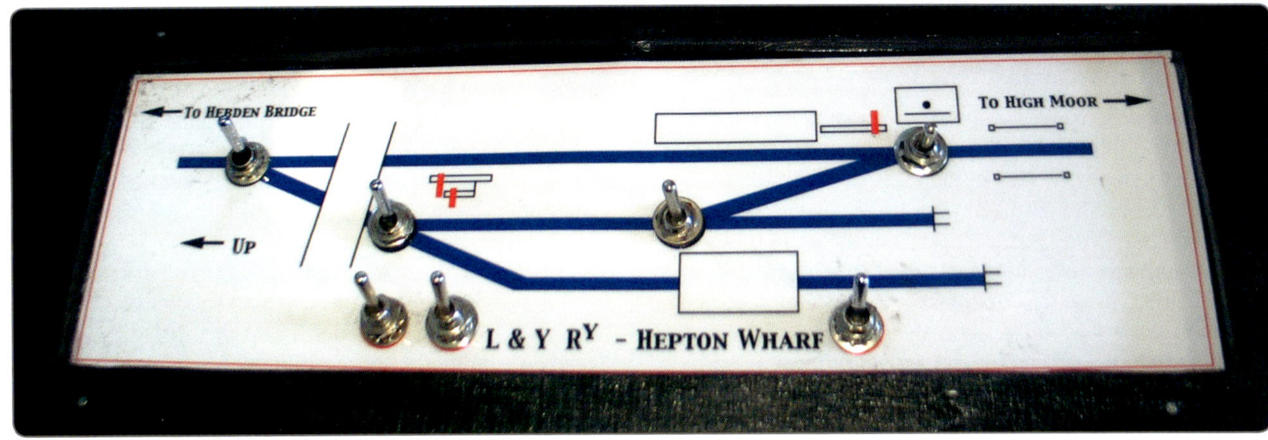

ABOVE: *The new geographical panel on 'Hepton Wharf:' point switches on the track diagram, signal switches at the bottom in line with the signal they control. Not very prototypical, but simple and easily comprehensible – important for an exhibition layout.* Author

twin-coil solenoid point motor and modern DC slow-action turnout actuators, to memory wire and semaphore signal servos with inbuilt 'bounce' characteristics.

CTC and DCC

While all of these devices can be linked to the sort of lever frame described, the purely electrical systems can also be controlled from a panel system or, using appropriate software and interface devices, from a PC. It is the pre-computerised route-setting CTC set-up using relays or solid-state switching and complex electrical interlocking that forms the toughest option here – definitely not something for the electrically faint-hearted! Outside the hallowed confines of MERG (the Model Electronic Railway Group), such things are rather a mystery, and as yet – so far as I'm aware – nobody has attempted to market a commercial off-the-shelf analogue CTC system. The whole thing has anyway, been rather overtaken by digital/DCC systems, which offer a somewhat similar form of control, albeit in a different way.

When considering applying any form of CTC to a layout, it is important not to lose sight of the fact that the whole foundation of the prototype control system is something that is completely absent from the vast majority of model railways: train detection by means of track circuits. Very few prototype UK CTC installations – usually those on remote lines like the Highland Far North section – have employed the American 'manual' approach, where train positions were reported by telephone or, more recently, by radio. The sheer traffic density usually found on most CTC routes here makes this method of tracking trains impracticable.

The days when open-line block signals were manually cleared or restored are also long gone, the whole process being automatic and triggered by the trains themselves operating those track circuits, which are also the means by which their position is 'reported' to the CTC operator via panel display or computer monitor. For authentic operation of a modern-themed layout by CTC, therefore, it is going to be necessary to come up with some form of train detection – either using working track-circuiting, optical/infra-red devices or magnets and reed switches – together with the necessary circuitry to switch searchlight or three/four-aspect colour-light signals, as well as controlling the panel indications. There is quite a considerable wiring challenge in that little lot – which may well make a DCC-based approach more attractive!

However, a lot of DCC model railway control systems appear to me to have been designed by people whose principal interest is in electronics rather than in authentic railway operation. I'm afraid that the keypads, sliders and LCD screens that characterise so much DCC equipment seem more like a cross between a microwave oven and a TV remote than the means of controlling a realistic model railway, certainly one owing allegiance to anything other than the strictly contemporary prototype. And, in terms of the definition of authentic operation on which I've hung my hat – the separation of the signalling and driving functions – most such DCC systems are a total non-starter, as they specifically set out to achieve the exact opposite: everything worked from a single keypad or panel. That's 'model railway'

RIGHT: *Keypad-style DCC control like this all-inclusive American NCE system, I personally find very fiddly and unsatisfying to use. As well as being somewhat far removed from any 'feel' of traditional railway operating hardware, such systems seek to integrate rather than segregate the driving and signalling functions.* Author

ABOVE: *Dispersed control on the author's layouts: handheld 'wander' controller and simple 'handbrake' section switches with mechanical hand lever push-pull point actuators on 'Trerice' (left), and a small lever frame panel for remotely controlled points and signals, plus hand lever point actuators and 'handbrake' switches on 'Cade's Green' (right).* Author

control, not model 'railway control'. This is not to say that DCC cannot be used in the context of authentic operation; it can be – but only when the signalling and driving functions are suitably divorced. Some DCC set-ups (notably, that offered by MERG) are designed for this approach, but most don't even recognise it. ZTC apart, almost none of the DCC handsets or panels attempt to provide any 'railway-like' form of interface. Where are the controllers consisting solely of a regulator, reverser, brake and warning device? That's all a *real* train-driver gets to play with!

If an 'authentic' form of control is somewhat lacking in the driving department, it is totally absent from the point and signal control functions. Personally, I find the basic DCC 'accessory control' approach of punching in a multi-digit address code followed by the hitting of an 'actuate' command to be unsatisfying and (to my erratic fingers), frustratingly error-prone – at least as bad as traditional section switching! Also, such button-punching is so far removed from any traditional form of real railway operation as to feel no more authentic a *modus operandi* than the crude finger-poking of a tinplate train-set, seeming to me, fully as inappropriate as manipulating overscale lineside hand-levers to change the points and massive 'balance arms' on the posts to work the signals. But then, I suppose, everything depends on the prototype timeframe of the model; go back before about 1860, and hand-worked levers on points and signals are a perfectly authentic way of operating, while in 2010, address codes and mouse-clicks are very much the way things are done! However, for me to contemplate digital point and signal control on a traditional steam or transition-era layout, someone is going to have to come up with an interface between an authentic-pattern traditional lever frame and the DCC command system. That I ain't seen – yet!

Dispersed control

Thus far I have largely been considering railway control that is essentially remote in nature – the things that are in reality linked to a signalbox or CTC centre. But even today, some aspects of control escape such centralised direction; the hand point lever can still be found in all sorts of yards, sidings and industrial installations, while other out-of-the-way track formations are worked by train-crews using local lineside ground frames, although often 'unlocked' by remote control. Go back in period, though, and far more railway infrastructure depended for its working on the man on the ground rather than the whims of some remote 'signaller'. This is particularly true of the humble occupational or minor-road gated level crossing, which in most instances was resolutely manual from first to last; only those surviving past the 1970s have known the automatic half-barrier – or, on minor lines crossing country lanes – relegation to 'ungated' status, with only flashing lights and audible warnings to keep road traffic and trains apart.

It was the turnout away from a running line that has always made up the bulk of the railway's 'ground-controlled' equipment. Even in large and important freight yards, only the points linking the yard entry and exit to the running lines would generally be worked from the signalbox. Heavily used or important pointwork within a yard might be linked to a ground frame, a small, non-interlocked frame containing a handful of levers and controlling the formation from a convenient location in the immediate vicinity. In the rest of the yard, all depended on the sweating shunter making his way to each turnout as required and heaving on the traditional hand-operated ground lever. So, in the cause of authentic control for our models, we need to draw a similar distinction between pointwork connected to the signalbox, that operated from a ground frame, and turnouts thrown independently by a ground lever. Traditionally, we modellers have gone in for a degree of 'overkill' in our centralised point operation; the cliché of the country goods yard with all the pointwork remotely controlled is quite unrealistic in this regard, being no more likely than a major main line junction worked by hand-thrown ground levers.

It won't have escaped your attention that the locally controlled turnout just described is associated very closely with shunting, ever the most demanding aspect of model railway operation. By and large, when shunting, as drivers/

shunters we need to stay close to the scene of operations, both to better see exactly what we're about, and to manage the tricky and contentious business of coupling and uncoupling – on which, much more in a moment. In my book, the greatest friend of the dedicated model railway shunter is the handheld controller, which permits him to 'ride with' his locomotive as it moves about the layout. Staying close to the locomotive when shunting means that you will also be in the proximity of any ground-controlled turnouts over which shunting moves need to take place – in which case operating locally sited actuators to throw turnouts is no sweat and closely replicates the prototype *modus operandi*. While it is doubtless possible to make a realistic working ground lever – certainly in 0 scale – I prefer a control (electrical or manual) set in an appropriate location in the layout fascia, where it obviates the need to reach over the layout, something that I find is best avoided. Local ground frames can be represented by grouping such controls appropriately, using the remote-actuating system of choice.

As well as the actuators for ground-thrown turnouts, other 'local' control functions can be handled by switches, levers or buttons set into the fascia adjacent to whatever it is they are controlling. I have already mentioned the 'handbrake' switches for locomotive-parking holding sections, but several other devices can usefully be worked thus – most notably, electro-magnetic, permanent-magnet or mechanical uncouplers. Manual level crossing gates are another feature that lend themselves to some form of local control, as are non-powered turntables that would in reality be a case of 'push hard and puff'. In fact, in many cases – not least, that of our country branchline terminal – there would be more devices subject to local 'ground' control than ever there were connected to the signalbox lever frame. So, in trying to replicate such a situation, we might well find we end up with a layout control system where only the signals and running-line turnouts are controlled from our signalbox frame or panel, with maybe a few more turnouts linked to a subsidiary and suitably sited ground frame. Everything else would be handled by individual controls set into the layout fascia in appropriate locations. Train control would, of course, be quite separate – for preference by handheld controller, DC or digital to choice. This mélange of differing control status and actuation method is what I term a 'dispersed' system. It is the total antithesis of the centralised 'mighty Wurlitzer' panel.

Offstage trackage: staging and fiddleyards

Thus far, I have considered operational design mostly in terms of what happens on the modelled, 'on show' part of the layout. But almost without exception, realistic model railways depend to a greater or lesser extent on 'offstage' hidden trackage to service these visible goings-on. Coming up with the most appropriate way of handling such 'backstage business' is a vital part of both operational and practical design – and something that is no sinecure, as whatever you devise not only needs to fulfil all the operational requirements, but to function smoothly and reliably while being space-efficient and easy to manage.

It is important to differentiate between the two alternatives named in my subtitle, for they are not the same thing and call for different design solutions. To take the simpler alternative first, staging is simply concealed trackage on which a complete train can be parked, unchanged, until the timetable or operating sequence bids it reappear. A fiddleyard, on the other hand, is somewhere that trains cannot only be stored unseen, but where they can be re-marshalled, turned around or re-engined, as appropriate. The big difference between staging and fiddling lies in access. So long as you can get at a staging track well enough to clean the rails occasionally and deal with any mishaps, that is all you need to provide for. A fiddleyard, by contrast, needs unrestricted access and enough space to work in.

LEFT: *Straightforward train-storage 'staging' tracks: the 'down Weymouth' hidden sidings on Andrew Duncan's 'Weymouth Lines' layout. Eventually, the branch terminus of 'Brideport' will sit above this trackage. Although the visible PW on the layout is fine scale bullhead, all the 'offstage' tracks use Peco Streamline on foam underlay for speed of construction and operational silence. The through running lines are at the rear.* Author

Balanced capacity

The basic problem with all hidden train storage is that our trains don't get any shorter when they trundle off into the wings, so the minimum dimensions of the hidden portion of any layout are a direct function of train length. On a very small layout, where the visible scene is little longer than a typical train, this can easily result in the non-seen portion of the layout being virtually as big as the modelled area; a 60:40 or even 50:50 visible/unseen split is not uncommon. Personally, I find that sort of proportion a little ungainly – and, on a small site, rather cramping of modelling space. I generally try for something closer to 70:30, even if that does call for some sacrifice in maximum train length.

The capacity – in terms of train length and make-up – of any hidden trackage needs to be appropriate to the capacity of the visible part of the layout. If the headshunt on your station or yard will only take a 4-4-0 and the run-round loop a strict five coaches, then there is absolutely no point in scheming offstage storage capacity around Pacifics and ten-coach trains. Particularly when space is tight, getting an accurate balance between all aspects of the offstage train storage and the visible trackage can save valuable inches. I always make precise measurement checks of actual train lengths for all the various formations I need to work, and match them carefully when specifying the dimensions of fiddleyards, cassettes and – particularly – headshunts. The only thing worse than wasting space by allowing unnecessary length is cramping your operational scope for want of an additional quarter-inch...

Where space is at a premium, striking the right balance is all about making the most efficient use of what is available. However, in less straitened circumstances, the requirements of prototype authenticity and good visual design may well mean that – like the prototype – we end up with a visible track capacity somewhat in excess of the normal traffic requirements. The fact that the loop in station 'x' *could* hold 35 wagons does not mean that every goods train on that line has to be loaded to '34 and a brake van'. In these circumstances, there is a strong argument for designing the offstage trackage around the *typical* formation rather than the absolute maximum capacity, particularly where that alters the balance of hidden/modelled trackage in favour of more modelling.

Staging

Arranging to hold complete unchanged trains offstage is by far the simpler proposition. In this country, such staging is most usually associated with the continuous-run oval-format exhibition layout run on 'parade' principles, using a simple sequence of set trains appearing as required. The usual solution for this requirement is a simple 'ladder' yard or parallel close-spaced loops accessed by normal pointwork, occupying the long side of the oval opposite the main modelled scene. Such a yard can be simply arranged using normal track and pointwork, laid, wired and operated like any other track. The only refinements might be some form of route-setting to select tracks by aligning the pointwork appropriately and providing traction power in non-DCC applications, and train detection systems to aid operators where the tracks are not in clear sight. The enormous advantage of such 'conventional track' ladder-style staging yards is that they can be operated totally 'hands off' and from a distance, by the same control system and operators as the rest of the layout. For these reasons, they are by far the most desirable option.

The problem is, of course, that ladder yards like this take up a lot of space relative to their capacity, particularly in the matter of the approach pointwork. In the context of the typical inside-viewed home oval continuous-run layout, often of restricted dimensions, giving over almost half of the available area to offstage train storage is often unacceptable. More compact solutions are required, of which the horizontally sliding traverser or its upright cousin, the vertically moving 'train stacker', are the most efficient.

RIGHT: *A train stacker or vertical traverser – a series of shelves on a backing board, the whole assembly mounted to slide up and down on ball-bearing door track and counterbalanced like a sash window. This under-construction four-deck double-track version is 9ft long (but only 8in deep) and has a capacity equivalent to eight ten-coach express trains (with locos); it will form the 'Westbury' staging for the 'Weymouth Lines' layout.* Author

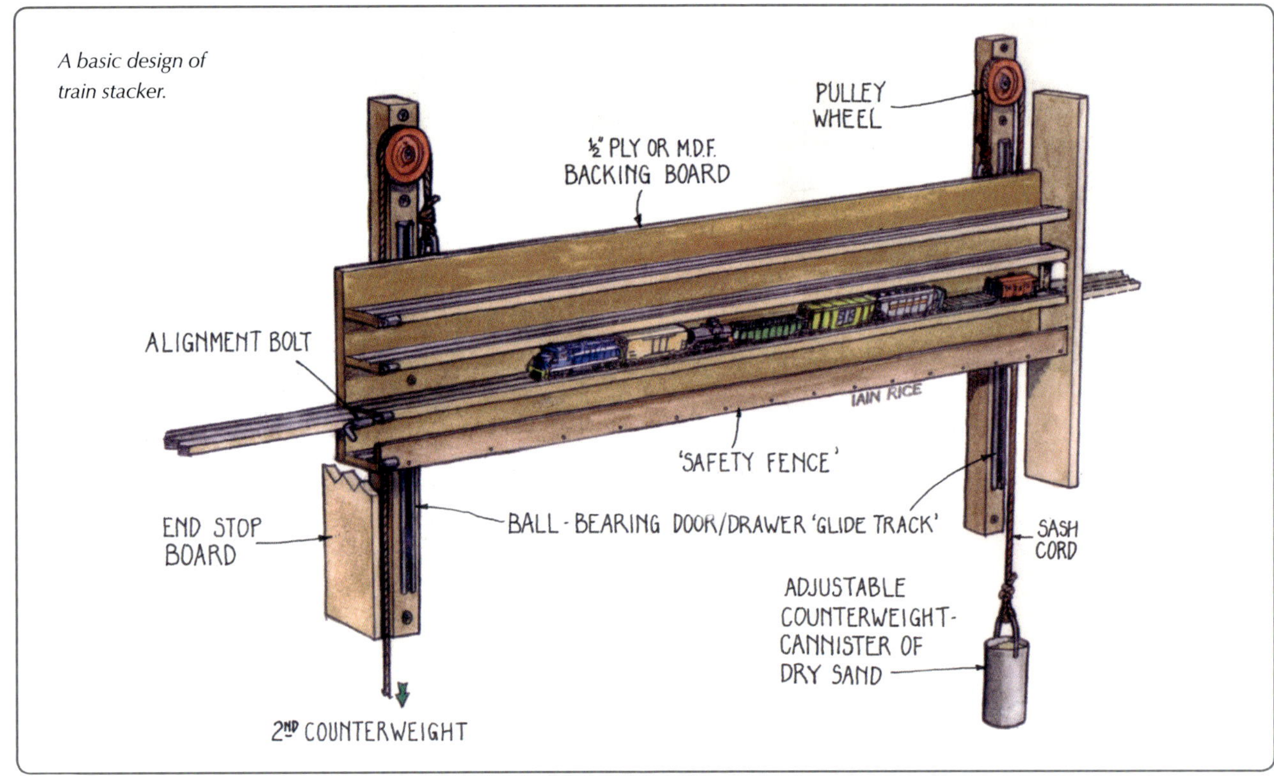

A basic design of train stacker.

Where space (especially width) is tight, the stacker wins out hands-down as its 'footprint' is minimal and the potential capacity large. A 6ft-long six-track stacker calls for a site only 6–8in wide compared with the 20in-plus width needed for an equivalent traverser with the lead-in track on the centreline. Traversers with offset lead-ins swallow up even more real-estate.

Although both traversers and stackers can be motorised for remote and even automatic operation, they are usually operated manually, which requires suitable access. Where access to staging isn't a problem, then even more manual systems can be used, in some form of removable 'complete-train cassette' that is inserted into a suitable 'dock' in the running lines. The train to be staged is run into the cassette and secured in some way before the cassette is lifted out and placed on a storage rack, being replaced by another containing the next train called for by the timetable. This approach can be very space-efficient, but there is an obvious limit on the possible length of train before things become impossibly unwieldy for single-person handling. I've found 5ft or so to be about the comfortable maximum. Due to the high degree of manual handling involved, such cassette systems are more generally considered in the context of 'return staging' and fiddleyards rather than as a straightforward staging/storage system.

Return staging

Thus far, I've been considering 'through' staging in the context of a continuous-run layout where a given train will always be travelling in the same direction. In a great many cases, however, it will be necessary to turn a train around before sending it back whence it came, even if the formation remains otherwise unchanged. This is the usual situation on virtually any 'terminal' layout, but may also apply on many continuous runs. There are basically three staging yard designs that permit this operation: the 'return loop' ladder yard, beloved of many a large American layout, the 'complete train cassette' described above, and the 'train turntable'. The first of these is, like through ladder staging, the most desirable option for its combination of hands-off remote control and general ease of working – but it requires a *lot* of space and in a British context

BELOW: *A train turntable under construction on the extended version of Mick Simpson's beautiful 2mm fine scale 'Wansbeck Road'. Such an arrangement is well suited to small scales, and drastically reduces stock handling. And yes, it did get a buffer-stopping end fence before going into service!* Author

is rarely found in scales above N. Even taking advantage of 00's curve-squeezing potential, you would still be looking for an area of around 10 x 8ft in 4mm scale. In 0 scale, stately home owners only need apply...

The train turntable requires a width equal to its length, so is also quite space-consuming for long train formations. It works very well in 2mm scale though, and Peter Denny has long had such a turntable (about 5ft long for a modest 4-4-0 and five 50ft coaches) on 'Buckingham'. In the 'housed' or in-line position, such a turntable is very compact, merely occupying the footprint of the actual tracks. So it is a solution well-suited to many exhibition layouts, where floor-space in operation is not usually a problem, but ease of transport is. The 'complete train cassette' also offers the potential for swapping ends, given enough space to carry out the turning manoeuvre, and bearing in mind the practical limitation on cassette length. Where two people are available to carry out the cassette twiddling, the whole process becomes a lot easier and the length of cassette possible is considerably greater.

The versatile fiddleyard

Most designs of staging yard do not permit any appreciable degree of 'fiddling' – the breaking-down, storage and re-marshalling of trains. This is the province of the true fiddleyard, which will be designed to facilitate such operations by providing excellent access. The ideal fiddleyard is one which is as far as possible from being 'fiddly' to work, being possessed of adequate illumination, and having adequate room for the safe manipulation and storage of stock. There is a sort of 'inverse ratio' that applies to fiddleyard design, along the lines of 'the simpler the fiddleyard design, the more you have to handle the stock' – and vice-versa. Where stock is delicate, cutting down or eliminating handling is an obvious design priority, which is why the popularity of complex and sophisticated fiddleyard solutions have grown in line with the development of finescale modelling and high levels of detail.

Unless you happen to enjoy building clever fiddleyards, there is little point in designing something more complex than the basic set-up that will do the job you need to do in the context of the layout as a whole. You can easily end up with the 'tail wagging the dog', with more space, effort and complexity devoted to the fiddleyard than to the actual layout. (I have that T-shirt in my collection too…)

Choosing the right fiddleyard option from the manifold possibilities is another one of those aspects of layout design calling for careful preliminary thought and accurate analysis of the real needs of the model. There is a whole book to be written on fiddleyard design and the various possible systems of offstage train-handling, so I'm afraid all I can manage here is a quick skit around the more obvious options. The essential point though, is that the fiddleyard is very much an integral and fundamental part of the overall layout design, not a casual afterthought.

BELOW: *Fiddleyards don't come any simpler than this: track on a plank! In this case, all that is required is to put the engine on the other end of the train, accomplished manually. These are the off-scene arrangements for the superb museum-quality Scaleseven model of mixed-gauge Edgware Road station, London, as it was in the 1860s, built by Mike Jolly and Paul Marchese.* Author

Basic fiddleyard options

At its simplest, a fiddleyard can consist of nothing more than a length of track nailed to a plank – the ultimate in ultra-compact offstage train handling. The only way you can work such a fiddleyard, of course, is either to send the train back unchanged whence it came – quite appropriate to a push-pull, railmotor or DMU – or to uncouple and manipulate the various items of stock individually by hand. Where all that is required is to 'top-and-tail' a train by swapping the engine or engine and brakevan from one end to t'other, this may be deemed acceptable; I have worked several of my 'shunting planks' thus. The next step up from a single plain track is several such tracks mounted in parallel on a sector plate (pivoted at the inboard end), sector table (pivoted on centre), or traverser, which enable the yard to cope with more than one train at once but don't call for extra length to accommodate pointwork. The tracks do need to be far enough apart to permit manual access – about 3in centres is the minimum. However, if more than basic top-and-tail rearrangement is called for, then I would regard any of these simple 'fiddle track' designs as non-starters.

Sector plates and traversers offer other offstage storage/fiddling options. A sector plate can feed a 'kickback' fiddleyard, serving as a sort of glorified stub turnout to receive the train from the layout then, suitably realigned, feeding it onto a hidden track or tracks located directly *behind* the modelled scene. Such an arrangement works particularly well in the context of a 'cameo' style exhibition layout, where the fiddleyard and stock storage lies concealed behind the backscene but remains highly accessible. At the cost of extra length, traversers can be arranged to provide a degree of 'hands-off' working by providing a 'loco neck' each side of the sliding table to facilitate running round a train. The drawback of all such arrangements is that it takes a while to handle trains in the 'offstage' part of the operating sequence.

Where more length is available, simple fiddle tracks can be arranged as a fan of sidings served by pointwork and

ABOVE: *A simple sector-table fiddleyard on Rodney Hall's 'Llanastr'. In this case, the table also takes the place of a couple of turnouts (the toe of the loop and the bay platform entry), simply being aligned and realigned as necessary. This saved valuable length on this pioneering minimum-space layout.* Author

ABOVE: *'Kick back' fiddleyard on 'Hepton Wharf'. The actual fiddle roads – a short holding spur for the steam railmotor and a long and easily accessible 'fiddling track' for train re-marshalling – are directly behind the layout backscene and are accessed by the sector plate, which also incorporates the loop toe point, another space-saving dodge along Llanastr lines. Note the integral stock storage shelving.* Author

spaced far enough apart to allow access. This is a very traditional approach, often described as 'hidden storage sidings'. Like the single track, such sidings are only really suited to the simpler levels of manual fiddling. However, they have an important further advantage: with the addition of 'dead sections' at the inboard siding ends, and the use of reliable auto-couplings, a siding-fan fiddleyard can be 'shunted' in the same way as the visible layout, permitting hands-off working. It is a very slow way of working, however, so more usually suited to a home layout than the 'keep something moving' imperative of exhibition working.

Complex fiddleyard systems

These, or cassettes, in some form or another, such as cassette fiddleyards, are very much a manual, hands-on sort of affair; it is just that what is being handled is a cassette containing a train or part thereof, rather than the models themselves. The usual form of cassette used nowadays is that devised by Chris Pendlenton, framed in small-section (1–1½in) aluminium angle glued or screwed to a ply or MDF sub-base. The inner

BELOW: *Fully enclosed and nicely finished 'showcase' whole-train cassettes on Henry Tasker's EM S&DJR layout.* Author

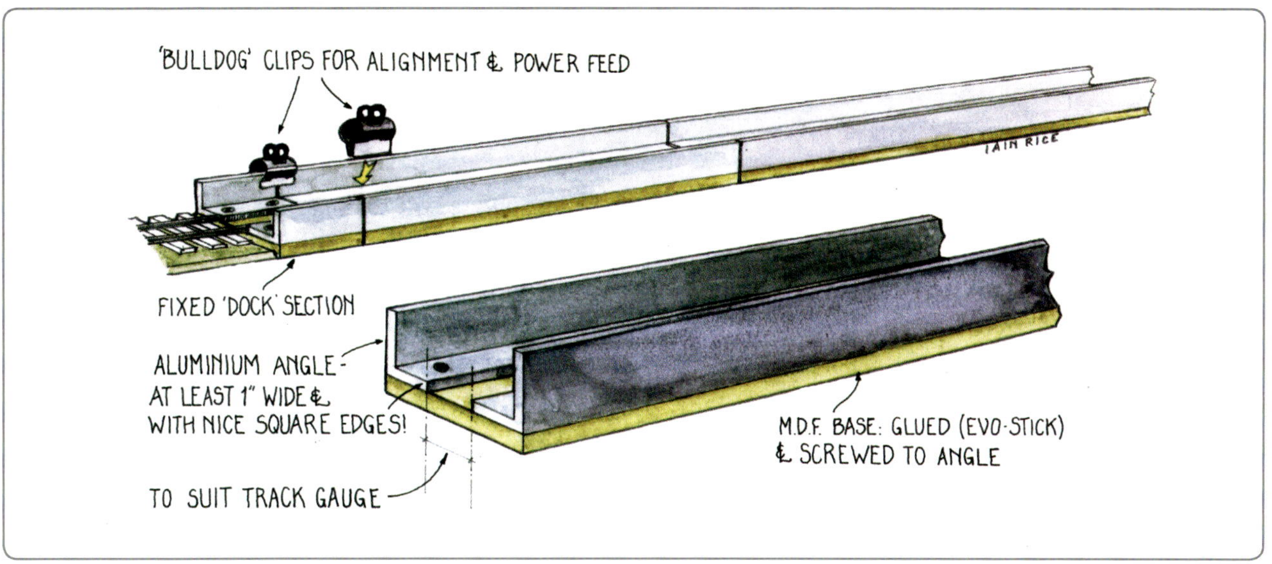

ABOVE: *The classic Pendlenton cassette – Rice's version.*

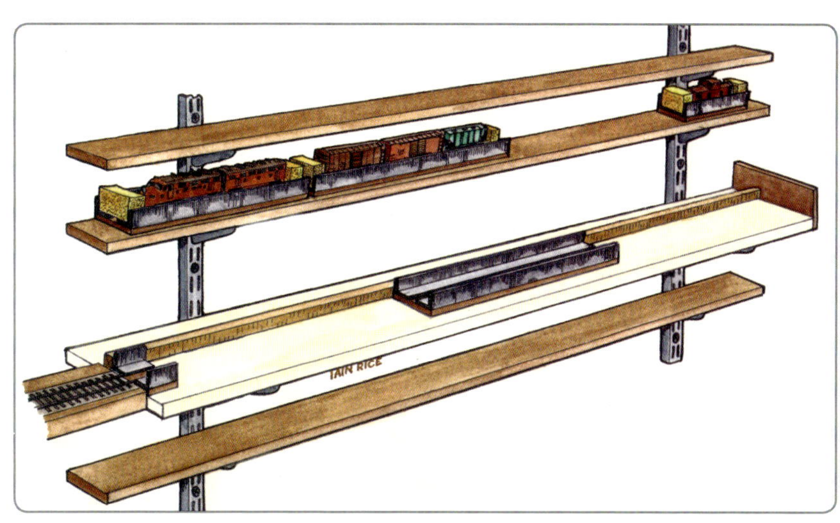

RIGHT: *A typical short-cassette fiddleyard arranged for wall-mounting using shelf track. The actual cassette deck – with alignment fence and 'dock' – is made from Melamine-faced Conti-Board to give a low-friction surface that allows the cassettes to be moved easily.*

edge of the base flanges of the angle forms the running-surface on which the stock rolls in lieu of rails, thus killing two birds with the proverbial single stone. The only real drawback to this form of construction is the relatively high cost of the angle – for which reason I personally use a simple all-timber 'removable shelf' design that achieves most of the same objectives at peasant prices. I know of other modellers who make their cassettes as fully enclosed storage units; my old friend Henry Tasker has some elegant whole-train cassettes on his 'Bath Green Park' layout with hardwood bases and Perspex sides and tops so that, when stacked on the storage racking, they effectively form a showcase for his collection of Midland/S&D/LMS coaching stock.

Cassettes of whatever precise design don't exist in limbo. To function, they need a supporting shelf (wittily called a 'cassette deck') fitted with some form of 'docking port' to link them to the actual layout, together with alignment and power-transmission arrangements and some sort of storage rack to hold the cassettes not linked to the layout. Some incredibly sophisticated and complex systems to achieve these simple objectives have been described, but being a 'bear of little brain' I have always gone for the straightforward option: a short, fixed length of cassette as a dock, a piece of straight stripwood as an alignment aid, and spring Bulldog document clips to hold things in line and transmit the power, and shelves to hold the spare cassettes. This simple set-up is shown in my drawing hereabouts.

The cassettes themselves can be made as whole-train units – as already mentioned in the context of staging – but are more usually made as individual short units designed to be placed and clipped end-to-end to form the necessary length to handle the desired formation. These 'sub train' cassettes are usually tailor-made for the particular items of stock they're intended to accommodate and described accordingly: tender or tank loco, brake van, 'x' coaches or 'y' wagons. Shuffling individual cassettes around, placing them in line to form whole-train formations and moving them into and out of storage is a task that demands care and takes time – which can be a drawback under exhibition conditions. One elegant solution to that conundrum is to use a splitting turnout to serve two docks per lead-in track, enabling a train to be held 'ready to go' while still enabling the fiddleyard to accept an incoming train.

Whatever variant of the cassette is used, no other

system can beat their combination of flexibility, versatility, protection of stock and efficient use of space. These days, they have become almost a 'default choice', whether or not the operational needs of the layout justify the considerable cost and complexity involved. Like everything else, cassettes have their drawbacks – chief among which are their labour-intensive and inherently fiddly nature. These are all factors that demand careful weighing from the depths of the modelling armchair.

Couplings

These are the other vital component in the operational scheme of things, and once again are very much something that needs to be considered at the outset of the layout design process rather than – as so often – being relegated to afterthought status. This is because the different types of coupling make widely differing demands on the layout design in terms of access and actuation. An extreme case is that most-authentic alternative, the manually operated hook-and-link coupling that replicates – visually, at least – the prototype arrangement. Quite apart from the practical limitations imposed by physical size – which normally confines this hair-shirt approach to 4mm scale and above – the use of scale (or even somewhat overscale, as many such things are) link couplings makes very specific demands in practical design terms. Link couplings are only ever going to be a workable proposition when access to the track at *all* relevant coupling/uncoupling locations is completely unfettered, and the combination of layout display height, depth of scene, headroom and illumination enables you get your head in a position where you can see what you're doing. Believe me, nothing is more detrimental to operational pleasure than trying to couple up link-fitted stock when you can't get at it or see what you're about!

There is also a debate to be conducted about the visual intrusion and consequent 'destruction of illusion' of the mighty 'hand from the sky' versus the appearance and lack of authenticity of the various forms of auto-coupling. Here, we can only envy our US colleagues, who enjoy the luxury of a reliable and fully functioning auto-coupler that also *looks* very much like the real thing! The manual access requirement intrinsic to the use of hook-and-link couplings creates many problems in terms of landscape, structure location, track levels and the provision of prototypically placed signalling – limitations that may adversely affect the realism, authenticity and visual balance of the whole layout. These are very much factors to be borne in mind when reviewing the merits of the various systems of coupling as a design preliminary.

As in so many aspects of layout design, the final solution to the coupling dilemma is likely to be a compromise. There is no clear winner as an all-round 'best coupling' solution in any scale; it is very much a case of 'horses for courses'. To be honest, the 4mm scale manual link coupling I regard as very much a 'limited option', especially for layouts on which much shunting takes place. Or at least I do until someone comes up with a functional 4mm scale shunter! While scale three-links can both look good and be perfectly functional

ABOVE: *Choosing to go with 'authentic' three-link couplings has big implications in layout design terms. It will mean that any location where coupling-up might ever take place will need unrestricted access and good illumination – plus a steady hand and excellent eyesight on the part of the operator! And that's before you consider the visual intrusion of the mighty 'hand from the sky'.* Author

on a 'trains passing by' parade layout, my experience over many years of trying to use them on the typical 'shunting plank' style of finescale layout has been one of frustration and frequent malfunction. Problems have included repeated attempts needed to snare the link and get it over the hook, links getting tangled, frequent derailments due to mishandling/'nudging' of the stock, wagons being moved or set rolling accidentally and problems getting the shunting pole safely out once coupling-up or uncoupling has finally been achieved. And as for trying to couple coaching stock 'under the gangways...'! These drawbacks are bad enough at home, but trying to fiddle like this at an exhibition with an audience breathing down your neck is far worse! Nowadays I limit the use of three-links to the coupling of wagons into short 'cuts' of two to five vehicles, with auto-couplers on the outer ends of each cut. Scale link couplers are nowhere near as problematic in 7mm scale, where the actual coupling hardware is getting on for twice the size, the links have enough weight to drop gracefully into the hooks and the rolling stock has a lot more mass and inertia, thus taking a bit more derailing! But I still wouldn't care to work an exhibition layout thus-equipped over many hours...

Mix and match

It is as well to bear in mind that there is no law which says you have to stick with one coupling system over an entire layout. Indeed, there are strong arguments for doing the exact opposite and using different couplings for different applications. That is, after all, what the prototype has been doing for some considerable time past; American-style 'knuckle' couplers (known as Buckeyes in the UK, after the principal US manufacturer from whom they were imported) have been fitted to a lot of corridor passenger stock since early in the 20th century, being standard on the LNER, SR and BR and in limited use on the GWR. So we can use US Kadee-style knuckles in those applications and be perfectly authentic, as well as enjoying reliable auto operation. Coaches are anyway often kept in sets or fixed train formations – in which case, we don't need to bother with autos at all except at the set ends or on 'supplementary' vehicles, otherwise using cheap, simple, trouble-free rigid drawbars. The fact that your principal passenger locomotives are incompatible, coupler-wise, with your 'loose' goods stock is of limited account; shunting with such locomotives, while not entirely unknown, can scarcely be described as typical operating practice... Only on smaller layouts with 'jack of all trades' motive power does overall coupler compatibility become an issue.

It may look fine on a main-line corridor coach, but a Kadee knuckle on a British wagon, at least in the larger scales, is a bit of an eyesore, although in N it is less so than the normal Rapido RTR fitment. The standard 4mm scale tension lock is also a rather unsightly device, although the miniaturised variant now prevalent is less of a carbuncle than the massive original. Both these RTR couplers are anyway somewhat limited in operation, being dependent upon unsightly mechanical ramps for uncoupling and lacking any 'delay' function. For all scales from N to 0 there are far less obtrusive and more functional home-grown alternatives, most particularly the various kit-form hook-and-loop' designs – Sprat and Winkle, DG and B&B – and, of course, the bent-wire 'hermaphrodite' couplings, of which the best-known is the Alex Jackson.

These aftermarket coupling designs are all DIY affairs, to a greater or lesser extent; I described them in some detail in *Railway Modelling the Realistic Way*, so I'll spare you any dissection of their anatomies here. All these devices offer 'light touch' auto coupling and true remote uncoupling, using some form of magnetic actuation. In common with the Kadee knuckle design, they can also offer a delayed uncoupling function – which enables a single uncoupling magnet to serve a fan of sidings. The S&W comes in variants for all scales from 2–7mm, whereas the B&B is a 2mm coupling, as is the DG – although it is popular in 3mm and can even be used in 4mm on reasonably wide curves. The Jackson will work in 3mm scale if you make it delicate enough, and 7mm if you beef it up a bit, but mainly it is a 4mm device.

All these couplings have their foibles, characteristics which need bearing in mind when designing a layout around their use. Apart from such basics as the need to design-in the relevant uncoupling devices, it is worth checking that the chosen coupling will be happy on proposed curve radii and is also compatible with the standards chosen. AJs, particularly, call for precise location both vertically and in centring, having a somewhat narrow 'gathering angle' – for which reason, they tend to work best in finer-scale applications with tight running clearances and wide curves. Even on dead straight track, the amount of vehicle skew allowed by a slack standard like normal 00 – with 1mm+ between the outer wheel flange faces and the track gauge – can easily cause the hooks to fail to engage. In any standard, sharp curves and bumpy track will also be enough to make the AJ unreliable. Hook-and-loop designs are far more forgiving in these matters, which is why I for one tend to favour them!

BELOW: *My own answer to the coupling dilemma is this simple and unobtrusive all-wire variant of the well-tried hook-and-bar system. The inverted bent-wire hook is lightly sprung upwards and engages with a fine wire loop. Uncoupling uses permanent magnets acting on the iron-wire links of the coupling chain. These magnets can either be fixed or arranged on a pivot-and-cam system to drop down when not required to act. I use a combination of both.* Author

8 VISUAL DESIGN AND PRESENTATION

LEFT: *An overall view of 'Trerice' – a very small layout incorporating careful visual design and several bits of visual trickery. Those clay dries, for instance, are proportionally compressed to about 85 per cent of correct scale, while the yard hut in the foreground is carefully placed to act as a scene-dividing view-block. The concave backdrop is also important in 'opening up' the scene.* Author

You may ask why a topic that, traditionally, has hardly merited much attention at all in layout designing should be placed before such apparent fundamentals as track planning. My response would be that visual design is the fundamental discipline on which all realistic model railways are based, and if you don't get this aspect of a design right you're wasting your time with the rest! The reason for this strident assertion is that the way we look at a model – or conversely, the way a model is designed to be looked at – has a profound effect on what can go into that model, how it is disposed and, most importantly, how much (and in what manner) it can be compressed to reconcile the age-old imbalance between subject and space. Understanding the art and mechanics of 'visual compression' is the key to squaring that ever-present circle.

Visual design goes a lot further than merely fitting everything in, however. Having in my time trotted out some pretty scruffy specimens of the railway modeller's art, I've learned the hard way that ill-considered composition and poor presentation can undermine even the best of modelling. The lesson is that the overall aesthetics of a model railway matter a *lot*. To fulfil its potential, a layout needs to be easy on the eye when viewed simply as an *object* – a work of art, even! Achieving a result that meets such stringent aesthetic criteria calls not just for the provision and careful finishing of appropriate presentation, but also for pleasing visual design within the actual model itself: a decent frame around a well-composed picture. Good layout composition demands attention to such matters as line and form, proportion, visual balance, sightlines and viewpoints, and lifelike and harmonious colour. Listed baldly like this, the whole business sounds a formidable mountain to climb, but in practice, good visual design usually costs little more than a modicum of thought and a rudimentary acquaintance with the basic principles involved – starting with a quick look at the way we actually *see* things.

Fields of view

What we can actually perceive when looking at something – anything – is determined by three basic factors: the degree of illumination, the restrictions of our field of vision and the focusing abilities of our eyes. The first of these I touched on back in Chapter 2; it's the other two that concern us here. 'Field of view' is defined as 'the angular extent of the observable world as seen at any given moment' (Wikipedia). In humans, our 'binocular vision' – the area within which both eyes can interact to give perception of form and distance – amounts laterally to an angular spread of 70° either side of our visual centreline. That is, we can survey a field of 140° without moving our heads when looking straight ahead. As we move out from the centre of this field, however, our visual acuity falls off until at the extremes we have only limited peripheral vision, which reacts to light and movement but not much else. Our vision is at it's most acute in the foveal field, which extends only about 3° either side of the centreline; that's why, when we want to see something as clearly as possible, we move our heads so we're looking straight at it! The closer something is to the centre of our

BELOW: *Field of vision.*

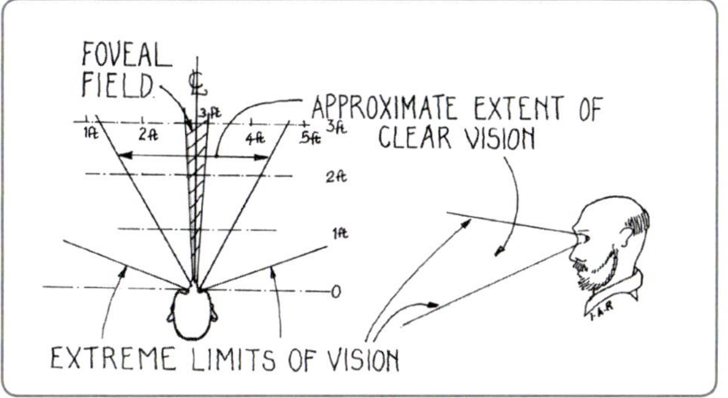

total field, the more clearly and comfortably we can see it; the extent of this 'field of clear vision' is relatively limited and varies between individuals; mine seems to equate to about 30° either side of centre.

In the vertical sense, our visual centreline is not normally parallel to the floor; rather, it's inclined downwards, favouring the ground ahead of us rather than the sky above. Which means our field of view is usually centred on what's directly in front of us and somewhat below our nominal eye level. We can readily look down and see the ground ahead of us without moving our heads, but normally we're only peripherally aware of objects much *above* eye level – something that's jolly useful in layout display terms, as already noted back in Chapter 2 when considering layout mounting heights and fore-mounted lighting fascias. The fundamental thing to understand about this field of vision is that it's unchanging; in other words, our angle of vision – the physical limits to what our eyes are capable of taking in from a given viewpoint – remains the same no matter what distance we are from whatever it is we're looking at. This means that the closer we are to something, the narrower our clear breadth of vision will be. To adjust our field of view beyond these limits, we have to physically move our heads (or our entire person) to alter our viewpoint.

To see more of what's in front of us, our normal reaction is to step back a bit and refocus for the more distant view. To obtain a 'wide' view, as of a landscape, we need to site ourselves at some considerable distance from our subject. When we're looking at things from a fair way away like this, our 'field of clear vision' is usually quite a lot wider than it is when we're 'close to' our subject – to an extent that depends on the particular characteristics of our eyes (ie, which sight defects we suffer from!). Viewing things at longer ranges also brings into play another facet of our visual perception – the way the focusing action of the lenses of our eyes alters the way we perceive the relationship between different objects in our field of view. Although nowhere near as pronounced as the acute compression produced by artificial multi-lens devices like telescopes – after which the effect is named – our natural vision does result in a degree of 'telescoping'. This is when verticals and laterals in the view appear to move closer together with distance, foreshortening curves and 'bunching' parallels – an effect already noted in Chapter 4 when considering curve radii. In addition to this visual compression, we also perceive distance through our colour vision. The filtering effect of the atmosphere alters the colour values of distant objects by refracting and reflecting light, as described in my look at natural lighting back in Chapter 2; the resulting changes in hue and fall-off in the intensity of the colours of objects gives us our 'dim, blue distance'. Along with the compression effects, this colour regression is a property we can make use of when composing the scenes making up our layout.

BELOW: *The wide view is the distant one, as in this atmospheric shot of the Devon side of the Tamar Valley taken from Drakewalls, on the slopes of Kit Hill in Cornwall; those sunlit fields are a good couple of miles away. And yes, it was raining where I was standing! No model could reproduce this sort of viewpoint without the use of a backdrop. This is also a very good example of distance regression by colour intensity – something we can replicate on a model.* Author

The model view

When it comes to looking at a model railway, we have to take account of various practical factors that rather limit our options when it comes to selecting a viewpoint. The key considerations here are our visual acuity – how well we can physically *see* the detail and texture that makes a model what it is – allied to the purely practical necessity of obtaining the right physical relationship with the model to enable us to get a good view or to operate it. In the case of almost all model railways saving the truly expansive affair in a large scale, the normal comfortable viewing distance as a spectator is of the order of a yard or less. When working on the model or performing delicate operating tasks like coupling-up, we're often a good deal closer – for some things, down to a range of a few inches. At these sort of distances, our field of clear vision is extremely restricted; if I stand a yard in front of 'Trerice' like a squaddie on parade (eyes to the front and head still…) I can *just* see either end of the model, which is a whole

ABOVE: *The typical viewpoint for a model railway: 2–3ft from the subject, with a 'head still' span of clear vision of about 3–4ft. It's this limited visual span that allows us to 'get away with' such large degrees of selective compression on our models; because we're so close, we can't see enough of the scene at one go to register those missing distances.* Adrian Colenutt

4ft 9in long. The bit I can see comfortably and clearly, however, is only the middle 3ft or so. To take in the whole four-and-a-bit feet comfortably I certainly swivel my gaze and usually turn my head slightly. On 'Cade's Green', which was originally 7ft long, I could comfortably view most of the model – say, 6ft or so – by simply moving my head and eyes. Now it's grown to a bit over 10ft, however, I find I have to move my viewpoint to take in the extremities. My conclusion is that about 6ft of layout is the most we can visually cope with from a fixed point at our typical viewing distance.

Distance recession

So where does this sort of view leave us in terms of distance recession? Well, in looking at our small-scale model from a yard or so away, what we're trying to reproduce is the outlook we'd get when looking at the real thing from several times that range – an equivalent distance that varies directly in line with the scale of the model. In terms of straight arithmetic, to determine how far away you are in scale terms, you simply multiply the *actual* viewing distance by the scale ratio of the model, keeping the unit of measurement (feet, yards, metres – it matters not) constant. Thus, a 4mm scale layout viewed from our nominal three-feet-away position would equate to looking at a real railway from 3 x 76.2ft = 228.6ft. Which is actually quite a 'long' view; enough to have noticeable implications in terms of the 'distance recession' brought about by a combination of altered colour values, and perspective/foreshortening effects. As a simplistic aid to visualising how far these equivalent viewing distances actually are, I think in terms of a queue of good old London double-decker buses – 'eight feet wide and thirty feet long', according to Flanders and Swann; (must be an 'RTW'…). Thus, the '4mm scale equivalent view' would be from a bit over seven buses away. Conjure that image up in your mind's eye and you'll soon appreciate that these are significant distances!

Obviously, when looking at a typical model from our actual distance of a scant yard or less, none of these distance recession factors is going to have much effect on what we see; only in the case of a really large model with very deep scenes – like Pendon – will there be any degree of 'natural' recession. This means that to create the right illusion in a small space, we're going to have to suggest the effects of recession by artificially introducing them into our modelled scene. Careful attention to colour values – especially those on a backdrop – is one obvious way we can

BELOW: *Only a model of the size of 'Pendon' can induce any natural feeling of distance recession within itself – as here, where the foot of the down is a scale distance of some 500 or more feet from the viewer. Few layouts can offer this kind of visual scope.* Pendon Archive

BELOW: *Although viewed from the typical yard or so, the restrained colouring used by Chris Lammacraft on his exquisite 4mm scale model of Hemyock station, is entirely consistent with the prototype when seen from some way away. The 'distant' object with 'upfront' colouring is a classic modelling giveaway.* Author

create a feeling of distance, but that still ignores the matter of perspective compression and foreshortening. As already argued in the case of curve radii, by carefully altering the relationships between objects and changing their relative sizes and dimensions we can create a 'distorted' version of reality that is actually *more* visually convincing than a mathematically exact scale replica. This sort of deceitful fiddling-about with reality is a technique known as 'selective compression', and I'd argue that in the cause of realism it is probably our most powerful tool. My experience is that almost every type of layout – even big, expansive ones – can benefit from a modicum of artfully-applied compression.

Selective compression; applying the visual squeeze

As with an artist painting a picture, creating a convincing and pleasing model railway is often more about creating an effective illusion than it is about achieving some slavishly-exact rendition of reality. The subject is regarded with a selective eye and 'edited' to preserve its essentials and character, with the aim of producing a result that tricks the eye into seeing a result which rings true while adapting it to the needs of the 'canvas' and 'medium' – which, in railway modelling terms, equate to the space available and the materials and techniques to be used to build the thing. It's the first of these – space – that poses the biggest visual problem, for railways as a subject almost invariably sprawl to an extent that rules out the simple numerically derived scale modelling approach in any but the smallest sizes. That's especially true of length; almost inevitably, we're forced to cram our subject into a scale distance that is frequently the merest fraction of what it should be. The trick is to carry out this cramming without the result looking cramped – the other end to which selective compression is a means.

This is all well and good in theory, but how do you actually arrive at a workable degree of compression in practice? After all, the dimensions of a lot of the elements in the modelled scene – the footprints of pointwork formations, engineering features and structures, curve radii, gradient lengths and so on – are either fixed by the scale of the model, or determined by practical considerations. So merely applying an overall compression factor – reducing everything by a given percentage – is not the answer. Apart from effectively altering the overall scale of the model, it wouldn't anyway produce the desired result, which is a form of controlled distortion. The real trick is to keep the basic scale fixed but achieving the necessary dimensional cuts and related distortions *without it noticing*. Fortunately, there are quite a lot of ways in which this can be done. The problem is that there's no way of summarising these in simple rule-of-thumb universal formula; rather, it's a case of understanding the various dodges and picking the right combination for a particular situation.

Compressing reality

The difficulties are obviously most acute when you're trying to design a layout depicting an actual scene, as the relative sizes and positions of the elements making up that scene are fixed by reality. If you're going to have any chance of producing a convincing representation, you obviously can't monkey about much with these fundamentals; any 'tweaking' will have to be subtle, so that it doesn't destroy the overall 'look' of the scene. The designer of a fictional/freelance layout has an easier time of it in this regard, as he can at least select elements that better fit the available space. Even so, it is rarely possible (or even, as argued above, desirable) to just add up the linear requirements of all these elements and simply set that figure as the layout length as some adjustment will be needed to compensate for lack of space as well as to balance everything up and create an appropriate degree of distance recession.

Therefore, the secret to successful compression lies in achieving it without upsetting the perceived *proportions* (including distance compression) of the scene as a whole. As proportions are effectively visual comparisons, then it's the *look* of something in relationship to all the other elements surrounding it which is important, rather than its strict scale dimensions. Compress only one element without adjusting those others to which it relates, and the result will usually stick out like a sore thumb! An example of this basic problem is that common candidate for the chop, the station platform. Curtailing the length of one of these has two immediate and obvious effects: First, it upsets the relationship of the platform length to that of the trains that need to pull up alongside it, so that engines which should be coming to a stand at the platform ramp, nicely within the starting signals, are suddenly away down the line somewhere (a 'SPAD'), or, at terminals, hard against the stop blocks with a coach or two left dangling out of the platform on the other end. Secondly, those station buildings that should be grouped neatly along a quarter or so of the platform length are sprawling over all but half of it.

Solving the first part of this conundrum is usually easy enough – adjust the train lengths to preserve the correct relationship with the truncated platform, either by dropping a vehicle or two out of the formation or, more subtly, by choosing shorter stock if you can do so. In fact, this need to shorten trains somewhat is almost a *sine qua non* on any layout that calls for much in the way of longitudinal compression in the first place. Apart from all the visual considerations, if you're short of length then you won't want to be allocating any more than you have to 'offstage' trackage/fiddleyards. If it is easy enough to trim the trains, though, the station buildings are a much tougher proposition. A lot will depend on how long the platform was to start with and by how much it has to be curtailed. Very short platforms rarely call for much in the way of compression anyway, so at one extreme the problem scarcely exists. At the other extreme, the very long platform – particularly those with the buildings all bunched up at one end of it – allows you to lop a fair bit out without the missing length being particularly apparent. You still end up with a goodish length of platform extending away from the buildings, which is the visually significant factor.

The real problem comes with that common scenario,

a platform of moderate capacity – six to eight coaches, say – allied to a goodly set of buildings extending along a third to a half of its length. Here, there is very little scope to take much length out of the platform before the buildings begin to look disproportionately dominant, rather like a classic two-coach tinplate toy-train station. This means two things: you haven't got a great deal of scope for platform shortening *per se*, which means you will have to look harder for length savings elsewhere, and secondly, you may well have to consider reducing the length of the buildings below their true scale value. On some designs of building – such as the LNWR's sectional timber structures – you can *sometimes* get away with taking a bay or two out of the woodwork without the subterfuge becoming too obvious. Similarly, on buildings hiding behind a GE-style multi-span ridge-and-valley platform awning, you can omit an up-and-down or two of awning and shorten the buildings accordingly without the deception shouting at you.

Proportional reduction

For most types of building however, just cutting length without doing anything else will destroy the basic proportions of the building, when bang goes authenticity and, usually, realism. The answer here is to reduce the modelling scale of the building *as a whole* slightly, reducing the *dimensions* while preserving the *proportions* – a ploy known as 'proportional reduction'. I pulled this trick on Andrew Duncan's 'Maiden Newtown', where the main station building and branch-line train shed are actually modelled at 93 per cent of their true scale size. This modest deception saved something close to two inches of vital length and allowed us to get away with a platform eight inches shy of scale value without it being too apparent. No one has yet spotted this particular piece of 'controlled distortion' without it being pointed out to them, not even Andrew!

In fact, tweaking scale but maintaining proportion is a very useful weapon in the realistic modeller's armoury, as it facilitates not just needful compression but also a mild degree of enhanced distance recession; a spot of such basic trickery is a great way to preserve visual depth when the necessary inches are absent from the available site. There are limits, of course, as to how far you can take this 'downscaling' or distorting of structures or other features. Much depends, I find, on the position of whatever it is you're intending to 'squeeze' relative to the viewer. The further back in the scene it is, the more you can squeeze it without the end result looking odd. In fact, it is surprising what you can get away with! As an example, the linhay of the clay dry, to use a West Country expression for an open-fronted shed, on my 4mm scale 'Trerice' layout – located at the rear of a very small cameo model and thus quite close to the viewer – is actually modelled at 1:90 scale, about 85 per cent of its correct-to-4mm/1ft size. This fairly drastic shrinkage keeps the structure looking right in proportion to the restricted dimensions of the layout and stops it being over-dominant, as well as placing it visually 'well back' in the scene.

ABOVE: *Selective compression, the modeller's saviour. The station platforms at Maiden Newtown are a scale 50 or so feet shorter than the originals at Maiden Newton. To keep things in proportion, the station buildings have been modelled at only 93 per cent of their true scale size; the giveaway is that phone box, which comes a tad too far up the windows.* Author

If you do 'squeeze' a structure this much, though, don't forget to adjust the scale of immediately-adjacent figures and accessories by a broadly similar amount. Thus, the clay-workers at Higher Trerice are all *gastarbeiters*, being German figures from Merten and Prieser in H0 scale, as are their tools and wheelbarrows. At 1:87 proportion, these are still fractionally oversize when compared directly with the scale of the building, being a compromise between that and the 1:76.2 scale of the trains. In this instance, I also had to maintain the elevation of the actual loading bank at its true scale value, as that related to the height of the top of the clay-wagon sides. To compensate, I tweaked the size of the linhay doorways and their 'elevator hoods' a bit to keep the general proportions of the façade as close to the original as

BELOW: *The squeezing of the scales deceives the eye; although the buildings seen here are modelled at 1:90 proportion and the loco is at 1:76.2, the subterfuge isn't too obvious, even in close-up. The accessories – ladder, barrows, conveyer – are H0 1:87 models, somewhere between the two!* Author

possible. The result of all this jiggery-pokery is surprisingly convincing, even in close-up.

Judging whether something is going to look OK when 'squeezed' like this is really a matter of trial-and-error judged by eye. It is just one of the many occasions during the layout-planning process when mocking up a proposed arrangement at full size – an invaluable designing tool on which you will find much more in the next chapter – can swiftly resolve visual and spatial problems. I'd love to be able to trot out a neat table of appropriate scale compressions for every situation, but I don't think that's possible; there are simply too many disparate factors involved. The only rule of thumb I can usefully offer are some rough limits from my own experience, which suggest that you can't usually get away with going below about 90 per cent of true size on objects in the foreground, dropping to around 65 per cent at the rear of a reasonably deep scene. The other inviolate rule is that proportions are more important than dimensions. This is true as much of things like landforms and earthworks as it is of structures; so, for instance, if you have to 'compress' a hill, be sure to take as much out of the height as you do out of the footprint. That way, you'll preserve the all-important slope of the ground and avoid ending up with an unintended Alp. Keeping true proportions when compressing landforms is particularly important where they meet the earthworks of the railway; the unstable-looking embankment and the cutting-side so steep as to be a landslide waiting to happen are modelling chestnuts as old as the hobby…

Composition

I have already advanced the notion that model railways can be made to work visually as artistic compositions in their own right, with well-balanced proportions, a pleasing arrangement of forms and harmonious colouring. Even a model depicting an actual location can be 'composed' thus by careful selection of viewpoints and orientation, much as a photographer seeks the ideal vantage point from which to take his picture. Happy proportions are arrived at by careful consideration of a number of factors: the precise layout footprint in terms of depth versus length, the height of the scene visible twixt lower (layout) and upper (lighting) fascias, and the relationship between the size of the actual models and the limits of the scenic 'envelope' by which they are contained. And yes, that relationship is to a large extent determined by scale and subject. On a given site size, the height and depth proportions appropriate to 0 scale urban/industrial modelling would be quite different to those suited to something open and pastoral in N.

Composing the scene of a model railway to look pleasing and well-balanced is all about being aware of the way the

BELOW: *Graham Hedges' 'Stoney Lane Depot' is one of the 2mm layouts I most admire. It is not only beautifully observed and modelled, but to my eye the composition, visual balance and colouring are all spot-on. The choice and placement of the structures, the lack of obvious parallels and right-angles and the subtle curve of the elevated main line make an interesting, satisfying and harmonious whole. It is also well presented and realistically lit.* Adrian Colenutt

LEFT: *Flowing curves and interesting angles always make for pleasing visual effect, as exemplified by Simon de Souza's exquisite P4 'Corrieshalloch', which does without an obvious parallel or obtrusive right-angle on the property. Precious little straight track, either – quite appropriate in the Scottish highlands.* Author

various visual factors over which we have some control can be handled. These factors include size, mass and scale of objects and their placement within the scene, the degree of compression as just discussed, and the detail level/texture and colouration of all the various elements making up the model. As with the need to be consistent in modelling standard that I have argued as vital in the cause of realism, it is the contribution of individual models to the visual quality and unity of the whole layout which is the priority here. The goal is to create a harmonious entity rather than some mere assemblage of individual components; each piece of the 3-D jigsaw which goes to make up the final result needs to be considered as part of the overall scheme of things, rather than in isolation. This 'overall scheme of things' very much includes the design of the presentation that sets off the actual modelling. The key to getting the best and most pleasing arrangement and balance between all these aspects lies not just in colour and texture, but also in careful attention to line, proportion and the 'composing' of the whole model.

Curves and lines

I think that most people would agree that nothing is more pleasing to the human eye than a flowing, lissom curve. Except, possibly, an assemblage of such curves, arranged in harmony and proportion – such as might be found in a beautiful landscape or the entrancing outlines of Catherine Deneuve. By contrast, nothing is more visually sterile than a series of parallel straight lines, intersected only by other straight lines aligned exactly at right angles to them. Why is it, then, that so many model railways seem to be designed as if tied somehow to a sheet of graph paper, with everything aligned on some arbitrary and implacable grid? Quite apart from the aesthetic sterility with which the model is thus imbued, it's almost invariably unrealistic; very little in nature and surprisingly little in artifice takes the form of unrelenting dead-straight parallels and normals exactly aligned with the plane of view.

As a lover of landscape and long-time admirer of '*la plus belle* Catherine', I'm firmly wedded to the curve as the principal design element for my model railways. Not that I go all Dali-esque; things that would in reality be straight are straight also on the model; it's just that where there's a choice – as in the shape of the overall layout footprint (especially the front edge), the nature of the track alignments, the courses of the various roadways, watercourses and boundaries in the scene and, of course, the forms of the landscape – then I go for curves every time. Not exaggerated, swoopy scallops, mind; subtle and gently sinuous is more the sort of thing. Circles and arcs per se are actually pretty rare in nature, so most of these curves are more-or-less irregular – usually pleasingly parabolic and of constantly varying radius. As with so many aspects of visual design, a bit of trial-and-error adjudged by the unerring eye is in my experience far more effective than any amount of theory, mathematics or micrometric measurement. That mock-up, again…

If I embrace curves with enthusiasm when mapping out my models, the one thing I emphatically seek to *avoid* is too many parallel alignments, especially straight ones. Some, parallels are of course, unavoidable, in that they are inherent in the prototype. Many man-made features – roads, ditches and canals, structures of all kinds – incorporate them; in the case of railway track they are decidedly desirable! But what is neither necessary nor desirable is the oft-seen sterility of a model in which the rear edge of the scene, the track, any roadways or waterways within the scene and the front edge of the model are all precisely and rigidly parallel – never more so when all these elements are also relentlessly unbending. The same goes for the preponderance of right angles that so often accompany such an obsession with regularity. I'd argue that the road that intersects the

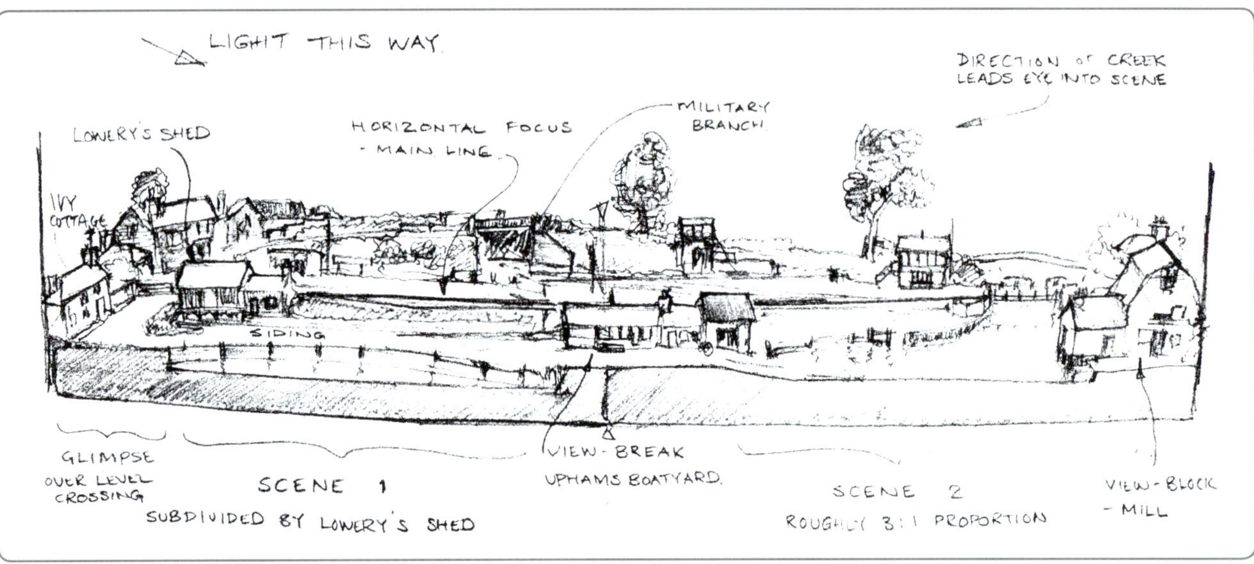

ABOVE: *Design sketch for 'Woolverstone', showing how the basic scene is broken up into discrete zones using foreground structures and dominant elements like the tall trees as view breaks. The result is to create a series of well-proportioned sub-scenes which direct and contain the eye.*

railway slightly on the skew *always* makes for a bridge or crossing that is both more interesting and more realistic. When you start to really *look* at the prototype, dead-square intersections are relatively rare. To me, a model railway that is based too much on straight alignments, circular curves, relentless parallels and abundant right-angles smacks irrevocably of the train-set; realistic and visually rich it ain't!

BELOW: *One of the sub-scenes on 'Woolverstone' – the level crossing and roadway, bounded by the buildings disguising the track exit to the left, and by the foreground view block of the corrugated-iron store on the right.* Author

Scenes and sub-scenes

Any scenic model railway is actually made up of a collection of disparate features – landscape forms, buildings, engineering features, trees, areas of water and so on – dispersed about a common space. The way these various components are arranged within the scene and the relationship they have one to another is what determines the visual balance of the scene, and the business of establishing the best location, size, colouring and degree of detailing for each individual feature is what I mean by 'composing' the model. In the case of the typical long but relatively narrow shelf-form scenic model railway viewed from the front, what we're basically talking about is the way that these elements are distributed along the length of the layout and how the result looks when seen from the typical yard-in-front spectating viewpoint.

The aim is to arrive at a disposition of the various elements that is broadly balanced, with the more dominant features – items in the immediate foreground, prominent landscape forms, areas of water, large buildings or groups of buildings, major engineering features and strong verticals like industrial chimneys or electricity pylons – dispersed along the length of the layout in a pleasing manner rather than being bunched together or scattered randomly. How you go about this dispersion depends to a considerable extent on the length of the layout in relation to the typical field of view which, as we have already determined above, is around six feet for the average human standing a yard or less in front of the layout frontage.

Small, self-contained 'cameo' layouts will fall entirely within this limited visual span; indeed, the cameo concept doesn't really work if they don't! Longer layouts will however, extend beyond a single visual span – and to appreciate them we have to move along the frontage to obtain a series of sequential views. Thus, even the longest of layouts is effectively viewed as a series of 'sub-scenes', each six feet or less in breadth. So it makes sense to *plan* our model thus – which brings the compositional challenge down to, effectively, the pleasing visual division of the layout along these 'sub-scenic' lines, together with the arrangement of elements in a balanced way within those sub-scenes. The trick is to get these divisions and elements into a harmonious visual relationship.

The Golden Mean

Most of the rules governing composition I learned back in art school are concerned with visual relationships based on the use of the 'Golden Mean'. This hallowed tenet of classical art and design is a proportional ratio derived from that point at which a line can be divided such that the ratio between the two portions of the divided line is exactly the same as the ratio of the longer portion to the original length of the whole line. I won't bore you with the algebra involved, but with a suitable fanfare will reveal that the magic ratio, rounded to a manageable number of decimal places, is 1:1.618. The unique mathematical property of this ratio is that when you express it as a fraction – 1 over 1.618 – and carry out the division, the answer is 0.618. I think I'm right in saying that this is the only fraction in which this numerical correlation occurs, which is why mathematicians get so excited about it. Visually, this 'golden' ratio of proportion is widely found in the natural world as well as forming a fundamental of art and architecture from the Ancient Greeks onwards. Much store is set by the 'golden rectangle' – one with the longer side 1.618 x the shorter; leaving aside the façade of the Parthenon (the most

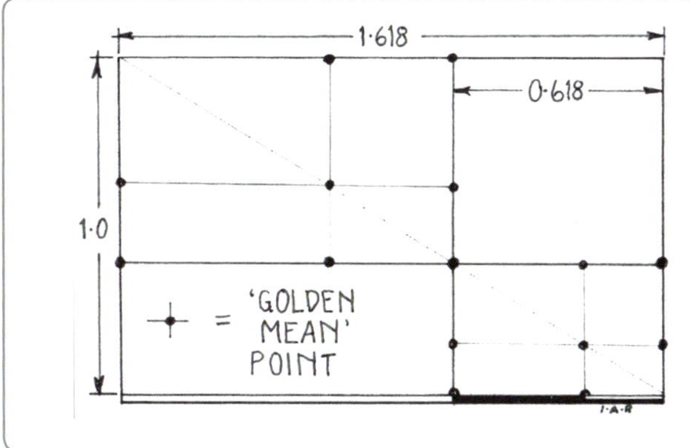

ABOVE: *'Golden mean' proportions.*

hackneyed example), many great 'old master' paintings are painted on canvases employing these proportions, while they are the shape of, among other things, a Georgian sash window, a traditional 'foolscap folio' book and many contemporary 'widescreen' TVs and computer monitors.

However, when it comes to the 'visual canvas' of a typical model railway – basically, the size and shape of the aperture left between the lower and upper fascias and whatever it is that defines the ends of the modelled scene – then we're faced with something only approximately rectangular and whose proportions are several country miles away from any 'golden mean'. Even if it is of the most modest length, a model railway looked at face-on has a basic outline more akin to a letterbox, if not a crack in the floorboards; 'slit-like' is the description often used to suggest a height-to-width ratio more in the range of 1:5 or so at the 'cameo' end to 1:20 and more on larger layouts. Where would *that* have left the ancient Greeks, I'd like to know?

However, the golden mean isn't just held out as an ideal proportion in which to lay out a perfect rectangle; it's also held to be the most harmonious manner in which to *divide* something – anything! For the ratio can be applied to any axis of any space or shape, whatever its outline. The 'mean ratio' can be used to divide, sub-divide and sub-sub-divide (ad infinitum) our visual space, these lines of division creating a whole series of 'golden mean points' within that space. Placing objects either on these mean points, or grouping them within the 'golden spaces' defined *by* the mean points, is the oldest principle of artistic composition or visual design, and is just as relevant to railway modelling as it is to fine art, architecture, or design. So just because the overall shape of the 'canvas' of our typical model railway departs so widely from the ideal outline does not imply that the principle of the golden mean has no relevance to our layout's visual design. We can use it to plot the boundaries of our 'sub-scenes' and the position of key objects or alignments within them – including elements depicted on the backscene.

Scene division

As already postulated, the main form of visual arrangement of a model railway is the breaking down of the overall longitudinal scene into the series of 'sub-scenes'. This form of sub-division happens on all model railways, whether intentionally arranged or otherwise; inevitably, the more dominant objects which go to making up the model visually 'chop it up' into a number of discreet areas. Arranging things so that these boundaries occur as close as possible to golden mean points is an obvious way of creating pleasing proportions within the layout. The principle can then be reapplied to the positioning of elements within each 'sub-scene', once again promoting good visual balance, as described below. Working to such alignments may seem a tall order – particularly when trying to re-create a real scene in model form – but my experience is that it's surprising how often arranging things to place them optimally with reference to the 'Golden Grid' is only a matter of tweaking them an inch or so. Once again, this is something that is easy and worthwhile to determine in the context of a sketch model or full-size planning mock-up. Even where it is not possible to place things *exactly* on 'mean points', getting them as close as practicable still helps; as always, a little compromise is almost inevitable in all aspects of layout design.

While you *can* spend a lot of time with a measuring tape and calculator plotting 'golden mean points' precisely on your mock-up or layout, this isn't necessary as you can easily make yourself a golden mean sighting bar', as used by the smart set c500BC. This sounds grand but is actually very simple, and as can be seen from the picture, mine is an ordinary plastic 12in ruler with a white line painted on at the appropriate point – which is, of course, 0.618 of the total length from one end. As my ruler is 323mm long, this 'magic line' is conveniently 200mm from datum. (It should

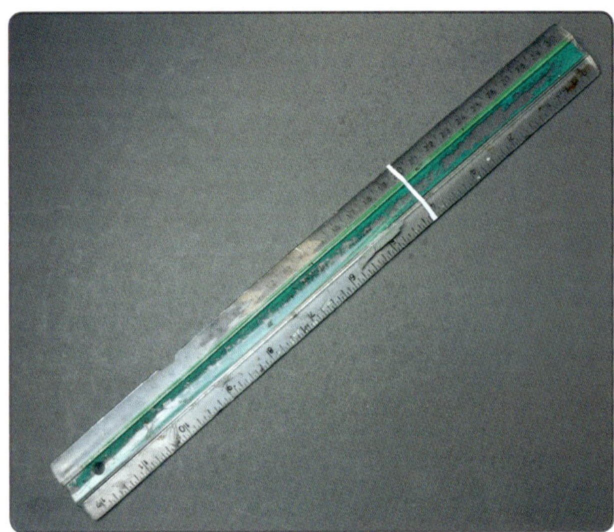

ABOVE: *Rice's long-serving sighting bar for judging the 'golden mean'; a scabrous old 12in ruler with a line in the appropriate place.* Author

be 199.6, but there are limits!) To use this ancient device in the best Classical manner, don a toga or other suitable garment and find yourself an assistant, preferably young and glamorous (one thing daughters are good for!). Holding the device at arm's length in front of you, shut one eye and squint at your bar. Step back (carefully!) until the ends of the bar line up with the points between which you want to establish your golden division, and direct your assistant while they move whatever it is you're trying to locate (or place a marker of some sort) in alignment with the mean point on the bar. Job done. If you're lacking the assistance, you can go by trial and error: squint and decide *roughly* where the object/marker needs to be by reference to established features. Stick object in place, step back, re-squint, correct location – and so on, until you get it right.

While this system of 'golden means' is usually held up as the ideal way of designing and composing things visually, it can't always be applied and it is by no means the only option. In some contexts – such as a model set in an urban environment where buildings, streets and so on are on some sort of grid – then symmetrical arrangements or things spaced at regular intervals may be more appropriate. However, in the sort of free-form landscape context typical of most British model railways, such four-square regularity tends to look stilted and unrealistic. The point about the golden mean disposition is that it manages to locate things in a relationship that's aesthetically pleasing but mathematically irregular. As a more general rule of thumb, using a proportional ratio of 3:5 – which, at 1:1.66 is pretty close to gold anyway – achieves a broadly similar type of disposition. However, it is worth stressing that *all* such aesthetic considerations are anyway subject to the over-arching rule of the artistic railway modeller's mantra – the one that starts 'If it *looks* right ...' It was, after all, the good old Mk1 human eyeball that discerned the 'golden mean' in the first place!

Visual balance

As well as the matter of carefully dividing the visual field of the model up in this considered way, it is also a good idea to take account of the 'visual weight' of the elements making up the sub-scenes, to try to get these into some sort of equilibrium. One way to do this is to imagine each sub-scene as a sort of visual see-saw, on which 'visually heavy' objects have to be counterbalanced either with another object of similar visual mass, or with a collection of smaller objects of lesser mass. As with any form of see-saw, the effect of each item will depend on its relationship to the point of balance. So if, for instance, there are 'heavy' objects such as large buildings or dominant landforms to be accommodated, from the balance point of view these can be sited in several ways: as equally massive objects sitting at either end of the scene; as a single mass

BELOW: *Achieving visual balance.*

situated directly over the mid-point; or as one of a series of objects of different sizes and visual weights sited at varying distances from the point of balance so that they 'cancel out' each other's mass. Of these options, the first can be described as 'sterile' – everything at the ends, nowt in t'middle; the second may be neutral in balance terms but will visually chop the scene clean in half – which, as we've just established, is proportionally undesirable; the third is by far the most likely to result in something that makes sense in terms of producing a realistic result as well as being interesting to look at while retaining good visual balance.

ABOVE: *A classic small-but-significant foreground view-block is the yard office on 'Trerice' which, together with the fence, gate, noticeboard and phone-pole (not forgetting Arthur Trewhin, resident shunter), forms a visually busy front-of-stage 'incident' that divides the overall scene in twain, in this instance in the ratio of 1:2 ($\frac{1}{3}$ / $\frac{2}{3}$).* Author

Determining and adjusting the 'visual weight' of a layout's elements such as buildings, landforms and engineering features is a subtle business, as it depends on a number of factors, of which the most important are: size and proportions (especially height); closeness to the viewer; degree of detail and texture, and colour. Thus, a small, highly detailed, strongly coloured object sited 'stage front' may well have a greater 'visual weight' than something much larger, but flatter and duller, set at the rear of the scene. So a 'small but weighty' foreground structure could be balanced, visually speaking, by a big hill painted on the backscene. As we have considerable control over most of the factors just identified, it is quite possible to balance-up a scene without compromising realism or practicality by simply adjusting things like fore-to-aft position, detail and relief and colouring. Where you want to create a 'scenic break' or division-point, you can readily do so by increasing the visual weight of whatever it is you have located at that point, either by 'upping' its detail, texture, colour, size and prominence or – more subtly – by downplaying other elements of the scene slightly in relation to the 'key point'. This is another instance where it can be very useful to apply the 'visual squeeze' and down-size structures and land-forms, or to adjust colour values and textures to make them 'recede'.

Viewblocks and sight-lines

I may have conveyed the impression that the division of the overall layout into sub-scenes is a matter of placing something large and obvious – like a big building or a girt great hill – to form the 'dividing point' between one sub-scene and another, Well, that is certainly one way of doing it, but we can be considerably more subtle – especially with the sort of eye-level viewpoint advocated in these pages. When an object is both close to eye level and close to your viewpoint, it does not have to be particularly large to have a considerable visual impact. Even quite a modest feature – a smallish structure, minor landform or tree of slight habit – will be sufficient to act as a viewblock if so placed, restricting the extent of the area of the scene that can be seen from that particular viewpoint. Creating such a 'blind area' by cutting off the sightlines in a given direction is a very good way of setting the boundaries of a sub-scene without, in visual terms, 'stating the bloomin' obvious'. Such a view-block boundary can be defined by quite a small and inconsequential object not calling for a lot of real-estate, being thus both effective but economical.

Near eye-level viewblocks created by carefully-sized and sited foreground objects have several other uses in visual design terms as they can both 'frame' and draw attention to what you *do* want to be seen and hide that which you *don't*. Arranging such a viewblock – a small rise in the ground surmounted by a modest tree or two, say – to conceal the point where the track leaves the modelled scene can often get around the 'hole in the sky' problem without always having to resort to a bridge or a tunnel mouth. Controlling sight-lines with viewblocks can also avoid awkward bits of perspective and hide over-tight curves and other visual intrusions. Where viewblocks are dispersed about the layout such that they briefly interrupt the view of the track from time to time, so that trains pass behind them as they traverse the modelled scene, then a further raft of benefits can accrue. First, the fact that our trains are frequently shorter than they should be is less apparent, as the whole length of them is not on view at once. Secondly, the sense of 'journey' is enhanced and the paucity of the overall length of run disguised as the trains pass through a series of 'short events' divided by the viewblocks rather than traversing a single none-too-long one. Thirdly, it is usually the case with reality that the view of trains is not entirely unhindered – in which case, the occasional foreground object impeding the view is more realistic than simply having every inch of track 'stage front'.

Perspective

Few model railways this side of Pendon extend far enough away from the viewer to exhibit much in the way of natural perspective or visual recession. I've already suggested some minor use of 'enhanced' perspective effects by reducing the scale, detail level and colour intensity of structures and other elements situated at the rear of a scene. However, there is only fairly limited scope for this sort of thing in the sort of depth available on most of the sites we have to work with, so over-much in the way of natural perspective effect is something we have to learn to live without. In a quest to trick the eye into believing there's more to a scene than is actually the case, various modellers at various times have attempted to incorporate a degree of false perspective modelling in their layouts by fiddling around with converging parallels. I have to say though, very rarely to convincing effect.

True false-perspective modelling involves not only the artificial reduction of scale and gradation of colour and texture, but also the manipulation of the *shapes* of the actual objects in view so that they mimic the appearance they would assume when viewed at a greater distance. The angles of the 'lines of perspective' – those parallel straight lines in objects or in the landscape that would in nature converge to a 'vanishing point' situated precisely on the eye-level horizon – are steepened, and the vanishing-point taken off of that true eye-level, to give a false impression of distance *when seen from a given viewpoint*. And there's the rub; as soon as you move even an inch or two away from the viewpoint around which this false perspective is arranged, the distortions become horribly apparent and the result, far from enhancing realism, destroys it. Only where there is only one possible viewpoint does such false-perspective modelling ever truly work. Those few successful applications I've seen on model railways have all employed viewblocks to hide the false-perspective element of the scene from all other points of view except the intended one, as in the brilliantly executed street scene on 'Pempoul'.

Unless you have a very clear idea of what you're doing – in which case you won't be bothering to read this sketchy summary! – then I'd strongly suggest giving any form of false perspective a wide berth in the visual planning of your model. In fact, I'd go further than that, and suggest that it is a good idea to avoid, as far as is humanly possible, incorporating any artificially fixed perspective elements into the modelled scene – *including* things drawn on the backdrop. While there's no

BELOW: *A brilliant (but rare!) example of effective perspective modelling on 'Pempoul': the village street, which uses forced perspective and scale compression to give additional depth to an otherwise too-shallow scene. It works because the possible viewpoint is carefully limited by confining view-blocks like the foreground 'transformateur' and the street structures themselves; the 'downhill' view is a touch of pure Gravett genius.* Gordon Gravett

ABOVE: *Effective use of perspective drawing on backdrops is a skilled business. Here, on Mike Clarke's beautifully subtle backdrop for 'Llanastr', the houses of the village are glimpsed in the visual gap between the station building and the road bridge – both of which act as view blockers to cut out the off-axis 'wrong view'. Note also the excellent colour blend of backscene and foreground modelling. Magic!* Author

ABOVE: *With backscenes, the rule is generally the simpler the better – as here, on Karl Crowther's beautifully restrained 'Kentside', which really catches the open, airy feel of the Morecambe Bay shoreline with this almost-abstract rendition.* Adrian Colenutt

doubt in my mind that the biggest contribution to successfully creating a feeling of depth and distance in a model comes from the appropriate use of backscenes – the only way I know of compressing umpteen miles of real-estate into the thickness of a sheet of paper – if you try to be too clever it's all too easy to end up with a result that looks decidedly 'odd' when viewed other than straight-on. And nowhere is this effect more evident than where the backscene attempts to incorporate 'converging parallels' and similar perspective elements, especially those that recede, such as roads and the sides of buildings.

The problem is, once again, that of viewpoint. Any given perspective of a view or object only appears as you see it – in terms of the location of the vanishing-point and the converging angles of the parallels – from a single fixed viewpoint. Move from that point, even slightly, and the perspective changes; the vanishing point effectively moves with the viewer (in nature, it is actually the point where your own visual centreline meets the horizon) and the angles of all the converging lines change accordingly. So any such lines painted on the backscene are only ever going to 'work' visually when viewed from the precise point from which they were drawn; all other viewing angles will simply look either odd or odder still! To avoid this anomaly, there are two answers: use viewblocks as already described, to cut out all but the desired viewpoint; or don't try and stick perspective elements into the backscene in the first place. The latter has always been my preferred option!

Backscene design

Perhaps this section should be headed 'Designing *around* a backscene'. So far as scenic model railways go, I'm a firm believer in backscenes – although, like a lot of modellers, I tried for a long while to 'do without'. Nowadays, I regard a backscene as an absolutely fundamental part of any model railway with any pretensions to realism, as necessary as the baseboards and track – and therefore something that needs to be designed-in from the outset and considered very much as an integral part of the visual design. A backscene has two prime functions: to cut out illusion-destroying distractions behind the modelling, and to add the 'distance' otherwise obviously missing from our inevitably compressed scenes. That said, there's no denying that providing an effective backdrop is structurally far from easy, especially on sectional/portable/exhibition layouts, and a few alternative approaches were advanced back in Chapter 3.

However it is arranged structurally, a backdrop will neither counter distraction nor add convincing distance if it draws attention to itself by being too 'busy', by using colour that is too strong, or is unrelated to the hues of the modelled scene, or if it incorporates disturbing visual elements like the sort of duff perspective just described. The most effective backscenes, in my experience, are those that fulfil their basic function in the simplest possible way. That such backscenes are also the simplest to contrive is a rather large added bonus! Few of us are good enough artists to paint something that can stand up as a piece of artwork in its own right, while no-one – no matter how gifted or clever – can overcome the laws of perspective just outlined. So my own 'take' on the whole backscene business has been to try to arrange the layout's design so that the contribution that the backscene is intended to make to the overall scene is limited to those areas that I feel I can handle: the provision of the all-important sky, and the suggestion of some *distant* landscape. Simple outlines of far-way hills, with perhaps some basic rendition of field boundaries and woodlands, or an urban skyline reduced to a series of dim silhouettes, is about all I ever attempt. Given that reduction in perceived colour and texture is a prime characteristic of distance

ABOVE: *Here's a classic way of blending foreground modelling with the backscene – rising ground topped by something (a hedge, in this case) that forms a natural silhouette against the 'distance'. To avoid shadows, that telegraph pole has the arms to the rear of the pole, firmly in contact with the painted backscene; it's a ploy that few notice, and a lot less obvious than an unwanted shadow.* Author

BELOW: *Sometimes shadows against the backdrop can be useful disguise; the overhanging trees bordering the roadway in the rear corner of 'Hepton Wharf' throw a pool of shade (bolstered by suitably dark paint tones) that effectively disguises the ever-awkward but sometimes-unavoidable point where the roadway meets the backdrop. The cottage at right conceals the exit of the tracks through the backscene.* Author

recession in nature, there's never any need for detail on a backscene. What is essential, however, is colouring that blends seamlessly with the shades used in the modelled part of the scene, and a believable transition from 3-D modelling to 2-D backdrop.

This last is almost impossible to achieve where the modelling is simply butted-up against the backdrop more-or-less at right angles; the change in plane between the basically horizontal modelling and the entirely vertical backscene is far too stark, and no amount of clever lighting will eliminate it. Even starker is the sudden transition from fully textured modelling to the flat painted finish of the backscene – something that will never look other than odd. If you study professionally built display dioramas, like those found in good museums, you will see that the horizontal modelled surface curves up and blends seamlessly into the backscene to form one continuous surface, with the colours and textures exhibiting a continuous gradation from fully modelled foreground to purely painted background. That's the pukka way to do the job, but it requires the backscene to be an integral part of the model – an arrangement that's usually only possible on either permanent layouts or on self-contained cameos.

Far more readily achievable on most model railways is the alternative approach, the 'disguised interface', where the point where the modelling meets the backscene is either hidden by viewblocks of one sort or another, or arranged in such a way that the rear of the modelled scene forms a natural silhouette to set against the distant view provided by the backdrop. Fortunately, both these approaches are easy enough to arrange – particularly on layouts using natural eye-level display, as advocated in these pages. Even something as seemingly inconsequential as a modest 'crest' in the groundwork a little way in front of the point of meeting can be enough to disguise the change of plane, as can artfully placed clumps of rough grass and other vegetation. Hedges, fences, walls, structures, trees and rock formations can all be used either as viewblocks or to form a 'silhouetted' landscape element. Just be sure you arrange things so that you don't throw unwanted shadows on the backdrop, as discussed in the lighting notes in Chapter 2.

There are some instances where

the nature of the model is such that it does not call for any landscape elements to be incorporated on the backscene at all, in that the modelling incorporates a full 'rear silhouette' giving a natural skyline – in which case, all that's needed is the sky. This is not always blue and full of nice fluffy clouds – in many instances it can simply be represented by an even expanse of an appropriate colour, which can take the form of a suitable screen erected behind the model, or even a coat of paint on some handy wall. This is the approach I've taken on my Dutch-prototype H0/P87 layout 'Bodesmeer'; the plain grey sky – in conjunction with 'cool' lighting – adds conviction to the November setting. Use of an 'independent' backscene like this also allows me to ring the climatic changes; a blue sky and a bit more warmth in the light (swapping LED bulbs for 'yellow' low-energy lamps) gives me a bright autumn day whenever I want it! One further advantage of designing around an independent backdrop is that it permits an 'in the round' presentation, where the model can be viewed from a range of angles rather than simply from the front, as in normal 'staged' presentation. The drawback is that the backdrop in this instance has to be considerably greater in extent than the mere length of the model, to ensure that there's sufficient 'sky' to back the model from any angle. It's an arrangement that works best where a relatively small model is sited against a decent-sized blank wall painted in some suitable shade.

BELOW: *The natural outlines of the buildings and trees on 'Bodesmeer' form a modelled background that does away with any need to provide a backscene as such; all that is required is a 'sky' ground, in this case provided by a plain painted wall. The effect here is the last of the (halogen) sunshine before that big grey cloud wins the day!* Dirk Schoemaker

Presentation

Any layout will benefit from well-thought-out and carefully executed presentation. In most cases, this will consist of four elements: The 'layout fascia' or 'front profile' is a finishing panel that conforms with the modelled landforms at its upper extremity and conceals the baseboard framing or sub-structure at its lower. This is usually matched to a 'top' or 'lighting' fascia, which is sited above and slightly in advance of the front edge of the layout, where it defines the upper limit of the visible scene as well as concealing overhead lighting fixtures. At either end of the modelled scene are usually found the 'side wings' or 'end viewblocks', often integrated with the panel-work or drapes concealing the fiddleyards or other 'offstage' elements of the layout. These side wings define the ends of the scene and conceal the ends of the backdrop. Taken together, these three elements serve to 'surround and set off' the modelling in the same way that a picture-frame enhances a picture. The last normal presentational element is some form of drape below the layout fascia to conceal the supporting structure.

I have already touched on the mechanics of these elements when delving into the practicalities of baseboard structures, lighting and backscenes, which leaves the all-important aesthetics to consider – to whit, proportions, colour and finish. The depth of the layout fascia *per se* is often influenced by practical factors such as the verticality of the layout's topography and the depth of its framing. I find this rarely gets much below four inches and can easily

stray to six or more – quite 'chunky' if allied to a layout 'scene height' of a foot or 15in. Whatever the layout fascia depth comes out at, the upper lighting fascia needs to be somewhat deeper. In fact, 'golden mean' theory would suggest that the ideal would be for the sum of the top and bottom fascias to equal the mean distance between them, with the actual fascia depths determined by the 'golden' split of 0.618 upper/0.372 lower. With a foot gap, this would work out, all bar the shouting, as 7½in aloft and 4½in below, certainly workable proportions; it would be a chunky light fitting indeed that couldn't hide behind a 7½in fascia. The end wings are a more variable feast and often call for a spot of trial-and-error; usually, I keep them in line with the mean depth of the layout fascia at around 4in.

ABOVE: *'Staged' presentation, with a landscape-profiled fascia, side 'wing' pieces, and an upper lighting fascia framing the modelled scene. This is 'Portpyn' – charming and exquisitely executed large-scale (1:34) narrow gauge.* Adrian Colenutt

BELOW: *Upper and lower fascias on 'Trerice' are roughly in 5:3 proportion, the top one being 5in deep and the up-and-down-a-bit lower fascia averaging 3in. The viewing gap mostly comes out at around 9in.* Author

Contrast colour

This leaves the matter of colour and finish. Conventional wisdom has it that such layout fascias and surrounds should be painted matt black, but I'm afraid this is one more bit of conventional wisdom I no longer subscribe to. Matt black is such a 'dead, dark and stark' shade that it tends to draw unwonted attention to itself; in fact, it is a total *absence* of colour – something that never occurs in nature except in caves deep below ground, when you

LEFT: *Matt black surrounds can provide dramatic contrast, but are often over-dominant and 'visually dead'. One of my personal bêtes noir is the all-too-common practice of plastering layout fascias with souvenir plaques and other such visual distractions. Well, would you slap an 'I've been to Blackpool' sticker on the frame of your prize Cuneo? This is 'Culm', a very nice EM layout that I feel would be even nicer with a more neutral and less cluttered fascia.* Adrian Colenutt

can't see anything anyway. The reason cited for the black is to provide the best possible contrast to the colours of the model – but too much contrast is not necessarily a good thing, and a shade that complements the colouring of the model without 'shouting it down' can be both more effective and aesthetically pleasing. After all, when did you last see a painting framed in dead matt black? If you must have a dark shade – and it can work well with the right subject – then a deep charcoal grey or a rich umber brown are more natural alternatives. Personally, I prefer a less 'obvious' contrast, and these days I tend to go for neutral mid-tones like a medium sage green, a moderate bluish-grey or a middling sienna earth shade.

As well as forswearing the black, I'm also none too sure about the matt finish; not only is it visually 'dead', but it's an absolute so-and-so to keep in shape, as it shows every kind of mark and blemish. Matt paints are also often a pig to apply without leaving brush marks. I find that a satin-finish oil-based paint over hardboard or MDF or a satin varnish stain over a decent grade of ply give the best all-round finish from both the durability and appearance point of view, although I've also recently seen some effective results using fine-textured automotive-type upholstery fabrics or very fine-grade carpeting to finish layout surrounds. What I would always seek to avoid, however, is anything that 'competes' with either the textures or colouring of the model – on which basis I am not a great fan of gloss-varnished veneers and similar 'furniture' finishes sometimes applied to model railway fascias; they tend to be too 'busy', especially if the veneer is 'figured'. On the whole, I find the modern synthetic satin-finish 'antique style' paints intended for woodwork and cabinetry to be the best all-round bet, although they can take an age to dry – not so good if you find the need for a spot of 'touching in' the night before an exhibition!

RIGHT: *Far more to my taste is this nicely uncluttered presentation in a sympathetic shade of satin-finish mid-green combined with a dark green drape. Tasteful and effective, setting off the simple but atmospheric P4 'Kitehouses' layout built by Dave Hawkins and Tony Sullivan.* Author

9 THE PLAN

ERNEST TUBB
RECORD SHOPS
NASHVILLE
PIGEON FORGE
FORT WORTH
edding
STAEDTLER
NOTTINGHAM (CASTLE) M.R.
CARRIAGE SHED
BRAKE VANS
ROADWAY

It may have seemed a long time coming, but it is now time to consider the one thing that the majority of modellers most associate with the whole concept of 'layout design' – the plan. This is often referred to (and drawn) as the 'track plan'. Well, as you'll have gathered by now, my contention is that layout design is about a whole lot more than any mere disposition of permanent way. In fact, I'd argue that the track formation is, in many ways, the most fluid part of any railway's make-up, be it model or full-size. I could cite you any number of prototypes where the track layout altered several times over a span of years to meet changing priorities or operating requirements. The same is true of many a model railway, including most of mine; indeed, as I write these words, I'm in the middle of a mild rework of the track at 'Cade's Green' to add a goods yard at the 'north end' of the layout. The essential point of all this in relation to layout planning is that it is the landscape features, general geography and structures (especially vernacular buildings and major engineering features) that form the *fundamentals* of the plan; the track disposition is as much determined by the constraints imposed by these 'fixed points' as by the needs of the running department.

Of course, as railway modellers we have a luxury denied the prototypical railway engineer; it's much easier for us to alter the 'environment' of our railways – and hence the possible track arrangements – than it was in reality. In fact, many aspects of British PW practice – such as the frequent employment of compact-but-complex point formations like three-way and slip turnouts – had their origins in the difficulties (and consequent high cost) of making earthworks; complicated track came cheaper than embankments or cuttings. This is in stark contrast to the traditional approach to model railway layout planning, which starts with a track plan designed in isolation and then adds the 'scenery' around the edges as a sort of decorative fringe.

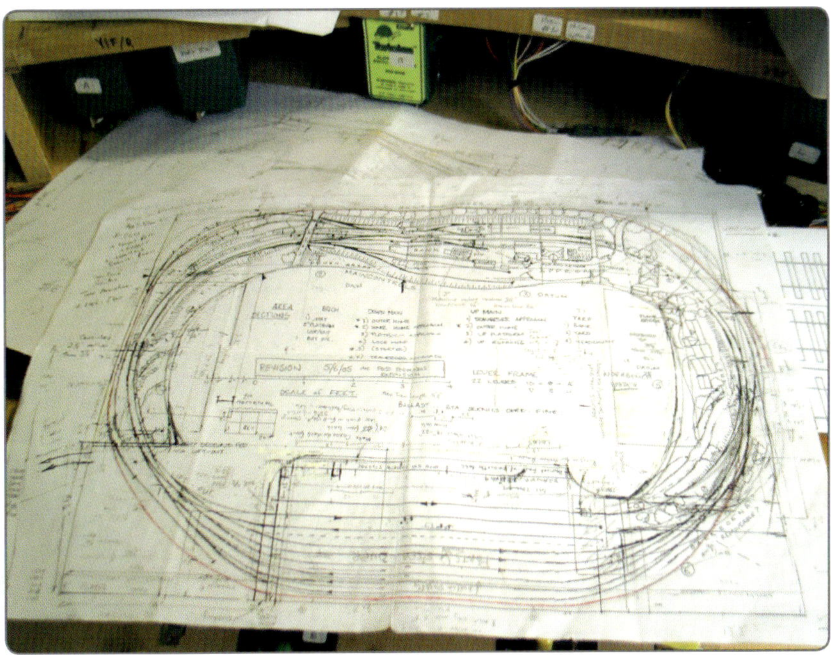

ABOVE: *A layout plan is the chief document from which a layout is actually built. Here is the plan drawn in 1990 for Terry Cole's 'Botley' project – now, 19 years later, well under construction. The somewhat dog-eared drawing has seen many an amelioration or deviation, and has acquired copious notes. But it is still the essential summary of what is intended and, indeed, what has been built.* Author

A quick flip through a few model railway magazines or a visit to the average exhibition will soon provide a plentiful selection of examples of the thoroughly unlikely landscape features, impossibly-proportioned structures and improbable bits of civil engineering such an approach engenders. No recipe for a realistic result, methinks…

BELOW: *The actual track disposition is, in many ways, the most flexible part of a layout design. After all, prototype track layouts are far from being set in stone, although few undergo such dramatic change as the eastern approach to Newcastle Central…* Author's collection/ Courtesy Mick Simpson

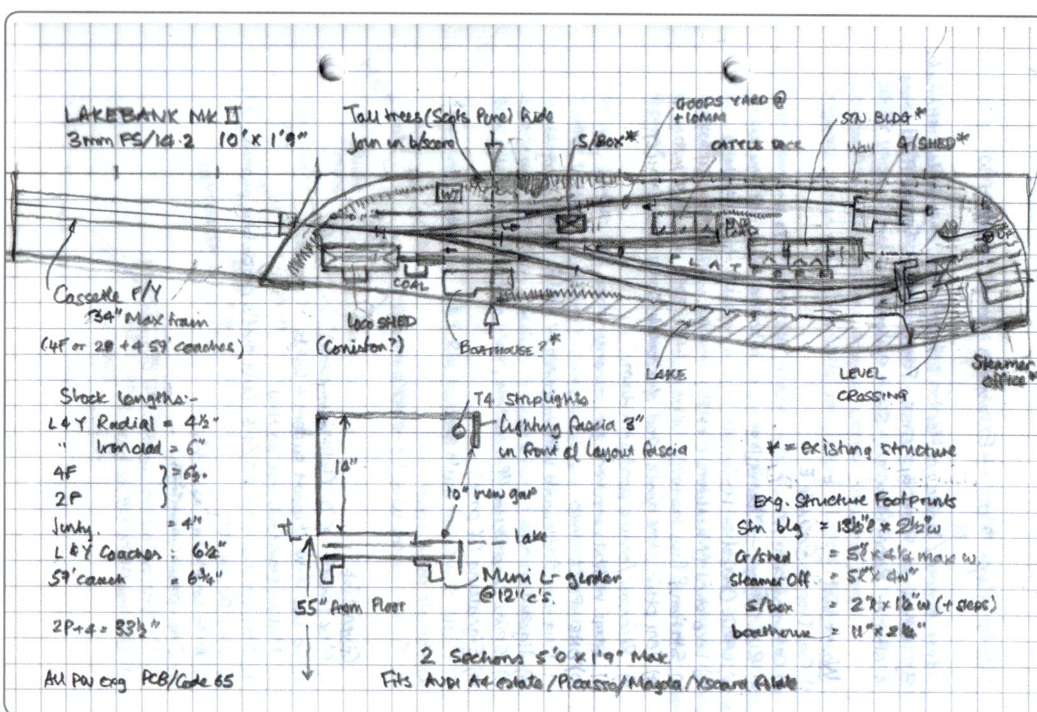

LEFT: *An initial design sketch for what has become 'Lakefoot' – the Launceston club's 3mm fine scale Lakeland branch line terminus. Note that the plan – rough though it is – is still drawn to scale. Note also, the amount of ancillary information included; this design reused structures and stock from an earlier layout which had to be scrapped when the club lost its former premises.*

To me, the plan-drawing process is more a bringing together of all the many strands – prototypical, practical and aesthetic – that go into a fully rounded 'holistic' layout design. To have any real value, a plan has to be accurate, well-informed and based on a sound set of requirements. Hence the long preamble that has led up to this point! That's not to say that ne'er pencil shall caress paper until every preliminary 'i' has been dotted and 't' crossed; far from it! Along the way, many a sketch plan will have been dashed off to record ideas, possibilities, and useful prototype information. These sketches will typically include track and structure dispositions, landscape features and practical details, as well as possible 'general arrangements' for the whole design. However, I draw a very firm distinction between these sketches and the final, definitive Plan, with a capital P. The point about a Plan is that it is complete and fully detailed and carefully drawn to scale to take account of all those 'do not ignore' practical constraints to do with curves, clearances, gradients and the location of baseboard joints, as well as all the aesthetic and authenticity requirements already pored over.

In fact, the final big-P plan is an amalgamation of three

BELOW: *If you can run to it, a perspective sketch of what the proposed design is meant to look like is a useful aid to the design process. This is a drawing for 'Hepton High Moor', a further cameo design based on the same theme as 'Hepton Wharf'.*

distinct preliminary planning stages: visual design (including landscape and presentation), track planning, and practical design. The first and last of these we've already covered at length, the second I'll come on to in a minute; it's the actual mechanics of the process I want to consider next: how do you actually nail down the final arrangement that's going to be the subject of 'big-P'? Well, not by wishful thinking, that's for sure; anything that makes it through to the final plan has got to be ruthlessly examined from all the standpoints mentioned. The time to find out something is not going to work is before it hits the page, not when the baseboards have already been built. (Voice of experience...) While much can be accomplished by careful and accurate scale drawing, that will only ever get you halfway there as it is a 2-D process and our models are 3-D. I tend to make a lot of perspective sketches of the sort illustrated hereabouts to try to nail down the 'general arrangement' I'm after, but they still won't tell you how something will look from every viewing angle and – even more tellingly – whether it will work operationally and practically. In this regard, there's no substitute for a bit of trial-and-error, in the invaluable context of the full-size mock-up or the convenient miniaturisation of a sketch 'study model'.

Full-size mock-ups

These are by way of being the ultimate arbiter of most design features. However clever and sure-fire an idea looks in 2-D on paper, it's how it cuts the ice in full-size 3-D practice that matters, and in my experience the surest way to determine what works and what doesn't is the suck-it-and-see arbitration of a 1:1 scale mock-up. A few lengths of flexible track, photocopied pointwork templates, Blu Tack, pins, carton-card, sticky tape, crumpled paper, a few blocks of wood or plastic foam and a felt pen or two are the basic ingredients, assembled upon a convenient surface of appropriate size and/or footprint. The idea is, first, to check the nuts-and-bolts practicality of the proposed arrangement, making sure that everything that needs to be located in the proscribed area does indeed fit, with workable gradients, proper track centres and adequate clearances between track and structures. The mock-up will also show whether there is enough length for the intended turnout angles and sufficient space for curves of appropriate radius. Much of this trial-and-error checking is accomplished using flexible track laid on the intended alignments, over which items of stock can be physically run to check radii and clearances, and trains made up to establish clearing points and track capacity.

The other great use of the mock-up is as a visual design tool, to judge how the proposed arrangement of track, structures and landforms will actually *look*. Structures are mocked-up with card and tape to the appropriate scale dimensions, with windows, arches and other features drawn on with felt pen, while landforms are roughed in with crumpled brown paper. It's at this stage that I usually find myself adjusting the size and position of features, often opting to 'scale down' structures to achieve better visual balance, or tweaking their positions to bring them closer to desirable 'mean points'. The Mk1 eyeball and the sighting bar are the tools for this kind of work. I record the results by measuring and drawing and by banging-off a few digital snaps to incorporate in the layout specification.

BELOW: *The ultimate design tool: a full-size mock-up of the proposed arrangement will show up any impracticalities and misfits as well as giving a very good idea of the final appearance. I reckon it's almost indispensable, especially in the context of a layout being 'squeezed' into a small site, where there's no margin for error. This is 'Boduan Junction' – see next chapter.* Author

Study models

Basically, a model of your proposed model, these come in two forms: sketch models, usually fairly rough-and-ready affairs used to check the design – or specific aspects of it – for composition, overall appearance and presentation; and plan models. These are essentially a 3-D version of the final plan, made accurately to scale to a good standard and often finished in full colour to give a detailed impression of what the final model is intended to look like and to act as a reference during construction. Well-finished plan models that show the layout in its intended setting are especially useful in presenting your intentions to a non-modelling audience (family or colleagues), to whom a bald layout plan may not mean all that much. They are also a valuable tool in the context of a group layout, where everyone can appreciate the proposal.

Sketch models are essentially mock-ups in miniature, and can be similarly rough-and-ready in their execution; card, paper, a felt pen and sticky tape are the usual stock-in trade.

ABOVE: *A 'plan model' is a scale model of the proposed layout, usually based on a blown-up photocopy of the drawn plan with 3-D elements added in paper, card, foam-core board and scenic materials. This is Terry Cole's study for 'Botley', a very well-executed example; mine are usually a bit more rough-and-ready!* Author

surely? Well, very rarely, actually, unless you've picked a truly miniscule subject or you have a modest aircraft hangar at your disposal. When you actually get to grips with the scale arithmetic, most prototype track arrangements sprawl to an impossible extent. It's sobering to realise that such 'modest' branch line terminals as that old chestnut, Ashburton, could, for instance, comfortably accommodate a six-coach train at their platforms and had a run-round loop that could swallow a 30-wagon freight. To be anywhere near true to prototype proportions in the matter of track layout, a 4mm scale 'Ashburton' would need to be 20-odd feet long! It is also worth remembering that in prototype terms, Ashy-B was a truly compact affair; many 'small' country stations sprawled a great deal more than that! In fact, just about the only prototype station layouts you'd have much chance of reproducing accurately at 4mm scale in less than that six or so linear yards are cramped inner-city affairs!

In this context; it is revealing to compare the 'footprints' of differing prototype locations; who'd have thought that the sleepy six-train-a-day GWR branch terminus at Moretonhampstead (one platform, a loop, three sidings and a single-stall loco shed) would effectively occupy more real-estate than frenetic four-platform Fenchurch Street terminus in the city of London, taken together with the associated Goodman Street goods depot? Or that the end-point of the Furness Railway's Windermere branch would sit alongside Marylebone in real-estate terms? In truth, the sort of subject so often favoured by we 'realistic' modellers verges on the unmodelable if you're bent on scale dimensional accuracy. Thankfully, we long-ago learned that it is possible to create a convincing illusion of most subjects in a great deal less than the true-to-scale footprint.

Alternatively, relive your childhood and get yourself a supply of Plasticine modelling clay, which is ideal for knocking up a rough representation of landforms and structures. Building a well-finished plan model, on the other hand, can be quite a demanding exercise as, like the plan itself, it needs to be accurately to scale and carefully constructed, with well-fitting components and a high degree of finish. A plan model is based on a photocopy of the actual plan, with the track left as drawn but 3-D form given to landscape and structures. Foam-cored 'featherboard' is a good basic material to work with, with layered card, 'glueshell' or shaped foam blocks to give form to the landscape and structures of laminated foam-core covered in a paper overlay with features drawn in as required. Trees and hedges can be added from regular scenic materials – I find Woodland Scenics 'foliage clumps' work well at the 1 inch = 1 foot scale at which I generally produce both plans and plan models. How far you take the level of detail and finish of such a model depends a bit on intent and a lot on personal inclination, but installing DCC is probably taking things a tad too far…

Track planning: accommodating the prototype

In my book, there are three basic tenets that underlie any worthwhile model railway track plan: it should be prototypical, workable, and compatible with the environment within which it is set. Taking these criteria in order, the first is, on the face of it, relatively straightforward, especially if you're setting out to model an actual prototype location: you just reproduce the real arrangement to scale,

Trackwork compression

This spatial conundrum is old hat in model railway planning; we have, for many years, accepted the need for 'selective compression' – the removal of unmodelable length from a prototype while keeping the basic disposition of the layout correct. Far from being a drawback, I'd suggest that in the cause of realism a degree of such compression is actually an advantage, something it would be desirable to do even if you *did* have that handy hangar to play with. Why? Well, quite apart from the saving in shoe-leather through not having to trek up and down a dozen yards of layout every time you carried out a shunt, it's my experience that 'dead scale' models – including true-to-length track formations – rarely *look* right, for the 'distance perception' reasons already dissected in the visual design notes a page or two back. In track-planning terms, the main thing we need to know about selective compression is how far we can take the process before the result either starts looking silly or just becomes plain unworkable.

RIGHT: *Mocking-up a proposed track arrangement at full size with flexible track enables clearing points and siding/loop capacities to be checked. This is the putative 'north end' extension to 'Cade's Green', which involves relocating the cattle dock.* Author

The practical side of length compression (which is what we're really talking about) is easy enough to get your head around. The key thing to bear in mind is that while you can shorten a track formation simply by deleting distance between turnouts, you can't compress the turnouts themselves without altering the crossing angles and hence the mean radii of the included curves – which may well have implications in respect of the locos and stock that can run over them. Overall train lengths, however, can usually be 'squeezed' a bit where space is tight, either by using shorter items of stock or by leaving vehicles out of the formation. So deciding, in practical terms, where exactly in a track layout you can 'prune' excess length calls not just for careful thought but almost certainly for some full-size trial-and-error with flextrack, templates and the actual items of stock to be used, paying particular attention to fouling and clearing points, shunting neck and run-round loop lengths and exact siding capacities.

It is often surprising just how much length you can lop out of some track layouts without losing either operational practicality or the general look and 'feel' of the prototype. However, taking out length from a track layout will often also mean you will need to trim the width as well, usually by omitting some peripheral trackage – maybe a parallel loop or a siding or so. This sideways trimming is partly needed to preserve as far as possible the overall proportions of the layout, ensuring that what should be long and thin doesn't end up short and dumpy. It is also often dictated by lack of available length for the pointwork needed to access multiple parallel tracks. Where such peripheral trackage *has* to be included for basic operational reasons, then there are a couple of further dodges to consider when squeezing in the necessary turnouts. Most obvious is to use shorter point formations, either by accepting sharper crossing angles or by tweaking the alignments to use a 'wye' in place of a straight turnout; wyes are notably briefer for the same crossing angle and mean curve radius. You can also 'close couple' successive turnouts by bringing the switch of the following turnout close up to the heel or switch of its predecessor; in yards and other locations where point locks aren't needed, the prototype can go down to a single sleeper twixt adjacent switch-toes or switch-toe and preceding wing rail. You will have to modify commercial turnouts or point templates to achieve this, however. Another useful solution is to 'overlap' turnouts into three-way or interlaced formations, common in British railway layouts and hence rarely looking out of place.

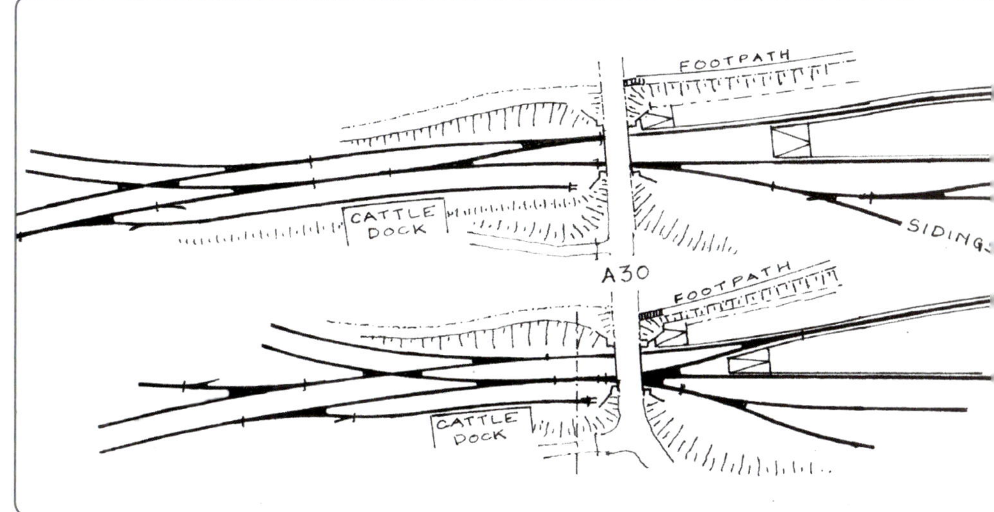

RIGHT: *Trackwork compression at Yeovil. Here's how we squeezed the south end of Yeovil Pen Mill to fit it into the available space: The double junction has been moved much nearer to the A30 bridge, and the crossover moved under the bridge and combined with the exit point from the down yard to make a three-way. The cattle dock spur has been shortened, and the entry point to the loco shed (extreme left) moved closer to the junction. The island platform has also moved towards the bridge. Overall saving: about 4ft on true 4mm scale length.*

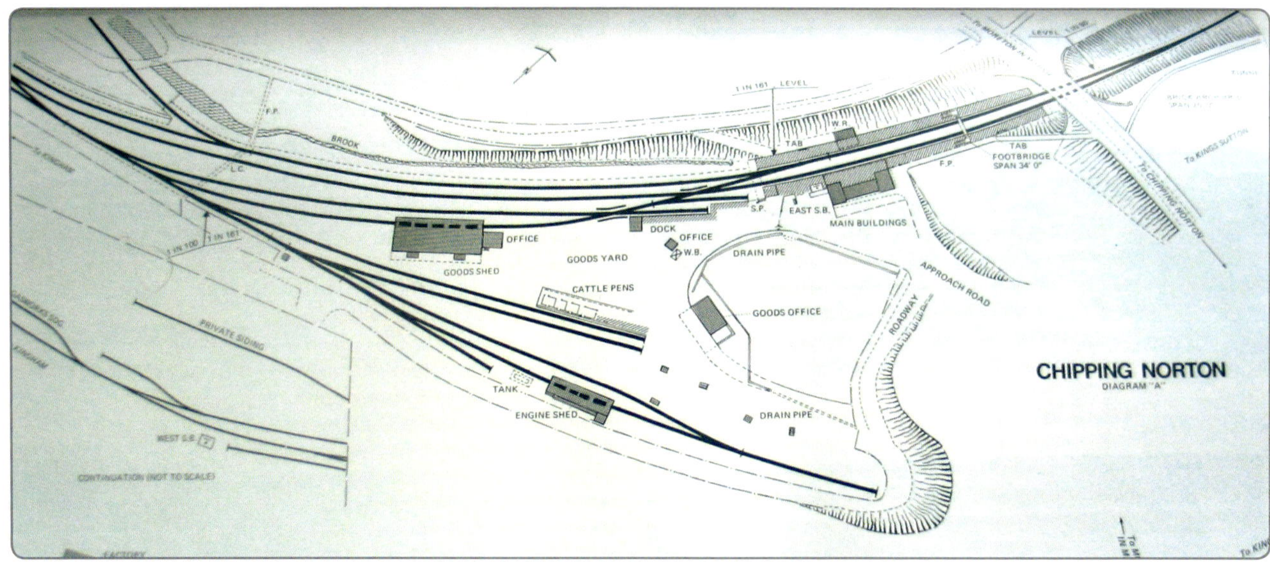

Designing like the prototype

So much for track planning in the context of trying to squeeze a prototype arrangement onto a too-small model footprint; what then of the business of dreaming up a track plan completely 'from scratch' in the context of a fictional subject? Well, my advice is – by and large, don't bother. I've rarely found such an expedient necessary, in that it is almost always possible to find a suitable prototype that can be adopted and adapted to suit the needs of your fiction. So my first reaction on being faced with such a requirement is to head to the bookshelf and photo albums to see what reality can provide, either in the form of a complete track layout or by way of characteristic track formations that can be combined as needed to create a 'composite' arrangement. The sources for such raw material are many and easy to find, with the better individual or generic line histories now including prototype track plans as a matter of course – often in the form of the highly detailed OS 25in-to-the-mile maps or the railway's own 40ft-to-the-inch plans. Some publishers – notably OPC, Wild Swan and Irwell Press – have produced complete volumes of such prototype track plans, usually associated with brief histories of the lines depicted and a selection of relevant photographs. Just the sort of material that should figure large in a 'prototype archive'.

ABOVE: *Here's a prototype track diagram (of GWR origin, in this instance), incorporating several characteristic and useful track arrangements (eg the goods shed trailing connection by the two slips) that could easily be 'borrowed' for a freelance plan. This one comes from the pages of* A Historical Survey of Selected Great Western Stations, *by R. H. Clarke, published by OPC. Solid gold.*

In fact, once you start to look at railway literature and photographic sources with an acquisitive eye, you soon find that, while there probably is a 'prototype for everything', certain basic track arrangements are used over and over again, with some design elements recurring at almost every station. Some of these arrangements centre on formations peculiar to the practice of a particular pre-Group or Grouping company, to the extent that they form a clear 'signature element' for that particular railway and an obvious 'must-have' ingredient for a fictional layout based on its practice. Examples include the old GER's predilection for double slips on the curve (something hardly anybody else seemed to contemplate), the Midland's paranoic avoidance

BELOW: *Goods yard trailing connections.*

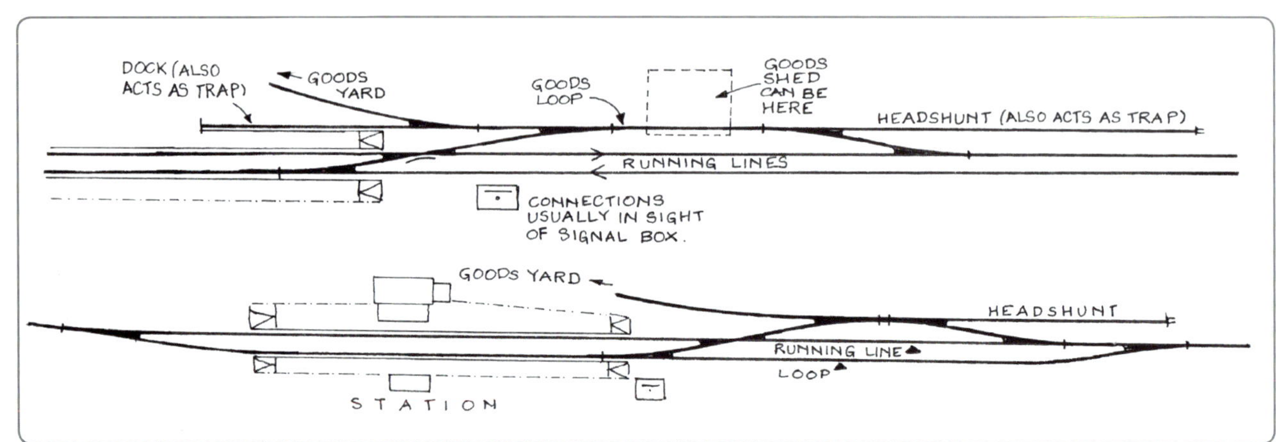

of facing turnouts and hence almost total lack of running loops (which must have made them top of the pops with the Railway Inspectorate – see below!) and the GWR's fondness for branch terminal goods yards accessed from the run-round loop by means of a diamond across the main running line. There are many other such PW quirks to be found and fallen upon with modelling glee.

Of course, many standard track formations were used because they were the best way of doing a particular job. If I had to nominate one layout as being utterly typical of traditional British PW design practice, it would have to be the arrangement shown in the sketch alongside. This depicts a goods yard based on a loop sited parallel to the running lines of a normal double-track railway, with 'double trailing' connections. That is, with access at one end of the loop being by means of a trailing crossover to the adjacent running line, and at the other by means of a trailing lead from the opposing running line across the near track by a slip diamond forming a trailing crossover. This enabled the goods yard loop to be accessed by means of a trailing shunt from either running direction, while the trailing slip connection provided a run-round facility if needed, as well as permitting 'wrong line' working in case of need. This use of slip turnouts was a great feature of British railway practice from very early on; in the Netherlands, a slip is still referred to as an 'Engels wissel' or 'English turnout'. If one formation can be cited as being characteristically British above all others, it must be the single slip – an item of trackwork all-but-unknown in Europe and the USA, where slips are almost always double.

I've already remarked on the prevalence of complex 'compound' pointwork in British PW design, and it is by no means confined to main-line locations. Even such exotica as four-way turnouts could turn up in the oddest places; leaving aside the famous specimens in the station throats at King's Cross and Birmingham Moor Street – unsurprising in such cramped and busy locations – what are we to make of a GE example that once graced the back end of the goods yard at Saxmundham, one road of which didn't actually *go* anywhere? (The French, of course, went one better than anyone's four-way; there's a *branchement à cinque voies* of the PO-Midi in the railway museum at Mulhouse). But throughout the British railway network, three-way turnouts and single slips were two-a-penny even at modest country stations, and overlapped or interlaced turnouts by no means unknown; in some places, it seemed almost as if the rarest thing was a plain straightforward point! Turnouts incorporating traps (see over) were also commonly found,

ABOVE: *This sort of complex and 'dense' trackwork, featuring many compound formations such as three or even four-way turnouts, single and double slips and interlaced or bisected turnouts, is characteristic of traditional British PW. King John picks his way through the approach to Bristol Temple Meads.* Author's collection

BELOW: *As a general rule, the earlier the period, the more complex and less standardised the track formations. Highly intricate and completely custom-built layouts were prevalent in the pre-Grouping era, with the old GER probably possessing the crown for the most convoluted PW; this is Bethnal Green Junction, on the approach to Liverpool Street, c1910.* Author's collection

especially on the GWR, which company was also fond of the semi-outside single slip. However, the old GER probably took the prize for convoluted, 'non standard' track; it seemed as if they just drew the lines where they wanted them to go regardless, and then built the resulting tangle – somehow! That said, such PW exuberance was largely a feature of the pre-Grouping scene; the general rule is that the later the date, the plainer the pointwork and by the 1930s, most of the fiercer PW tangles had been largely ironed out.

Railway Inspectorate requirements

There are also certain traditional PW design elements that stem from the stringent requirements of the Railway Inspectorate of the Board of Trade with regard to passenger-carrying railways (most goods-only lines were exempted). These requirements were universal and unvarying, with very few deviations. Chief among them was the famous aversion of the board's inspectors toward facing points in running lines, especially those on which trains would be travelling at speed. Of course, such things were sometimes unavoidable: at junctions, on the entry to running-line loops, in 'diverting' crossovers between adjacent pairs of running lines in a common direction, in the approaches to stations having many routes or platform faces and, of course, on single-track lines – where what is a trailing point in one direction is facing in t'other. Facing turnouts in running lines, whatever their purpose, are always fitted with facing point locks, either actuated via treadle-bars by approaching trains or mechanically locked via a release lever in the signalbox lever frame. But, point locks or no, what was almost unknown on a normal double-track running line in the 'traditional' railway era was a facing crossover; only on the modern railway have such things been permitted. Given that two recent railway accidents – Greyrigg and Potter's Bar – have involved high-

BELOW: *Facing crossovers in main running lines – especially high-speed running lines – were rare but not unknown, as here, where such a crossover links the down fast and down slow lines of the LSWR's four-track main line through the south-western suburbs of London.* Author's collection

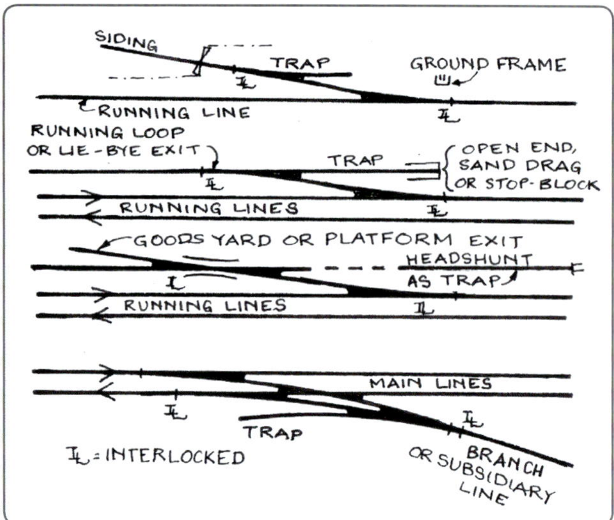

ABOVE: *Typical trap arrangements.*

speed derailments on just such facing crossovers, you can't help but wonder if the traditional aversion had much to commend it!

The other bee-in-the-bonnet requirement of the BOT inspectors that modellers are apt to overlook was their insistence that any track on which passenger trains ran should be fully protected from the effects of runaways, over-shoots or unauthorised movements on any other trackwork – sidings, loops, junctions – connected directly to it. This was achieved by 'trapping', either involving the interlocking of turnouts facing the exit of connecting track such that a vehicle moving towards the running line would be diverted into a headshunt or loop parallel with, and clear of, the running line or, where no such suitable trackage existed, by the provision of a 'trap point'. This was linked to, and operated in conjunction with, the running-line turnout and was positioned to derail and deflect the errant vehicle before it fouled the running line. Trap points could be 'complete' turnouts, sometimes leading onto a short spur with a sand-drag or stop-block, but often they were simply a set of 'catch points' – a double- or single-bladed switch leading off to the appropriate side, intended to tip the runaway into the dirt. Whatever form they take, the point about trapping arrangements is that they need to be there – and on a lot of model railways they ain't!

Another characteristic track arrangement that has its origins with BOT requirements is the junction between single lines that is 'double at the point of junction', usually in the form shown in my sketch. As with most of these mandatory track arrangements, it only applied to passenger-carrying lines, but did result in some rather odd and seemingly inexplicable bits of trackwork on occasion. In the case of light railways, junctions between freight-only and passenger-carrying lines and some later minor branchlines, the requirements were relaxed and single-point or point-followed-by-a-crossover junctions permitted. As time went by, this 'doubling' of junctions was gradually abandoned,

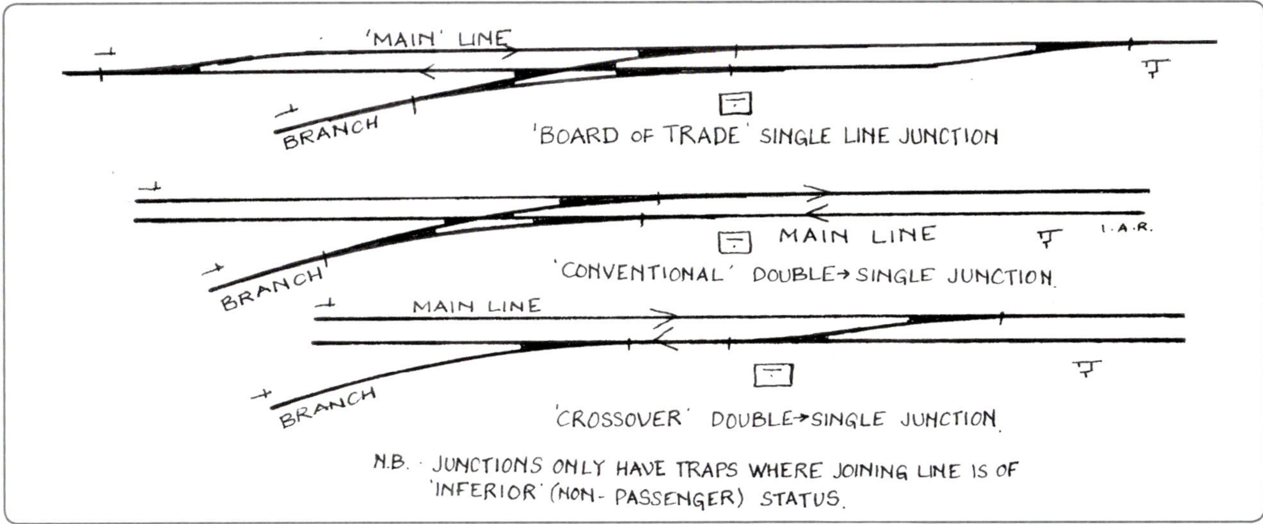

ABOVE: *Single-line junctions.*

and many single-track junctions that had started out double were later simplified. As with a lot of aspects of PW design, the date of the installation being modelled is significant – the general rule being that the later the timeframe, the simpler and more standardised the layout was likely to be.

Go with the flow...

If traditional British track layout design has one overriding visual characteristic, it is the 'flowing' look that results from the extensive use of custom-built (ie curved) pointwork. This is in stark contrast to the situation found on many model railways, where the exclusive use of 'standard' turnouts (those having a straight 'main' road and a curved divergence) often imparts an oddly 'angular' look to the formation, full of awkward curves and kinks where things don't quite line up. When you study many prototype layouts, it is remarkable just what modest proportion of the pointwork came off the 'standard' peg; there are whole complexes where not a single such turnout can be discerned, and everything on view is a curved turnout or wye of some sort – albeit many of them only subtly so. This use of trackwork tailored to site might seem an extravagant way of proceeding, but in fact with the way much British PW was traditionally constructed, from a wide range of standard switch and crossing assemblies linked by configured-on-site 'closure rails', there was precious little practical difference between building 'straight' and 'curved' turnouts. As time went by and off-site prefabrication became more prevalent, new track layouts did start to become a bit more 'regular', but given that a lot of British track had an in-situ life of half a century or more, the traditional smooth-and-sinuous look predominated until well into the diesel age.

It is this distinctive visual aspect of traditional British PW that forms the strongest case for taking the trouble to learn to build your own turnouts, whatever the scale, gauge and standards you've chosen to work to. Plain track isn't a problem – any make of flexible track can be curved to conform to the 'sweeping look' without undue difficulty,

BELOW: *Flowing, transitioned curves and the extensive use of curved turnouts characterise much British PW. This is Temple Meads again, with a 4F on a west-to-north goods working.* Author's collection

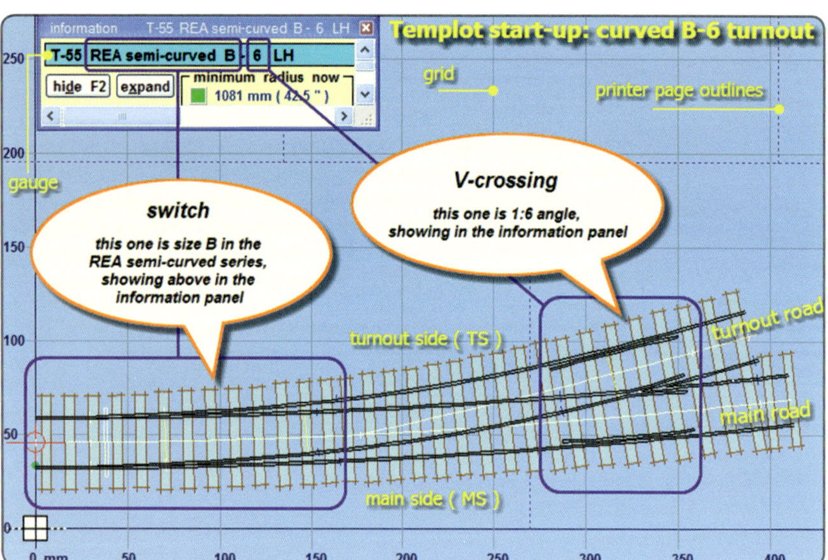

LEFT: *Templot is a piece of computer software that enables you to custom-draw templates for any turnout or track formation your layout design calls for. It will also produce accurate scale plans of track formations that can be used as a basis for, and integrated with, 'whole layout' designs.* Courtesy Martin Wynne/Templot

OPPOSITE: *Some modellable prototype loop-and-siding through stations.*

but trying to design a truly 'flowing' track arrangement when you're restricted by the geometry and configuration of off-the-peg turnouts is never easy. This is even when, as with the Peco range that forms the 'default' choice for the British modeller, you have got a reasonable selection of types to choose from. Often, it is the prototypical turnout configurations and subtle curvatures and alignments attainable with hand-laid track that give 'finescale' layouts that edge in the realism stakes, rather than any vast superiority in the track *per se*. Trying to come up with an arrangement of standard turnouts that preserves the subtle sweep of an overall PW formation is something I find is best accomplished by trial-and-error at full size in the context of a mock-up, preferably using the actual track and pointwork. Failing this, Peco supply full-size templates for planning purposes, or you can simply use photocopies of the actual track sections.

The template problem and Templot

Even when it comes to laying out prototypical 'free form' track arrangements for hand-laid track, then traditionally you encountered some of the same problems found with ready-made pointwork – due mainly to the limitations of the templates on which the track is actually built. Only the most accomplished of model platelayers are in a position to 'wing it' and build pointwork entirely from first principles; most of us need a bit of help, and for normal mortals there was little point in drawing some super-smooth and sexy track formation on a plan if it couldn't actually then be built due to the lack of the necessary templates! While a wide selection of traditional pre-printed track-construction templates have long been available from the various specialist gauge/scale societies as well as from several commercial sources, like the ready-made track, they are generally limited to those straight-road 'standard' formations – albeit in a much wider range of configurations and crossing angles. So for all those subtle curved and wye turnouts, you were either down to adapting 'straight' templates by cutting and pasting them to achieve the appropriate curvatures, or plying the pencil to draw custom ones of your own.

Not any more, though! Once again, the home computer rides to the rescue. Sophisticated specialist track template drawing software has now been developed by Martin Wynne, software capable of producing any type or radius of turnout in any gauge, scale or standard using prototypical geometry, sleeper arrangements and rail locations, even to the extent of being able to incorporate detail constructional features following the practice of a specific prototype railway. Such pointwork can be drawn, not only in isolation, but as part of an overall integrated formation, enabling you to replicate just about any arrangement no matter how subtly sinuous. This invaluable magic wand is 'Templot', from 85A Models (www.templot.com), which will not only draw the templates for you at full size, but – as already hinted above – will produce the overall track layout in the form of a scale plan at any size required, thus forming a truly-useful bit of computer-aided layout design (although in that context it's only a *track*-planning tool, not a complete layout-designing system). The only drawback to Templot is that it is only available as a PC/Windows programme and so, alas, inaccessible to dedicated Mac-users like Rice.

Typical track arrangements

I think it was Bob Barlow, founder-editor of the *Model Railway Journal*, who remarked that, when it comes to creating a believable fiction, then the 'Art of the typical is the art that convinces'. While there are some truly off-the-wall track arrangements to be found on the prototype (try Wells Priory Road, where the GWR Cheddar Valley line ran smack across the middle of the S&D's good's yard), the vast majority of stations conformed to a relatively restricted palette of basic configurations. On minor rural single-track railways, for instance, a very large percentage of stations consisted, in some form or another, of a 'loop and two sidings'. Similarly, most branchline termini were laid out to be shunted 'trailing' from the 'throat' end. The 'wayside goods yard' based around a loop accessed by trailing connections in both

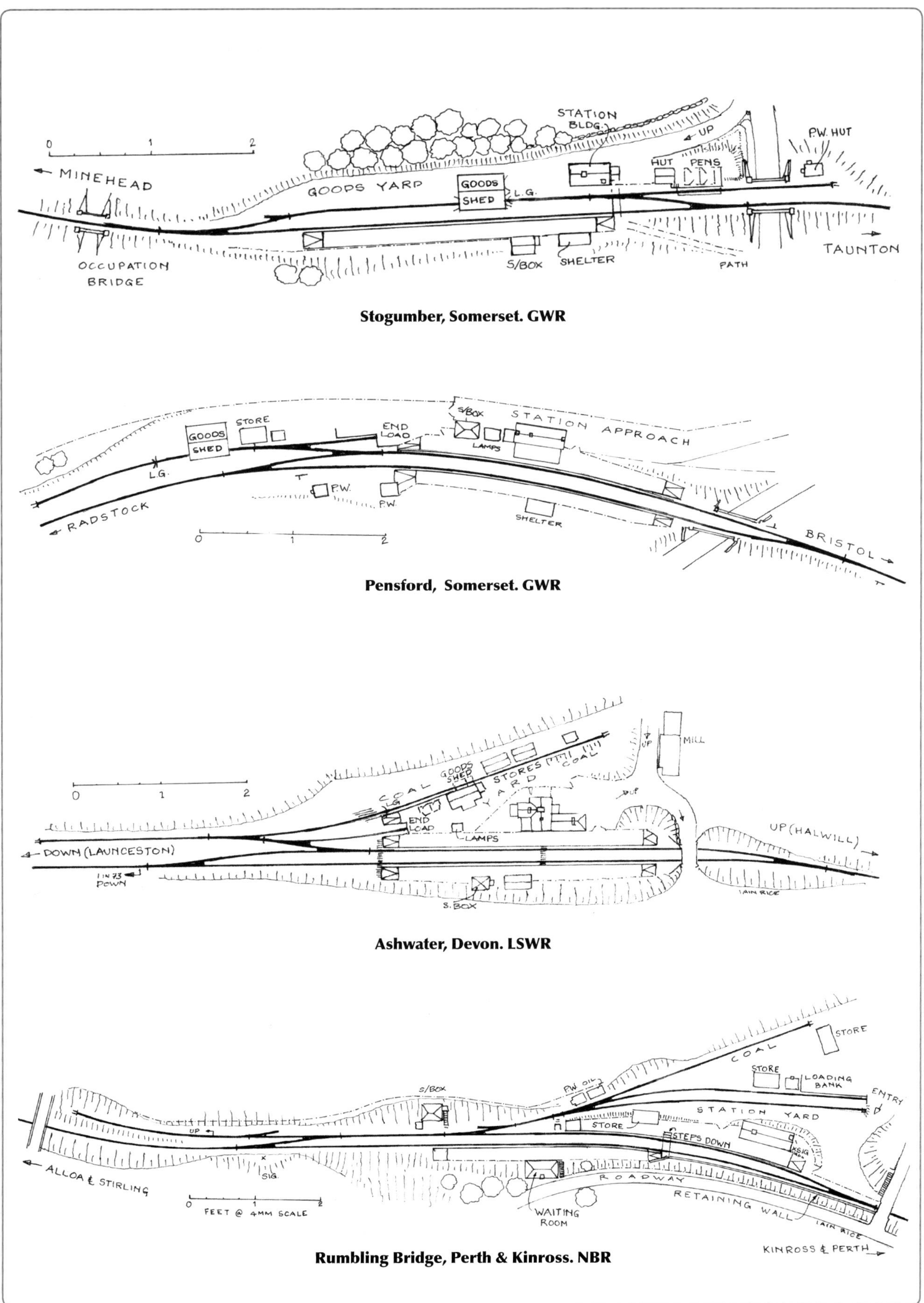

Stogumber, Somerset. GWR

Pensford, Somerset. GWR

Ashwater, Devon. LSWR

Rumbling Bridge, Perth & Kinross. NBR

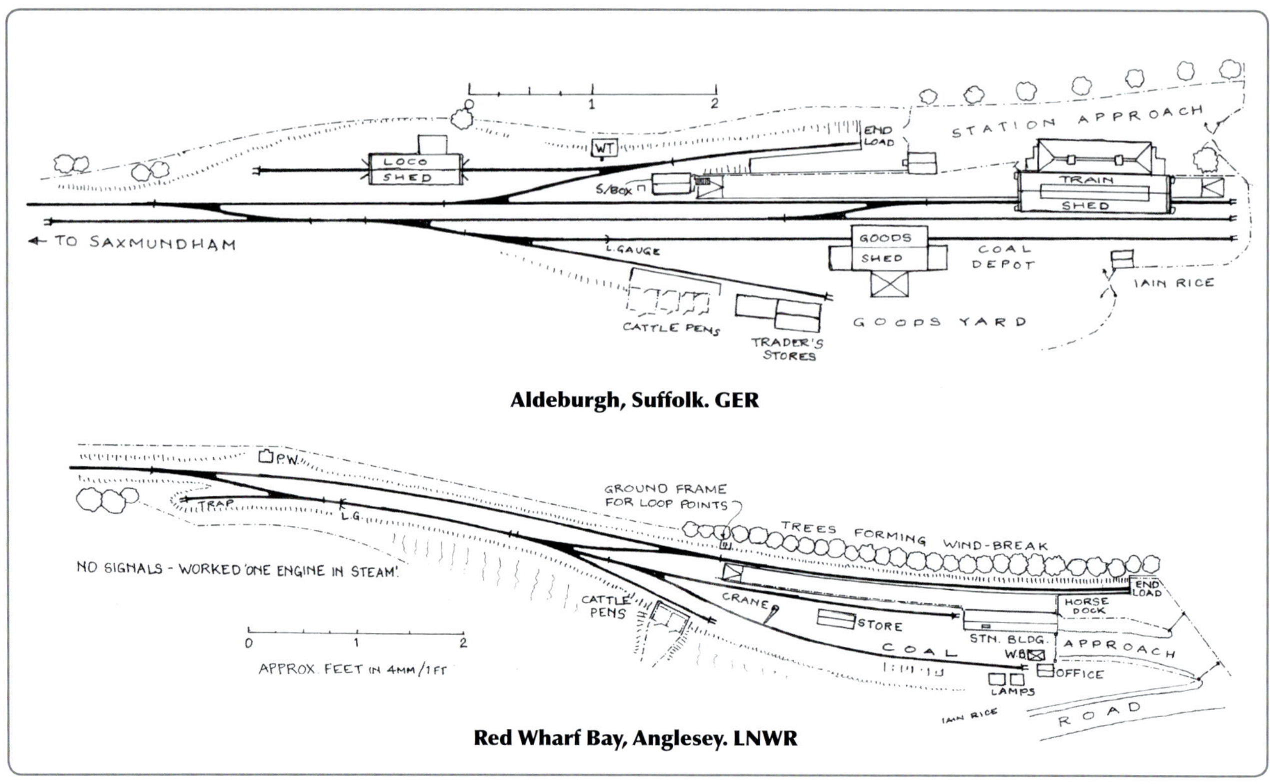

Aldeburgh, Suffolk. GER

Red Wharf Bay, Anglesey. LNWR

ABOVE: *Two 'model' branch termini.*

directions has already been made an example of, and many goods yards themselves employed a basic generic layout that saw the goods shed on a loop of some sort while all the other sidings were single-ended.

But such generalisations apart, individual stations or other railway installations saw almost infinite variety in the precise disposition of the same relatively few basic features, rather in the way that the immortal Bach can come up with seemingly endless but satisfying variations on some simple theme of a few notes. Often, it was the relationship of the trackwork to adjacent structures and landscape or engineering features that gave character, interest or charm to a particular location. Such attractive and modellogenic groupings of track and adjuncts are just the sort of 'layout design elements' around which I construct my 'composite' designs and are, I'd suggest, the basic building blocks of realistic layout design, both with regard to track layout and the composition of the overall scene.

Baseboard joints

These are the bane of the sectional layout, and if not carefully handled in terms of visual design can be an unmitigated eyesore; many an otherwise-convincing model railway has been badly compromised by a ruler-straight crevasse every few feet. While there are various 'after the event' dodges for hiding these carbuncles, I prefer to tackle the problem by, as far as possible, 'designing it out'. How I'm going to join my sections invisibly is always a big item on the 'givens' list, and in the cause of such invisibility I often resort to radical and fundamental design solutions with respect to the nature of the baseboard structure or the way the scenic elements of the model are constructed. That's where I can't skate around the problem by either locating joins on non-scenic parts of the layout, or by doing away with them in the first place by accepting (and designing around) larger baseboard sections. I have never subscribed to the 'modular' approach (all baseboards must be the same size and shape) precisely because it usually results in far more joins than are strictly necessary and locates them with no reference to the modelling. In other words, I stick to my basic tenet that the baseboard is subservient to the model, not the other way about.

Even if you keep them to the minimum by using the maximum size of section that meets transport and handling needs, some joins in scenic layout areas are inevitable; the question then becomes one of mitigating a necessary evil. The dead-straight baseboard join at right-angles to the axis of the layout is obtrusive because it's almost always completely alien to the nature of the topography through which it runs. The British landscape, as already noted, is notably short on straight lines and right-angles; the natural boundaries – river-banks, contours, the spread of vegetation – are invariably irregular, as are many of the man-made ones. One way to 'lose' a baseboard join is to have it follow a natural boundary within the scene – a river-bank, lane-verge or hedge line. Engineering a curved and convoluted 'jigsaw' joint following such a boundary is, however, no sinecure in baseboard-structural terms, although glued-ply 'eggbox' construction can accommodate such frolics.

Far simpler is to keep the structural joint straight and simple, but to 'lose' it beneath one or more removable jigsaw-format scenic segments that 'bridge' the gap and

fit in with 'natural' boundaries either side of it. In fact, as outlined under the concept of 'jigsaw' layout construction described in Chapter 3, it is not difficult to contrive a layout where *all* the scenery is made up of such removable chunks, which means you can hide as many baseboard joints, structural elements, mechanical devices and electrical circuits as you like; 'Bodesmeer' is arranged thus. However, where you are faced with the need to render a conventional straight join less visible without going down the 'removable overlay' route, there is another ploy that I've used with some success, the 'scenic gasket'. As can be seen from the sketch

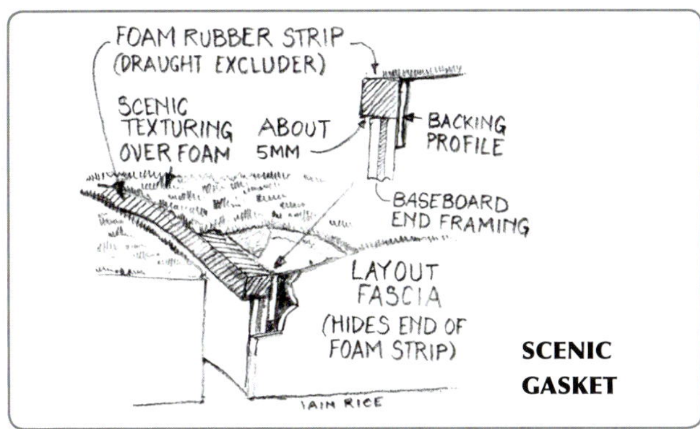

SCENIC GASKET

hereabouts, the basic idea of this is to finish the visible surface either side of the join with a strip of compressible, flexible material – foam rubber or similar – that follows the contours of the landforms accurately and is textured on its upper surface to match the adjoining groundwork. This strip is made to project a few millimetres out from the joining faces of the baseboard sections such that when the sections are bolted or clamped together the soft 'scenic gaskets' are brought firmly together and 'squashed up' tightly so that there is no readily-visible gap. Bob Barlow and I used this system successfully on the 'East Suffolk Light'.

Graceful exits

One of the other visual and practical chestnuts of realistic layout design is the eternal problem of allowing trains to leave the modelled scene without looking unnatural or indiscrete. The usual solution, of course, is to disguise such exits by having the departing train pass under a bridge or

ABOVE: *Bridges as exits: sharply skewed spans, like the timber occupation bridge on 'Hepton Wharf', are harder to see through and work well positioned tight to the backdrop. A subtle alternative is a close-arched bridge set (highly prototypically) in a cutting a little way in advance of the actual exit point, as on Corrieshalloch at right. Notice the bend in the road avoiding a 'head on' with the backdrop.* Author

enter a tunnel. In many British landscape settings, one or other of these can usually be arranged in a credible fashion – although bear in mind that there aren't too many tunnels in the fen country and few real railway engineers deliberately aimed their line at the middle of a hill, as many models appear to do! If you do use a tunnel, allow it enough length to permit the lining to look convincing and keep the interior

BELOW: *If you opt for a tunnelled exit – as I have on 'Trerice' – then arranging matters so that there are at least a few inches of actual lined 'tunnel' makes a big difference; keeping it 'tight' also helps conceal the actual exit into the fiddleyard. I must improve my soot-stains, though; highly unconvincing!* Author

LEFT AND BELOW: *Strategically placed structures make excellent disguises for unseemly exits, as here where Maiden Newtown's goods shed hides a thoroughly uncouth hole in the wall.* Author

dark. If a bridge is the chosen option, skewed spans are much more effective as they are harder to see straight through, but if the bridge is 'square', choose a 'tight' prototype to avoid unwelcome glimpses of the fiddleyard.

It is by no means always possible to contrive such a conveniently engineered exit, especially if you're modelling a 'flatland' subject where the natural topography doesn't produce the differences in levels that favoured overbridge construction; I have found that even in rolling Suffolk – let alone on a Dutch polder – level crossings are far more common than road overbridges, which in reality demand artificially elevated approaches – rarely justified if the road was other than 'main'. In these circumstances, introducing such a bridge to hide an exit can easily strike a false note. Fortunately, in the context of a realistic layout viewed at or near eye-level, there is another viable alternative – the use of a foreground view-block to disguise the point at which the train does a 'platform nine-and-three-quarters' job on the backscene. A slight rise in the ground topped by a hedge, a small stand of modest trees, an advertising hoarding, or a suitably sized structure carefully placed can easily be sufficient to hide the actual point of exit.

Plan drawing

Having expended a great deal of verbiage on what might be regarded as mere preliminaries, we come at last to that pinnacle, that end-point, that *ultima dictum* of the layout-designing process – drawing The Plan. Except that, so far as I'm concerned, plan-drawing is far from being a conclusion; rather, it's a step on the way, the point at which you stop dreaming the layout up and start to think about building the dratted thing. The last status I award a plan (however beautifully-drawn!) is that of finality – far from it! I fully expect the *final* result – the finished layout – to depart in all manner of ways from what is shown on the plan – which is anyway, let us not forget, only a *part* of the overall layout design.

ABOVE: *Road and river exits: The creek at one end of 'Woolverstone' sneaks off-scene beneath a low-arched road bridge – the road making an exit behind the old toll-house. The railway bridge, although further drawing the eye from the creek's abrupt exit, would not in itself provide an adequate camouflage. Backing the bridge-openings with a slightly angled mirror can create the illusion that the creek continues beyond the margins of the modelled scene.* Author

Chez Rice, a plan is more by way of a guide than a directive, a basis rather than a conclusion.

That said, a plan is no use as a guide if it is inaccurate, unclear and badly executed. So creating it demands a little effort and understanding. It needs to be drawn to a scale that is large enough to be clear without resulting in a document so large as to be unwieldy. All my British-prototype plans (preliminary or finished) are initially drawn at one-inch-to-one foot scale, for all that a lot of them end up being re-sized for publication. Only on really large projects – which tend to be American in subject – do I use a smaller scale. By sticking with one scale as far as possible it is possible to develop an instinctive feel for what is workable, while keeping commonality of scale between the rough sketches and the final plan lessens the chance of transcription errors creeping in. Inch-to-the-foot enables you to use an ordinary imperial ruler, which normally gives you a convenient minimum drawing unit of 1/16in – equal to 3/8in (or pretty much 10mm) at full size. I wouldn't see any layout plan as calling for greater accuracy than this; if the ultimate dimensions are that critical, you're cutting things too fine!

Computer-aided design

Despite my enthusiasm for the information-handling abilities of computers, I don't rate them over-much as a layout plan-drawing tool. There are a number of reasons for this, starting with the availability of suitable software. Most of what's sold specifically for the task is non-British in origin, with all the more sophisticated systems – 3rd PlanIt, CadRail, Xtrack, AnyRail, the Mac-based EmpireExpress – coming from the USA. Many of the more popular 'model railway' programmes available – such as the Hornby 'Virtual Railway' – are more by way of computer games, while others, like Atlas's 'Right Track', are pure track-planning tools, often tied to specific commercial track systems. Even the fully fledged programmes mentioned have 'libraries' of commercial products almost exclusively American in origin (although most do include Peco track, widely used Stateside), while their inbuilt track geometries and railway engineering features are derived from full-size US practice. Similarly, a lot of the landscape elements and structures provided are specifically American in origin. As far as I know, Templot aside, you can't buy even basic track-planning software with a comprehensive library of British prototype trackwork configurations, let alone fully fledged layout-design systems that incorporate typically British landscape, structures and engineering features.

My main aversion to computers for layout design drawing is because I find them unsympathetic – lacking in any intuitive qualities and, in my hands at least, painfully *slow*. I much prefer the directness and simplicity of pencil on paper. Call me a Luddite if you will, but I find I can get on a lot quicker pushing a 2B about a sheet of layout paper than I can waggling a computer mouse. But then, I *enjoy* the spontaneity of drawing; doing *everything* on-screen makes it all seem a bit too much like the day-job! It also ties you to the computer for the drawing process, whereas a pad of paper, ruler, rubber and a pencil or two can be deployed just about anywhere – the garden, the pub, down at the club....

No, I don't rate a laptop as an alternative; the combination of a relatively small screen and a track-pad rather than a mouse I find even more user-unfriendly in this context.

All this isn't to say that computers have no place in layout design or plan-drawing. They have many virtues, particularly if you don't get on all that well with pencil and paper. There are a number of general-purpose CAD packages – Turbo-CAD, Corel-draw, Claris-CAD and the like – that can be used to draw layout plans just as readily as any other sort of plan, in which context they are capable of a high degree of accuracy and consistency – much better than anybody's hand-drawing. This is very useful for plotting things like exact alignments, curve radii and turnout footprints – tasks that Templot is also very good at. General-purpose CAD packages also permit you to draw elements such as engineering features and structure footprints and manipulate them on-screen. In the case of a large, complex or 'dense' layout, their extreme precision may well be a distinct advantage – but in the context of the typical modest-sized, low-density 'realistic' British style of layout design, it smacks somewhat of technological overkill! Where CAD software almost always falls down is in the ready drawing of the sort of subtle, random curves that characterise so many elements of the British landscape, and which can really only be reproduced 'freehand'– something I find a lot more readily achievable with a pencil than it is with anybody's computer!

This is not the end of the story. In the context of the sort of detailed 'topographical' layout design drawing I've always favoured – which seeks to add a 'pictorial' element to the bare bones of the plan in an attempt to convey the look and feel of the subject in a fairly graphical way – any CAD technical drawing system is a non-starter; it's simply not designed to do that sort of job. To produce fully developed pictorial colour artwork – which is what we're talking about here – you need an all-singing colour graphics programme like Adobe 'Illustrator', as used by *Model Railroader* for their impressive layout renditions. But 'Illustrator' is a very powerful and sophisticated piece of software that takes a *lot* of learning! It also calls (as do the full-house CAD programmes) for plenty of computer power and memory, together with a high-quality, large-screen monitor; this is not the sort of work you can readily do with a basic home PC set-up. To my eye, at least, even the best and most expert of computer graphics still lack the ultimate subtlety, character and individuality of hand-drawn artwork. There may well be a case for drawing the basic footprint and track-plan with a CAD system, then printing it out and adding the rest by hand and where precision is paramount this could be the best bet.

Drawing materials and implements

Having with lordly disdain dismissed computers as a drawing tool, just what does one use to produce an accurate and usable plan? Basically, pencil and paper, in my case. For the nuts-and-bolts of layout planning, I usually start by drawing fairly freely in soft pencil on translucent designer's 'layout paper', which both allows greater drawing freedom while being easy to erase. I stay with pencil while I gradually refine this 'working plan', introducing a reasonable degree of precision as the design crystallises and only moving on to ink, paint or more permanent media once I'm satisfied that I have a workable and dimensionally accurate solution. Often I'll use the usually much-altered 'working plan' as the basis for a 'fair copy', either by tracing it in a refined, inked form on normal draughtsman's tracing paper or, more laboriously, by redrawing the design carefully on heavyweight cartridge or watercolour paper if I'm intending to go the whole hog and produce a set of fully developed 'layout artwork' in full colour.

My tally of hardware for accomplishing all this is actually pretty modest. Yes, I do possess a drawing board – an A2-sized tabletop affair with the plainest and most basic of parallel-motion rulers; it came from Walton designs and cost about £40 a decade or so ago. I find I rarely use it though, at least for British-subject plans – mostly because the majority of the projects I work on are relatively modest in extent and can thus be accommodated on a far more portable A3 designer's layout pad. To go with the pad I have a clear plastic 15in drafting rule, a small wooden T-square, a good-sized (10in) 60° square and a 360° protractor. For going round the bend, I have a couple of pairs of decent-sized compasses, one of them with a bar extension that will draw radii up to about 10in, together with a circle-drawing template and – most importantly – a set of

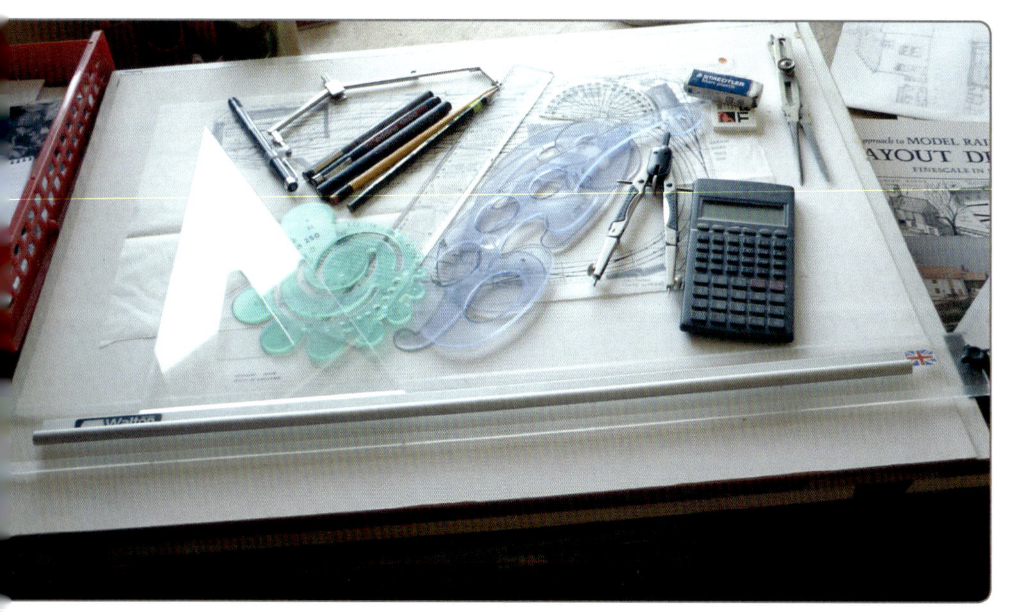

BELOW: *Pretty much the sum total of the drawing office equipment chez Rice. For modestly sized plans, the drawing board can be dispensed with in favour of a pad.* Author

ABOVE: *Nothing fancy about what I actually draw with, either: Cheap Tesco HB pencils and fibre-tip technical drawing pens mostly. There are three main ranges of these, as shown; get them from art supply shops, about £3 a time. I use these pens in a variety of widths and colours, as can be seen.* Author

draughtsman's French curves which, like railway track with spiral easements, are parabolic in nature. The other two essentials are a pair of dividers and a pocket calculator.

To actually draw with I use ordinary traditional wooden pencils of a fairly soft grade: HB is as hard as I go and 2B is preferable. I may like my pencils soft but I also like 'em sharp – in which context I wouldn't be without my whirl-the-handle schoolroom desktop pencil sharpener; £3.99 from Lidl. I get through a lot of pencils, and find that the plain yellow HB that Tesco will flog you at a pitiful 66p for 12 (!) serve perfectly well most of the time. Only if I come over all artistic do I yearn for something more refined. To change my mind with and correct my many errors, I use a good-quality soft eraser which I keep clean. If you want a brand, then the Faber-Castell 'Plastic' erasers are good and sold at proper art or draughtsman's supply stores. When such an eraser gets dirty, give it a bath in warm washing-up suds.

For inking 'final' drawings, I use fine-line fibre-tip drawing pens, either the German Edding 1800-series 'ProfiPens' or the Japanese 'Pilot' DR drawing pens. Both of these ranges can be bought in line widths from 0.25mm up to 0.7mm (Pilot) or 0.8mm (Edding), in a range of colours. Generally, I use 0.25, 0.5 and 0.7/8mm line widths: 0.25 for landscape, structures and engineering features, 0.7/8mm for principal trackage and 0.5mm for subsidiary. At 1in/1ft scale these trackage line-width dimensions are OK for 2mm and 3mm scales but a bit wimpy for 4mm, when a 1mm line width would give a truer idea of trackwork footprint. For 0 gauge, I draw a double 0.5mm line for track, of about 1.5mm total width. To use these liquid-ink pens while avoiding smudging – especially on impervious tracing paper – you will need a proper draughtsman's rule with a rubber strip to raise the ruling edge clear of the paper, thus avoiding ink being drawn beneath the ruler by capillary action. To make sure the same thing doesn't happen when using the French curves, I use some little dots of Blu Tack to keep the ruling edge from touching the paper.

On a monochrome plan, I often use a fine grey felt pen to add tints and shading in order to bring out the three-dimensional nature of what's intended and to pick out structures and engineering features. To develop full-colour layout artwork – usually for publication – I transfer the design to suitable paper, usually in the old-fashioned 'square by square' manner using the 'scale foot' grid for reference. For small plans falling within the compass of my scanner and printer (A4 size) I have had some success with scanning a pencil 'working plan' and then printing it out on an art-grade paper with in inkjet printer, taking care to keep the scaling constant. My printer has a 'card' feed which will cope with fairly stiff paper. As a basis for coloured artwork I use a good-quality heavy (130–150g/sq m) cartridge paper 'stretched' onto a drawing board or, better still, a smooth watercolour paper such as 'Cotman'. The transferred drawing is inked with the pens as above, then carefully coloured with decent artist's watercolours and sable or synthetic brushes – a slow but rewarding process.

BELOW: *For colour artwork, the plan is transferred or redrawn and inked on a suitable grade of paper and tinted with watercolours – a satisfying but laborious process. The end result looks nice but is usually little more useful than a monochromatic plan.* Author

Drawing technique

If I may so dignify my ameliorated scribblings… In any recognised sense of the term, I am no draughtsman, so what follows has nothing whatever to do with 'proper' technical drawing; rather, it's a set of expedient dodges. The only 'formal' rule I do always abide by is to choose one corner of the drawing (usually the bottom left-hand, as I'm right-handed) as a 'datum point' from which all significant measurements are made. To save time in constantly re-drawing the layout 'footprint' accurately following fresh starts or erasures, I prepare an outline of this as an underlay, a template drawn in dense black ink that can be slipped beneath the translucent layout sheet to show through and give me a clear guide as to where the datum point and site boundaries lie. Often, I'll put a grid of inch squares (ie scale feet) in red over the footprint outline as a further drawing aid, and that's about as technical as I get.

As you may have gathered by now, when it comes to layout design I'm all about curves. Straight lines don't interest me very much, and one of the reasons I so enjoy replicating the British scene is the predominance of curvature in infinite, subtle variety, both in the landscape and – as noted above – in much of the trackwork; only in the flatter parts of the Eastern Counties do you find much in the way of unwavering track and rectangularity of landscape feature. On many of my layout designs, pretty much the only dead-straight lines are those edges of the footprint that follow a wall – so being able to draw curves is a key aspect of my approach to drawing. Here, I make a clear distinction between curves in the landscape and those forming part of the track layout – which last, have to make functional as well as aesthetic sense. So while I'm happy to sketch in contours, outlines, boundaries, roads, waterways and other such sinuous landscape features freehand, curved track – as with *all* track – is very carefully and accurately set out.

Drawing track

This is the only part of my plan-drawing process which lays any claim to real precision. Obviously, to be meaningful in a planning sense, the PW has to be rendered with exactitude in terms of footprint and location, and in its relationship to other features. Curves are often the most critical factors in making a layout design 'fit' its site, so it is vital to get them in the right place and of correct radius and form. The most critical point in any railway curve is the limiting radius – the 'tightest' part of the curve and the determiner of compatibility with locos and stock. So in setting out such a curve on the plan I position and draw in this limiting portion first, using compasses carefully set to the true scale radius; minima like this are one thing that can't be 'squeezed'. I extend this circular 'guide' curve for some distance either side of the limiting portion, so that I have plenty of scope for striking an easement off of the basic curve to link with adjoining trackage. Only once this limiting segment of the curve has been established do I move on to set out the transition to straight or (more likely) gently curved track, using the French curves to ensure a smooth parabolic progression from the circular to the more-or-less straight.

Pointwork is another critical factor to get right when drawing track. Here, two things matter: the crossing angle and the 'lead' – the distance between the nose of the crossing and the tips of the switch blades, which will depend on the switch length of the turnout – A, B or whatever. If there's one error that can throw the validity of a plan right out it's getting these turnout leads wrong – and thus not allowing sufficient length to accommodate the necessary pointwork. I use the protractor to measure off the crossing angle in degrees, but for the turnout length I use actual dimensions taken from ready-made turnouts or the appropriate templates, suitably reduced to scale. I include some of the more common turnout lengths and crossing angles in degrees in the little table reproduced alongside, which I compiled a long time ago and have found invaluable ever since. Bear in mind also that turnout lead values increase with gauge: a P4 B6 turnout is all-but an inch longer than the 00 equivalent. Multiply that discrepancy a few times and you've soon arrived at the difference between 'fits' and 'doesn't fit'! When drawing plans for 4mm scale, I always use the P4 turnout lengths 'plus a bit', on the basis that a little bit of breathing space never hurts. What would be truly useful would be a set of accurate inch-to-the-foot point-drawing stencils; I'll have to talk to my etchers!

Other key dimensions to get right (or erring on the right side) when drawing PW on a plan are track centres and track-to-lineside-structure clearances. This last is one aspect of on-paper plan drawing where the convention of representing track by a line of well below true scale width can be misleading, so it's important to check such clearances by measurement from the track centreline. Of course, this being Britain and the nominal standard track gauge being 4ft 8½in, the track centre-to-centre distances for 'six foot' and 'ten foot' ways don't come out at some nice round number on an inch-to-the-foot plan: 0.141076in and 0.19357in respectively (my pragmatic 4mm scale values) hardly leap off of the ruler at one! Sticking with normal rule divisions, I find that 5/32in (0.15625in) and 7/32in (0.21875in) serve well enough, erring as they do on that 'right side' of the critical. Similarly, the 7ft 6in track centreline-to-lineside-structure clearance – a handy 0.09842in on our plan – is best nudged out to a full 1/8in (0.125in), on the basis that a generous 'miss' is always a good idea, particularly when tighter-than-scale curves and long vehicles are involved. For 2mm scale, half these 4mm values are appropriate; in 3mm scale, I opt for 1/8in, 3/16in and 3/32in respectively and in 7mm, values of 9/32in, 3/8in and 7/32in. I'm afraid I've never done the sums for S scale! These are only representational values on the plan, don't forget; when laying out the final model at full size, true scale values (or pragmatic adjustments) can readily be applied. I use a pair of appropriately set dividers as the most convenient and accurate way of establishing and checking these centres and clearances both on the plan and in reality.

Conventions and symbols

As with most specialist disciplines, model railway plan-drawing observes a few conventions peculiar to itself. I've already mentioned the somewhat nominal line-widths used

RIGHT: *Drawing turnouts to scale.*

TABLE OF ANGLES/LEADS

CROSSING NUMBER	ANGLE °*	LEAD IN INCHES (SWITCH CODE) EM/P4	OO	O(fs)
1 IN 5	12½	8" (A)	7" (A)	13½" (A)
1 IN 6	10	9¼" (B)	8" (B)	15¾" (B)
1 IN 7	8½	9½" (B)	8¼" (B)	16¼" (B)
1 IN 8	7	10" (B)	8¾" (B)	17" (B)
1 IN 9	6½	10½" (B)	9¼" (B)	17¾" (B)
1 IN 10	6	11¼" (C)	10" (C)	19" (C)

THESE FIGURES ROUNDED TO THE NEAREST ¼ INCH

* ANGLES TO NEAREST ½°

1) DRAW CROSSING ANGLE (1 IN 6 SHOWN)

10°

CROSSING NOSE

2) MARK IN APPROPRIATE LEAD (P4 VALUE SHOWN)

LEAD

3) BLEND IN USING FRENCH CURVE

B6 LH TURNOUT, P4

to represent track, to go with which approximation there are various bits of miscellaneous shorthand dotted about, mostly connected with things like board-crossings and inspection pits, the limits of gradients, stop-blocks, over-track features like loading gauges or portal cranes, and the position of such necessary-but-unprototypical features as uncoupling ramps or magnets. Other diagrammatic symbols relate to such practical necessities as baseboard joints, the boundaries of 'jigsaw' scenic sections and the positioning of fixed wing-pieces and other viewblocks or presentational aids, as well as the arrangement and depiction of fiddleyard systems such as cassettes, stackers, traversers and sector plates. My own plans sprout a further raft of more pictorial idiosyncrasies intended to convey an idea of the intended topography and the nature of the various structures. I use hatching – inspired by the older pre-contour-line OS maps – to suggest landforms, with suitably organic outlines to represent trees, hedges and other boscage, and roof-ridge, chimney and skylight detail to give shape and purpose to buildings. I illustrate a selection of these cartographic quirks in the 'sample plan' below.

Design conclusions

With the prototype painstakingly researched, the rationale thoroughly thought through, the detailed specification exhaustively set out and the plan precisely drawn, we're at last in possession of a complete and thoroughgoing Layout Design. All that now remains is to put down the pen and pick up the saw, and actually make a start on building the resulting breathtakingly-realistic model railway. In many ways, the easy bit!

BELOW: *Layout plan symbols.*

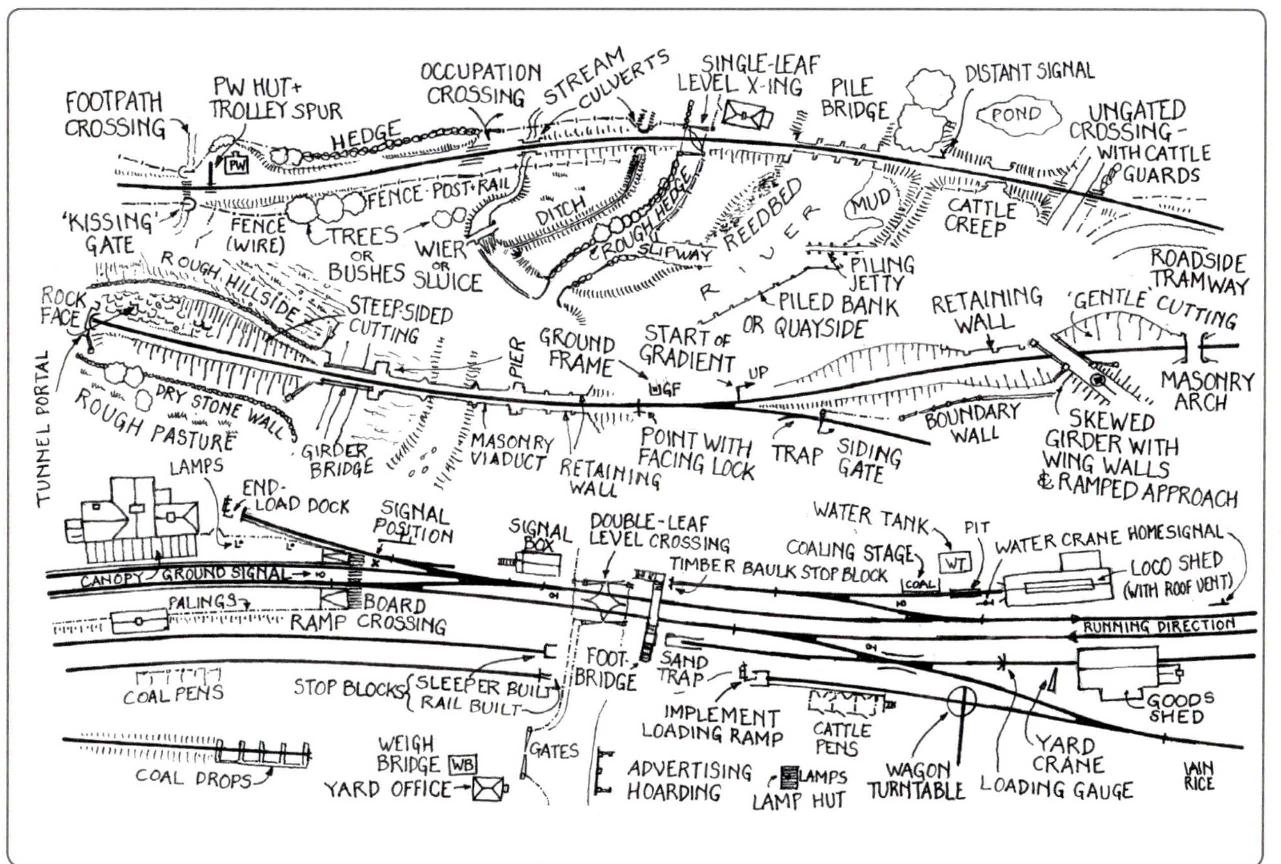

10 SOME LAYOUT DESIGN EXAMPLES

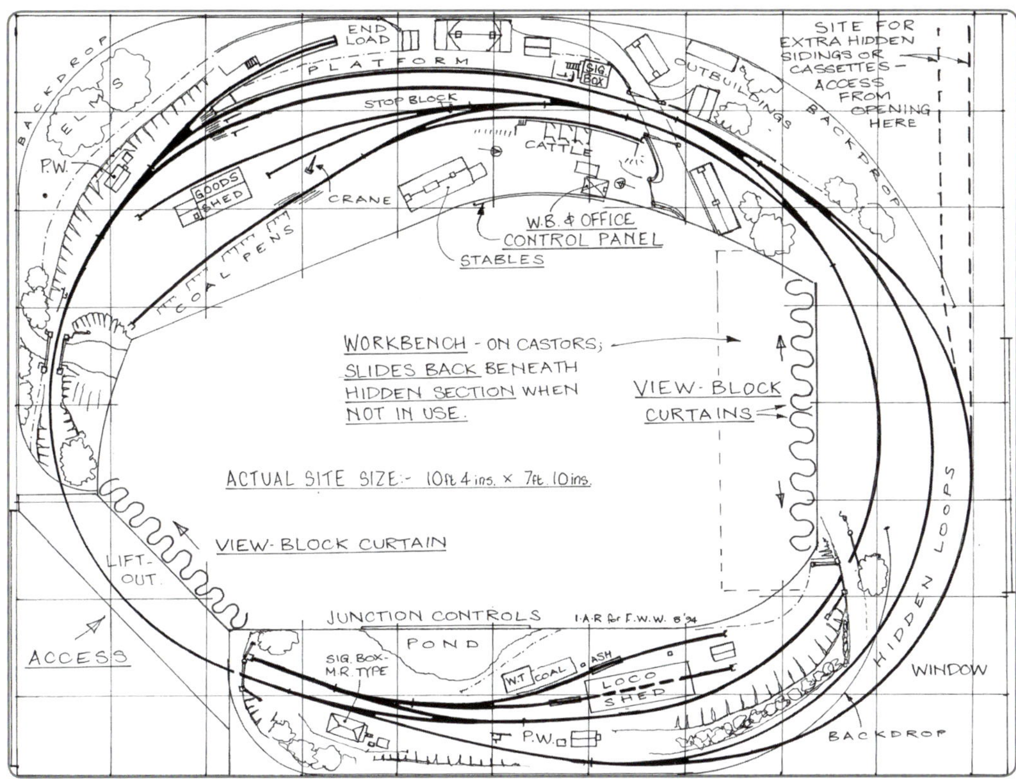

LEFT: *The design for a compact home layout: a somewhat unusual inside-viewed 4mm scale oval with an M&GN theme, designed for my old friend Frank Watts (primarily a loco-builder) as a 'glorified test track with an engine shed'. The site was a small room partitioned off within a double garage. Rather than fixed fascias and 'wings', the layout was framed and off-scene areas hidden with ceiling-hung drapes that could be drawn aside for access. Note the detail and amount of ancillary information incorporated in the layout plan.*

To round off this rambling dissertation, here is a small selection of finished layout designs espousing the principles expounded in this book. For reasons of page space, these are mostly for the sort of smaller scheme, which anyway, form most of my output, as least in a UK context. With the exception of the design for Shaftesbury Town, which I have detailed fully as a 'worked example', each scheme is accompanied by an abbreviated summary of the initial brief, the rationale and the specification, plus – I hope – just enough explanation to make sense of any unusual features.

Worked example: 'Shaftesbury Town'

This is a scheme for a typical home layout using a mid-sized 'U' footprint, intended to be transportable rather than portable. The design *could* be adapted for exhibition use,

BELOW: *Shaftesbury was one of the few towns of any consequence in the West of England never to have a railway station; this layout proposal sets out to give it one!* Frith collection

BELOW: *The 'given' and 'druthers' lists for the layout that – eventually – became 'Shaftesbury Town'. Commendably brief and to the point, if a trifle ungrammatical in places!*

<u>Shaftesbury Layout: Lists</u>

Givens list:

1) Site: Office/study 14'10" x 7'9". 1 long wall (facing door) and 1 end. Could use part of other long wall if needed.
2) Layout to go above filing cabinets (3-drawer – 42" high).
3) Window to be completely unobstructed.
4) Layout not to take up so much space as to obstruct existing uses of room. Must be room for desk, filing cabinets, stationery cupboard, bookshelves, display case, TV and stereo.
5) Doorway not to be obstructed when layout not in use.
6) Lighting to be ceiling-mounted and use existing lighting circuits. 2 ceiling roses at present, 1 available for layout
7) Layout to be movable if needed.
8) EMGS 1979 standards to be used; min radius 36".
9) Budget: £3000 over 3 years.

Wants list:

1) Layout to be similar in size and content to Peter Denny's 'Buckingham' in Mk. II original version (Denny book P.16). 'Important' branch-line terminus.
2) Setting to be Wessex/West Country. SR or GWR (or both). Exactly where not critical, but prefer real place rather than fictional. (Unless Hardy!)
3) To be fully signalled with proper lever frame & block instruments (working).
4) To be capable of prototypical operation by timetable.
5) Must be capable of solo operation or up to 4 people.
6) Preferably DCC control. MERG system?
7) Need reliable auto-couplings with remote operation.
8) To have some interesting/prototypical trackwork.
9) Mostly RTR locos + stock. Don't mind a few kits but don't want to spend a lot of time building stock.
10) To be capable of handling reasoonable-length trains (5-6 coaches) and tender locos. So need a T.T.
11) Scope for plenty of tail traffic/special workings
12) Not too much scenery or non-railway structures.
13) Would like a level crossing if possible.
14) Scope for PO and some 'special' wagons.
15) Must have nice signals + signalbox.
16) Mustn't take too long to build; want to run ASAP.

using an alternative fiddleyard arrangement to give an 'inside-viewed' L-shape. I've chosen it as my 'worked example' as it is very much a mainstream choice of subject with a consequent wide appeal. This design was originally conceived for a friend who wanted something based on 'a railway to a real place, about the size and complexity of early Buckingham MkII, but set in the West Country, and capable of proper timetable operation.' In other words, a branchline terminus – but a larger and busier one suited to a reasonably important town, rather than some bucolic twig with four trains a day.

'Buckingham' is one of the longest-lived and best-known of British model railways. In creating it back in 1946, the Rev. Peter Denny took a real place and gave it an imaginary railway – a branch from the erstwhile Great Central main line. (Buckingham was in reality served by the LNWR.) 'Buckingham Great Central' has evolved over the years – more than 60 of them in fact – from a comparatively modest single-platform terminus to a large and imposing multi-platform affair suited to the Denny 'Buckingham's' enhanced status as a 'small cathedral city'. In the 'middle period' of this development, Buckingham GC was a medium-sized terminus with a couple of platform faces, a reasonably comprehensive goods yard, a gasworks, a canal wharf and a modest loco depot.

ABOVE: *As there wasn't a railway – even on paper – to link Shaftesbury to the LSWR main line, it was necessary to invent one. Mocking up the line's prospectus was a bit of fun as well as a useful way of giving the model a detailed and believable rationale.*

In search of a 'prototype'

The first task in designing a comparable layout was to identify a West Country town of reasonable actual (or potential) importance that either didn't have a railway at all, or was sufficiently poorly served to merit a 'rival' branch from a competing railway – the Buckingham scenario. It's when you undertake an exercise of this sort that you realise just how comprehensive the British railway network actually was! At the end of several hours of poring over maps and head-scratching, I had a list of just six rail-less possibilities: Lyndhurst, in the New Forest, Charmouth and Shaftesbury in Dorset, Wedmore in Somerset, and Modbury and Salcombe, in South Devon. Lyndhurst has distinct possibilities, but is not really 'West Country'. Charmouth has already been 'done', more than once. The two Devon towns and Wedmore, while of undoubted local importance, were never likely to get big enough to warrant more than fairly basic railway provision. This left historic Shaftesbury, sitting aloof on its Dorset hilltop while the LSWR's West of England main line ignored it and passed by some three miles to the north.

Shaftesbury's nearest rail access was at Semley, a minor wayside station served solely by Yeovil–Salisbury stopping trains; expresses stopped at Templecombe or Salisbury, respectively 11½ and 18 miles away. A cursory check through the various standard railway histories failed to turn up a single putative Shaftesbury railway scheme; in fact, my trawling barely turned up a single reference to the place! But then, in 1856 – when the Salisbury & Yeovil bill was before Parliament – Shaftesbury was in a state of some decline, with a population of less than 2,000; being ignored by the railway didn't help! Nevertheless, it did have a market, a castle site and a romantically ruined abbey, and several steep streets of ancient buildings – consequent upon a long and noble history. Gas lighting had arrived as early as 1836, so there must have been a gasworks. In a nutshell, the place had potential, as Tim Lambert says in his concise online historical note (http://www.localhistories.org/shaftesbury.html): 'If the railway had passed through Shaftesbury it would almost certainly have boosted the growth of the town.'

Developing a believable rationale

My rationale for a Shaftesbury layout thus rests on the foundation of such a rail-boosted blossoming – very much on the lines of what did happen nearby at Gillingham. Once smaller and less important than Shaftesbury, that town went through a veritable post-railway boom that saw its population and prosperity soar; today, it is nearly twice the size of Shaftesbury. Unsurprisingly, there are lots of instances of towns that 'missed out' on main line status in this way, connecting themselves by means of a short, locally promoted branch line. Cirencester is a classic example. So, I've supposed that just such a local company – The Shaftesbury & South-Western Junction Railway? – was formed in the later 1860s, to promote a connecting line. By my 'survey', it would have been some 3½ winding miles long without any intermediate stations, leaving the main line at Hatch, some 2½ miles west of Tisbury, and climbing steeply to approach Shaftesbury from the nor nor' east. After the usual vicissitudes, this line might have been opened around, oh, 1872 or so.

Such a railway would doubtless have developed over the years, with the train service and facilities increasing to reflect the ensuing expansion of the town and its trade. As well as promoting a growth in agriculture, industry and population, a rail-connected Shaftesbury would also have been in a strong position to exploit its unique and lofty situation, romantic history and literary associations (it's in Hardy) to develop a tourist trade of the more refined sort. It might, indeed, have become very much the sort of genteel resort Hercule Poirot could have visited while investigating an Agatha Christie mystery ('A town *most* quaint, my dear Hastings…') Such a visitation would fit nicely with the late-1920s Southern Railway timeframe envisaged for the model, firmly entrenched in dignified Olive Green and still very much LSWR in character.

Topography and engineering

Any Shaftesbury railway would have been quite a difficult proposition in engineering terms, as this is pretty hilly country – almost certainly the main reason the Yeovil line passed it by. The station could not anyway have been situated right in the town itself; at some 750 feet above sea level, hill-top Shaftesbury is one of the highest towns in southern England! Any erstwhile branchline would have had to content itself with a terminus nestled some way below the crown of the hill – a situation very akin to that at Launceston, another hill-top town with many similarities to Shaftesbury. A first job was therefore to select a suitable station site, as this would have an impact on the orientation and basic track-plan of the layout. In fact, the problem became inverted; as the nature of the available layout site really only allowed one orientation of a terminal station viewed from the 'platform' side – buffer stops at the right-hand end, approach track coming in from the left – then I was perforce looking for a location that would tally with this pre-determined footprint.

Fortunately, I often pass through Shaftesbury, so it was no great hardship to pause awhile for a bite of lunch and a leisurely stroll around to size-up the terrain and assess the possible station sites – which, I soon realised, were precious few! Two, in fact: somewhere around Ivy Cross, on the broader swell of the high eastern flank (700ft or so) of the hill, a little way to the north-east of the old town; or at Enmore, crouching close below the town square on the north-western flank of the hill. The hillside here is much steeper but the topography allowed of a considerably lower station elevation – around 600ft – albeit at the cost of piercing the 'saddleback' of the ridge with a short tunnel at Little Down. The road up from the station to the town square would also have been a stiff pull – although nowhere as bad as at Launceston!

In the event, the Enmore option won hands down because it tallied very nicely with the area available for the model, giving the right track orientation with the station nicely set against the background of that steeply rising hillside and, in the shape of Littledown Tunnel, possessed of a ready-made 'exit' to the fiddleyard. The alignment through Enmore would also have favoured an extension of the route in the general direction of Sturminster Newton to form, ultimately, a possible direct route (the 'Central Wessex'?) to Dorchester and Weymouth, superseding the 'round-the-houses' of 'Castleman's Corkscrew' via Wimborne and Wareham. Many a local railway was conceived with just such a wishful 'eye to the main chance'.

Plotting a route from the main line at Hatch up to Enmore (courtesy of the OS and Google Earth), I soon found that even to get this far up would have called for a winding alignment and gradients steeper than 1 in 60 in places as the branch scaled the flank of the chalk-and-greensand ridge on which Shaftesbury sits; the line would have needed to climb some 180ft or so in its 3½ miles, an overall average inclination close to 1 in 100. The hardest going would have been in a sinuous climb around Semley Hill and in the final approach to the short-ish (650 yards or so, by my reckoning) tunnel at Littledown. The eastern portal of this tunnel would have formed the 'summit' of the route, which then drops gently down through the tunnel to the station approach. Such a branch would almost certainly have been built single-tracked and probably none-too-generous in the radii of its curvature – so maybe not too suitable as a putative main line, however wishful the thinking!

Train service and traffic demands

The precise facilities needed at any terminus being dictated by the nature of the train service, sketching out a working timetable for a 'developed' Shaftesbury was a key next step. Producing this WTT was quite an involved exercise, requiring much study of actual timetables for the Salisbury–Yeovil section, a realistic appraisal of possible traffic, and a study of what went on in comparable situations. (Not to mention some serious head-scratching to fit all the bits together!) Part of the result – the summer weekday service – is reproduced hereabouts, rather wonkily typeset (as they often were).

I determined at the outset that the Shaftesbury branch should enjoy a direct through passenger service to Salisbury rather than suffering a simple shuttle to Tisbury, the logical location for a junction station. By about 1910 (allowing a reasonable period of development, and also a year for which I had a 'Bradshaw'), I reckoned that a service of 7 trains each way daily was not unreasonable, this still forming the basic service current for the 1927 timeframe of the model. Four

BELOW: *Draft working timetable for the Shaftesbury branch.*

Shaftesbury Town Working Timetable: Summer (Based on Bradshaw 1910)

Up Trains - Week Days

			TC	*Mlk*	*§TC**		*⌿ Gds*		*⌿ Gds*	*Mlk*
104¾	Shaftesbury Town	6.03	8.32	11.42	**1.56**	2.32	*2.45*	5.42	*6.44*	8.12
101¼	Hatch Junction.	6.14		11.53	**2.07**	2.43	*3.02*	5.53	*7.01*	8.23
96¼	Tisbury	6.25	8.54	12.05	**2.18**	2.54		6.04		8.36
92	Dinton	6.33		12.14		3.02		6.15		8.48
86¼	Wilton	6.43		12.25		3.12		6.25		8.56
83¾	Salisbury	6.48	9.16	12.30	**2.38**	3.17		6.31		9.01
82½	*Salisbury (Goods)*						*3.50*		*7.49*	
00	**London Waterloo**		11.03		**4.40**					

Down Trains - Week Days

			¶Gds	±	*§TC**		*Gds*	±		
00	**London Waterloo**				**11.00**				3.50	
82½	*Salisbury (Goods)*		*9.23*				*2.42*			
83¾	Salisbury	7.11		10.07	**12.45**	1.27		4.32	7.09	9.17
86¼	Wilton	7.16		10.12		1.32		4.37		9.22
92	Dinton	7.26		10.22		1.42		4.47		9.30
96¼	Tisbury	7.34		10.30	**1.07**	1.50		4.55	7.31	9.40
101¼	Hatch Junction	7.45	*10.08*	10.41		2.01	*3.27*	5.06		9.51
104¾	Shaftesbury Town	7.59	*10.22*	10.54	**1.31**	2.15	*3.45*	5.20	7.54	10.05

* Diagrammed to Salisbury Loco
± Conveys empty milk vans
§ Summer timetable only: Conveys through coaches from B'mth
⌿ All up unfitted gds pin down brakes Shaftesbury to Hatch Junc.
¶ Additional working as required market days (Thursdays)

Cleaner/firelighter books on 4.14 a.m. Early turn crew book on 5.30 a.m. off at 2.30 p.m. Late turn book on 2 p.m off at 10.45 p.m.

of these 14 workings convey through coaches for Waterloo, with a further four being designated to handle milk traffic, thus allowing extra station time en route. A 'summer timetable only' footnote sees the principal early afternoon train also conveying through coaches from Bournemouth. Freight traffic is handled by two daily trip workings from Salisbury (Milford Goods), with additional trips 'as required' to meet the needs of the Thursday livestock market.

This timetable threw up a number of specific requirements for Shaftesbury Town station: platform capacity for at least five bogie coaches and a van, a milk dock for churn-handling, a good-sized cattle dock, overnight stabling for a through coach as well as the branch set, and a 55ft turntable for the mpd. Consulting some old trade directories for the town (courtesy of Shaftesbury library) added a few more: a loading facility to handle abattoir traffic, end-loading for farm implements, at least three agricultural merchant's stores, an oil depot and a spur for the gasworks. All that in addition to the usual warehousing for general merchandise, craning capability, sack and sheet storage, dray-horse stabling and, of course, space for the town's coal factors (up to five!). Also required within the station complex, is somewhere to load/unload horseboxes and to deal with carriage trucks – essential facilities for a Victorian resort town.

The traffic analysis also suggested the motive power and stock needed (and hence the associated facilities). A dedicated branch loco is the core provision – almost certainly an M7 0-4-4T, crewed by early and late turn men, aided by a cleaner/firelighter and visiting fitter. This called for a small, single-road shed with basic maintenance and coaling facilities. In the summer, the early afternoon through working needs more substantial power – a T9 4-4-0, perhaps, or a 'Woolwich Mogul' from Salisbury shed. Goods trips would also be a Salisbury turn, for a Drummond 'Black Motor' 0-6-0 goods, or perhaps a Mogul on market days. The turntable avoids the need for tender-first running on the main line. The branch passenger set would probably be a trio of ex-LSWR 48ft compartment coaches, with 'Ironclad' or Maunsell stock for through workings. Milk traffic (still churns in 1927) would call for a small fleet of four-wheel milk vans, while a couple of meat vans would be loaded daily and worked out by the late goods. An adequate supply of cattle vans would be needed for the market traffic, while the oil depot would receive paraffin, probably in 'Royal Daylight' tank wagons. Agricultural implement traffic would call for flat implement or 'low machinery' wagons. All that in addition to the usual general traffic mineral and open merchandise wagons, ventilated and unvented vans, flat and bolster wagons.

Station layout and facilities

Traffic needs apart, my approach when designing a believable and appropriate set of railway facilities for a fictional layout is always to study similar situations in reality – so I went in search of suitable role-models for Shaftesbury. The LSWR main line is not too well-provided with branches, but Swanage and Sidmouth both seemed to offer useful pointers. Of the rest, the Yeovil Town branch was double-tracked and served a much bigger town, while Chard was a unique situation (a joint

LEFT AND BELOW: *Shaftesbury motive power in the 1920s – all very attainable in 4mm scale. The 'branch engine' would undoubtedly have been an M7 0-4-4T – as handsome a specimen of the breed as you could wish for. The main through train of the day rates a tender engine, for which a T9 is a credible choice with a 'Woolwich Mogul' as an alternative. All three of these locomotives are available as high-quality RTR models.*

Goods working would most probably have been in the hands of 'Black Motors'– Drummond '700' class 0-6-0s, first cousins to the T9 and currently calling for a kit-built model. Again, the Mogul could substitute. Author's collection

'double terminus' forming an end-on junction with a GWR branch). Seaton was too small and the Lyme Regis line a much more recently constructed and minimalist affair built under the provisions of the Light Railways Act of 1896.

Swanage and Sidmouth, however, had striking similarities and provided useful starting points. The 1874 Sidmouth branch – with its single-track, cramped site and steep approach – had particularly strong parallels with the fictional situation at Shaftesbury. The Swanage branch – opened a decade later – enjoyed notably more generous goods provision, with a goods loop and long headshunt. Not to mention a loco shed oddly sited directly off the running lines and accessed only over a turntable. Otherwise, the basic station recipe is the same: a single platform with one long face and a bay, a full range of goods facilities and a small locomotive depot. In essentials, my 'Shaftesbury Town' is a mirror-image of Sidmouth, but with a Swanage-like loco shed location and the goods yard amended to suit the identified traffic needs and to fit the awkward topography of the supposed site. The entrance to the short but sulphurous Littledown Tunnel lies only a few hundred yards from the platform end.

The resulting track layout does have a couple of quirks, most notably the connection to the gasworks spur from the extreme end of the platform road, which thus effectively ends in a short trap siding beyond the gasworks turnout; note the single-bladed trap situated just inside the spur's roadway gate to protect what is still technically a running line. The bay platform is double-faced over part of its length to provide a dedicated 'churn bank' for milk traffic and a further bank for horsebox and carriage-truck traffic lies alongside a short spur off the bay. The loco facilities, as at Swanage, are tucked away on a cramped site accessed direct from the running line on the station approach. The shed access is, however, direct; the 55ft turntable – deemed to be a later addition – is sited alongside.

Train working and signalling

The nature of Shaftesbury's train service – in particular, the need for more than one locomotive to be on the branch at any given time – would have determined the system of single-line working adopted and the nature and extent of the signalling provided. With its 14 passenger and four goods movements daily, there would have been long periods during which passenger workings overlapped with goods shunting at the terminus – so the Shaftesbury branch would have demanded a reasonably full and flexible signalling provision, probably involving the use of the Tyer's 'electric train tablet' system much favoured by the LSWR. This in turn would have required the signalbox at the terminus to be situated on the station approach adjacent to the running line, being duly provided with a suitable tablet exchange platform.

The need for goods shunting and passenger working to occur simultaneously at the terminus also dictated the need for a dedicated goods headshunt together with sufficient yard trackage to enable the goods traffic to be kept clear of the running lines. Any conflicting movements would be under the control of ground signals, and full trapping would, of course, be provided. There would also be a home signal rather than a fixed distant on the station approach, to protect any fouling moves on the running lines. These signalling additions would call for more levers in the locking frame and consequently a larger signalbox. My tally gives 16 active levers (including the lock for a ground frame of three levers controlling the engine release crossover and the gasworks spur entry). With a few spares, that suggests a 20-lever frame. When opened, the line would have had a much more basic signalling and control system; the present set-up is deemed to have resulted from a late-1880s resignalling, suggesting the provision of an LSWR Type 3 signalbox. Liphook – also with a 20-lever frame – was the prototype I selected; there is a nice set of drawings in *A Pictorial Record of Southern Signals* by G. A. Pryer (OPC).

Layout site and presentation

The prospective site for this 4mm scale, EM-gauge layout was a ground-floor room in a 1930s semi – actually, the original attached garage, now converted and taken into the house. Like many such older domestic garages, designed around the modest cars of the day, it's small by modern standards; originally 15ft 6in x 8ft 6in, necessarily reduced to 14ft 10in x 7ft 9in by an inner skin of cavity blockwork. The primary use of the room was as a study/home office, but one side and one end wall were available, plus a shelf's-worth of the full-height bookcase on the opposing long wall. Not over-generous, but adequate. The original connecting door fortunately opened inwards to the house, which eased one problem as we could safely 'bridge' the doorway and link the bookshelving to the rest of the layout, which permitted a fiddleyard long enough to handle decent-length trains. If we'd stuck strictly to the logical L-shape, the approach curve would have needed to be even tighter and the fiddleyard a great deal shorter.

The resulting U-shaped design presented here uses ruling curves (non-visible, over the doorway link) of 3ft radius to permit a still-tight (but visually acceptable) transitioned curve of 3ft 9in mean radius for the station approach. It would have been nice if that old garage had been six inches wider… The model was to be sited with rail level 50in above the floor, a dimension partly determined by the need to house a bank of three-drawer filing cabinets (42in high) beneath the goods yard, but mostly chosen as a good compromise between standing viewing and 'walkaround' operation and seated operation using a bar stool. The hilly nature of the scenery made the resulting viewpoint perfectly natural, while a backdrop extending to 7ft 9in above floor level (ie the ceiling!) ensured an eye-level horizon-line. Lighting was to be ceiling-mounted using linked fluorescent tubes concealed by a deep ceiling-hung fabric pelmet supported by domestic curtain-track and powered from the existing domestic lighting circuit via a ceiling rose (relocated). This pelmet would match the (deep green) material chosen for the main layout drapes, allied with layout fascias finished in a medium sage green.

In keeping with the prototypical-operation brief, the design features a comprehensive and realistic 'signalbox' control console, mounted below the layout fascia and incorporating a 20-lever frame with working catch-handles

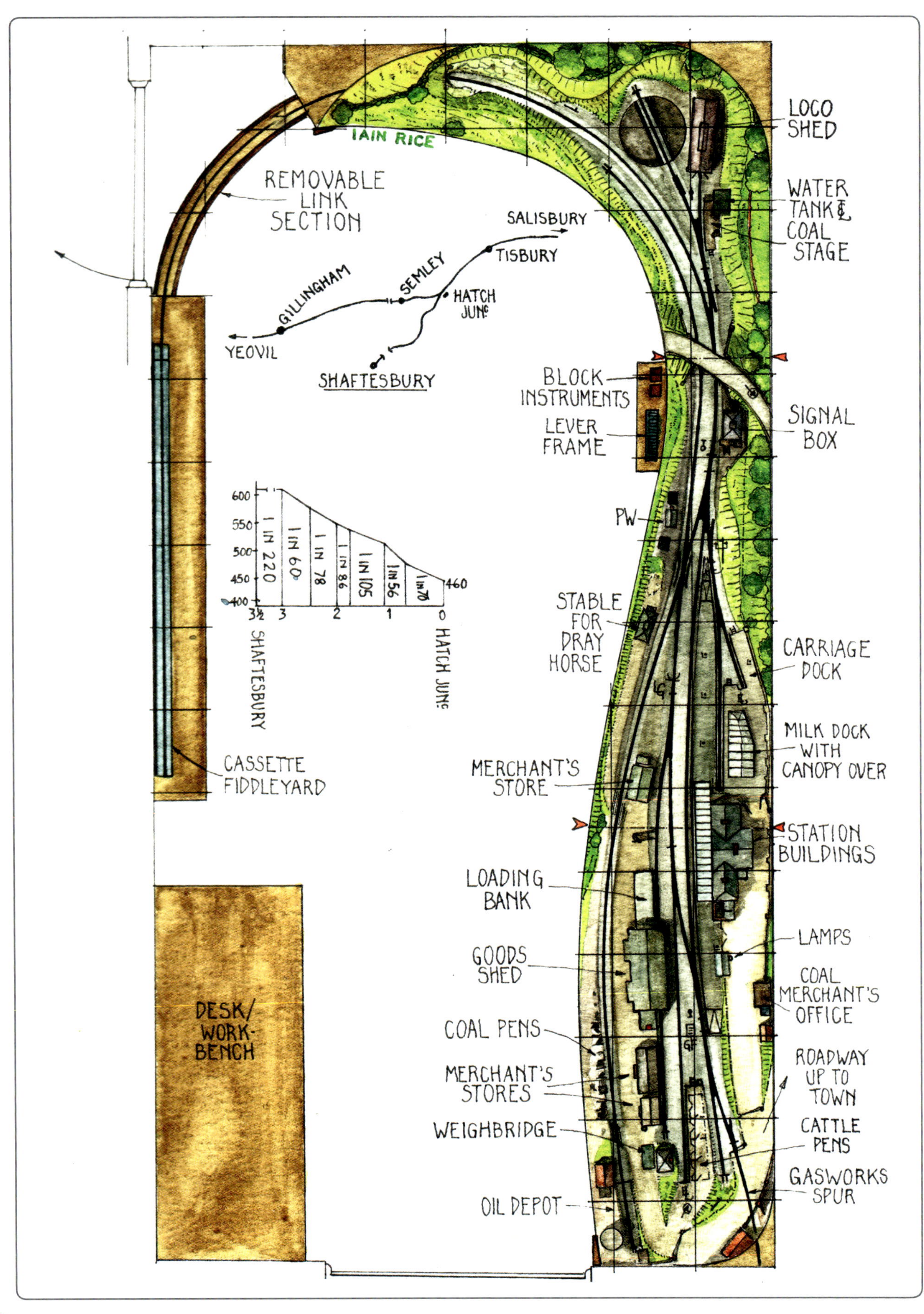
IAIN RICE
REMOVABLE LINK SECTION
SALISBURY
TISBURY
SEMLEY
HATCH JUNC
GILLINGHAM
YEOVIL
SHAFTESBURY
600
550
500
450
400
1 IN 220
1 IN 60
1 IN 78
1 IN 86
1 IN 105
1 IN 56
1 IN 70
460
3½
3
2
1
0
SHAFTESBURY
HATCH JUNC
CASSETTE FIDDLEYARD
DESK/ WORK-BENCH
LOCO SHED
WATER TANK & COAL STAGE
BLOCK INSTRUMENTS
LEVER FRAME
SIGNAL BOX
PW
STABLE FOR DRAY HORSE
CARRIAGE DOCK
MILK DOCK WITH CANOPY OVER
MERCHANT'S STORE
STATION BUILDINGS
LOADING BANK
LAMPS
GOODS SHED
COAL MERCHANT'S OFFICE
COAL PENS
ROADWAY UP TO TOWN
MERCHANT'S STORES
CATTLE PENS
WEIGHBRIDGE
GASWORKS SPUR
OIL DEPOT

LEFT: *Shaftesbury layout plan.*

and related to a proper track diagram, functional block instruments and simulated electric tablet apparatus. All the signals (LSWR lattice-post types) would, of course, work. Structures follow suitable prototypes drawn from a variety of West-of-England locations: the loco shed favoured Swanage, but the station building owes a lot to Sidmouth, while the goods shed is an abbreviated version of Axminster – which place also provided the water tower and coal stage. As operation was based around the summer timetable, the layout would perforce be set in scenery in the verdant garb of 'high summer'.

Trains were to be DCC-controlled using Lenz equipment and handheld controllers. Couplings were modified Sprat-and-Winkle with drop-magnet actuation, with the branch passenger set as a fixed formation using drawbars. Although capable of solo operation, the layout would be able to keep three people busy: a signalman, a dedicated driver running the train service, and a third operator looking after the fiddleyard, shunting the goods yard and acting as the Hatch Junction signalman. This operator could also wear the 'control' hat and instigate or oversee 'special' workings such as tail traffic or market-day 'extras'.

Specification

This layout was intended for construction by 'one man assisted from time-to-time by a couple of mates'. The main modelling interests of the principal proponent were track and signalling; he wasn't into loco-building per se, while buildings (apart from signalboxes) were 'an utter bore'. Scenery and structures could anyway mostly be left to one of the 'mates'– me! Otherwise, the baseboards were to be modified L-girder, wall-supported off heavy-duty 'Spur' shelf track, with trackbeds in 12mm MDF and ply scenery profiles; there would be four baseboard sections in case the layout ever needed to be moved. The backdrop would be wall-mounted using 2mm MDF on a stripwood frame. A 6ft-long cassette fiddleyard – integrated with the track-supported bookshelving otherwise occupying this wall – featured additional cassette storage on shelving above and below layout level.

Plain track was to be C&L EM flexible, which conveniently features the three-bolt 'S1' chairs used by the Southern Railway; most sidings, though, would be laid with pre-Grouping 9ft sleepers and Exactoscale LSWR four-bolt chairs. Matching pointwork would be handbuilt from C&L components, with point actuation by slow-action 'Hoffman' motors – along with a few hand-operated turnouts in the goods yard. Signals would all, of course, be lovingly scratchbuilt from MSE components and fitted with Full Stop 'bouncing' signal servos. Architectural models would use plastics, mostly the Wills scenic series sheets and Plastikard. Glueshell-and-card scenery would be used to keep weight down and the speed of construction up.

The electrics were based around a standard 16–20V ac DCC BUS with four 'power districts' (station, goods yard, approach/loco depot, and fiddleyard) and an off-layout programming facility, with a separate 12V dc supply for point and signal actuation and layout lighting. The required locos would be mostly adapted RTR with 'drop-in' EM conversions: a brace of Hornby M7s and a T9, plus a Bachmann N or two. Only the 'Black Motor' would call for a kitbuild. On the stock front, the branch passenger set *would* need etched kits (Roxey), augmented by the odd Hornby Maunsell; but freight stock could be mostly plastic kit-built or RTR. The standard of modern RTR, lightly titivated, was set as the overall benchmark. The budget for the whole project was to be £3,000 spread over 3 years, the intended basic 'build time'.

Summary

In describing the evolution of 'Shaftesbury Town', I've gone into considerable (although by no means exhaustive) detail in an attempt to show how all the various factors discussed in the text of this book were brought together in the design of what is, on the face of it, a pretty straightforward and modest layout. I wouldn't like to estimate how many hours the whole process took (the timetable alone consumed a week of evenings!), but it was no five-minute task – and one which included several visits to the town. (No hardship; it's a delightful place.) There was also a good bit of time spent on-line or down at the library. I like to think that the end result is realistic, both visually and operationally, as well as eminently buildable. Has it been built? Not yet: my unspeakable friend (nameless to avoid blasphemy!) went and moved house at the eleventh hour, so the scheme is slated for a total reworking to suit a different site. Such is the life of an itinerant layout-designer!

'Fen Drove'

This ultra-compact, highly portable and very straightforward 'shunting plank' scheme was originally conceived as a first

BELOW: *The perspective drawing is a useful design tool, even if as rough-and-ready as this sketch of my long-running 'shunting plank' layout 'Fen Drove' – a basic scheme which exists in a wide range of variants. This is a cameo version.*

ABOVE: *Confected to essentially the same simple recipe as 'Fen Drove', 'Butley Mills' was a similar East Anglian agricultural tramway terminus, albeit with an East Suffolk rather than Fenland setting. The J39 seen here was a bit OTT for motive power; a 'Buckjumper' or 'J15' was more normal.* Author

step in finescale modelling, a 'toe in the water' or glorified test-track. Over the years, I've come up with umpteen variations on the same basic theme to suit a variety of sites, footprints and presentations; it's a concept that works for 2mm, 4mm and 7mm scales – on site sizes from 4 x 1 to 13 x 2 feet. My 1984 layout 'Butley Mills' (7ft 6in x 15in or so) was essentially built to the same design. Whatever the scale, size or presentation, 'Fen Drove' needs but a simple baseboard, few structures and only the simplest of mechanical and electrical ingredients. Here, I illustrate two versions of the basic design: one in cameo format with integrated backscene and presentation, and a 'plain Jane' variant designed to stand in front of a blank and suitably coloured wall which can act as a background. In this case, the rear of the modelled scene is specifically contrived to give a natural 'rear profile' which can be simply silhouetted against a plain sky ground. A mounting height that puts the track close to the viewer's eye level is a *sine qua non* for fenland models like this.

The subject is the terminus of an East Anglian freight-only agricultural branch, inspired by the lines to Benwick and Burwell Fen. The design offers a range of loading facilities for fruit and produce traffic, livestock, timber, agricultural implements and sugar beet. Inward traffics include coal, lime, fertiliser and animal feeds. There's also a wharf onto a fen waterway, with transhipment facilities for coal and lime, as at Outwell Village on the Wisbech & Upwell. All of this offers reasonable scope for operation and a good variety of wagon types. Motive power could be a 'Buckjumper' 0-6-0T, a J70 tram engine, a Class 03/04 diesel, or even, at a pinch, a J15 0-6-0.

Given the 'trial layout' brief, tracklaying for this design was kept simple; five straightforward turnouts. Fine-scale 'apprentice piece' intent apart, the layout *could* be executed in any of the popular scales in ready-to-use Peco track; in 7mm, it would even be to 'fine' standards! Electrics are conventional DC using a handheld controller and 'dispersed' control, with the turnouts and uncouplers (drop magnets) manually operated. For 2mm and 4mm scales, this version of 'Fen Drove' uses a cameo format with lightweight glued-ply baseboards. For 7mm, conventional baseboards and a separate backscene would make better sense. Whatever the precise construction, the basic design makes a viable and compact home-cum-exhibition layout in almost any scale.

'Goodman's Wharf'

This is another 'shunting plank' exhibition-orientated mini-layout, but a very different animal to the rural minimalism of 'Fen Drove'. Urban-dense, ultra-compact and ultra-portable, 'Goodman's Wharf' is a self-contained folding cameo specifically designed to be moved in the boot of an ordinary saloon car or small hatchback – to which end, the thoroughly unconventional baseboard uses a backscene/back board made of half-inch building ply as a main structural member. This is hinged vertically to allow the layout to fold from a 6ft long cameo some 15in deep by 14in high into a 'box' 3ft long by

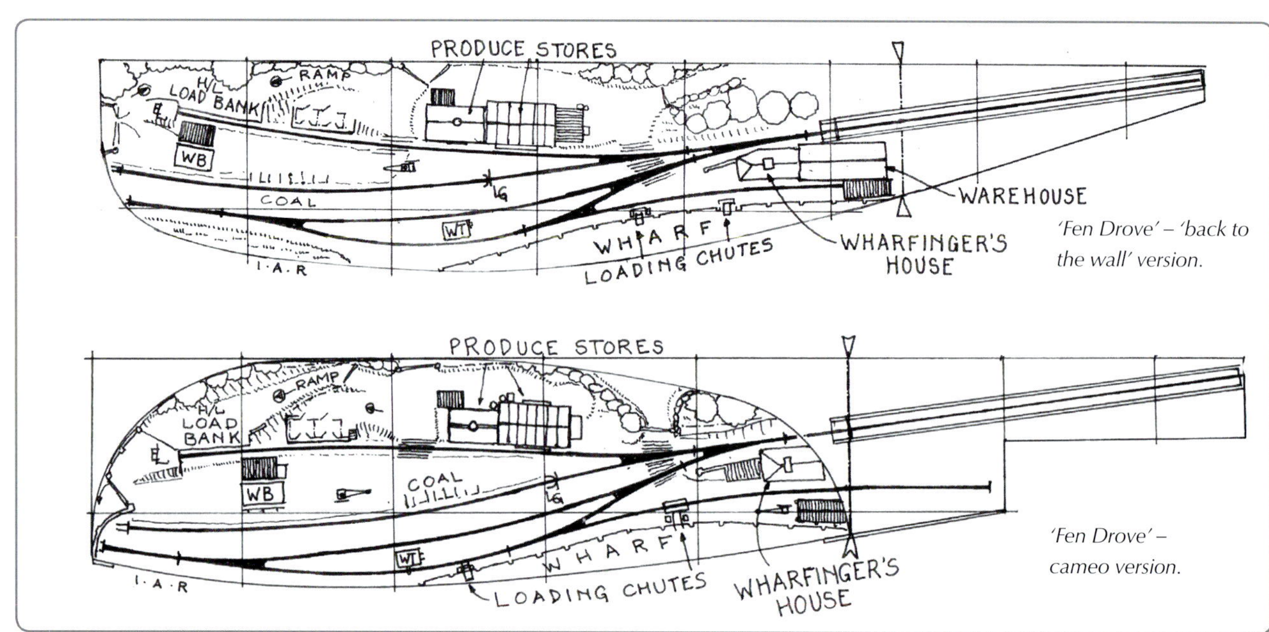

'Fen Drove' – 'back to the wall' version.

'Fen Drove' – cameo version.

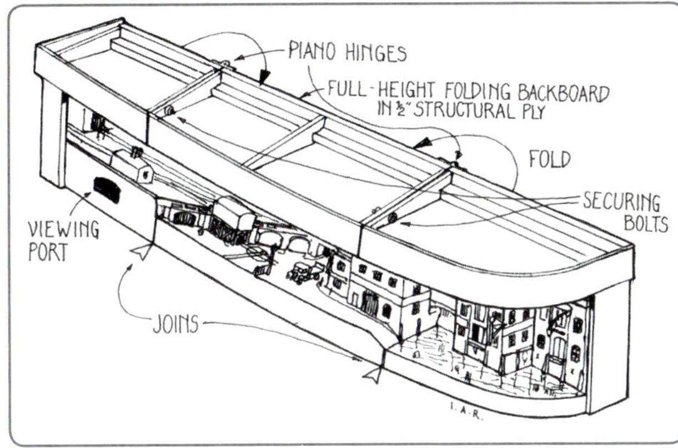

ABOVE: *Folding cameo baseboard for 'Goodman's Wharf'.*

30in wide by 14in high – a size which went neatly into the boot of an Audi A4 saloon with enough room to spare for a stock box, a pair of table-top mini-trestles, and the usual exhibition paraphernalia of drapes, extension leads, tools and so on.

The subject here is an old Rice favourite, an East London riverside goods depot 'somewhere off the Mile End Road'. Think London Docks branch, Goodman's Yard, Shadwell, Poplar Dock, and all points east in the general direction of Woolwich. The basic recipe is track elevated on brick arches (Wills) and tall, grimy buildings. The recipe also includes a wagon hoist (à la Bishopsgate) and a small stretch of Thames-side mud. There are a lot of buildings, some of them fairly large (although mostly only in low relief). The fold-lines in the sky are disguised by the tall hydraulic tower on the left and hidden behind the big foreground warehouse on the right. A novel 'extra' is the modelling of part of the 'basement level' accessed by the wagon hoist, viewed through a port cut in the front fascia and appropriately (ie dimly) lit.

The specification is otherwise pretty basic. The design was for 4mm scale/P4, but as the track is either inlaid in granite setts or hidden by bridge girders and parapet walls, this doesn't call for anything fancy or fully chaired in the way of PW; rail soldered direct to PCB sleepering was the intention. The fiddleyard uses single-ended cassettes, located through a 'port' in the backscene and supported on a drop-down hinged flap. As with all my cameos, this one is designed to sit on mini-trestles atop a table, which also provides a convenient parking-place for spare cassettes. Electrics are straightforward dc, with a handheld controller and solenoid-operated turnouts controlled from a 'ground frame' panel on the end of the layout. Couplings are my customary 'imprecise' auto type with fixed magnets. Stock-wise, a 'Buckjumper' and a handful of wagons are all you need.

'Boduan Junction'

At 6½ft long by just over 2ft wide, this coffin-sized cameo layout designed for Don Leeper is about as big as you can take the all-in-one self-contained format to, without the result becoming impossibly unwieldy to move. Intended principally as a 4mm scale/P4 'occasional exhibition' showpiece with cassette fiddleyards at either end, 'Boduan' represents the junction of two railways planned in reality but never actually built: the Cambrian Railways' extension northward from Pwllheli to Nefyn, and the LNWR's scheme

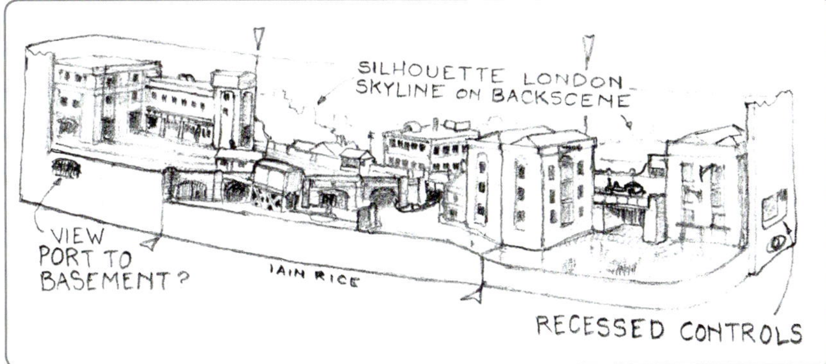

RIGHT: *A perspective rendering of 'Goodman's Wharf', shown sans lighting fascia – which could be replaced with a demountable 'flying light beam' as on 'Hepton Wharf'. The arrowheads denote the fold lines.*

BELOW: *'Goodman's Wharf' layout plan.*

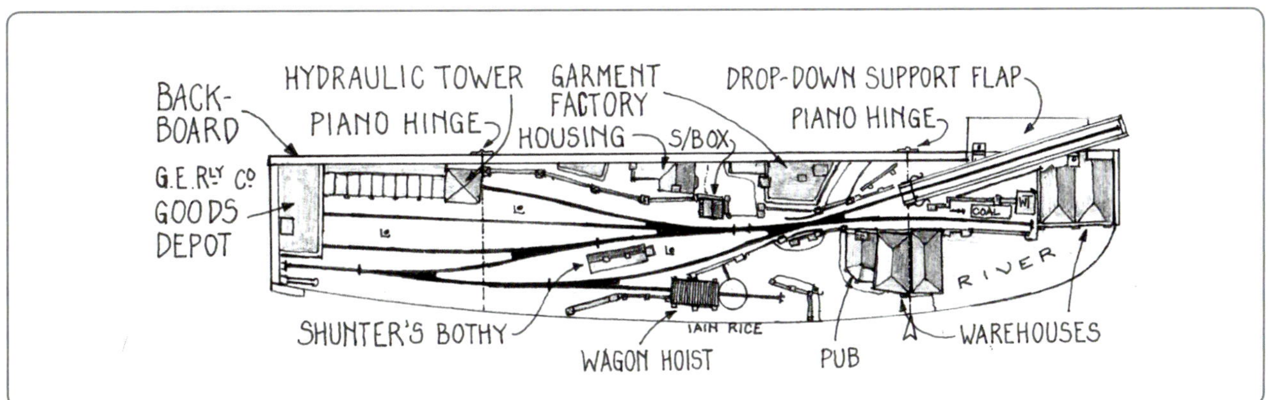

ABOVE: *'Boduan Junction' – perspective rendering.*

to develop Morfa Nefyn/Porth Dinllaen as an alternative Irish ferry port by means of a line approaching from Caernarfon, away to the north-east. In realising this bit of 'might have been', the supposition is that Cambrian got there first, but the LNWR acquired running powers over the last couple of miles of their metals into Nefyn and then built its own line on a further mile to Porth Dinllaen.

This scenario explains the rather odd disposition of the track layout; the tiny Cambrian wayside station of Boduan (or Bodfean; Victorian Welsh spelling is ever variable!) is deemed to pre-date the arrival of the LNWR branch running down the north coast of the Lleyn peninsula from Bryncir (or Brynkyr or Bryncyr). So the actual junction – of 'Board of Trade' pattern – is unrelated to this station, which is thus served only by Cambrian trains; LNWR passengers have to make do with a tiny halt for the railmotor service from Bryncir. Also at Boduan is a siding serving a quarry; originally linked to the Cambrian, this siding now connects to the LNW, making for some nicely convoluted shunting when quarry traffic needs to go south over Cambrian metals! The 'facing-both-ways' Cambrian goods yard also makes for tricky working.

BELOW: *'Boduan Junction' – layout plan.*

Otherwise, Boduan is intended as an exercise in high-quality, fine scale pre-Grouping historical modelling; small but exquisite are the watchwords, with an exacting specification. The track, for instance, is to be entirely handbuilt, using custom-etched brass fold-up Cambrian chairs on ply sleepers. The locos and stock are a mixture of hard-to-find etched kits and scratchbuilds, including a delightful Cambrian 2-4-0T started by the late Frank Watts and completed by the author, along with a trio of exquisite Cambrian 45ft tricomposite coaches from D&S kits built and painted by Ian Rathbone. Electrics are designed to be DCC compatible, although the layout will initially be worked with conventional dc. Display design, cabinetry and lighting will be similar to those of 'Hepton Wharf', illustrated elsewhere in this book. All that Don and I have to do now is live long enough to build it!

'Altguish', BR Far North Line

A fruitful hunting-ground for railway modellers bent on a little light fiction has always been that dusty pile of unfulfilled dreams, the prospectuses and parliamentary bills of railways that were planned and authorised but – for one reason or another – never built. The pages of railway histories are full of these footnotes to ambition, and the basis of this particular 'might have been', the Garve & Ullapool, was trawled from H. A. Vallence's classic account of the Highland Railway. This is rather Rice treading on the toes of good friend Simon de Souza, whose exquisite pre-Grouping P4 'Corrieshalloch' (as featured elsewhere in these pages) is likewise based upon the original standard gauge G&A proposal of 1890. (Later proposals were for narrow gauge lines.)

My design, for a modestly dimensioned 2mm finescale or 'N' exhibition layout, portrays this 'prototype', at a much later period in its history – to whit, the BR 'Blue Diesel' era of the early 1970s, a timeframe for which much of the appropriate motive power – BR TOPS classes 24, 25 and 37 – is available from the revitalised and much-improved

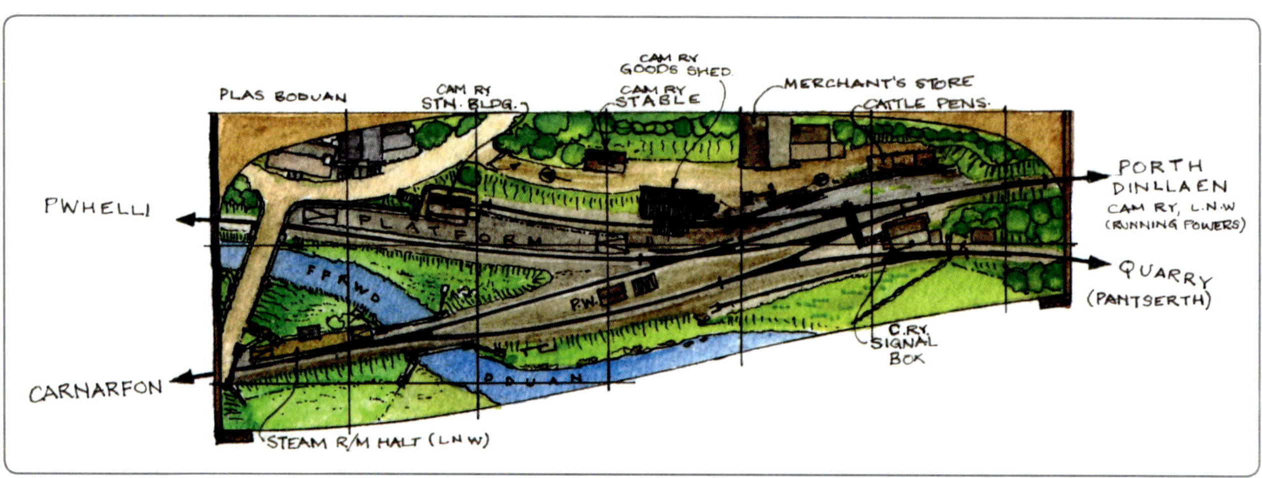

ABOVE: *A 4mm scale P4 exhibition layout which treads very much the same 1970s-era Highland turf as 'Altguish' (although on an L-shaped end-to-end layout) is Mark and Ciaran Tatlow's excellent 'Portchullin'. This represents a fictional additional station beside Loch Carron on the Dingwall to Kyle of Lochalsh line – the route from which the Garve & Ullapool would have branched.* Author

Bachmann/Graham Farish range. These are models that not only look good and run like watches, but are readily converted to 2mm fine scale standards by simple wheelset substitution, using the wheel re-profiling service offered by the 2mm Scale Association. Combined with the Association's new plastic-sleepered bullhead track system, this approach would take most of the sting out of choosing the fine scale option.

The actual subject of the layout is Altguish station, which (say I) is the summit and principal intermediate passing-place on the 32-mile-long branch from Garve, on the Kyle of Lochalsh line, to the northerly fishing- and ferry-port of Ullapool on Loch Broome – a railway which, as with rest of the Far North Line, would have been single track. For the purposes of my scheme, I've promoted Altguish itself from merely being a (very) remote roadside inn to a tenuous highland settlement, a straggling village recently boosted in importance by the construction of the mighty Conon Hydro-electric scheme, with its ugly concrete dam at nearby Glascarnoch, creating a 4½-mile long loch that wasn't there when the railway was built! My Altguish station is a very typical Highland Railway Far North passing place with two platforms, a set of 'cottage' buildings (patterned on Rogart), a 'north' and 'south' signalbox, a modest goods yard with hip-roof timber shed, a modern loading ramp installed for handling earthmoving equipment in connection with the dam works and the remains of a small locomotive depot, originally built to service banking engines but now home only to a solitary snowplough.

I'm afraid I've taken a few liberties with the topography of the place (it's a wide strath, very open and bleak and a thousand feet up) so that a short distance to the east of the station, the line crosses the wide, shallow and stony 'Black Water' by means of a typical Highland Railway lattice girder bridge (inspired by the Dulnain River bridge) before plunging into a tunnel through a spur of the hill – which is *just* about plausible. West of the station the railway crosses the old construction road to the dam over an ungated crossing (with new-fangled flashing lights) and runs into a convenient cutting through a belt of fir trees – which does actually exist! The southern flank of Strathvaich (deer) Forest that forms the main background is likewise real enough, as is the view of the distant 2,500-odd foot peak of Meall a Grhroniain that forms the centrepiece of the backdrop – which also features a distant view of the Glascarnoch dam.

Primarily, then, this is an exercise in dramatic and ambitious scenic modelling, designed to take full advantage of the potential of 2mm scale to portray the broad span and sweep of the landscape of the Western Highlands. To this end, I've used the 'Omega footprint' I first devised for the Launceston Club's 4mm/00 'St Teath' layout (another victim, alas, of the club's premises debacle). An 'omega' layout uses a compact circular or oval track plan combined with paired 'up' and 'down' fiddleyards *outside the circle*, to give a modestly sized but versatile continuous-run format that offers a lot of 'viewing frontage' and a surprising amount of train-handling capacity in a small area. It's a useful arrangement for a through station, as the layout can be operated in continuous-run or point-to-point format at will. The 'omega' is designed to be worked by a minimum of two operators – one for each direction of traffic – who are sited outside the oval at the 'corners' of the visible scene, handily adjacent to the fiddleyards – of which they also have one each to manage (that opposing the direction in which they're driving trains). Signal control would be likewise split – each operator taking responsibility for the adjacent box, and hence setting their own 'road'; rather an unrailway-like proceeding, but expedient in the context of a 'lineside' exhibition layout. The fiddleyards are linked by an independent access track, which permits locos or compete trains to be readily exchanged with the opposing fiddleyard 'off scene' and without affecting trains running on the main circuit. To increase yard capacity and facilitate train-swapping, it would be no problem to incorporate a cassette 'dock' into these fiddleyards, as shown on the down side.

The other main feature of the 'omega' is the solid centre of the oval, combined with the shallow-arc backdrop – not dissimilar to the set-up so effectively employed by Tim Venton with 'Clutton'. In this case – as with the original 'St Teath' design – this central landscape section is designed to represent hilly ground which, when combined

BELOW: *'Altguish' layout plan.*

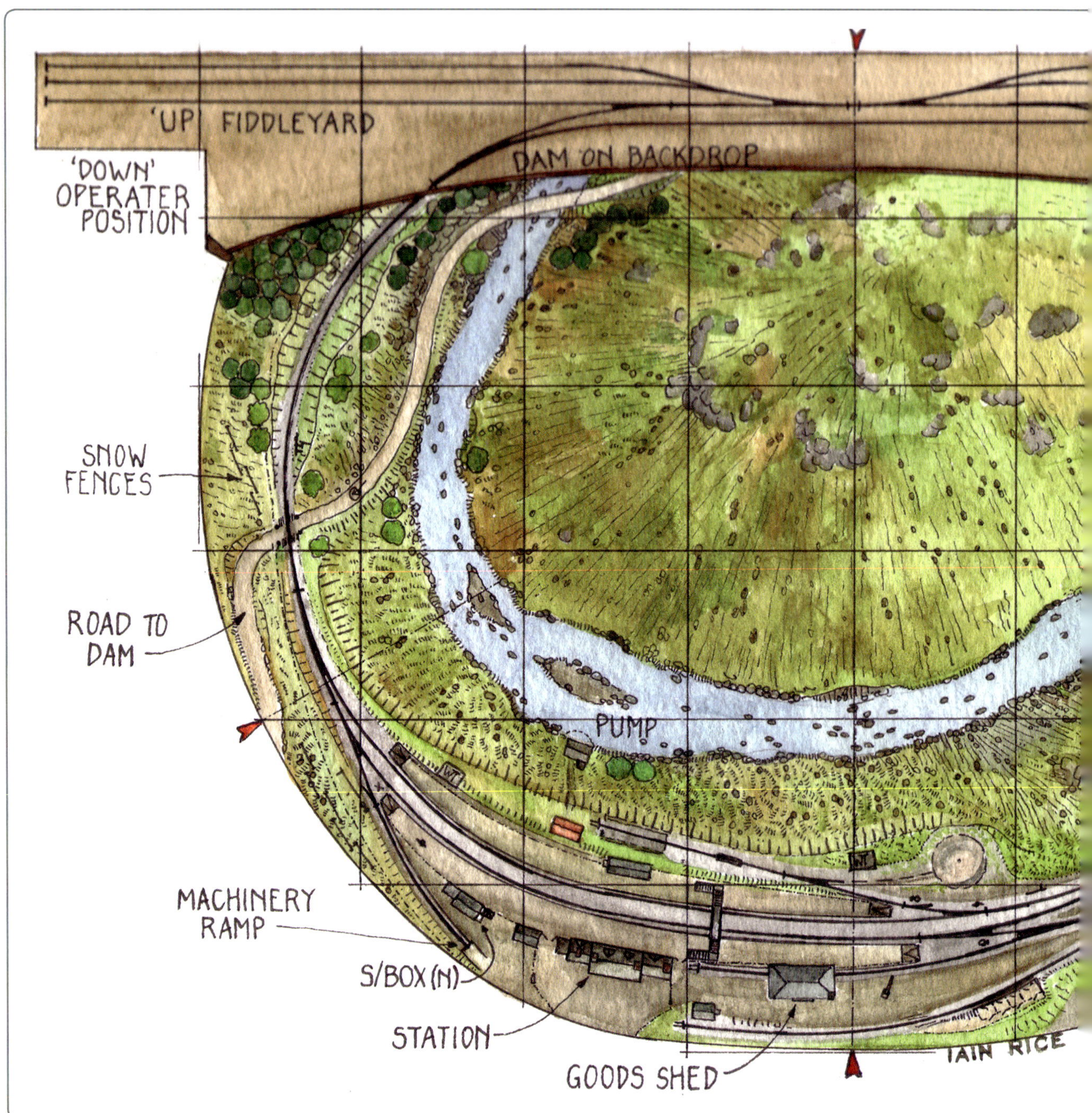

with a reasonable layout elevation and sufficient size, is a visual barrier big enough to conceal whatever is going on at the opposing side of the circuit from the viewer. To maintain easy portability, these central landscape sections do without baseboards as such, being conceived as self-supporting lightweight lift-out structures made of laminated styrofoam sheet carried on the inner edges of the four compact baseboard sections supporting the actual track and foreground scenery (maybe also foam structures?). The joins between these four track sections are disguised with 'scenic gaskets', the 'cracks in the river' being hopefully hidden among the many rocks in the stony shallows. The edge of the lift-out forms the far bank of the river, using the jigsaw approach outlined earlier in this book. The all-important backdrop would be a rollable fabric affair, as on 'Flintfield' or 'Pempoul', supported on a timber frame carried by the two rear 'fiddleyard' baseboards.

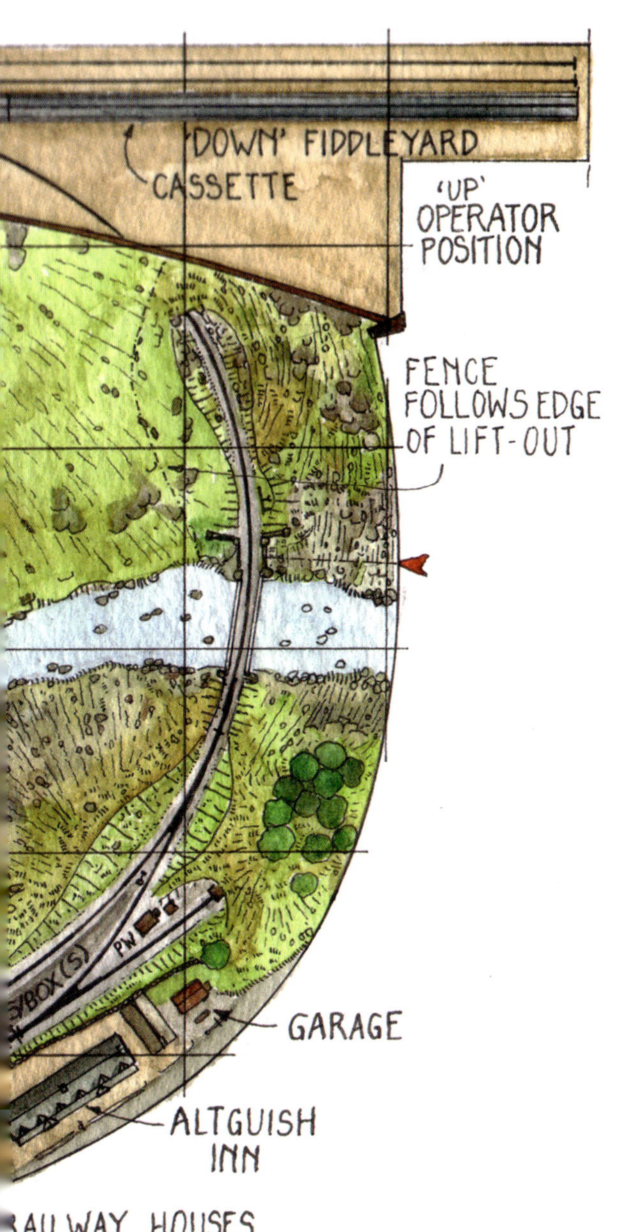

The 'omega' system thus offers a winning combination of compactness, versatility, ready portability and good viewing potential around most of its circumference. The downside (of *course* there's a downside) is that it is an absolute pig to light effectively! Making and supporting a conventional front-of-scene lighting beam is almost impossibly difficult and complex; the best answer is undoubtedly a series of lightweight flying light beams cantilevered out over the layout from the rear, high enough to be above the heads of the audience and thus out of sight – very much as Don Leeper has done with 'Hepton Wharf'.

I reckon Altguish would be best with three 'front' beams and an intermediate ancillary beam to light the background. Even in the case of compact Altguish, the longest of these cantilevers would need to be a few inches over 6ft, calling for careful design and construction; I'd use a tapered T-girder made in glued ply, pivoted on a pin on the top of the uprights carrying the backdrop and anchored by counterweights sitting on the floor behind the layout – in which role, I'd use five-gallon poly-containers of water, transported to shows empty and filled as required on arrival. With a potential weight of 50lb apiece, these should do the job OK! The actual light beams would carry minimal GU10 fittings taking a mix of LED and ordinary 50W quartz-halogen spotlight lamps, both sources which are both light in weight, but high in lumens. The quartz lamps should be far enough above the layout to mitigate radiated heat problems.

BELOW: *Cantilever lighting for 'omega' layout.*

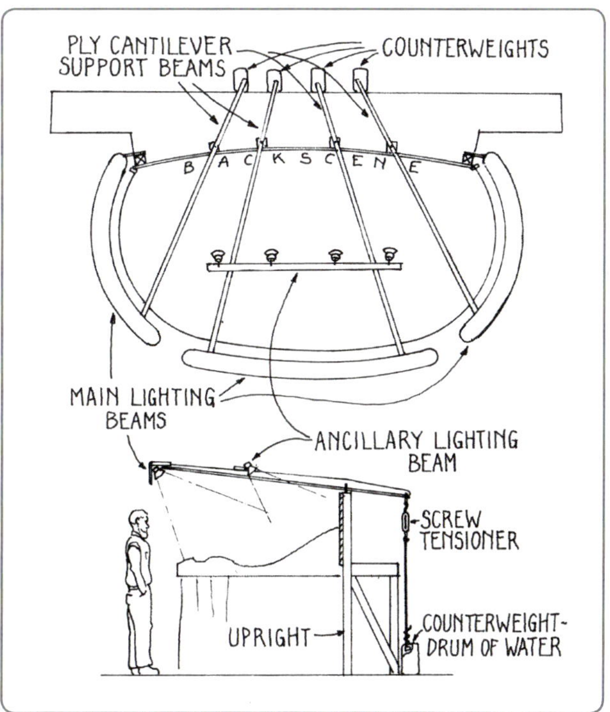

SOURCES

Line and Specialist Societies:

Historical Model Railway Society (HMRS)	www.hmrs.org.uk
Railway and Canal Historical Society (RCHS)	www.rchs.org.uk
Irish Railway Record Society (IRRS)	www.irrs.ie
Industrial Railway Society (IRS)	www.irsociety.co.uk
LMS Society	www.lmssociety.org.uk
LNWR Society	www.lnwrs.org.uk
Lancashire and Yorkshire Railway Society	www.lyrs.org.uk
Midland Railway Society	webp1.mimas.ac.uk/~ zzaascs/mrsoc/mrsoc.html
Cumbrian Railways Association	www.cumbrianrailways association.org.uk
North Eastern Railway Association	www.ner.org.uk
Great Eastern Railway Society	www.gersociety.org.uk
Great Northern Railway Society	www.gnrs.150m.com
Great Central Railway Society	www.gcrsociety.co.uk
M & GN Society	www.mandgn.co.uk
Brighton Circle (LBSCR)	www.lbscr.demon.co.uk
South Western Circe (LSWR)	www.lswr.org
SECR Society	www.southeasternand chathamrailway.org.uk
Highland Railway Society	www.hrsoc.org.uk
Caledonian Railway Association	www.crassoc.org.uk
Great Western Society	www.gwsmainline.org
Welsh Railways Research Circle	www.wrrc.org.uk

Some sites for railway history research

Public Record Office, Kew	www.nationalarchives.gov.uk
British Railways records	www.ndad.nationalarchives.gov.uk
National Railway Museum, York	www.nrm.org.uk
Scottish Railways archive	www.nas.gov.uk/guides/railway.asp
Railway study links	www.york.ac.uk/inst/irs/irshome/ links/links
Railway archive website	www.railwaysarchive.co.uk
GWR Archive	www.greatwestern.org.uk
GWR Links	www.r.heron.btinternet.co.uk/ ulinks.html
Somerset & Dorset History	www.sdjr.net
LNER History Encyclopedia	www.lner.info/index.shtml
Northumbrian Railways website	www.northumbrian-railways.co.uk
Great Central history archive	www.gcrailway.co.uk

Photographs of British and Irish Railway Stations:
www.mulehouse.demon.co.uk/stations

Disused Stations In The UK:
www.disused-stations.org.uk

Major Library Collections:

NRM Library, NRM, Leeman Road,York, YO26 4XJ. Access by appointment – request on 01904 621261. Search Engine for library/archives available whenever museum open.

HMRS Library (Members only): Midland Railway Centre, Butterley Railway Station, Ripley, Derbyshire DE5 3QZ. Normally open Wed – Fri, 0900 – 1500hrs. 01773 745959

Railway Studies Library, Newton Abbot. Public collection, housed in Newton Abbot Library, Market Street, Newton Abbot, Devon, TQ12 2RJ. 01626 206422. e-mail: railway.library@devon.gov.uk (Limited opening). Downloadable information sheet: www.devon.gov.uk/fs_16_-_railway_studies_library.pdf

Historic Maps Source

Reprints/extracts from old OS maps in various scales
Alan Godfrey Maps: www.alangodfreymaps.co.uk
Alan Godfrey Maps, Prospect Business Park, Leadgate, Consett, Co. Durham, DH8 7PW

LEFT: *Convincing proof that you don't need a lot of space to create a truly convincing layout. Rodney Hall's exquisite and influential P4 Llanastr is a scant yard long, but once again a good backscene expands the visual scene dramatically, while fine-scale standards, acute observation and beautifully executed modelling create realism and atmosphere in spadefuls. This is indisputably South Wales – and the rain isn't far off!*